The Gilded Age

or,

The Hazard of New Functions

Mark Wahlgren Summers

University of Kentucky

Joe Moore

Prentice Hall   Upper Saddle River, New Jersey 07458

Library of Congress Cataloging-in-Publication Data

Summers, Mark W. (Mark Wahlgren)
    The Gilded Age, or, The hazard of new functions / by Mark Wahlgren
Summers.
       p.   cm.
    Includes index.
    ISBN 0-13-576679-6
    1. United States—History—1865–1898.
E661.S96   1997   96-31040
973.8—dc20   CIP

Acquisitions editor:	Sally Constable
Editorial/production supervision, interior design:	Alison Gnerre
Copy editor:	Pamela Price
Buyer:	Lynn Pearlman

This book was set in 10/12 Baskerville by The Composing Room of
Michigan, Inc., and was printed and bound by Courier Companies, Inc.
The cover was printed by Phoenix Color Corp.

Printed in the United States of America
10 9 8 7 6 5 4

ISBN 0-13-576679-6

Prentice-Hall International (UK) Limited,London
Prentice-Hall of Australia Pty. Limited, Sydney
Prentice-Hall Canada Inc., Toronto
Prentice-Hall Hispanoamericana, S.A., Mexico
Prentice-Hall of India Private Limited, New Delhi
Prentice-Hall of Japan, Inc., Tokyo
Pearson Education Asia Pte. Ltd., Singapore
Editora Prentice-Hall do Brasil, Ltda., Rio de Janeiro

To the memory of Isabel M. Stampp, this book is fondly dedicated.

Contents

3   "Gentlemen, We Are Not Yet Over": Reconstruction   28

4   Redeeming the Past, 1875–1898   43

Part Two: The New World: America Transformed

5   Wasteland   56

Acknowledgments

Many people made this book possible and plausible, as it lurched and staggered, often in a slovenly and unseemly condition, from one draft to the next. For the time and care that Philip Harling, Kathi Kern, Dan Lykins, and Andrew McIntire put into reading it, my most heartfelt thanks; for their sage and sumptuous comments, all honor goes to Thomas Cogswell, David Hamilton, and William Childs. They knew better than I what would work best. In some cases, readers will suspect, they *still* know better—and, of course, the readers are quite right. Finally, and as ever, the best and most thorough critics, draft after draft, were my parents, Evelyn and Clyde Summers, glints of genuine gold in this, America's second Gilded Age.

Introduction

Alive from Root to Core

> The promised land flies before us like a mirage.
>
> *Henry George*, Progress and Poverty

A Gilded Age?

How far apart the images of the late nineteenth-century America stand! On one side, the Gilded Age shines as an era not of novelty but of charming antiquity: high-button shoes and gingerbread houses, and boys squirming in the dresses and tresses that *Little Lord Fauntleroy* made fashionable. In this fabulous world of wistful memory, gay '90s gentlemen sporting waxed mustaches tip their derbies at overdressed, overfed ladies on a stroll through the park and every ride down the boulevards takes place on bicycles built for two. One might almost imagine that unkempt customers looking for a shave in lather drubbed up out of their own personalized mugs faced no hazard worse in life than a barbershop quartet interrupting the strokes of the straight razor with "She's Only a Bird in a Gilded Cage."

Historians think they know better. For them, the era has earned the name that it first received in 1873, with the appearance of a best-selling novel by Charles Dudley Warner and Mark Twain, satirizing the way the pursuit of the almighty dollar fostered political corruption and speculative manias: *The Gilded Age*. Beneath the thinnest of gold coatings lay a leaden world, where everything was judged by its price in the market. Greed, graft, poverty, misery, upheaval, and bigotry stained the age indelibly. An image sticks in the mind of material accomplishment and spiritual paucity. It is reflected in a traveler's description of the railroad line across the Missouri River into Omaha. "This bridge is of an immense length," he wrote. "The bed of the river was quite dry."[1]

One historian has made a good case for the late nineteenth and early twentieth century as an "Age of Excess," in which Americans, buffeted by change, lost control of their lives by holding too long to "old moral creeds," and by lacking any far-reaching vision for where they wanted society to go. With even shrewder insight, another scholar chronicles how the era brought the breakdown of "island communities," independent of larger, national forces, and of the moral order on which Americans had thought they stood. By the 1890s, an atomized world stood waiting for the new, more centralized, more bureaucratic system that progressive reform would give. Finally, many scholars see the injustice, the thwarted opportunity of industrial America, and sense in it a crisis, the makings of what might have been a genuine social revolution.[2]

Figures don't lie—neither the statistical ones on which historians can make their case, nor those smiling ones facing, however uncertainly, the snapshot cameras of the 1890s from the beaches of Coney Island and the front porch of Mentor, Ohio. Yet neither has done the age full justice. Fear and frustration shaped the age for many: this included miners in the coalfields of the Midwest, Indians civilized into an early grave, sharecroppers bound to worn-out soil and to the prices given in Liverpool's cotton markets, and agitators hauled before Chicago courts and hanged on flimsy evidence. Such individuals saw the promise of democracy at its hollowest.

Still, for many Americans, the Gilded Age was the Age of Progress and Promise, where even the past could be restored in a new, improved edition. "Island communities" losing control over their own destinies were repaid in all the consumer items that a national market economy could provide. Given the choice between the corner store and the welter of goods that a Sears Roebuck catalogue could provide, or between the old log cabin and one made from planed boards, most Americans would have felt that by discarding the old for the new, they had made the best bargain. It is well to remember how hard many immigrants found adjustment to American life. The bottom line, though, is that, for all the problems, they kept on coming.

A sense of progress, not just in material, but in moral ways, allowed some Americans, like the poet J. T. Trowbridge, to write anthems to their "children's children," who would someday inherit the present's blessings:

> *Yours the full-blown flower of freedom, which in struggle we have sown;*
> *Yours the spiritual science, that shall overarch our own,*
> *You, in turn, will look with wonder, from a more enlightened time,*
> *Upon us, your rude forefathers, in an age of war and crime!*
> *Half our virtues will seem vices by your broader, higher right,*
> *And the brightness of the present will be shadow in that light;*
> *For, behold, our boasted culture is a morning cloud, unfurled*
> *In the dawning of the ages and the twilight of the world!*[3]

In Trowbridge's optimism, something else should catch our eye, the apologetic for his own time. It is a more common note than we may think. Americans certainly had plenty to be proud of in the late nineteenth century. And yet, many of them were not proud—and certainly not content—with the way life was changing. This uneasiness affected not just radicals and professionals naysayers writing for genteel New York journals, but also middling Americans—churchgoers and clubwomen—who saw things that had gone wrong and wanted to change them—sometimes in big ways, sometimes in little. Money and machinery transformed America, but so did moral sense. Reformers' successes were flawed. Some of their failures and blind spots were monumental. Still, without seeing that impulse to make anew and make better, the Gilded Age will appear to us much bleaker, much emptier of content than it was.

Age of Energy

So convenient is the term "Gilded Age," so familiar, that we cannot help using it, but another fits better: the Age of Energy. The striving that went into getting rich or achieving greatness also went into just about anything else people did, from taming the Great Plains to redeeming the sinful cities. Not all of this energy was well used, and it often flowed in contradictory directions. Indeed, the era can be explained by the historians' best friend, the paradox, which was embodied in disastrous success, splendid failure, creative destruction, and an embrace of the new as a means of restoring the old.

The last paradox may be the most important. Amid signs of society fragmented and disintegrating, or building anew, the United States ended the Age of Energy with many of its old ways intact. At times, the values to which the American people held had outlived the world in which those beliefs made sense. Just as often, ancient values took on fresh meaning even when conditions had changed. How the conservatism of thought and radicalism of technological change remade the Gilded Age, and how society tempered the application of each, is part of this story. So, too, are mainstream politics and religion. Indeed, I hope that this story will restore politics in its larger sense to its rightful place, as the shaping force on people's lives. What governments did or failed to do was nowhere near the whole story. But in some way, it touched everyone and everything in the fabled Age of Laissez-Faire.

This story of the Gilded Age will certainly not appeal to those scholars for whom the period represents a dark time of injustice, complacency, and shallow thinking. All these the late nineteenth century displayed; this book will conceal none of them. But there is another America, a nation of creativity and idealism. In business, culture, and politics, the Gilded Age showed American resourcefulness at its best—as well as worst. It is not with contempt or in criticism alone, but also with admiration, that historians should approach the Age of Energy.

Chapter 1

Progress
Backward, 1876

Centennial, 1876

When the great Centennial Exhibition opened its 450 acres of exhibits in Philadelphia's Fairmont Park in the spring of 1876, it won an unusual success: it became a must for every historian to treat as a symbol of the times.

Those belittling the Gilded Age have the easiest time proving their case. Eight million people paid to gape, if not to learn. They could spot machines to cut out shingles, Swedish schoolhouses, pyramids made from crayons or grindstones, and a bust sculpted from butter. They could hear America's greatest symphony conductor, German-born Theodore Thomas, and his orchestra playing the Georgia poet Sidney Lanier's bizarre, forgettable cantata, the "Song of the Centennial," with 800 voices for added effect.[1]

With so many exhibits, every historian can make a different case for what the Exhibition said about the times. In fact, the variety may be what mattered. One might take away two contradictory impressions: a country revolutionized by machinery and invention, and an America where traditional values held true. Technology and tradition, progress and principles, idealism and self-interest: any true "Song of the Centennial" would have required such a bewildering mixture of beats and tempos that neither Lanier, nor Richard Wagner, who wrote a Centennial March, could have done it justice.

At first glance, the Exhibition seemed to celebrate hard fact and heavy metal over idealistic theory. Its centerpiece was the immense Corliss Engine in Machinery Hall, driving eight thousand devices, including half a mile of sewing machines. Visitors could marvel at the latest in transportation (the bicycle), or the newest thresher-separator, which was able to clean and thresh up to a thousand bushels of wheat a day. In the hodgepodge of exhibits, many people overlooked Alexander Graham Bell's device for transmitting voices across a long distance, but the Emperor of Brazil tried out the model and was dumbfounded. "My God!" he is reputed to have cried, "it talks!"[2]

Age of Invention

Americans boasted of their know-how. Applied science they lagged in, but they led the world in invention—the practical kinds that saved toil. American soil no longer bred Thomas Jeffersons, admittedly; but what about Thomas Edisons? "A *genius* who held there was no such thing as a *genius*," in one biographer's words, Edison stood for all those qualities that Americans thought were theirs alone: innovativeness, practicality, and resourcefulness. Leaving school at age seven, to the relief of a teacher who pronounced his mind "addled" and his future bleak, Edison couldn't stay away from chemistry and physics. He earned the money to pay for his supplies by selling candy and newspapers on the railroad, until one lucky day when he saved a stationmaster's son from being hit by an approaching train and was rewarded with training in telegraphy. Edison liked his new job so much that he nicknamed his two children "Dot" and "Dash." By developing a wire that could send as many as four telegraph messages both ways simultaneously, he saved Western Union millions of dollars.

In the Centennial year, Edison was still pretty much unknown, but already he and a staff of like-minded tinkerers had gone into the "invention business" in a white clapboard building at Menlo Park, New Jersey. Their goal, he explained, was "a minor invention every ten days and a big thing every six months or so." Before they were done, the team at Menlo Park would develop the movie camera, the electrified railroad, the fluorescent lamp and the fluoroscope, the electrical battery, dictating machines, prefabricated housing, and tools to crush rock and grind cement more finely. But the breakthrough that made Edison famous was the phonograph in 1877. Months of work went into a revolving cylinder that could play back noises impressed on its tin-foil surface. The inventor shouted, "Mary had a little lamb, Its fleece was white as snow," into a diaphragm with a needle attached and the needle cut grooves into the cylinder as it spun. Then another needle ran down the grooves as the cylinder revolved and out came doggerel, rough, but undoubtedly his own. Edison was gratified but alarmed. "I was always afraid of things that worked the first time," he explained. His fears were groundless. The device was an instant sensation. Paying customers flocked to auditoriums to hear a machine that could speak any language or even crow like a rooster.[3]

Three years later, the electric light made the inventor's name a household word. Other inventors had patented lamps illuminated by an electrical current, all of which were costly. Some were smelly, too, and others painfully bright. A gas jet might produce ten to twenty candlepower; an arc light, with a glare numbering in the thou-

An advertisement for Edison phonograph. (*Collier's*, March 9, 1901)

sands, did fine only in lighthouses. What was needed was a cheaper, longer lasting filament and a new lighting system that would permit any one bulb in a system to be turned on and off separately. Edison's team devised both. The scientists tried filaments of platinum, paper, cork—even beard hairs. A carbonized cotton fiber proved the solution and later it was discovered that a breed of Japanese bamboo worked even better.[4] In September 1882, the lights went on down Wall Street. Before his retirement, Edison had seen his promise kept, to make bulbs "so cheap that only the wealthy can afford to burn candles."

By then, indeed, his original phonograph was an antique, and therein lay an important lesson about American inventiveness. Technology bred technology. New devices made way for newer ones. Emile Berliner, the son of a Talmudic scholar, invented the flat phonographic record to replace Edison's cumbersome and expensive cylinders. In 1914, a German firm found ways to run grooves on both sides of the disc. A small machine-shop owner, Eldridge Johnson, improved Berliner's record player and founded the Victor Talking Machine Company. All of these changes came about because the demand for the phonograph outran Edison's own imagination. The "Wizard of Menlo Park" thought he knew all the uses for recorded sound: books for the blind or telephone answering machines, for example. What he overlooked was entertainment—especially music. The twentieth century had barely begun before Italian slumdwellers in Brooklyn could hear the world's greatest operatic singer, Enrico Caruso, in their own parlor, and Kansas farm families could laugh at the Yiddish comedy routines of Weber and Fields a thousand miles off Broadway. By 1914, half a million records were produced each year and by 1921 this number had grown to over one hundred million.[5]

Then there was George Westinghouse, inventor of the air brakes, electrical switches, and signaling devices that had made railroad yard work a somewhat less deadly profession. He stood among the crowd of engineers and inventors to whom the Wizard gave his first public demonstration of the lamp. Westinghouse was impressed, but not, perhaps, only with Edison's genius. Why not make and sell lighting cheaper than Edison did? Westinghouse decided to try. He turned to the flaw in Menlo Park's electrical system, the power it used to light the filament. Direct current traveled badly. Along the wire, bulbs glowed dim, then dimmer; two miles from the generator they shed no light at all. Industries with great motors needed great power but Edison's system could not provide it. Nor could it light the countryside. Alternating current could perform these tasks. It lost nothing in transmission, and, carrying a thousand volts, it had more jolt to deliver from the start. Thanks to Hungarian immigrant Nikola Tesla's induction polyphase motor, it improved, just as the original phonograph had.[6] The Corliss engines at the next World's Fair in 1893 got no notice at all. The AC dynamo had replaced them as the symbol of progress.

Hail, King Steel

Another technological wonder had already come into common use by the Centennial year, though it had none of the romance of electricity: industrial steel. After 1892, the country produced more steel than iron, and, twenty years later, it produced fourteen times more. Though steel's quality had improved, it had always been tougher and harder than iron. What had changed its advantages to buyers was the asking price for making it. "The eighth wonder of the world is this," boasted Andrew Carnegie, America's most famous steelmaker:

> two pounds of iron-stone, purchased on the shores of Lake Superior and transported to Pittsburgh; two pounds of coal mined in Connelsville and manufactured into one and one-fourth pounds of coke and brought to Pittsburgh; one-half pound of limestone mined east of the Alleghenies and brought to Pittsburgh; a little manganese ore, mined in Virginia and brought to Pittsburgh; and these four and one-half pounds of material manufactured into one pound of solid steel and sold for one cent.[7]

Carnegie, Edison, Westinghouse, and Bell won a lasting fame in their own right, but they also became symbols for that creative spirit of invention that made some Americans christen the late nineteenth century the Machine Age or the Age of Invention. In the seventy years leading up to 1860, the U.S. Patent Office issued 36,000 patents. In the next three decades, it granted 440,400 more (including those for illuminated tin cats, tapeworm traps, and combination cannon and plow).[8] "We live in an age iv wondhers," the wry bartender Martin Dooley (himself of the Gilded Age's finest inventions—a literary one) would admit early in the new century:

> Th' shoes that Corrigan th' cobbler wanst wurruked on f'r a week, hammerin' away like a woodpecker, is now tossed out be th' dozens fr'm th' mouth iv a masheen. A cow goes lowin' softly in to Armours an' comes out glue, beef, gelatine, fertylizer, celooloid, joolry, sofy cushions, hair restorer, washin' sody, soap, lithrachoor an' bed springs so quick that while aft she's still cow, for'ard she may be annything fr'm buttons to Pannyma hats. I can go fr'm Chicago to New York in twinty hours, but I don't have to, thank th' Lord. Thirty years ago we thought 'twas marvelous to be able to tillygraft a man in Saint Joe an' get an answer that night. Now, be wireless tillygraft ye can get an answer befure ye sind th' tillygram if they ain't careful.[9]

Had he not been a bachelor, Mr. Dooley might have looked closer to home and found changes just as revolutionary. He would have found sewing machines making clothing in hours where once thread and needle had taken days, iceboxes and canned goods where fifty years before only those people in the country could keep food, and then only the few items that a buttery or root cellar could keep from spoiling. By the time of the Civil War, the open hearth had given way to woodstoves, which were able to cook several things at once. Before the century's end, oven doors came with temperature gauges, allowing the cook some control over heat.[10]

In that sense, the last half of the nineteenth century might just as well be called the Age of Gail Borden as of Thomas Edison. Borden was a Texas surveyor and land agent just bursting with nutty inventions. There was the locomotive bathing house that allowed shy swimmers to change their clothes on the beach and step straight into the water; the dinner table with the revolving center that spared people the bother of passing the food around; and a sailboat able to blow across the prairies. Eventually, Borden developed something that made money and opened the way for a national market in other perishable foods: condensed milk.[11]

The Rise of the City

One reason that Carnegie's cheap steel became as indispensable as electric lighting was the ways in which builders and designers put it to use to refashion city life. Newcomers crowded the streets and tenements; with vacant space so scarce, the old "walking city" would have to spread outward or else push upward, with taller buildings. But the further population pushed beyond the city center, the harder it became to make the daily commute from home to work for those too poor to afford a horse and pay the stable rates. Brick could not bear the weight for buildings higher

A skyscraper is built on Broadway, 1900. Nothing could be more up-to-date—if you don't count the last three floors. (*Collier's*, December 1, 1900)

than five stories. Stone was too heavy. And what tenant could bear the daily trudge up six flights of stairs?

Affordable steel and electrical wiring made all the difference. Creating a skeleton of steel girders, hammering on exterior pieces to make the whole rigid, architects could erect towering edifices, and, after 1866, the development of passenger elevators driven by steam or hydraulic power made it possible to pack these buildings with of-

fices and people. The first true "skyscraper" (or "cloud presser," a short-lived nickname) rose in Chicago in 1885. It was ten stories high and was steel-framed. As early
as the 1830s, chartered companies had begun investing in horse-railways, horse-
drawn cars that were carried on iron rails at breakneck speeds of six to eight miles per
hour. Cheap steel rails set transit companies free to spread beyond city limits and
charge affordable fares for the affluent end of the working class. Rates were fixed by
the distance traveled. Starting with New York in the 1860s, metropolitan centers
started ridding themselves of the horses and the tons of manure they dropped, as well.
The change began with steam-railroad lines, constructed at a level above the street
and able to carry thousands of passengers a day. In the 1880s, electricity-run streetcars and "els" were introduced. By the 1890s, electric trolleys had turned the cable
cars and horse railroads into antiques just about everywhere except San Francisco.
Early in the new century, 97 percent of all street railways ran on electricity.[12]

The new web of transport did not simply create suburbs. Along with other
forces, it spread the city and helped segment it. Until the early 1890s, wealthy
Chicagoans made Hyde Park their country retreat in summer. Then trolley lines made
it half an hour's travel from downtown. In came apartment buildings, along with food
and dry goods stores. The Chicago "el" turned exclusive Ravenswood into a working-class neighborhood, with factories where vast lawns once ran. But then, America
had some of the biggest, most densely populated cities in the world by that time.
Added together, the twenty biggest urban centers accounted for less than two million
people in 1850; but New York alone had more than three million half a century later;
Chicago and Philadelphia had more than a million; St. Louis, Boston, and Baltimore
had more than 500,000. Defining anyplace with more than 4,000 people as a city, two
New Yorkers in three were city dwellers, and one Pennsylvanian in every two.[13]

The "walking city" of old gave way to a metropolis where rich and poor, white
and black, business and residential neighborhoods were set further apart. Once, most
cities had home and place of work within close range. For small shopkeepers, things
stayed that way. But thanks to the skyscraper, land values in the commercial parts of
town soared; thanks to the streetcar lines, the wealthy found their homes beyond city
limits, far from the noise and congestion. Nearer to the city center, but beyond the factory district, might stand the row houses and apartments of the skilled laborers,
though many of them could afford to live in the "streetcar suburbs" themselves. Nearest of all, within walking distance of the heart of town, lay the financial district, and
within close range, the factories. Where once the poorest lived on the outskirts of
town, they now found themselves with the city growing up around them, in tenements
and railroad yards, shantytowns and warehouses.[14]

Yet trolleys transformed the quality of inner city life, as well. Downtown stores
were able to thrive. The tracks that scattered people outward also drew suburbanites
inward to the business district. Indeed, they made the business district possible: not
until the 1870s did most cities have streets devoted to shops and department stores
and many establishments relocated to spots along the main suburban lines. By 1900,
"downtown" in New York and Chicago meant the department stores along Fifth Avenue and State Street; it also meant the "Great White Way" of Broadway, where the-

aters and restaurants did a boffo business. But without the commuter lines, even good musicals would have closed after a short run, and, of course, without Edison's electricity, the blazing light of street lamps, theater marquees, and swanky eateries would have been the dim, tawny glare of gaslight.

Just a few blocks away, where the immigrants and poorer classes lived, the old lights flickered and fewer trolley lines ran; theirs was a city increasingly invisible to the downtown and increasingly alien from the professionals, who came to the city to work or for pleasure. But even inner-city residents gained from urban growth. More business meant more jobs, more opportunity, and more chance at leisure. They might not mingle with the crowds on Broadway; their neighborhood groceries met their everyday needs. Still, in the broiling summer weather, it was the mass transit of electricity, steam, and steel that allowed them to flee their own neighborhoods for an outing. A nickel fare might carry them to the amusement park or the seaside.[15]

The Limits of "Progress"

Sundays by the sea and brighter kitchens at home: Americans called that "progress." But even if the benefits were shared by all, defining it only in material terms would prove "progress" a great misstep forward. Materialism might harness the torrents of Niagara to turbines, the way an Englishman proposed. What was the awesome spectacle of water tumbling over a falls, compared to five million horsepower a year? What wealth King Steel had showered on Pittsburgh and what a sight it made of the place! "Every object the eye falls upon is black," a traveler wrote, "—houses, roads, buildings, people's clothing, children's faces." Materialism might leave Americans with outlooks as proselike as that of the lady on shipboard, who glimpsed her first iceberg glistening in morning sunlight and pronounced it "just like one of our grain elevators."[16] Clearly, a nation's greatness lay not in its prosperity alone. "I can't get up anny kind iv fam'ly inthrest f'r a steam dredge or a hydhraulic hist," Mr. Dooley protested. "I want to see sky-scrapin' men."[17]

And where *were* those "sky-scrapin'" men and women in this centennial year? Wandering through Machinery Hall, they seemed as outmoded as the quaint exhibits of Indian life. "Murmur of many voices in the air/Denounces us degenerate," James Russell Lowell, the dean of New England poetry, cautioned in his ode to the centennial's Fourth of July:

> . . . *Is this the country that we dreamed in youth,*
> *Where wisdom and not numbers should have weight,*
> *Seed-field of simpler manners, braver truth,*
> *Where shams should cease to dominate*
> *In household, church, and state?*[18]

These were common doubts, and in their commonness, perhaps, we can capture a little hope. Old values and old habits were *not* cast aside as readily as cylinder records and last year's calendar would be. Gilded Age, Machine Age, Age of Enterprise: all these titles fit the centennial year like suits of readymade clothing. But the country had many suits for many occasions.

Two images, infinite distances apart, speak of quaintness and modernity: the gingerbread house and the electric bulb. Look closer at each. It took the new, strong bandsaw blades to shape such filigrees and fancy work, while Edison's achievement was aimed at recreating the old gas lamp that city-dwellers were already so familiar with, minus the smell, the flickering, and the heat. It was *as* an imitation of gaslight that advertisers acclaimed Edison's innovation—safer, perhaps, steadier, but not a bit more intense. Even the earliest light switches themselves *twisted* on, just like the gas tap, and were located on each individual light, rather than in the wall next to the door.[19]

With all the achievements of Edison and Westinghouse, it might be thought that by 1900 the dynamo would stand where the steam engine had. In fact, electrical motors produced less than three percent of all horsepower that year. Water-wheels supplied nearly six times as much, and steam-engines' share stood at an all-time high: 77.4 percent. There were many more factories in 1900 than in 1860. But there were also many more farms—two-and-a-half times as many. Cities grew, but most people still lived outside them: more than three out of every five.[20]

The moral values of the past lived on, too. Anyone who kept an eye open at the Centennial Exhibition could attest to that. From the number of ways in which the image of the first President appeared, and made "from every conceivable material," an observer commented, artists must have assumed George Washington's face wholly unknown. Sightseers stared at the bolt-and-nut screwing machine and the atmospheric gas engine. But they also came to gaze on statues of a shepherd with one of his lambs in his arms, and to approve of the caption, "Safe in the Arms of Jesus." Machinery Hall, seen properly, might testify to the success of Christian values and the heritage of liberty and opportunity that the American Revolution had left its children. What pagan country could match the Corliss engine? Christianity, obviously, was "the main-spring that drives the machinery of the age, . . . the source of the material prosperity as well as the moral excellence of the people who yield to her beneficent reign."[21]

Moral excellence was a value that defined the age as plainly as materialism did. It was not a source of self-congratulation only, but a call to arms. No matter how far the Remington typewriter, dry yeast, and canned goods on display might someday carry women from their nineteenth-century kitchens, it would take human effort to bring them to their proper place in American life. On that 4th of July, Susan B. Anthony, Elizabeth Cady Stanton, and a host of other veterans of the fight for women's rights gathered in Philadelphia to read the "Women's Declaration of Independence." For them, the Woman's Pavilion, funded by women and dedicated to showing their own share in the mechanical achievements of the day—as telegraph operators and inventors alike—missed the point; worldly success was still defined in men's terms there. The fact that there had to be a Woman's Pavilion at all, that the Exhibition managers had shut the main building to women's displays, exposed how far the country lay from its original promise of equal rights.[22]

The Women's Crusade

Above the roar of the Corliss engine and the self-plaudits of the Centennial Exhibition crowd rose that "murmur of many voices." Not all echoed Lowell's or Stanton's. Late in 1873, a veteran temperance lecturer found, to his astonishment, that his message was being accepted all across Ohio. Out of the churches, wives and mothers came to kneel at the barroom doors in song and prayer. In their eyes, the fight was one for homes threatened by the drunkenness that went along with what politicians defended as "German liberty." Across the Ohio valley, petitioners called on their local governments to turn down every request for a liquor license that came up.[23]

Comfortable churchgoers with investments in the liquor trade, as well as the German and Irish immigrants who saw the movement as a personal attack, had the votes. But for a brief spell that winter, they must have wondered. The streets were thick with temperance crusaders, black and white—in some places marching side by side. In Columbus, Chicago, Philadelphia, and Boston, they blocked saloon doors and courted arrest. When the city council of Springfield, Ohio passed an ordinance directing police to keep sidewalks clear of obstructions—including people bowed in prayer—the women simply took their stand on the curbstone.[24]

The Women's Crusade may have hoped to turn off the taps in America's

Old and New, 1894.
New York's skyline has changed; but tradition holds on. Liberty Street stays the same: cobblestoned paving, gas lighting, and German small-shopkeepers. (*Scribner's*, March 1894)

beerkegs. In that respect, it failed utterly. Hardened offenders pelted temperance workers with crackers and bologna, and one bartender threatened to drive them away by taking a bath out on the sidewalk. Hard times closed many more rumholes than high morals. Yet the fervor in the streets awakened Protestant women across the North to how much they might do, and how many concerns they shared. Hitherto silent, shamed by the valor of what Victorian America called "the weaker sex," male voices in school and pulpit arose against the liquor traffic. Lost as this crusade might be, its leaders knew there would be others: they had organized to carry on the fight in Sunday schools and in local elections for more than half a century. In February 1874, Ohioans took the first steps that led to the founding of the Women's Christian Temperance Union.[25]

The quest to improve American life went far beyond protest movements, but it showed the same energy, the same intensity that Stanton or the crusaders brought to their lives. It might be seen in the Chautauqua movement. Meeting in the countryside, seated in tents or on the rude wooden benches of amphitheaters, millions of men and women gathered yearly to hear public readings, illustrated lectures, organ recitals, and scientific demonstrations.[26] Across the North, the improving instinct showed itself in the village-improvement societies that women created, to salvage what little of nature the towns still had. The spirit could stir itself in matters as small as the spring day that the ladies of Guilford, Connecticut, set aside for raking the village green—as expansive as the Catholic utopian women's community that Martha White McWhirter founded in Texas—as broad and far-reaching as the movement to create women's colleges with standards as rigorous as those for men: Vassar in 1865, Smith, Wellesley, Mills, Bryn Mawr, and then, as adjuncts to universities exclusively male, Radcliffe and Barnard.[27]

It is in that idealism, that sense of possibilities and responsibilities, that the gold in this "Gilded" Age shines brightest. Nothing bad had to exist unless Americans willed it so. Society was just open enough, government just representative enough to allow change and to apply moral belief to all things. Americans could reinvent themselves in a new, improved form, different from but resembling the best of generations past. So to Lowell let the last word go, and this time in a hopeful key:

> *I ask no drowsy opiate*
> *To dull my vision of that only state*
> *Founded on faith in man, and therefore sure to last.*
> *For O, my country, touched by thee,*
> *The gray hairs gather back their gold;*
> *Thy thought sets all my pulses free;*
> *The heart refuses to be old.*

Chapter 2

A New Stillbirth
of Freedom?

As New York rallied to the nation's cause in April 1861, the city was awash with flags. On one street, a reporter wrote, "the rustling of banners in the wind [was] like the noise of wings overhead."[1] No poet was so unpatriotic as to associate those wings with the Angel of Death. But then, the Great Rebellion was a war that too many people welcomed and almost nobody expected.

War Becomes Revolution

It began as a fight to keep the union of states that the founders had created, not to end slavery. Both sides looked to a quick win. Both were wrong. Thanks to the repeating rifle, the breechloader, the Minié ball, and the old-fashioned battle tactics, more died in this conflict than in any other that Americans had entered. Some 623,000 soldiers lost their lives. Half a million more were wounded. Countless survivors would carry their scars until they died; surgeons performed nearly 30,000 amputations. Many patients never got off the opiates that hospitals first gave them to ease their agonies. "The dead in this war," Walt Whitman wrote,

> there they lie, strewing the fields and woods and valleys and battlefields of the South— Virginia, the Peninsula, Malvern Hill and Fair Oaks, the banks of the Chickahominy, the terraces of Fredricksburg, Antietam Bridge, the grisly ravines of Manassas, the bloody promenade of the Wilderness; the varieties of the *strayed* dead . . . ; three thou-

sand drowned; fifteen thousand inhumed by strangers or on the march in haste, in hitherto unfound localities; two thousand graves covered by sand and mud, by Mississippi freshets; three thousand carried away by caving-in of banks, etc.; Gettysburg, the West, Southwest, Vicksburg, Chattanooga, the trenches of Petersburg; the numberless battles, camps, hospitals everywhere; the crop reaped by the mighty reapers—typhoid, dysentery, inflammations; and—blackest and loathsomest of all—the dead and living burial pits—the prison pens of Andersonville, Salisbury, Belle Isle, etc . . . . Two hundred thousand graves! They say we have no monument. . . . Let them be our fame, our monument.[2]

Of such sacrifices are revolutions made, both in what a government does and in what its people think. To keep the Confederacy going, white women had to sacrifice husbands, sons, luxuries, and necessities. Some found it easier to surrender the meek, obedient role that society had set out for them. "Pshaw! There are *no* women here! We are *all* men!" a plucky Louisianan wrote, as she took up carving knife and pistol to fend off forward Yankees. Angrier at politicians who fiddled while the home front suffered, mobs of women in Savannah and Richmond smashed store windows and helped themselves to bread.[3]

To win the war, the United States had to tax, borrow, muster, and control as never before. Through Jay Cooke's Philadelphia banking house, the country bought savings bonds in record numbers. Financiers held the most, but clerks, saloonkeepers, widows, and wives subscribed, investing not in their own future only, but in their country's. Four hundred million dollars in "greenbacks," government paper money, was issued, and another $300 million in national banknotes. An income tax of 3 percent provided $55 million a year but that was nothing compared to the excise taxes, so extensive that it took more than twenty thousand words to cover them all.[4]

With the Southern representatives gone, Northern congressmen who had long wanted the government to promote economic development had their way. Land grants and loans sailed through Congress, to build one transcontinental line, then another. The Morrill "war tariff" imposed high duties (on average, 47 percent) to protect infant industries, and would keep doing so until many of those frail babes went as hulking giants into the next century. Before the war, banking had been every institution for itself. Seven thousand legitimate ones issued notes, not to mention six thousand swindling concerns. Now the country required a system of banks—nationally chartered and nationally controlled. The Homestead Act of 1862 opened 160 acres of public domain to each would-be settler. Homesteaders simply paid a filing fee and lived on the land for five years. The Morrill Land-Grant College Act provided each state with vast tracts to support "agricultural and mechanical colleges." Out of this sprang the Universities of Illinois, Wisconsin, and California, and institutions of higher learning in nineteen other states, as well.[5] Most important of all, the war made the Union into a nation that was permanent, indivisible, and run by the North. From Washington's inauguration to Lincoln's, southern presidents held office in two years out of every three. Not for nearly a century after the Civil War would a politician from the Confederate South be elected president; not for a generation would one of them become Speaker of the House.[6]

It was a revolution, sure enough. White men of the North and South brought it about. But there was another upheaval, even more dramatic, and Southern blacks, women and men, helped cause that one, by fleeing in wartime and using what freedom they were given in the peace that followed. Let Congress disclaim any wish to meddle with slavery; let Union soldiers serve as slave catchers for Confederate planters. Liberty and Union *were* inseparable. Every slave hoeing cotton freed one more white for Confederate service; every black man donning a Union suit spared one more white from Mr. Lincoln's draft-law—as over 180,000 blacks did eventually. Destroy slavery, and the United States would strike a blow at the Confederacy worth a dozen battles. For the praying millions, the killing fields of Virginia only pressed the moral issue home. If the Union was blessed by the Lord, why did He will the slaughter to go on? Could it be a punishment for the sin of holding human beings as property, a sin that the North allowed and had long profited from? "I hear Old John Brown knocking on the lid of his coffin & shouting, 'Let me out, let me out!'" an abolitionist wrote prophetically, as the fighting began. "The doom of slavery is at hand."

Together, the Lord's will and the war's needs brought Abraham Lincoln, a cautious, rather conservative Republican president to proclaim the slaves free wherever a Confederate flag flew in 1863. The war's opportunities also permitted hundreds of thousands of blacks to set themselves free by escaping; and in many cases to advance the cause by enlisting. Soldiers who wrinkled their noses in disdain at black people became the proud commanders of black regiments. "I never believed in niggers before, by by Jasus they are hell in fighting," a cavalryman admitted. The slaves and underclass of just the day before won twenty-one Congressional Medals of Honor and a nation's gratitude.[7] In 1861, Congress had passed an amendment (never ratified) guaranteeing slavery forever, but four years later it adopted an amendment ending slavery everywhere. By then, the Republican party had taken a big step further still. A bare freedom, its leaders agreed, would not be enough. The basic rights of all Americans must be protected.

Civil Rights: A Catalyst for Change

But what *was* basic? The right to own land, change employers, marry, inherit, or take a dispute into court—most Republicans counted those. Beyond that, they faltered. Radicals like grim Congressman Thaddeus Stevens of Pennsylvania and Senator Charles Sumner of Massachusetts warned that until the South was remade and given that "republican form of government" that the Constitution guaranteed, the nation had won nothing it could count on keeping for long. If the radicals had their way, blacks would vote and Confederates stay home; after all, the only rights rebels deserved, as one senator joked, were "funeral rites." The national government might set up public schools or even hand out the planters' estates as homesteads to the former slaves; take some four hundred million acres from seventy thousand "proud, bloated and defiant rebels," Stevens urged, and there would be forty acres for every freedman, plus enough left over to pay off the public debt and pension Union veterans.[8]

Radicals could make themselves heard. Well past the age of seventy, failing in health and voice, Stevens still knew more parliamentary tricks than the rest of the House put together. Any member who took him on in debate risked a scathing reply—though, when the day's work was over, like as not, Stevens would clap his victim on the shoulder and invite him out to dinner. Observers in the galleries would look for him specially, hobbling the floor of the House on his club foot, his ill-fitting brown wig askew, that sardonic smile just about to let loose some barbed quip at a Democrat's expense. He was the one Northerner white Southerners loved to hate, and they predicted for him an afterlife hotter than the forge of his ironworks. Lofty, literary Sumner, by contrast, knew nothing about pushing a bill through. Jokes baffled him, and, unlike Stevens, he would vote against a half-step forward rather than compromise true principles. In his gaiters and olive gloves, he looked the English dandy. But Sumner's speeches were polished works of art, widely read and influential. Beyond Capitol Hill, thousands of veterans of the antislavery movement, men and women, blacks and whites, argued the cause of equal rights. Hundreds of Southerners, slaves but yesterday, called conventions to appeal to Congress for the vote, and, in Louisiana, staged a mock election and cast the only Republican ballots in the state.[9]

And yet, with all those advantages, the Radicals never had a chance. The moderates had the votes. Mainstream Republicans respected property rights—even those of traitors—and legal precedents—even inconvenient ones. "Only a fool would look into the Constitution to find an apology for making forced loans," Thad Stevens once exclaimed; but if so, the Republican party was full of that kind of fool. Moreover, they saw practical snags in the Radical program. "Thad will be all right when he's dug up a few hundred years hence, I reckon," Lincoln once commented. "I must look out for these four years, and as much further as I can see." Moderates were of the same mind; they looked to the distant future, but kept an eye on the next set of elections. When the question of letting a few thousand Northern blacks vote was put on the ballot, white Northerners went against it just about every time. Giving the suffrage to hundreds of thousands of former slaves, mostly illiterate, unpropertied, and disarmed, might be bloody down south and could be political dynamite up north. Acting as federal governess over the South for a generation would cost millions, but radical schemes required nothing less. Without an army of government agents to play poll watcher, for example, Confederates would make disfranchisement a joke. Most Republicans were ready to settle for much less, "progress at a good round trot," as one paper put it, and nothing faster. As long as the South gave blacks their basic rights, treated loyal men fairly, and sent the worst traitors into retirement, that would be enough.[10]

Andrew Johnson's Reconstruction

But once again Southerners nudged the revolution forward—two Southerners in particular. On April 14, 1865, while Lincoln sat watching a second-rate comedy at Ford's Theater, a first-rate Confederate sympathizer and actor, John Wilkes Booth of Virginia, shot him from behind. That night, the President's life ebbed away. In the gray of a drizzling morning, Vice President Andrew Johnson of Tennessee was sworn into office. It was a terrible beginning to a terrible presidency.

Johnson was no traitor. He was an honest democrat, proud of his humble origins and prouder still to call himself an American. In 1861, when secession fever swept Tennessee, he had risked his life defending the Union. When Union troops took back the state, Johnson returned to Nashville as Lincoln's military governor. Born in a log cabin, taught to read by his wife as he sat sewing in his tailor's shop, working his way up from alderman to governor and then senator, Johnson was as rough-hewn a success story as Lincoln himself, with two differences: he was a Southerner and a Democrat. Success let him become a slaveowner. It agreed with him so much that he once longed for the day of true equality—where *every* white family could have a slave to do the work. For him, a humane bill was one that gave free blacks two years to leave Tennessee, before having them driven out by force, and wartime changed Johnson very little. He did give up his slaves before Republicans put him on their ticket in 1864, but he never got over his notion of America as a white man's country nor the idea that by owning them, he had been doing his slaves a favor. Democratic gospel told him that the best government was one where the states had a free hand in most matters and the president, not Congress, led the way as policymaker in everything else. That would not sit well with Republicans, who saw the partnership the other way round.[11]

It would take a smooth talker to bring them around. Johnson wasn't a smooth anything. "He is always *worse* than you expect," one of his longtime supporters complained. The truth was, this self-made man had botched the job. Where Lincoln's origins made him humble, Johnson's gave him bragging points. "If Johnson were a snake," a foe commented, "he would lie in the grass and bite the heels of the rich men's children." Everywhere he spotted enemies; he believed they were lording it over him, trying to keep him down, menacing the republic. They were planters, fanatics, traitors. He had risen to the top by giving no quarter to those who disagreed with him. The people stood by him and always would. Johnson had no give in him—no lurking thought that he might not have all the right on his side.[12]

On May 29th, the president issued his proclamation setting up a provisional government, the first of several. For just about all Confederates worth less than $20,000, the administration gave a full amnesty, as soon as they swore loyalty to the Union and emancipation. The rest must sue the president for pardon. All summer, petitions for pardon piled up on the president's tables, a foot high, while "pardon brokers" peddling influence thronged the anterooms of the White House and wore out the carpeting and furniture in the attorney-general's office. By fall, Johnson was signing hundreds of pardons a day, and, one visitor complained, the whole population consisted of "Rebels wishing defiantly for mercy." There were no mass arrests, no treason trials, no confiscation of Confederate estates. Promised title to farms carved from the abandoned properties off the Carolina coasts, former slaves were gathered together by General Oliver O. Howard, head of the Freedmen's Bureau, to hear the bad news. "Why, General Howard, why do you take away our lands?" one black cried. "You take them from us, who have always been true, always true to the government! You give them to our all-time enemies! That is not right!" As Republicans watched, Johnson picked governors and pushed through new constitutions across the Confederate South. In the process, he set conditions for readmitting the states to their full rights. The "ironclad oath" barred former Confederates from becoming postmaster,

In Thomas Nast's savage cartoon, President Andrew Johnson pipes a tune to charm the Confederate snakes. Looking on the black victim quizzically are Secretary of State William Seward, Secretary of the Navy Gideon Welles, and Secretary of War Edwin M. Stanton. (*Harper's Weekly*, 1866).

tax collector, or government official—if, that is, the president had obeyed the law forcing his appointees to take it. He didn't.[13]

Such generous treatment might have worked had Johnson's governments shown the same generosity to the former slaves and Union men. By their own lights, they behaved wonderfully well. The fire-eaters who shouted for secession took the back bench to Johnny-come-lately Confederates. Lawmakers gave up the right to secede and passed the Thirteenth Amendment. They settled "the negro question" by setting up the Black Codes, defining just what freedom meant. Former slaves had the right to marry and own property, sue and be sued, and testify in court in cases where blacks were involved.

The Failure of Self-Reconstruction

It was enough for Johnson, but not for Northern Republicans. Even after the shooting stopped and Confederate President Jefferson Davis was behind bars in Fortress Monroe, Northerners could not reckon the Union as secure. Far from being universally repentant, some South Carolinians declared that the federal government would have to pay them for the slaves set free and exempt them from any taxes to pay the war debt. "What, ruin us, and then make us help pay the cost of our own whipping?" a Southerner exclaimed. "I reckon not!" Men freshly pardoned filled the Southern legislatures. Chattanooga theatergoers hissed the American flag when it appeared on stage; elsewhere Union men were insulted and sometimes killed. In July 1866, Louisiana radicals tried to call a long-adjourned constitutional convention into session to give blacks the vote. No sooner had a remnant of the original delegates met in New Orleans than a white mob attacked their supporters. "O! it was a bloody deed," one witness wrote north. "*One hundred* corpses in the lapse of one single hour, men, struck by two or more shots, unable to fly, beaten to death with clubs like mad dogs!" Wounded whites and blacks were butchered. The police and firemen helped do the killing. "Treason a crime?" one Unionist cried the year before. "D——n it, loyalty's the only crime, I think!"[14]

Planters held the whip hand over the landless workers they once had held title to. Giving the vote to blacks was out of the question. As one of Johnson's governors explained, they were "mere children—great big, laughing, overgrown, greasy, lazy children" (which, he added quickly, he said as one who loved the Negro). Under the Black Codes, employers who broke their labor contracts got fined. Black employees got a taste of the whip or stood in the pillory. In some states, blacks were kept from renting land in town or punished for "disrespect." In others they were forced to find a job or a "master" by New Year's. Vagrancy laws allowed the state to find countless excuses to put former slaves to work against their will, and "vagrants" multiplied wondrously in flood season, when the Mississippi levees needed repair. Apprenticeship laws let the courts pluck black children from their homes and make them "apprentice" fieldhands and scullery maids. Maryland and North Carolina alone made "apprentices" by the thousands. In some states, blacks could not own guns or dogs, move about freely without passes, or take on a trade. To enforce this, of course, the state could depend on white policemen and white militiamen, often still wearing their Confederate uniforms. With blacks forbidden to testify against whites and whites sure that every black killed had a healthy effect on the ones left over, justice was unworthy of the name. At least five hundred whites were indicted for killing blacks in Texas in 1865 and 1866. Not one was convicted. Blacks paid taxes, but found the poor relief, parks, schools, and orphanages their money went to were for whites only. North Carolina wiped out its school system, for fear that blacks might want schools, too, someday. "If you call this Freedom," a black veteran protested, "what do you call Slavery?"[15]

The Union needed a changed South. If black labor was to be free in more than name, the power of the plantation must be broken, and with it the political power of the Lords of the Lash. If the white South would not do these things on its own, the nation must. Already the New England Freedmen's Aid Society had promised to send teachers enough "to make a New England of the whole South," but government had to act, too. By the time Congress assembled that December, radicals knew they had an enemy in the White House. Only when moderates tried to fiddle with Johnson's Reconstruction did they find the same thing. Having stretched his own rights like India rubber to allow him the power to make a new political system, the president insisted that the Constitution kept Republicans in Congress from behaving the same way. In February 1866, Congress gave a new lease on life to the Freedmen's Bureau, which provided food and care for Southerners in need and gave blacks military courts in which they could appeal for justice across the South. Johnson vetoed it. A month later, he vetoed a bill guaranteeing the former slaves' civil rights. Moderates tried to find a middle ground. Wherever it was, Johnson had no intention of meeting them on it. "Sir, I am right," he told his secretary. "I know I am right. And I'm damned if I don't adhere to it." The civil rights bill passed over his veto, and a new freedmen's bureau bill went through that spring. "I don't wish [the president] any harm," a congressman joked, "but I shouldn't care if the Almighty took a fancy to him."[16]

The Fourteenth Amendment

Goaded by Johnson, fearful that mere law would never pass a presidential blockade and an unfriendly Supreme Court, Congress had all the more reason to fix the terms of peace for the eleven Confederate states into the Constitution. That spring, Congress produced a fourteenth constitutional amendment. To have their old political privileges restored, Southern states needed only to ratify it (Tennessee did immediately). Nobody got the vote; nobody lost it. But the Fourteenth Amendment was more than the "foundation of wood, hay, and stubble" that radicals branded it. The basis of apportionment for the House would be adjusted, the national debt guaranteed, the rebel debt repudiated, and prominent Confederates cut out of federal office—though Congress could let them back in again. Most of all, the Amendment guaranteed the rights of citizenship and equal protection of the laws to all persons born or naturalized in the United States. No longer could a Court decree, as Chief Justice Roger Taney had done before the war, that a Negro had no rights which a white was bound to respect (by 1864, indeed, a black had been admitted to practice law before that very court).[17]

And still the struggle went on in Washington. Between the president and Congress, relations went from awkward to poisonous. An outcast in both of the existing parties, Johnson had to create his own—a National Union movement open to all who put reunion ahead of equal rights. "We want the Union back—not merely pinned together with bayonets," one of his supporters explained. Between the northern Democrats who put the white man first and conservative Republicans hungry for peace, Johnson calculated votes enough to elect a Congress more to his liking. For one brief instant that August, things seemed to be going Johnson's way. The National Union convention met in Philadelphia to call for peace on the president's terms. As delegates cheered and wept, the delegates of South Carolina and Massachusetts—breeding grounds for secession and antislavery at their most unyielding—marched in, arm in arm, the very picture of sectional peace. Soon after, Johnson took his case to the people on a train tour across the North. The "Swing Around the Circle" went wrong almost at once. Before it was over, the president was trading insults with hecklers, branding Republican leaders like Sumner and Stevens as traitors and would-be assassins, and comparing himself to Christ. Mayors fled town to avoid being seen with him. General Ulysses S. Grant, the great Union war hero, went on a binge and dropped out of the tour. That fall, from Minnesota to Maine, voters sent their answer. They elected a more radical Republican Congress than ever, and the National Union party vanished unmourned.[18]

Radical Reconstruction

Johnson fought on. He weighed in against the Fourteenth Amendment. That killed whatever hope there had been of his Southern governments accepting it. By the end of the year, even moderate Republicans were being crowded closer to where radicals had stood the year before. To make the South safe for the Union, they would have to do what Johnson had done: remake politics across the former Confederacy. New state governments friendly to business promoters and small farmers, and a robust Republican party open to loyal white and freed black alike, should do the trick. So in 1867 Congress passed the so-called Military Reconstruction Acts. Under their terms the ten former Confederate states that had refused to accept the Fourteenth Amendment must rewrite their constitutions to guarantee the right of blacks to vote and hold office. A majority of registered voters would have to elect new governments, which would ratify the Amendment. Until they had done so, the army would keep order and preserve the peace. Commanders would administer five military districts; register voters, both white and black; and fire any official who tried to thwart Reconstruction.

But no one could fire Johnson. Through that spring and summer, he used every legal technicality and loophole in the Reconstruction Acts to stymie the Republicans. He dismissed military commanders and reinterpreted the law to help Confederates register. Congress had to hold a special session in July, just to make its will plainer with one more Reconstruction. It had to adjust the law the following winter to stave off a court challenge and to ease the conditions for readmitting Southern representatives to Congress. Already, Republicans had tried to tie Johnson's hands with the Tenure of Office Act, which prevented him from dismissing appointees outright, even Cabinet members, and gave the Senate final say. Most of all, they wanted to keep the president's hands off the army and hoped to protect Secretary of War Edwin Stanton, who clung to his job long after Johnson made him unwelcome. In August, the president suspended Stanton from office, as the law allowed. When the Senate restored the secretary to his old place, the president tried to eject Stanton by force. This was one exasperation too many. "Didn't I tell you?" Thaddeus Stevens exploded. "If you don't kill the beast, it will kill you." Moderates had beaten impeachment three months before. Now they, too, had had enough and voted to bring Johnson to trial. For radicals like Summer, the trial was merely a formality. If not for Senate rules, he complained, he could vote as he wanted: "Guilty of that, and infinitely more." But those who predicted that the president "ad interim" was about to be one "ad outerem" spoke too soon. At the heart of the House managers' case was the Tenure of Office Act, and its provisions were so cloudy in meaning that reasonable senators might differ about whether Johnson had actually broken it. That gave Johnson the seven Republican votes he needed—that and his promises to leave Reconstruction alone from them on. On May 16th, the Senate mustered thirty-five votes for conviction, one less than the two-thirds needed.[19]

Reconstruction culminated early in 1869, when the Fortieth Congress put through a third constitutional amendment, forbidding the use of race as a bar against a citizen's voting in the North or South. In 1870, the Fifteenth Amendment became part of the Constitution. Together, the three Reconstruction amendments would survive long after the rest of the Republicans' framework collapsed.

It *did* collapse, though, and keen-sighted people could have seen it tottering before the foundation stones were laid. From the first, the revolution mixed very fragile advances and very conservative underpinnings. In their faith in states' rights, private property, and an America where most people took care of themselves, the president and Republicans differed only in degree. Congress had not remade the South from a sense of simple justice, but because Johnson and white conservatives left them no alternative. If remaking the South was the only way to protect what the war had won, Republicans would do it, but that didn't mean they liked it. The sooner they were rid of the whole Reconstruction tangle, the better. If blacks "could be colonized, sent to heaven, or got rid of in any decent way, it would delight me," Congressman James A. Garfield of Ohio confessed—and he was one of the radicals! By 1867, though, it seemed that the only way to banish the "Negro question" from national politics was to make a South that could handle the problem itself. Ideally, giving the blacks the vote and the right to contract freely would let them protect their own interests, and Congress could go back to its peacetime responsibilities. By the year's end, moderates felt that they had gone as far as they dared—and, if the Democratic gains in the elections that fall were any guide, farther than most voters wanted. Only a few realists like Thaddeus Stevens questioned the assumptions under the Reconstruction settlement: that former slaves, new to politics, largely illiterate, landless and dependent on an aggressive conservative elite, could prevail. The North was doomed to disappointment, and black Southerners would get the blame for not achieving the near impossible.[20]

Persistent Inequalities

The Fifteenth Amendment shows how limited the new birth of freedom was. It could have given every adult male the right to vote. But that would have done away with Northern tests that cut immigrants out of the suffrage. Rhode Island forced the foreign born to own real estate in order to vote; other states had literacy tests or taxpaying qualifications. Nor did Congress make a serious effort to extend the vote to women. "Think of Patrick and Sambo and Hans and Ung Tung, who do not know the difference between a Monarchy and a Republic, . . . making laws for Lydia Maria Child, Lucretia Mott, or Fanny Kemble," one leading woman's rights champion protested. But even she understated how conservative the Amendment was. Quite deliberately, it uttered not a word about the right of blacks to hold office. In spite of Democratic predictions that rich men would bring on hundred million "Pig Tails" from Asia, at two dollars a head, just to vote down American workers, the Chinese in California, like Indians across the West, never got close to the polls—no closer than a bill to provide public education for all was able to get to a vote in the House.[21]

Women's moment never arrived. Radicals like Sumner called woman's suffrage "the great question of the future," but that future receded ever further. Between 1875 and 1890, the cause gained a little ground. Wyoming extended the vote in 1869, Utah in 1870, Colorado in 1893, and Idaho in 1896. Seventeen states enfranchised women for school board elections. In three others, they were permitted a vote on taxation and bonds. But most of the story was of constant defeat. Not until 1910 would they win their sixth state, though they mounted 480 campaigns to put the issue on the ballot.

Women might imagine that the Fourteenth Amendment gave them the rights of citizens to vote or practice law. The Supreme Court thought differently.[22]

For Indians, the Civil War actually marked a more ominous moment. The old Union might negotiate with tribes as if they were sovereign states, but not the new Union. After 1871, there would be no more treaties, no more pretense of Indian "nations" to deal with as equals. Inside the reservation, white man's law covered Indians, the Supreme Court declared, and blotted out any tribal law that got in its way. They were wards of the state, not citizens. Voting, selling alcohol, sitting on juries—all were denied them. In spite of the obvious intention of Congress in the Fourteenth Amendment, the high court ruled that citizenship was out of the question even for Indians who had left their tribes for white society. There was only one way for a native-born nonvoter to get the rights any male immigrant could get, sometimes within a few days of getting off the boat: he had to get a special act of Congress. (In fairness, it must be added, veterans of the Reconstruction Congress were appalled. The decision, one of them wrote, was "the strangest, if not the wickedest decision since the fugitive slave cases." Two years later he wrote citizenship into the law—but only for those who took up white civilization's ways).[23]

"Let Us Have Peace": The Passing of the Radicals

And where were the champions of human rights? Some turned conservative. Others fell away. In the wake of the Fifteenth Amendment, the women's suffrage movement split. Abandoning black suffrage to concentrate on feminist issues entirely, Elizabeth Cady Stanton and Susan B. Anthony set up the National Woman Suffrage Association, a rival to the broader, if less radical, reform spirit of the American Woman Suffrage Association.[24] Still other leaders retired or died. Barely kept alive by his passion for bringing Andrew Johnson to book, old Thad Stevens just outlived impeachment. Committed to equal rights to the last, he had himself buried in a black churchyard, the one in town that barred nobody on the basis of color. Other radicals lived on, but nobody seemed to be listening. Every year Charles Sumner seemed more irrelevant to the Republican party, a conscience his colleagues were sick of heeding.

The truth was, the war had shifted some Northerners' thinking, and even then only in some things, not in all. It had actually rooted some of the familiar institutions more deeply than before. The war hardened party ties more often than it snapped them. How could it be otherwise, when most of the Southern "traitors" stood with the Democrats, and yesterday's slaves voted with the party of Lincoln? or when Republicans had saved the Union, as most Democrats saw it, by mauling the Constitution? War made Americans appreciate the conservative virtues afresh. Ministers and intellectuals saw a new respect for order, a new emphasis on obedience among the Northern people, a keener appreciation of the past.[25] Wartime rhetoric translated smoothly into peacetime concerns, with the same warning of threats to law and the public order, the same emphasis on a need to uphold authority, and an authority whose main duty was to keep the peace. The more the old world they knew was changed, the less Americans like upsetting what was left.

By the time of Johnson's impeachment, Republicans had already tacked to the conservative breeze. Passing over their statesmen in May 1868, they nominated a war hero for president. As the hero of Union triumphs at Fort Donelson, Vicksburg, and Petersburg, General Grant deserved recognition from his country. A plain, close-mouthed, modest man, Grant kept the widespread love of those who, in the words of a poet, remembered him as the "Great Captain, Glorious in Our Wars."[26] All the same, he was no radical with ideas or a vision for a more equal America; he would uphold Reconstruction and keep order, and not much else. His was a calming presence and his letter of acceptance gave the country the winning slogan: "Let us have peace."

When the Democrats nominated shy, sickly Horatio Seymour, New York's wartime governor, their choice made the Republicans' job all the easier. Like most Democrats, Seymour had supported the war, and, like most of them, he had carped at Lincoln for winning it the wrong way, by freeing slaves and locking up dissenters. His running mate, General Frank Blair, Jr., rampaged across the country, accusing blacks of polygamy, demon worship, and lust after white women. If Democrats won, Blair promised, they would use the army to put whites back in control of the South. Did Congress object? If so, there were bayonets enough out there to take care of that problem, as well. Southern Democrats got the message, and sent one that no Northerner could mistake. They threatened black voters, most of whom were voting Republican. White terrorists shot and killed opposition candidates, and, in Georgia and Louisiana, committed full-scale massacres. Those two states went Democratic. If Alabama hadn't canceled the presidential election, it might have gone the same way, and through the same raw, bloody revolution. (A weary Congress had to re-Reconstruct Georgia; Republicans got a political reprieve—for all of another ten months). If Seymour and Blair meant that there would be four years of bloodletting and that the whole Reconstruction settlement would be undone, many conservatives wanted none of it. Prosperity needed peace. Financiers like Philadelphia banker Jay Cooke saw a campaign contribution to Republicans as the best business investment they could make. So badly did the Democratic campaign go that three weeks before the election, party leaders actually considered dumping their ticket and putting up a fresh one. Yet, with all those advantages, Grant won with less than 53 percent of the vote.

A Loss of Faith in Government

Grant's election signaled more than a pause in the reform movement. The mandate to use government as a solution to national problems had vanished. Legal scholars did discover new potential in the Constitution and in the use of state power. Plenty of experiments were tried in peacetime, using the lessons drawn from wartime experience. But every year innovations that cost anything or made government bigger became a harder sell. When the debt of Providence, Rhode Island, went up 529 percent in fifteen years, or when Newark's rose by 2,658 percent, the less positive government those cities had, the better taxpayers would like it. As the states rewrote their constitutions in the 1870s, they cut back on what public authority could do. One delegate to California's 1879 convention actually proposed a provision that "There shall be no legislature convened from and after the adoption of this constitution, . . . and any person who shall be guilty of suggesting that a Legislature shall be held, shall be punished as a felon without the benefit of clergy."[27]

Weary of war's expenses, the people demanded that Congress cut taxes and disband the military almost immediately. By 1866, the army had been reduced to puny proportions—too little to protect Southern Republicans—and the cheese paring had just begun. A decade later, the army could spare but 3,000 men to keep the peace across the South. Congress abolished the income tax in 1870. Excise taxes shrank by seven-eighths. Year by year, lawmakers forged new hobbles on departments' ability to use their money as they saw fit.[28]

If Americans distrusted their government, they had cause. Readers of *The Gilded Age*, Twain and Warner's bestseller, knew the indictment by heart: the desire for wealth was a moral cancer that had gone metastatic. It raised a host of speculators, like the promoter of the up-and-coming town of Corruptionville ("And patriotic? why, they named it after Congress itself".) Religious papers used "sentimental snuffle" to hawk bonds. In Washington, fictional statesmen like oily Senator Abner Dilworthy (modeled on a real senator, Samuel "Subsidy Pom" Pomeroy of Kansas) used pieties about human rights to cover their stealing, knowing well that lobbyists paid higher for the "high moral ones, . . . because they give tone to a measure." Was this fiction? Newspapers gave the reality: congressmen were expelled for selling West Point cadetship appointments, senators were shown up as bribe givers, and Washington reporters played the market on inside information. The less lawmakers did, the better. One chief executive was asked how he got on with lawmakers. "I won't say they are bad men," he told the interviewer, "but the pleasantest sight of the year to me is when at the end of the session I see their coat tails go round the street corner."[29]

A Less Manifest Destiny, 1865–1877

The impulse to withdrawal and restraint did not stop at the water's edge. Back in the 1840s, the future seemed certain to the "Young America" crowd. They would see the Stars and Stripes carried west to California, south to Panama, and north beyond the Arctic Circle. Among those shaped by that vision was William Seward. Toothless, scarred from ear to lip by a would-be assassin's knife, Lincoln's secretary of state had held on through Andrew Johnson's administration. It was hard not to like him but nearly impossible to trust him, especially when he was thinking up new schemes. The older he got, the larger his dreams grew, of an empire sprawled across the Caribbean—or perhaps the Pacific—or both! He wanted coaling stations halfway around the world, American rule to replace French rule in St. Pierre and Martinique, a base at Samana Bay, or, failing that, the whole island— Santo Domingo and Haiti included. Westward, Hawaii could be ours; why not Fiji? and Borneo? The Danes would part with their West Indies for $7.5 million; might they hand over Greenland and Iceland, too?[30]

Seward could dream and scheme all he wanted. Most of his ideas never got beyond chitchat. Other ideas failed almost at once. Americans wanted the French and their puppet emperor Maximilian out of Mexico, and the State Department gave the foreigners 50,000 reasons for quitting—all of them lined up along the border, guns in hand. France pulled its troops out and left Maximilian to face a firing squad, but American troops let the Republic take care of itself. Hawaiians were willing to come into the Union, but the Senate barred the way. It even refused a treaty giving them a break on sugar duties, and would not have taken the Danish West Indies as a gift. Only two of Seward's advances got anywhere. Twelve hundred miles west of Hawaii, a navy commander planted the flag on Guam in 1867. Since nobody lived there, there was no price tag. But there was a price for Alaska, which had been costing the czar of Russia more than it was worth. When Seward expressed an interest in the territory, Baron Edouard de Stoeckl, the Russian minister, leaped at the chance. Within days, the State Department had drafted a treaty buying what one derisive reporter dubbed "Walrussia." The price was $7.2 million—or about $2.2 million more than Russia had hoped to get.[31]

President Grant made even less headway than Seward. Before his administration was over, he had arranged a commercial treaty with Hawaii. From Congress, the authoritative voice of Senator Charles Sumner, head of the Foreign Relations Committee, called for Great Britain to pay damages for the injuries that the *Alabama* and other Confederate ships built in England had done the Union in wartime, and hinted that one way of settling the debt would be to hand over Canada. With Cuban patriots fighting to overthrow Spanish rule, congressmen clamored for American aid to a fledgling republic that might, in time, join the Union. Most of all, there was Santo Domingo, ruled by Buenaventura Baez, a tinhorn dictator ready to sell his country cheaply. Everyone knew how valuable Samana Bay would be for a naval station. Who could calculate the value of the island's coffee, sugar, fruit, and tobacco? It might even give blacks a nation within a nation of their own—a nation free from bigotry. President Grant felt so strongly about annexation that one winter night he called at Sumner's house to persuade him.[32]

But nothing happened. Sumner beat Grant's annexation treaty in the Senate, and crushed it every time it came up afterwards. Not even the saber-rattlers wanted a war over Cuba, much less Canada. Spain polished off the rebels and babied the State Department along with empty promises that Seward's successor, the genteel Hamilton Fish, chose to believe against all the evidence. "Scarcely beneath the Stars and Stripes," an angry poet wrote,

> *Beats there a heart so lost, so low,*
> *That struggling Freedom's cause will fail*
> *To fire with sympathetic glow.*
> *Alas! could hope itself expect*
> *More than Spain's myrmidons can wish*
> *When a misguided nation's pulse*
> *Throbs through the cold heart of a Fish?*[33]

Instead of joining the United States, the Canadian provinces joined each other in one dominion and built a railroad line across to Vancouver to bind British Columbia the tighter. Though orators talked about annexing Canada, policymakers never got very far. In the Treaty of Washington, they compromised their quarrel with England by putting the main issues in the *Alabama* claims case up for arbitration.

What had made Manifest Destiny so much less manifest? Opponents gave plenty of reasons. Big empires required big armies, and a navy better than the leaky wooden tubs limping along in the 1870s. How would a country so deep in hock from the Civil War pay for either one? Taxpayers wanted the income tax abolished, the tariff duties lowered, the national debt retired. As a reporter put it, "*Imposts* concern us, at present, quite as much as outposts."[34] Two other arguments, however, may have been more telling. Men like Sumner, who feared that annexation would spread to Haiti and wipe away one of the few black republics in the world, were rare. Much more commonly, critics warned that taking Caribbean islands meant more "barbarians black as the ace of spades and ignorant as horses," "the scum of the tropics."[35] Reformers smelled a swindle in Santo Domingo, with rings of speculators using Uncle Sam to make themselves rich. The House debate over Cuba, it was said, pitted Spanish gold against Cuban bonds, with congressmen taking liberal amounts of both. And wasn't that the story of Alaska, too, where Russian gold bought statesmen wholesale? (It didn't).[36]

The Liberal Revolt, 1872

The retreat of government power and of national vision may seem remote from the story of the North's failure of will in Southern Reconstruction. It wasn't. The leaders discredited were the ones whose name made Republican promises good, but more than that, the message the enemies of Manifest Destiny spoke went straight to the heart of the Reconstruction debate: government of, by, for the people was not working—at least, not well enough to absorb *more* black voters or give politicians *more* ways of lining their wallets.

The New York *Tribune's* great radical editor, Horace Greeley, indicated just where the disenchantment and moral exhaustion might lead. From land reform to slum clearance, Greeley had earned his reformer's credentials. Earlier than most Republicans, he hectored Lincoln to free the slaves and called for giving southern blacks the vote. But Greeley was growing old and tired. The North had won, the South had Reconstructed, and that to the old editor seemed enough. He wearied of defending "an easy, worthless race, taking no thought for the morrow," at the expense of the South's "best men." In 1867, he raised his voice for letting Confederate President Jefferson Davis out on bail, and put up some of the bond money himself. Longing for a renewal of the good will the North and South once felt for each other, and disgusted by the corruption in Washington, the editor found himself leagued with other Republicans of a like mind. In May 1872, the so-called Liberals made him a candidate for president. Democrats would take anyone to win, even Greeley, who had once declared every horse thief a Democrat. The "Sage of Chappaqua's" famous old white coat might cover their true colors, which, down south, were still a Confederate gray.[37]

Greeley never had a chance of beating Grant. The country was too prosperous to care about scandals yet. The South was quieter and richer than it had been in years. The Treasury was wiping out the public debt, and brand new rules had gone into effect to ease government hirings towards the merit system. Greeley had so many odd friends and crazy ideas: "free love and free farms, and all that." Was secession really dead? Were the war's results really secure? Once again, Grant seemed the safer choice. The old crusader lost in a landslide. His mind gave way. Within a month, he was dead.

Yet time stood with the conservatives. Each day, the arguments from high ideals lost force, until very nearly the only case for Reconstruction was the one of preserving the gains a war had won. But the more Reconstruction was put on that footing, the shakier it became. Every new western state admitted lessened Republicans' need for Southern votes. Every year, the Union looked a little safer. As that happened, Southern loyalists of both races went from indispensable to insufferable in Republican lawgivers' eyes.

Race prejudice was nowhere near the whole story. Still, it played a leading role in the so-called "redemption" of the South from Republican rule. Bigotry in the North varied, from the black-face impersonations of funny "darkies" in minstrel shows to an ugly lie, circulated by Democrats, that Republicans had a master plan to make a master race by blending white maidens with plantation Negroes. It touched the Women's Christian Association in Hartford, which raised charity funds from black and white alike but gave aid only to whites and shut the doors of its home for wayward girls to those of other races. It even infected Republicans who supported Reconstruction and remained steadfast for equal rights. As Sumner lay dying in 1874, he saw his work unfinished still. "My bill," he murmured to callers, "my civil rights bill—don't let it fail."

A chastened Congress took the measure up, only to find that a federal law opening juries, hotels, schools, cemeteries, streetcars, and railroads to blacks stirred an uproar from New Jersey to Illinois. "Either the law will have to be a dead letter or the negroes will be dead negroes," a Cincinnati reporter warned. The final law left out graveyards and schools. In practice, it might as well have left out everyplace else, too. Most communities ignored it. Just the same, the Supreme Court overturned its provisions in 1883. The "equal justice" part of the Fourteenth Amendment applied only to what state governments did, said the Court. Private individuals could discriminate as much as state law let them.[38]

Increasingly, the drive for equal rights seemed an obstacle to the first great purpose of the late war. If the country was to be reunited, some reconciliation seemed in order. The "natural leaders" of society ought not be cut off from power forever, whatever oaths they had broken. By 1868, even Jefferson Davis had received a pardon; four years later, a Republican Congress put through an amnesty act covering all but a corporal's guard of onetime Confederates. Within less than a decade, the South was back in their hands. "Peace with the old master class has been war to the negro," Frederick Douglass lamented.[39]

Chapter 3

"Gentlemen, We Are Not Yet Over": Reconstruction

One night in the Gilded Age, so the story goes, a Yankee visitor passed the night on a Louisiana plantation. It was all that legend would have led him to expect: a welcome warmer than the climate and a dinner as lordly as the landowner's manners. And yet, through all the lively conversation ran a thread of melancholy. Nothing, it seemed, could match the splendor of the Old South. When plates and palates were cleared and the room was fragrant with the smoke of a fine cigar, the wayfarer strolled out into the moonlit garden, the mild summer air flowing with the perfume of unnumbered flowers. The guest was overcome. "What a beautiful night!" he burst out. "Ah," an old servant observed mournfully, "you should have seen that moon *before* the war." [1]

The Self-Emancipation of the South

"The youngest of us," as an abolitionist had written in 1864, "are never again to see the republic in which we were born." Nor did they. The Union held for all time. Slavery was dead beyond resurrection. Steps were taken to give free blacks more chance to make good, and to make a Southern economy rather more like the North's. Reconstruction was no failure. It was something less pathetic, more tragic: as one historian put it, "America's unfinished revolution."

Emancipation was just the beginning. Blacks made their slave marriages legal. They held property and acquired it: cows, horses, plows, carriages, farm equipment, even some land. Scrimping pennies from their meager earnings, cashing in bounties for wartime service and lottery winnings, ten thousand former slaves put money into Freedmen's Savings Banks, chartered by the federal government. Blacks moved where they pleased, and many, especially single and widowed women, migrated to Southern cities, where opportunity was greater than in the countryside. They built and supported a host of churches, hired their own ministers, and heard those parts of the Scriptures so long denied to them. New Orleans congregations set up missions on outlying plantations and became missing-persons bureaus, helping freed slaves find their kin sold away from them across the years. Wives and children withdrew from field labor, where the family could afford it, and, when their husbands were hired to tend the cotton, black women set their own price for kitchen service.[2]

Long after being emancipated, Charles Whiteside remembered his master's words: "Charles, you is a free man they say, but Ah tells you now, you is still a slave and if you lives to be a hundred, you'll STILL be a slave, 'cause you got no education, and education is what makes a man free." Blacks wanting to read the word of God for themselves or the labor contracts their old masters pressed them to sign knew that well enough. Transforming cattle pens, warehouses, even slave markets into schools, paying Northern "school ma'rms" in eggs, vegetables, and fruits, thousands learned to read, write, and figure. "Thank God I have a book now," one Georgia black wrote his teacher. "The Lord has sent us books and teachers. We must not hesitate a moment, but go on and learn all we can."[3]

Compared to the privileges that whites enjoyed, the ex-slaves' was a skimping freedom, even after Congress did away with the Black Codes passed just after the war. For black women, emancipation often meant subjection to a husband's will nearly as absolute as it had once been to the master's. "When I married my wife," a Tennessee freedman explained to an employer hoping to exploit her labor as well. "I married her to wait on me and she has got all she can do right here for me and the children." Still, even in 1865, black rights stretched far beyond what the Old South had allowed. Laugh though one might at the new names that ex-slaves took, be it Alexander Hamilton or Chance Great, the right to name oneself, to carry a cane or a parasol, to go hunting with a pack of dogs, or to keep to the sidewalk when whites were passing was a token of rights any white would have taken for granted.[4]

"Negro Rule"—So Called

The Republicans who took power in 1868 would push black rights further still. To many angry conservatives, Radical Reconstruction meant little more than the ugly consequences of the three Reconstruction amendments—uneducated Negroes swarming at the ballot boxes and flaunting sheriff's badges; Northern intruders so poor that a carpetbag held all their possessions when they came and so greedy that a bank could hardly contain all their graft when they left; and scalawags, the native white rabble, thrusting their hands in the till. While the gentility watched helplessly, Republican "Negro rule" brought race-mixing in the railroad cars, fraud at the polls, political anarchy, public bankruptcy, and private insolence. "This is truly a government of the nigger, and by the nigger, and for the nigger," one Democratic journalist snarled.[5]

That Reconstruction certainly existed. Looking in on the South Carolina legislature, one observer saw next to nothing but African-Americans, ranging in color "through dirty white, chrome yellow, molasses color, ginger, cinnamon, and mahogany, to coal black." (That they might also differ in honesty, ability, and background escaped him entirely.) "I have a son I sent to school when he was small," a black Georgia legislator explained, when quizzed about his illiteracy. "I make him read all my letters and do all my writing. I keep him with me all the time." In a very few states, Reconstruction did cut thousands of whites out of the vote, briefly. In Alabama and Florida, both sides applied brass-knuckle tactics in close elections. "Damn it, corruption is the fashion!" Governor Henry Clay Warmoth of Louisiana shouted to a delegation of protesting businessmen. Mississippi's black superintendent of education pilfered public funds; a leading black politician sitting on the New Orleans Park Commission bought land from himself and used inside information to speculate in state bonds. Black magistrates and mixed juries did not dominate, but they existed. Having to address Negroes as "gentlemen of the jury," a white lawyer mourned, was "the severest blow I have felt."[6] Now and then, children of both races attended the same schools, and thousands of ex-slaves went from tenant to landowner.

Conservatives, then, were right in every particular. They just got the generalities wrong. Over all, Reconstruction brought about the fullest, fairest elections in Southern history. Former Confederates ran for office as Democrats in Republican states and sometimes won. Nowhere did voters elect a black governor. If the freedmen chose one of their own, they preferred ministers to fieldhands, and the educated class, free before the war, rather than those emancipated since: leaders like William Whipper, a South Carolina rice planter. Of six hundred blacks serving in ten states' legislatures, two-thirds of them came from Louisiana, Mississippi, and South Carolina. Most were one-termers. So were the only two black senators elected. Whites ran the important committees and wielded the gavel in most places. Black congressmen, some twenty state officers, mostly chosen from the three states with black majorities and nearly all of them born free, sheriffs and justices of the peace in plantation counties, constables in town—all this seemed radical by any standards the South had known before the war, but it was a far cry from Negro rule.[7]

Reconstruction remained firmly in white hands. So did the land, the industry, and the wealth of the South—plus the plunder. Roguery knew no party lines. If Republican lawmakers robbed, Democratic businessmen received stolen goods. It was they who bribed their way into control of state-owned railroads in the Carolinas and Georgia. Taxes were certainly higher than before the war. They had to be. The new society of social services that Republicans hoped to build took money.

Along with the carpetbaggers had come a multitude of other Northerners, many of them ministers and schoolteachers. Now the states built hospitals and asylums. Courts provided lawyers for poor defendants in Alabama and made white fathers pay for supporting their mulatto children. Law and jurisprudence both gave laborers a margin of advantage over their planter-employers. Across the Deep South, public schools arose, enough to educate one child out of every two in states where no facilities had existed before. For upcountry farmers, states provided debtor relief and broadly exempted what property could be sold to satisfy creditors.

Railroad executives from Boston and Philadelphia sent money and contracts southward, hoping to build or buy a network of lines and forge an empire of commerce. Reconstruction governments sped construction with subsidies and bond guarantees: $10,000 a mile in Mississippi, $20,000 in North Carolina. To foster development, they chartered banks and factories, funded levee repair, and lifted the limits on how much interest lenders could charge. Pulling 2 million acres from lands dedicated to sustain the public school fund, Mississippi lawmakers endowed them on a railroad project. In four years, Southern railroads expanded by 40 percent: an additional 3,300 miles of track. "We thought that railroad and bank directors would no longer have it all their own way, and fill all the chairs in our Legislatures," a Republican newspaper lamented. "But money is ahead of us yet."[8] All these inducements to business, too, Reconstruction meant.

Yet the new governments neither won the acceptance of most white Southerners nor fund the funding to turn impoverished states into prosperous ones. The railroad companies they aided went broke—many of them before completion—leaving state governments saddled with debts that they had never imagined would fall to them to pay and that they found ways of evading. As for the black electorate, it mostly stayed as it had been in the beginning, working the soil that white conservatives controlled. "Our wives, our children, our husbands, has been sold over and over again to purchase the lands we now locates upon," one freedman had protested in 1866. ". . . And den didn't we clear the land, and raise de crops ob corn, ob cotton, ob tobacco, ob rice, ob sugar, ob everything. And den didn't dem large cities in de North grow up on de cotton and de sugars and de rice dat we made? . . . I say dey has grown rich, and my people is poor."[9] There were a lot of ways the states could have helped bring lands to the landless. Except for South Carolina, none of them bothered.

Within the new governments, bickering reached the point of near war. Because banishment from office meant poverty in a society where white conservative Democrats owned all the resources, Republicans quarreled savagely with each other as they shoved their way to the public trough. Florida Republicans framed and impeached their governor three times in as many years. South Carolina's Republican governor escaped that fate by buying his accusers off. With hired bullies and federal gunboats to back them up, black Louisianians and Custom-House appointees made war on Governor Warmoth, and ultimately impeached him, but not before he had used his Returning Board to count in a Democratic governor, and two self-proclaimed governments vied for sole title. "Mr. Cheerman," one North Carolina black shouted at a party convention, "Judas Iscariot betrayed our Savior for thirty pieces of silver, but dar is men right here on dis floor who can be bought for less dan dat."[10] In the case of the self-proclaimed Republican governors in Virginia and Tennessee who handed their states over to the Democrats, charges of treachery did them simple justice.

"Redemption"

Where economic clout could be used to keep blacks home, Democrats used it, but they relied still more on organized violence. Whether they were called the Knights of the White Camelia or the Ku Klux Klan, the terrorist societies founded at the war's end had the same aims: to put blacks in their old place and smash the Reconstruction governments. With respectable white community leaders covering for them, Klansmen killed legislators, congressmen, ministers, and schoolteachers. "Impudent" blacks were hauled from their homes and whipped for refusing to step off the sidewalk when whites passed or for dressing up "like they thought anything of themselves." Where terrorism cowed the courts, grand juries dared not indict. Petit juries brought in acquittals regardless of the evidence. In some states, governors had the nerve and white Republicans the manpower to fill the state militia. There, the Klan could be broken. Federal action under the "Ku-Klux Act" of 1871 finally broke the masked terror elsewhere and even got some convictions in the federal courts.[11] But within a few years, violence returned, this time in broad daylight. Conservatives organized private armies called the White Leagues. Parading with guns, using any pretext to protect whites in danger, they backed up their candidates with open military force. By 1871, Democrats had "redeemed" nearly all the Upper South from Republican rule, and Georgia, too.

With planters and businessmen threatening their black tenants with ruin, and with white Republicans terrified into silence or forced to convert, the Reconstruction governments turned north for help. They got it, but they could not shake that first, fa-

(Thomas Nast, *Harper's Weekly,* 1874)

tal belief that a more manly people would not have needed to ask for extreme measures. If Negroes with governments of their own could not defend their own interests, the argument went, were they worth anybody's defending from elsewhere? Every intervention made the next one more politically costly. By the early 1870s, most Northerners were sick of stretching government's powers several times a year, so that carpetbaggers could keep the vow one of them supposedly made, of "five more years of good stealing" down South. Even among earnest Republicans, the suspicion hardened into belief that blacks were unfit to rule themselves.

The Grant administration could hardly lend its prestige to the cause of Reconstruction. By 1876, it had no prestige left. Reformers found their way into the Cabinet. So did rogues. Grant's first Attorney-General, Ebenezer Rockwood Hoar, had a flinty integrity but he lasted barely a year. Then the president swapped the Justice Department for some badly needed Senate votes. Neither landgrabbers nor party fundraisers got anywhere with Jacob Cox running the Interior Department. In late 1870 he quit before Grant could fire him. His successor let the spoilsmen and Jay Cooke's western railroad interests do what they wanted on public lands. The longer the administration went on, the fouler the stench of corruption grew. Hoar's successor and Cox's both resigned before the House could investigate them. William W. Belknap, the genial Secretary of War, should have done so, too. In March 1876, with incriminating testimony already in the public record, he rushed to the White House in tears to resign, before the House could impeach him for accepting kickbacks to keep his wife in silk. Just a week before, a federal jury in St. Louis had acquitted the president's private secretary, Orville E. Babcock, of taking bribes from tax-dodging whiskey distillers. Plenty of revenue officials, with less political pull, ended up in jail for their part in the "Whiskey Ring." Admittedly, the Cabinet still had two ardent reformers in it. President Grant fired them both. A Republican platform, quipped one reformer, was simply a conjugation of the verb "to steal."[12]

In good times, Americans had not taken administration scandals seriously but, in 1873, a panic on Wall Street began six hungry years. Railroads and factories went broke. Trade slowed; cotton prices plummeted. Jay Cooke's banking house closed. So did the Freedmen's Savings Bank, where former slaves had saved what little they could. Cooke had cleaned out the vaults to pay for the Northern Pacific—the transcontinental line he was building—which was bankrupt, too. Voters turned even more sharply against big-spending government and self-enriching politicians. In 1874, Democrats won the House for the first time since before the war and started hacking government expenses. They turned a searchlight on every dark corner of Grant's administration.

Even radical movements blamed government action for the people's woes. And why not? Gold wrote the laws. As long as lobbies and campaign funds decided what the parties in power ought to do, the Cookes would always be spoiling the broth. Out among the farmers of the Ohio Valley, the skilled workers of New York, and in the coalfields around Scranton, agitation by 1876 ran strong against the government's alliance with the private bankers and the national charters that let private firms issue banknotes. Those wanting easy credit protested a Treasury determined to return the

The Royal Tattoo.
Hawaii's king tattoos President Grant with scandals of the
day—some of which he had nothing to do with. (Library of
Congress)

country to a standard where every paper dollar could be redeemed in gold. To do that, there had to be fewer paper dollars circulating. As the "greenbacks" were withdrawn, prices fell, wages were cut, and construction stopped. Clamoring to drive the money-changers from the capital, a Greenback party ran a gentle millionaire ironmonger, Peter Cooper, for president in 1876.[13] Cooper did badly even for a hopeless candidate. He got barely 80,000 votes (two more hard years raised the Greenback vote tenfold). The feeling that government was part of the problem, rather than part of the solution, was widely shared.

Reconstruction died slowly and painfully. Federal officials took pains to interpret the Reconstruction Amendments as narrowly as possible. Did the ban on involuntary servitude include sentences to the chain gang for petty criminals? The Attorney-General thought not. Alabama law forbade blacks to marry whites; did that deny equal treatment under the law? Not according to the Justice Department. What about states that kept blacks from testifying in state courts? That, two Attorney-Generals protested, was none of the federal government's business. Indictments of Klansmen in the Carolinas never got to trial; the government dropped prosecution in the feeble hope that its generous behavior would be repaid.[14]

By 1874, only Louisiana, South Carolina, and Mississippi could expect Republican rule to last out one more election. All three had black majorities, but that was not enough to save them. In September of that year, Louisiana conservatives took to the streets, routed the police under former Confederate General James Longstreet, seized the statehouse, and forced the governor to resign. Federal soldiers put him back in place, but could not protect a fair vote that fall, or roll back the Democratic *coup d'etat* in the Louisiana House. The following autumn, gunmen scattered Republican meetings in Mississippi, and, after one set-to, rampaged across the county shooting blacks "just the same as birds." Whites came to the polls with rifles, and, in one case, a six-pounder cannon. Yazoo county had given Republicans an 1,800-vote majority in 1873; this fall, they got seven votes, total. Incorruptible, able, and sure to be deposed, Governor Adelbert Ames resigned. In 1876, South Carolina's "Redeemers" adopted the "Mississippi Plan." The red shirts worn by mule-riding armies of Democrats made the campaign colorful, but the red on their victims' shirts was not so easily removable. Across the uplands, Red Shirts whipped and killed Republican organizers. They would win, a white landlord told his black tenant, "if we have to wade in blood knee-deep."[15]

Hayes's "New Departure"

They did win, but only by wading in betrayal knee-deep as well, for 1876 was a presidential election year. With scandals breaking in every government department, Democrats made reform their warcry. For president they nominated Governor Samuel J. Tilden of New York. Tilden had no war record to explain away, no freakish notions to scare away business leaders. He was simply a canny political wire-puller and corporate lawyer, who had gone after the thieves in his own party. Now he promised to bring cheap, honest government to Washington and "home rule" to the South. Playing down race, Democrats swore to uphold the three Reconstruction Amendments. It was not equal rights they wanted to overthrow—just the crooks, fools, and tax eaters that were turning the South into a wasteland. Leave those states alone, they assured Northerners, and the voters would elect the South's natural rulers, those well-mannered, well-to-do conservatives who called themselves "Redeemers." Everyone would gain, blacks included. South Carolina would be as clean and as prosperous as New York.[16]

Against Grant, the Democrats' good, gray governor could have won. But Republicans chose a good, gray governor of their own, Rutherford B. Hayes of Ohio. Hayes had commonplace qualities, the kind Grant's administration so lacked: simplicity, honesty, courage, and a strong sense of duty. No one could blame him for the mess in Washington, though Democrats tried. Nor could anyone pin the blame for Southern Reconstruction on him: neither side had a good word to say for the "carpetbag-scalawag" governments. Imagine, then, the shock on the dawn after Election Day when the two parties discovered Hayes's victory resting on one electoral vote, 185 to 184, and then only if the last three Republican strongholds in the South did their duty in how they counted the ballots.[17]

Democrats were properly enraged. Having cheated, frightened, and "bulldozed" Republicans' natural majority away from the polls in most Southern states, they now lost a "reform" victory they had stolen fair and square. The most indignant among them shouted "Tilden or Blood!" They vowed to march people's armies on the capital to enforce the people's will. Tilden's nephew quietly tried to buy the vote-counting boards down South. Congressmen threatened to filibuster the official count of electoral votes to death in the House. Nothing worked. On their side, Republicans had the Senate, the president, and the army. What they needed was a clearer title. Both sides agreed on a compromise that no one much liked, an electoral commission with fifteen members. The commission was a makeshift judicial body in theory. In practice, it simply ranged partisans against each other. By eight to seven, the members certified Hayes's right to all three states.[18]

Hayes would be inaugurated now, but how peacefully was less certain; the Southern Republicans would be abandoned, but how willingly and how soon was anyone's guess. "As matters look to me now," wrote a Kansas partisan, "I think the policy of the new administration will be to conciliate the white men of the South. Carpetbaggers to the rear, and niggers take care of yourselves." With Tilden's hopes flickering, Southern Democrats snuffed them out entirely. In return, they won a guarantee that the new Republican administration would withdraw its support from what little remained of Republican governments in South Carolina and Louisiana—that is, a handful of buildings in the capital city. Plenty of other half-promises were made: Southern Democratic votes to make a Republican the next Speaker of the House, Republican aid for a transcontinental railroad west from Texas, and guarantees for blacks' basic rights. None of them amounted to a thing in the end.[19]

1877 was an end, not a beginning. With no money for the army and a clouded title, Hayes could hardly have done anything but go along with the deal his friends worked out. Still, he hoped for the best. Everybody would benefit from a well-run South, blacks included. With proper coaxing, the new president thought, white leaders might drop old issues and old hatreds. Then the planters and industrialists who took first rank among the "Redeemers" could find their true home, outside of Democratic ranks. So former Confederates and old Whigs got plenty of patronage, and reconciliation plenty of lip service in the North and South. The president even laid wreaths on Confederate graves. Only one defect marred the Southern strategy: its utter failure. After two years of mutual sweet-talk, the House elections of 1878 were held, and with what result? There was violence against blacks; ten Southern Republican seats in the House were cut down to four; the black vote was driven from the polls, the white vote was more solidly Democratic than ever; and not one single Republican governor was elected. Good organization did not deserve the credit. Timely killings did.[20]

Where Democrats needed black votes locally, they shared petty offices. Wade Hampton, South Carolina's Redeemer governor, made one black a captain in the state militia and put another on the board of the orphan asylum. His party sent half a dozen to the general assembly.[21] But these honors were rare, and outside of Democratic ranks they grew ever fewer. Those offices that most affected blacks' own condition—those involved in enforcing the laws locally—sheriffs, constables, jurors, state militiamen—were the first lost.

"Bulldozing" a Solid South

Against all odds, Republicanism survived. Down the Appalachians ran a belt of Republican counties, strong enough to elect congressmen of their faith (eight in 1888). There, upland whites who stood by the Union in wartime stood fast against the Democrats now. Along the Mississippi and across the richest cotton counties, blacks voted Republican, given the chance free of cash or coercion. Between the two groups, the upper South gave Republicanism a fighting chance. Further south, things were less hopeful, but the party did take enclaves. One or two blacks made it into nearly every congress. Nonwhite legislators and city councilmen were rarer than before, but they persisted.[22]

But the odds kept getting longer. Redeemers changed the political rules right away and kept adjusting the voting regulations year by year. Mississippi Democrats gerrymandered the heavily black counties along the Mississippi River into one district, known as the "Shoestring." That way the Republicans got one congressman rather than three. Alabama Democrats carved up the "Black Belt" to give all six districts a share. With 40 percent of the vote statewide, Republicans took no seats at all. A careful drawing of city ward boundaries in Wilmington ensured that a community 80 percent black had only one alderman in three. Where no geometry could keep Republicans from winning, white legislators gave them nothing to win. They wiped out local self-government and let the state authorities choose justices of the peace. When all else failed, they counted votes their way. As one Alabama editor protested, "some ballots that are cast are so secret they are never heard of again."[23]

What could break the Redeemers' grip? Party strategists tried to wipe out the stigma of "Negro rule" by making a whites-only Republican party. In Georgia, former Confederate General James Longstreet proposed separate Republican organizations for each race; Alabama partisans actually tried it. They soon found out the obvious: blacks, who provided most of the votes, could find leaders a lot more easily than the handful of white leaders making up the other faction could find followers.[24] Alternatively, Republicans could act as though the race issue did not exist. By stressing issues of economic development—for example, tariff protection—they might win go-getters away from the Redeemers. The only catch came in persuading *Democrats* to go along with the change of issues. It happened every so often. So angry were Virginians over the way conservative lawmakers scrimped on schools to pay the state debt that they threw them out and brought in the Readjusters, who put money back into education, gave the Old Dominion a new tax system, and incidentally legislated on behalf of both races. Within five years, Democrats had won their way back into power by waving the bugaboo of Negro rule. And though the American Iron & Steel Association churned out high-tariff pamphlets in 1884 and orators thundered about infant industries, the Solid South did not even crack.[25]

The Ignorant Vote.
Nast meant to show why Republicans with black support
had as much justice on their sides as Democrats with the
Irish on theirs. But it also showed how far the champion of
equal rights had fallen from faith in universal suffrage in ten
years' time. (*Harper's Weekly*, 1876)

Without outside pressure, their government would rest with whites almost exclusively and the bitter truth was that in any contest left to white voters, Redeemers
owned the South, lock, stock, and ballot box. Let white voters be assured a thousand
times that equality would mean neither a Negro governor nor, worse, a Negro son-in-
law, and they would refuse to believe it; and the Democrats were demagogue enough
to tell them just the reverse, as loudly and crudely as they could.

To win in their own right, Republicans needed a second Reconstruction, where
federal marshals backed up blacks' right to organize and vote. By the time the party
got the House majority it needed in 1890, it had lost the will. In both chambers, Massachusetts had sent worthy heirs to Charles Sumner to lead the fight: Henry Cabot
Lodge and George Frisbie Hoar. One of those "fawning fellows with running noses,"
as a Missouri congressman described reformers, Lodge had entered public life to reclaim it for men of character. Practical politics had dimmed his early idealism considerably, but even in 1890, his commitment to reform was so strong that it gave way
to nothing except partisanship. In this case, since Democrats did most of the vote-

stealing everywhere, an honest count served both ends. So Lodge's bill provided for enforcement not just in the South, but in every American city with more than twenty thousand inhabitants. An active opponent of slavery before the war, Hoar stood for the faith that brought the Republican party into being and had given it meaning. Now he did his utmost to align younger colleagues with Lodge's so-called "Force bill" in the Senate. But merchants trembled for their trade and labor unions panicked lest bayonet rule extend to them. High-tariff interests shoved the bill into the lame-duck session, where Republicans from mining states cut a deal with Southern Democrats in return for a bill to coin more silver dollars. "The question will not down," Hoar wrote, determinedly. "Nothing is settled that is not right." He knew better. Neither he nor Lodge tried any such crusade again, and Southern white Republicans, who had hoped for so much from the bill, played their lily-white strategy more than ever.[26]

The Color Line Goes National

The war had been lost by that time, not just in Washington, but in every bookstore and playhouse in the land. If anything, race prejudice had become more respectable, even in Charles Sumner's Massachusetts. Colonel Mulberry Sellers, inextinguishable speculator of *The Gilded Age,* was not so far from the real spirit of too many Gilded Age philanthropists when he admitted a willingness to elevate the Negro's soul: "you can't make his soul too immortal, but I wouldn't touch *him,* myself." Not even the evidence before them could convince Northern reporters of the obvious. In 1884, one visited Greeneville, South Carolina, and spotted a separate world of institutions that blacks had created since the war:

> All who can afford it study vocal and instrumental music from competent instructors. Connected with their churches they have their temperance organizations, their 'Bands of Hope' composed entirely of children, and their Young Men's Christian Association, at which they have debates and declamations. They have . . . some very creditable fire companies, one or two fine roller-skating rinks, and several companies of militia. They often have amateur theatricals, minstrel shows, public suppers and festivals. . . . They issue printed invitations for full-dress balls, calico hops, or masquereades, . . . and church weddings, with a large bridal party, are by no means infrequent. The negroes here have a paper, which they edit, print, and sell themselves.

And the one lesson to be drawn from all this was the blacks' slavish imitation of a superior race! There was, the reporter concluded, "but little to admire in the Southern negro. . . ."[27]

The same could not be said of the Old South. Around it swirled a mist of fanciful, wistful recollection, based on the sentimental plantation novels from before the war, and the imagery of a land devoted to cavalier ancestors and Sir Walter Scott's virtues. A pioneer in literature with Southern dialect and a sugary flavor, Joel Chandler Harris's "Uncle Remus" stories won a national audience. The Negro folktales he adapted often taught harsh lessons about trickery and brute force. Like blacks in a white-run society, Br'er Rabbit needed all his cunning to overcome Br'er Fox and Br'er Bear. But tricked out with doting white children and a sweet, harmless old ex-slave storyteller, the moral was easy to miss. By the 1890s, Northerners were echoing the same nostalgia for "the old-time darkey," and regaling readers with pictures of a colorful ("like the exterior of chocolate creams") people, for whom the watermelon was their "whole existence." Rural audiences still flocked to theaters for *Uncle Tom's Cabin,* but what would Harriet Beecher Stowe have thought of her antislavery classic, if she had attended? Pure farce and extravaganza, cornet bands, performing dogs, trained alligators, and milk-white doves carrying Little Eva to Heaven, all had replaced the plot. Whites in blackface sang wistful songs about good times on the old plantation, when folks like them lived high on the hog.[28]

So when the Supreme Court took up the case of *Plessy v. Ferguson,* it ranked as one of the most significant nonevents of the Gilded Age. Louisiana had mandated separate railroad cars for whites and blacks. With only one dissent, the justices put their stamp of approval on the state's right to use its police power to ordain "separate but equal" facilities (without ever having bothered to look into the question of how equal those facilities were). Legislation, wrote Justice Henry Billings Brown for the majority, "is powerless to eradicate racial instincts based upon physical differences, . . . [and] if one race be inferior to the other socially, the Constitution of the United States cannot put them upon the same plane." That *if* was a mere courtesy; expert opinion now weighed heavily on white supremacy's side. Only a onetime slaveholder from Kentucky, John Marshall Harlan, dissented. As he reminded his colleagues, any assumption that two races were unfit to associate with each other cast a stigma that the Fourteenth Amendment had meant to remove. "Our Constitution is color blind; and neither knows nor tolerates classes among citizens." Yet so unremarkable was the majority opinion in an age that took prejudice as a given, and so consistent with eighteen years of legal precedent was the case, that most newspapers did not see fit to cover the story. The *New York Times* did report it—under its regular column of railway news![29]

Redeemer Rule

Race relations were the most important retreat from Reconstruction's promise, but not the only one. The new leaders of the South were much like Northern voters in the mid-1870s. They wanted cheap government and precious little of that. So Redeemers made a positive practice out of leaving things alone—except for tax rates. Spending was slashed, revenues cut off. North Carolina halved its budget in a dozen years, while Texas put the government on a strict pay-as-you-go basis and then set up a revenue system that made it almost impossible to find the pay. Annual legislative sessions became biennial. Lawmakers' pay fell to four dollars a day. Alabama dispensed with a lieutenant-governor entirely, Tennessee with a governor's mansion (the chief executive had to board at a hotel). For what little the state did, the treasury laid a general property tax and a poll tax, substantial by past standards and measly by later ones.

Convicts were a special case. Florida did away with the penitentiary entirely. In other states, authorities applied that Republican invention, the convict lease. Businessmen needed cheap labor; the state needed cheap punishment. In return for a few pennies a day, a corporation could take over the lodging and feeding of criminals and turn a profit by putting the convicts to work. The more convicts, then, the better for the state treasury. As a result, measures meting out harsh punishments for petty offenses assured a lavish supply, largely black. So cheap and plentiful was labor that it could be used thoughtlessly. In Louisiana, 14 percent of all convicts died one year, 20 percent the next, and 14 percent the next. In effect, a seven-year sentence for selling cotton after nightfall served as a death penalty. Survivors went through unspeakable treatment. "We actually saw live vermin crawling over their faces," a grand jury reported, after one examination, "and the little bedding and clothing they have is in tatters and stiff with filth." That was in the prison's hospital section.[30]

Even by nineteenth-century standards, the custom in New Orleans of lodging lunatics in the city jail excited indignation. It was a virtual death sentence. Visiting the asylum in Jackson, Louisiana, a legislative committee found no furniture, clothing, or medical supplies. Inmates wandered around naked, and did so at faster speed in winter, since the asylum had no heating system. There were no beds, and the dining hall's stench so overpowered the investigators that they fled.[31] Alabama solved the public health problem by closing Montgomery's public hospitals.

North and South, the war had reinforced in substance, as much as it transformed in detail, the conservative basis of the nation, and Reconstruction's end revealed how strong conservative forces were. Still, it is important to see that, for all the reaction, matters did not go back to where they had been in 1860—or even in 1867, before radical Reconstruction got under way. Without the black vote in the North, Republicans might have lost the presidency in 1880 and 1888; even their electoral landslide in 1896 would have melted away. There *were* black landowners, black voters, and, in much of the upper South, a lasting two-party system.[32]

Public schools certainly were starved, but they were there to stay. True, where Massachusetts spent $21.55 per pupil at the turn of the century, North Carolina spent $1.65. A traveler early in the new century likened one dilapidated rural schoolhouse to "something like an old Virginia rail fence grown up with weeds." Negro children got a third as much per pupil as white children in Virginia, a sixth as much in South Carolina. What use was there, an editor demanded, in wasting money schooling "dusky dudes and dudines?" As for black higher education, the New Orleans *Picayune* may have been kind in calling Louisiana's college "A Colored High School with Grammar School Characteristics."[33] Yet over all, Southern schools got more funding than before the war. Even in Georgia, they ranked among the state's biggest budget items, and all across the South, spending for education started rising again in the 1880s. Between 1870 and 1890, the proportion of children of school age enrolled had tripled, bringing it close to Northern standards. Literacy rates rose prodigiously for both races. True, one black in every two remained illiterate at the turn of the century; but in 1865, nine out of ten had been unable to read their own names.[34]

That advance may give a clue to the hill-country opposition that every so often erupted against the Redeemers. However sparing the social services that conservative governments offered, white farmers unhappy with their leaders were likelier to think that the government was doing too much than to complain that it was doing too little. By wiping out the tax exemption that Republicans put on personal property, Redeemers were loading down assessments on the tenant's mules and furniture and on the carpenter's hammer. Taxes were higher than before the war, and for farmers with little, a mere dollar poll-tax took food off the table. When Tennessee Redeemers took fiscal responsibility too seriously, taxpayers revolted and swept the incumbents out.

Perhaps the right note for historians to take towards the postwar South would be that of an Arkansas Republican, present at the constitutional convention that wrote the document on which a Reconstruction government would stand in 1868. As other delegates celebrated, he hesitated. Eight years had seen the blacks brought out of bondage, through a sea of blood, like the children of Israel that Moses had led. Fondly he hoped that the convention might help Arkansas "pass over Jordan. But it is a hard road to travel, to get into the Promised Land. Gentlemen, we are not yet over."[35] Nor were they, thirty years later. But the journey had carried them far, and it would carry their descendants farther still. In a sense, the whole Gilded Age would tell a like story: not only of work completed, but of larger purposes begun.

Chapter 4

Redeeming the Past, 1875-1898

Try as they might, Southerners could not recapture the past. Not all of them wanted to. "Next to the grace of God," a North Carolina divine asserted, "what Salisbury needs is a cotton mill." Henry Grady, the pudgy editor of the Atlanta *Constitution*, became the prophet of a new order of things. Not for him the land of slavery, cotton plantations, and gentlemanly languor. For Georgia to rise again, it must change its estates into small farms, its cotton patches into peach groves and peanut fields. The night sky must be lit up not just with a Southern moon, but with the red glare of iron foundries. Coal mine and cotton mill, immigrant and toiler, would make the South anew, free from race hatred or base desires for Negro equality. Grady believed in his vision. Before he died in 1889, he even convinced himself that it had come true.[1]

The New South Vision

Other Redeemers practiced what the editor preached. Georgia's former Confederate governor, Joseph E. Brown, was a sterling example. When the war ended, Brown joined the Republicans. They made him Chief Justice. Redeemers made him senator. By the 1880s, the one-time champion of small farmers had become president of railways and coal and iron companies. His predecessor, former Confederate general John B. Gordon, not only invested in the Central Pacific Railroad; he let it invest in him, and, as senator, provided it with a very reliable return. With friends in power, corporations found the South quite the place to do business. Any factory built in South Carolina got a ten-year tax exemption (except for a property tax on the land it covered). Any community that wanted to pledge funds to aid a railroad got the general assembly's permission. Publicity campaigns touted Southern resources across the North.[2]

It sounded like an ideal cast for a melodramatic production of "The Great Barbecue, or, The South Sold Out," which is how some saw it. Not just government action, but national markets were reshaping the countryside. With the rest of the country clamoring for timber, coal, iron, and turpentine, Southern forests and mines supplied the raw materials for many of the finished goods that locals ended up buying from the North. Railroad passengers in the Southeast could smell a depot miles before they got to it, from the hundreds of tons of phosphates locally dug and bagged, waiting to be shipped away as fertilizer. North Carolina built tobacco factories and had its share of the four hundred Southern cotton-textile mills in operation at century's end. In 1900, the South employed one textile worker in three. Birmingham, Alabama, turned out more iron than the rest of the Confederate states put together. (It did so well at it that the owners saw no reason for retooling, even after most businesses took up steel instead. So the iron sewer pipe came from Birmingham, but along steel railroad tracks forged in Pittsburgh.) "If all the saw mills, cotton mills, tobacco factories, new towns, and other enterprises [announced as begun] had really been erected and put into operation, there wouldn't be surface room for them to stand on, water enough under the earth to supply their boilers, nor room enough in the sky for the smoke from their chimneys," a skeptic complained in 1908.[3]

Not far from town, a world remained that had barely been grazed by industrialism. For most farmers, market day remained the big event, when they went to the nearby village for talk and trade. Well into the twentieth century, a Mississippi boy remembered what a curiosity the county's one-mile strip of graveled road was. "I used to drive out there sometimes just to hear the buggy wheels click and scrunch," he wrote. Even city newspapers ran weekly sections discussing farm problems. Farming did not stand still, of course. Technology turned sugar making into a big business. Rice plantations along the swampy Carolina coast lost out to those on Louisiana's upland prairies, where ground was solid enough for harvesting machines and growers used rice seed from Japan. Still, the same old cash-crops—sugar, tobacco, and cotton—defined the New South. Grady might talk of diversifying crops; farm families knew better. Anyone who grew corn and potatoes would have to compete with produce from Maine and Illinois that was just as good. "I grow green peas and everything I know of," one Georgian lamented. "I have raised horses, cows, and hogs, and I have diversified it for the last three years and have not been able to make a dollar."[4]

King Cotton Rules Yet

Average farm size actually rose. By 1910, it was 724 acres, or twice that of 1860. Only on a plantation's scale could cotton planting make a good living, but many small farmers grew a bale or two, as a side venture, to get the consumer goods they needed.

They actually became less self-sufficient than before. Cultivating an alternative supply in India, Brazil, and Egypt during the war, British mill-owners never returned to their old dependence on the Deep South, but the South needed foreign markets more every year, as railroads opened up new lands to commercial farming. Twenty-two cents a pound was enough to make a fortune. With the Panic of 1873, though, cotton fell to ten cents. By the mid-1890s, market prices had dropped to less than six cents, and those farmers who brought their bales in at harvest season often could not even get market price. And still the Cotton Kingdom expanded. In 1873, 9.35 million acres had gone to cotton, in 1894, 23.6 million—but at 4.6 cents a pound—brought in less money in all.[5]

"A magnificent yield of cotton leaves the people unclothed," a bitter Georgian fumed. "A magnificent yield of corn leaves them scantily fed. Strange state of things, when abundance brings want and success means failure." In 1880, over half of the farms in Georgia were tilled by their owners. By 1920, over two-thirds would be operated by tenants, and half were white. Forty-seven out of every hundred Georgians was black in 1900, and they held one acre in twenty-five. As one bitter refrain put it,

> *An ought's an ought,*
> *And a figger's a figger*
> *All for the white man*
> *And none for the nigger.*[6]

Grady's vision had been blighted from the beginning. In 1865, when the Confederacy collapsed, the doom of the planter seemed sure. War had wrecked the cotton economy of the South and had undone its labor system. Planters themselves shared the glum forebodings. Some went off to Brazil or Mexico to start over, though most came home again soon. Others dropped planting entirely, and became lawyers or businessmen in New York. Those who stayed on the land might be as luckless as Alexander Stephens, Confederate vice president, now compelled to make ends meet by endorsing Darby's Prophylactic Fluid.[7]

Yet the planters survived. Northerners came south for bargains in real estate. Only a few made money. Most found that the skills suited to a Yankee farm could lead a cotton plantation straight to foreclosure. Merchants found that extending credit and furnishing supplies to the planters did not make money enough to go from storekeeper to landholder. Instead, a new generation of planters rose from the middling farmers of the South, those with fifty- to one-hundred-acre plots, or from the sons of planters from elsewhere, arriving with money and connections to back them. Many of the old established families kept their place at the top, as well.[8]

How could this be? The answer is simple. In a poor South, the cash-poor planters still had an edge. All the connections that family and commerce with Northern firms had given them still remained. Loans and credit came more easily. A poor real estate market actually protected cash-poor landowners. Who would buy their property? Who could afford to? Tax sales brought vast estates under the hammer, but not many blacks could afford to buy. Old planters could, for a pittance. So in Mississippi, 95 percent of all forfeited land ended up back in the original owners' hands.[9]

The big landholders could also depend on the same old labor supply. Free or not, black workers made a much more dependable force than Chinese or European immigrants (planters knew: they had tried both). For those masters who had varied the penalties of slavery with little rewards—a gift at Christmastime, support for the slave too old to work—emancipation meant freedom from costly obligations. Health and housing were now the employees' responsibility; laying down the law was left to court and constable.[10]

Some planters prospered. By 1900, four thousand of them in Georgia owned their own cotton gins. Many built sawmills on their estates, though few could match Colonel James Monroe Smith. His plantation was a virtual community—with a cotton gin, a dairy, gristmills, fertilizer and brick factories, two stores—and his very own railroad spur, tying him into the main line near Athens.[11] Like the colonel, many planters would help define the new part of the New South. They set up shops, invested in banks, sat on the board of railroad directors, and provided the capital for founding cotton mills. But for every Colonel Smith, there were a thousand poor Joneses, the field hands and landless tenants of the South.

"The Mortgage Worked the Hardest. . . ."

Tenant farming came in many forms, sharecropping being among the most common. For all its ill fame, it did have real advantages. White owners would rather have hired their labor on the wage system. That way, they could keep a closer eye on what employees did. Blacks could live in the old slave cabins, labor under the same gang discipline and perhaps the crack of the same overseer's whip. Specific contracts set forth how many hours of work would be done; which tasks would be carried out; what punishments would be given as a result of failure to work, absence, or sickness; and what rights blacks would be allowed to exercise. Any visitor to the employee's home on the planter's land might need a permit. A contract could forbid blacks to keep pets or livestock on their own, to talk to one another while working in the field, or to take a drink, even on their own time. Contracts required employees to show perfect obedience and respect—that old-time respect where the cap came off and the eyes were averted before the employer's face.[12] There would be a master and a servant and free labor would mean that most of the labor was on one side, and most of the freedom on the other, just as in the good old days.

Not too surprisingly, blacks did not like the arrangement. They changed employers. Some struck for higher pay. "If ole massa want to grow cotton, let him plant it himself," one freedman protested. "I'se work for him dese twenty year, and done got nothin' but food and clothes, and dem mighty mean; now, I'se freedman, and I tell you I ain't going to work cotton *no*how." Ideally, blacks would rather have been landowners themselves, grown what they pleased, worked when it suited them, and run their lives like free people anywhere. By 1890 one black Southern farmer in five would own some land—a remarkable accomplishment.[13] But in the first years after the war, most blacks had no chance of getting one acre, much less a few hundred. Even if whites agreed to sell to a freedman and the cash could be scraped together, the purchase was only a first expense. Ramshackle estates would cost a small fortune just to be put back in running order.

Gradually, both sides found a compromise in the rental of land for a share of the crop. If they wanted, tenants could live far from other families, put in a little garden of their own, buy a goat or a cow and graze it near the home, and decide when to work and how long. In theory, the system rewarded hard work and could have turned renters into owners. The more the tenant grew, the more bales of cotton he would end up with, to dispose of as he chose, and the more money it should have brought him.

To turn the theoretical into the real took two unattainable conditions: a good price for what farmers grew and a fair price for what they bought. A farmer free from debt had the best chance of getting both. At least he could shop around. But at the start of the growing season, tenant farmers typically had no money for seed and tools, or for rations to carry them through to the harvest. That drove them to the merchant, who sold on "time prices." As security for the goods advanced, the merchant took a lien on the crop. When selling time came, he took out his due first. Charging interest of 5 percent a month on whatever he sold, a storekeeper could end up with just about the whole crop, and sometimes more. As long as the farmer remained in his debt, he had to do his shopping there, rather than look for a better deal. Come spring, he would be back, doing business at the same counter. When the merchant happened to be his landlord, too, that welded the chains even tighter. As one lament put it,

> *We worked through spring and summer,*
> *Through winter and through fall—*
> *But the mortgage worked the hardest*
> *And the steadiest of all.*

Debt bound laborers to the soil. It also bound them to cotton. Lienholders might not like the price that a bale went for, but at least they knew something about the product, enough to feel comfortable selling it. Letting a small farmer retool—pledging him the funds necessary to make a go of some crop he neither knew how to raise—or how to market—almost invited disaster. Creditors might even object to farmers' taking out time to raise livestock and sweet potatoes. If debtors wanted a further loan, they must keep to the old ways.

And if the Redeemers wanted to keep power, so must they. It was no coincidence that when Mississippi Democrats mounted a campaign in 1875, they headed their ticket with the Grand Master of the state Grange, nor that a typical Redeemer legislature in South Carolina would have three manufacturers, three merchants, thirty-three lawyers—and sixty-three planters and farmers. If there was help to industry, often it was because the farmers, even spokesmen for the Grange, saw the factory as a way to save themselves from a costly dependence on Northern goods at Northern prices. Leaving the South without manufacturing, the president of a farmer's club warned, would "give this noble heritage over to log cabins, bushes, dogs, and gutters." Business interests could still obtain a welter of privileges: tax-exemptions, rigged assessments, land grants, convict-labor, and state troops to suppress disorderly employees. Rural representatives were glad to oblige developers that way up to a point—the point where the public purse had to be opened. Restoring the railroad aid programs that Republicans had created and then repealed was unthinkable. New South conservatives might prate about the sacredness of the public debt, but small farmers behaved far more irreverently, "scaling" or "consolidating" state obligations when they could, and sometimes throwing them off entirely.

Instead, when Redeemers expanded state power, it was on farmers' behalf. Georgia set up the first state department of agriculture in the nation in 1874. Other states followed suit and Alabama's bureau took on power "second only to the governor." Experimental farms were established and there was money for geological surveys. If a state agricultural society held a state fair, it did so thanks to a government subsidy. Farmers demanded usury laws to put a ceiling on interest rates and got them.[14]

In getting public action, landowners spoke more loudly than tenants and planters spoke the loudest of all. Plagued by vanishing livestock and food out of the field, they pushed through laws turning petty theft into grand larceny, where stealing a pig worth several dollars could earn several years in the state penitentiary. Irate at tenants' cotton-pilfering just before the crops were harvested and divided, Granges and agricultural societies put through "deadfall" laws to forbid sales after nightfall. Laws against trespass increased their fines tenfold, and the landlord's lien on his tenant's crop was given priority over the merchant's. Together, the laws made sure that any New South agriculture would stay very like that in the Old South: the laws guaranteed cheap labor, tightly controlled and suited for growing the same old cash crops. As long as planters could rely on a huge labor supply, they would. There would be no flood of displaced tenants to the cities to provide hands for the mills.[15]

Even then, there was altogether too much change, of the wrong kind, to suit many small farmers. New South spokesmen sneered at the naysayers as "Bourbons," who, like the French royal family, forgot nothing and learned nothing. Bourbons might have replied that Gradys and Gordons had nothing to teach worth knowing. "Progress" meant a retreat from the values that the white South had once cherished, of social harmony and freeholders' democracy. For poet Sidney Lanier, that farmers' commonwealth remained the most compelling vision, a world where

> *mild content rebukes the land*
> *Whose flimsy homes, built on the shifting sand*
> *Of trade, for ever rise and fall*
> *With alternation whimsical,*
> *Enduring scarce a day,*
> *Then swept away*
> *By swift engulfments of incalculable tides*
> *Whereon capricious Commerce rides.*

Nor was it Southern commerce that did the riding. "Farmers are all laborers," a country editor exclaimed, "and they are not going to rely on the money kings of the East for relief from financial troubles any longer—but each says to the other—'Trust not for freedom to the banks/In farmers' votes and farmers' ranks/Our only safety lies!'"[16]

If the postwar South had a hundred-proof Bourbon, it would have been Robert Toombs, the vainest and maddest of Georgia's elder statesmen. Long years of boozing had not quenched his fiery spirit, nor had the defeat of the Confederacy broken his will. Implacable against Northern interlopers, financial as well as political, Toombs showed the paradox at the heart of the Bourbons' revolt. To preserve the Old South would require new means. "Better to shake the pillars of property than the pillars of liberty," Toombs exclaimed. To counter the Georgia Railroad's power in politics, he shoved a state regulatory commission into the state constitution. No longer could the railroads win rebates, nor any corporation gain special legislative privileges.[17]

Bloody Shirts and Empty Sleeves

However much New South spokesmen would have like to have harried Toombs into obscurity, they could not do it. His Confederate credentials gave him and countless others cover. Indeed, for forty years, each section would make the wartime experience sacred: the Lost Cause of the Confederacy and the Won Cause of the North. If the Old South heritage was too strong for the New South to overcome, the war that ended it stayed too vivid, too traumatic for participants to overlook it. "Listen!" a Yankee poet appealed to readers:

> *Again the shrill-lipped bugles blow*
> *Where the swift currents of the river flow*
> *Past Fredericksburg; far off the heavens are red*
> *With sudden conflagration; on yon height,*
> *Linstock in hand, the gunners hold their breath;*
> *A signal rocket pierces the dense night,*
> *Flings its spent stars upon the town beneath:*
> *Hark!—the artillery massing on the right,*
> *Hark!—the black squadrons wheeling down to Death!*[18]

At the heart of both causes stood the veterans' societies to keep memory alive, or at least an attractive imitation of it. Foremost in power as well as in numbers stood the Grand Army of the Republic. By 1868, the North had 2,050 GAR posts, by 1885, 5,026 and well over three hundred thousand members.[19] There were plenty of other groups, moreover. The South had its Sons of Veterans, Order of the Stars and Bars, Confederate Choirs of America, and United Confederate Veterans. The North boasted its Armies of the Tennessee, the Potomac, the Ohio, and the Cumberland. Every year, cities hosted veterans' "encampments," which only got bigger as the war receded further into the past. Founded in 1889, and soon some 80,000 strong, the

UCV's annual reunions became mob scenes. When the soldiers gathered in Richmond in 1896, the *Dispatch* devoted twenty pages in twenty-four to the Lost Cause. Ten thousand veterans and ninety thousand other celebrants came to town, sleeping wherever space was available, from porticos to roofs.[20] North and South, the rituals were the same. Survivors spoke eulogies on the dead and honored the living with titles. Union veterans led the campaigns to raise a statue to General William Tecumseh Sherman in Washington or a national park on the site of the battle of Chickamauga. Everyone relived the most terrible, and most meaningful, days of his life.[21]

A war record was such an asset that both parties began recruiting soldiers to show off even before the war ended. A good political procession might feature wagonloads of disabled veterans or former prisoners from the notorious Andersonville camp. From Bangor to Baton Rouge, an empty sleeve made up for an empty mind at election time. A Confederate vice president sat in the House, his voice too weak to be heard, his frame too shattered to raise him upright. At the battle of Fredricksburg, General Ambrose Burnside had made such a mess of things that his men marched into certain slaughter before the stone walls on Marye's Heights. Thousands more had died of exhaustion and sickness after he sent them slogging through the mire of northern Virginia. Rhode Island rewarded him by making him governor and then senator until he died.[22]

Voters had not really swapped their ideals for a handful of medals. Instead, both sides were reaffirming something essential: their faith in the cause for which they sacrificed and their gratitude to the men who kept it alive. With Democratic "Rebel Brigadiers" taking seats in Congress, the veterans that the North sent would send a message loud and clear: the people who beat the Rebellion still kept the spirit of '61 alive.

> *We whipped them before, we can whip them again;*
> *We'll wipe treason out as we wiped slavery's stain;*
> *For traitors and slaves we've no place in our land—*
> *As true loyal men to our colors we stand.*

Those colors included more than the nation's flag in the two generations after the war. Alongside them, Northern Republican politicians waved the "Bloody Shirt." As the story goes, a Yankee congressman was giving a speech about atrocities committed on Union men down South. Holding up the tattered, blood-stained shirt from one victim, he got so worked up that soon he was waving it over his head; from then on, the term applied to every emotional appeal of North against South. "Every unregenerate Rebel . . . calls himself a Democrat," shouted one Indiana governor, in a model of bloody-shirt oratory:

> Every bounty jumper, every deserter, every sneak who ran away from the draft . . . who murdered Union prisoners . . . who contrived hellish schemes to introduce into Northern cities the wasting pestilence of yellow fever, . . . every one who shoots down Negroes in the streets, burns Negro school-houses and meeting-houses, and murders women and children by the light of their flaming dwellings, calls himself a Democrat.[23]

Other orators warned that a solid South could always run a divided North. It might pay off the Confederate debt, repudiate the federal bonds, pay masters for the slaves that Mr. Lincoln had set free, and—who knows?—in time build up state militia big enough to start another war. And this time, the Rebels would win. Predictions like those sound sillier now than they did then, and much that Northern Republicans were saying was not silly at all. The blood on the Bloody Shirt was real—and fresh.

There was something quite real—quite necessary—in the Lost Cause romanticism, too. Former Confederates could rub away the bitter facts that Southerners of both races had broken the power of the Confederacy and that Southern commanders had squandered what little chance they had of winning. Lost Cause ideology gave the Union credit where credit was due—and then some. Exaggerating the industrial might of the North made it easier to explain its victory as a dead certainty from the first, even *if* Southerners had all the talent and the Lord on their side. Everyone had won; everyone deserved prizes, even Jefferson Davis. As Confederate president, no insult had been too cruel to load on him. As a relic, he became a popular hero. When he came to a cornerstone-laying at Montgomery in 1886, as one newspaper described it, his apartment was strewn with roses: "he walked on a bank of flowers."[24]

Woe, then, to that politician who belittled the veteran's contribution! Senator Charles Sumner of Massachusetts found that out when he tried to wipe the name of wartime victories from the battle standards of existing regiments in 1872. Even his own legislature censured him. Fifteen years later, President Grover Cleveland offered to restore those Confederate battle flags captured in wartime. The banners were rotting unnoticed in federal arsenals, but the uproar about transferring them south was terrific. Protest memorials arrived at the Oval Office, written on blood-red paper. "May God palsy the hand that wrote that order," screamed General Lucius Fairchild, a one-armed veteran of Gettysburg and head of the GAR. "May God palsy the brain that conceived it, and may God palsy the tongue that dictated it." Instantly, Cleveland found an excuse to reconsider.[25]

"The Old Flag and an Appropriation!"

Bloody-shirt politics made the Treasury bleed, as well. Southern states sometimes provided a pittance to disabled soldiers and their widows. Texas gave land. Union veterans' families did better; they could depend on the federal government. Any soldier with a crippling war injury, and any spouse or orphan of one, could apply for a pension under broad legislation. Under an 1879 law, they could collect benefits all the way back to the day the regiment mustered out at the war's end. The Pension Bureau usually gave it to them. Special bills—4,127 in six months—took care of many others who could not meet the requirement. Congressmen could hardly turn any appeal down, and until 1886, presidents signed every such measure they got, sometimes hundreds in a day. Cleveland was the one holdout, but when Republicans took back the White House in 1889, they made a legless veteran, Corporal James Tanner, head of the Pension Bureau. "God help the surplus!" Tanner roared. On his old comrades' behalf, he promised to "drive a six-mule team through the Treasury." With the right interpretation, the requirements hardly shut out anybody at all, and a few veterans got pensions without even bothering to apply. The Disability Act of 1890 did away with the need for most special bills (or the danger of vetoes) by extending $144 in annual benefits to anyone disabled or any veteran's widow, even if the injury or cause of death had nothing to do with military service. Every ninety-day volunteer could collect. By 1907, that one law had cost the government over $1 billion. Pensions took up 21 percent of all government revenues in 1880, over 40 percent in 1893, and yearly outlays kept rising until 1913.[26]

To hear critics tell it, pension legislation stank with partisanship and corruption. In effect, Southerners were taxed to pay for Northerners' support. Blacks got little, and immigrants who arrived after the Civil War got nothing. A Pennsylvania family whose son deserted and drowned in a canal six miles from home demanded compensation; so did an Illinois soldier injured by a 4th of July cannon while on furlough. Modest reforms were proposed in the House: denying a pension to wives betrothed five years after the groom mustered out, say, or giving disability payments only to those applicants making less than $600 a year. None passed. When a local GAR post condemned abuses in the pension laws, the state headquarters expelled it. If pensions were one of the pathbreakers on the way to the welfare state, where government took responsibility for those in need, they also made a case for slamming the Treasury door shut, even in the faces of widows and orphans. ("If it wasn't f'r thim raypechious crathers," Mr. Dooley exclaimed in another context, "they'd be no boodle anywhere.")[27]

To those who gave, of course, the purpose of the pensions went beyond supporting individual recipients, however destitute the women who constituted the vast majority of beneficiaries happened to be. It served as solid proof that the government had not forgotten those who had rallied to the cause when they were needed most. Onetime soldiers were more than a mere interest group. The GAR reminded veterans of their worth as individuals; this new nation was their work, more than anybody else's. What could old soldiers find to talk of, year after year, one general's wife asked him early in the next century as he packed for the latest reunion. "My dear," he explained, "we don't go to talk; we just go there to meet together and to *feel.*" In a materialistic world, the reunions were a way of reaffirming values beyond personal gain, and an identity beyond material circumstances. "If there ever was an army on the face of the earth which resembled an affectionate family it was . . . *the Army of the Cumberland,*" one of his colleagues declared.[28] Generous with the government's funds, they gave freely of their own. In ten years, the GAR spent over $2 million in private charity for soldiers, much of it administered by the Woman's Relief Corps, the auxiliary of soldiers' wives and ladies loyal to the Union in general. Outside of the South, most states had private hospitals, which were built for disabled veterans by their comrades.

Memorial Day was more than a ritual to keep old hatreds alive. The custom began in 1865, possibly with the women who decked the graves of the Union dead in Charleston that first of May. Within two years' time, Northern veterans had turned the celebration into an annual event. Starting in 1868, May 30th became the official holiday. This date was chosen for the most practical of reasons: by then, the North would be awash with spring flowers, enough to decorate every resting place. Five thousand mourners showed up at Arlington to put a flag on each of fifteen thousand graves that year. Twelve months later, the crowds were four times as large; by 1872, the festival included ceremonies at the Metropolitan Opera House, orations, and a full-dress parade. Nothing showed better the moral obtuseness (or moral courage) of President Grover Cleveland than when he went fishing on Memorial Day. But then, he was the only president in a thirty-two-year span who hadn't worn Union blue.[29]

A holiday where Union veterans posted guards around the Confederate graves at Arlington to keep them bare, and where fife and drum corps played "Rally Round the Flag, Boys," as marchers bore bullet-torn banners down Fifth Avenue, certainly stirred up bitter memories. As time went on, however, Memorial Day took the edge off old hatreds. By 1895, Union soldiers could hold their annual meeting in Louisville without worrying about Rebel yells drowning them out. Mutual respect marked the gathering, with former Confederates serving as the masters of ceremony. Elsewhere, the GAR linked arms with Confederate veterans' societies to decorate every warrior's grave across the South. Did General John B. Gordon of Georgia want money for a home for disabled Confederate soldiers? Union officers helped pay for it. Was a battlefield to be dedicated? Generals from both sides rode there together.[30]

Properly expressed, the Lost Cause had not given unhappy whites no country to love, but two. They were better Americans precisely because they could cherish a past that nobody but a fool would dream of reviving. Instead of serving to lament the slain, veterans' organizations hurrahed for the living. The greatest Confederate general of all, Robert E. Lee, became a hero in the North as well as the South because he died a good American. He was the head of a college—the symbol of the rebuilding that Southern society needed. Every time the UCV held a reunion, crowds would sing "Dixie," and homes would put pictures of Lee and Davis in the windows; but among them other veterans carried the Stars and Stripes.[31]

The Power of the Past over the Present

Eventually, the wartime spirit became an awakener of national pride. The issues for which men died faded from Civil War memoirs. Instead, writers concentrated on the common sacrifice of foot soldiers, the gallant rush, the Yankee hurrah. Author John Hay might sniff at all this "blubbering sentiment," but it sold—and quite a lot better than the frank picture of war that veteran Ambrose Bierce put out in his horror stories. Admitting the true steel in a foe only made one's own heroism shine brighter. It also turned the war into a gallant, increasingly distant moment, in which North and South shared the glory. The time would come when Gordon would lecture about the last days of the Confederacy to a sellout crowd at Carnegie Music Hall. Eyes brimming with tears, the father of a dead Union soldier approached, hand outstretched. "I have hated you for more than thirty years," he told the general. " . . . I will never hate you any more."[32]

The survival of the cotton economy and evocations of the war clearly illustrate the power that the past held over the present, and how those keenest on upholding tradition could become forces for change. But examples abound. Anyone studying law would notice the increasing force that precedent carried in judicial decisions, and the near dread that legal scholars came to have of defending matters on the basis of such gauzy nothings as natural law, abstract principles, and moral equity. By the 1890s, the leisured classes were buying colonial antiques as if they were going out of style, and acquiring colonial furniture, much of it still warm off the laths. Midway through the decade, nearly fifty patriotic societies had come into being, to gild the living with connections to the worthy dead: the Society of Mayflower Descendants, the Colonial Order of the Acorn, and the Society of the Colonial Wars. Another ten years, and the First Families of Virginia and the descendants of the signers of the Declaration of Independence would have their own organizations, too. So attractive were Howard Pyle's illustrations for the life of George Washington that they outlasted the essays in *Harper's* that young Professor Woodrow Wilson had written, and the originals were given to the Boston Public Library. Newly founded in 1892, the University of Chicago had no heritage to make traditions of so graduate students proposed inventing them on the spot and decreeing them by a two-thirds vote. Galveston's blacks celebrated "Juneteenth," honoring that 19th of June, 1865, when the Union army ordered slavery's end in east Texas.[33]

Cast by society as protectors of the home and transmitters of culture, women, separately and through their organizations, stood foremost as keepers of the sacred past. The wealth of Mary Hemenway saved Boston's Old South Meeting-House and sent off an expedition to uncover the relics of the Hopi and Zuni tribes; another Boston lady financed the diggings around Serpent Mound in Ohio. Founded in the 1890s, the Daughters of the American Revolution saved Paul Revere's house and Independence Hall. Another ladies' association had already rescued Mount Vernon twoscore years before. Still another group saved Virginia's colonial capital and what had once been Jamestown. Two women, one Anglo and one Tejano, shamed Texans into buying up the Alamo in 1905, though no one could shame the state into admitting that people of Mexican descent had an equal claim on the shrine, where many of them had died alongside Davy Crockett and Jim Bowie.[34]

From These Honored Dead We Take Increased Devotion

Some of those who looked backward may have been turning their backs on a grubby, mechanical present, just as the historian Henry Adams did. His awe and admiration focused instead on the medieval cathedral at Mont-St. Michel in France. Before him it rose, a monument to faith and idealism, so lacking in modern American life. Among intellectuals and the mournful children of noble sires, there were plenty of complaints that modern America was, as one critic described it, a "chromo-civilization," where fat living replaced the wealth of the spirit. Machinery could make millions of chromolithographs, cheap enough to plaster every parlor wall with its own Currier & Ives tinted print, but where was the culture to produce one Old Master? For others, like Robert Toombs, the past lit the right road into the future. Founded though they were to inspire loyalty in wartime, the Union League clubs found a new mission in creating a government worth citizens' loyalty, free of corrupt ballot boxes and boodling spoilsmen. Building on the principle that veterans' pensions had set, women's groups a generation later would argue for "mother's pensions" for well-behaved widows with children in need. (By 1931, twenty-nine states had heeded them.)[35]

Thus memory and renewed purpose merged in the aging veterans' last campaign, as the century waned. The war's patriotism must live after them; and so they lobbied to see that history, from their own section's point of view, would appear in the school textbooks. The GAR raised money to put an American flag in every schoolhouse and classroom; to make children salute it and recite a Pledge of Allegiance that had been written for the occasion; and to turn Flag Day into a national holiday.[36] In this last crusade, the South's lost legions gave no resistance. It had become their flag, too. "The army of Grant and the army of Lee are together," President William McKinley told listeners, ". . . one now in faith, in hope, in fraternity, in purpose, and in an invincible patriotism."[37]

An invincible conservatism, itself made anew to suit a world of corporations, was also in evidence. All veterans were equal in the GAR and UCV but commissioned officers were less equal than others when it came to offices. On both sides, the veterans' organizations channeled their members' energies in safe directions. The values they extolled—of temperate habits, self-control, love of family, and public order—were certainly worthy in themselves. But what was left out was no less important. The idealism—the commitment to equal rights that fired radical Republicans—had no place in veterans' oratory. The Union for which the soldiers had fought had shown no room for improvement, still less for disorder. The middle-class and professional men who filled the veterans' organizations were ready to enlist, whenever called upon, against strikers or protest marchers, and with the old enthusiasm rekindled. In exalting the Lost Cause, ladies raised monuments to a world where every woman knew her place, a world from which, however briefly, the war had seemed to shake her free. "We meet not as new women clamoring for rights," an Alabama group assured outsiders, but merely as dependents "under the protectorate of the United Confederate Veterans."[38]

Thanks in part to organizations like the GAR, a nation took increased devotion to the honored dead, rather than to the new birth of freedom for which many had given their last full measure of devotion. Thanks, too, to those wistful for a past world richer in spirit than in canned goods, the prospect of making a fresh set of honored dead became increasingly attractive. Away with cash-register heroes and store-bought experiences! The fighting that proved an individual's manhood was what counted. It bred the manly virtues—courage and stoic endurance—rather than the sickly feminine ones—sentimentality and compassion. It hardened young men for a man's hard world by putting their convictions to the test of life and death. Noblest of all was he who imperiled his life from duty alone, understanding neither the high ideals nor the simple tactics of the fight in which he was engaged. "War, when you are at it, is horrible and dull," the onetime veteran, now jurist, Oliver Wendell Holmes, Jr., told Harvard's graduating class in 1895. "It is only when time has passed that you see that its message was divine. . . . We need it in this time. . . . We need it everywhere and at all times."[39]

Chapter 5

Wasteland

Buffalo Bill's Wild West Show

Everybody knew William F. Cody's real name. "Buffalo Bill" was as familiar as the Wild West Show that he took on tour. Dime novelist Ned Buntline turned him into a folk hero, galloping from one thrilling adventure to the next. One adventure, to Cody's fury, killed him off. "Authentic" biographies were just as wild. The youngest Indian-killer on the Plains (at eleven), the youngest rider on the Pony Express (at fourteen), chief of scouts for the Fifth Cavalry, Cody bore 137 wounds and scars—everything from bullet to lance. And as his name suggested, in one year, he had killed 4,280 bison.[1]

Still, "Buffalo Bill's" fame arose most from his show. Other circuses' fame lasted longer. Together, master mountebank Phineas T. Barnum and James A. Bailey put on what they pronounced the Greatest Show on Earth, while the Ringling Brothers' Congress of Trained Animals proved so popular that in 1906 they bought out Barnum & Bailey. But nobody could match Buffalo Bill. Where else could audiences watch "Indians" attacking a real stagecoach or a genuine artificial battle, where "Buffalo Bill" made a chief bite the dust every day—sometimes with an encore? Where in the real West could you find performers able to do such fancy riding, roping, and shooting? For that last, Phoebe Anne Moses, better known as Annie Oakley, was Cody's star. She could slice a playing card held up edgewise at thirty paces, or, using a mirror for aim, fire over her shoulder and break a glass ball that her equally talented husband, Frank

Butler, whirled around on a string. Chief Sitting Bull, having found life on the reservation as tiresome as the government rations he drew, let himself be billed as the slayer of "General" George Custer at the battle of Little Big Horn, and joined the rest of the cast on tour. "Buffalo Bill's" show made a hit with European royalty (and with German officers, who jotted down notes on the professional management of the show, for use in making a more efficient *Wehrmacht*). At one performance, Cody bragged, he held four kings and a prince; if that wasn't a royal flush, what was?[2]

Buffalo Bill's show recaptured the child in grownups and gave children the hero that a gritty, material age lacked. Long after he died, his extravaganza shaped the West movie makers showed, where cowboys wore ten-gallon Stetsons and every Indian warrior rode in a feathered warbonnet. Most of all, Cody triumphed because he captured and put under electric lights a West that Americans wanted to believe in: the wide-open spaces, where women handled six-shooters or fainted just in time for Fred Fearnot to rescue them, and where Nature bred the manliest of men, self-reliant, tough, and violent, taming chaos with personal heroics, harvesting a world of unlimited abundance and opportunity.[3]

The West was all those things, but to look no further at it would be as foolish as to take the showman at his own word. Cody's past was as phony as a chromolithograph's colors—boyhood bloodletting and all. When he died in 1917, his image as the clean-cut hero was marred slightly by the appearance of six of his mistresses at the funeral, as well as his wife. Ohio Quaker Annie Oakley was no more a western wildcat than Sitting Bull the slayer of Custer. Small deceits, these—hiding a much bigger illusion of the West made by larger-than-life heroes acting on their own. Cody had roved the frontier, not as an individual but as an emissary. The army sent him, just as the Kansas Pacific hired him to kill all those buffalo. Look at "Buffalo Bill" more closely, and a different West appears, created by people working together, shaped by Eastern institutions.

Garden of the World?

In 1850, the frontier stretched from eastern Kansas into Minnesota, with white settlers spilling from the Pacific coast across California to the foothills of the Sierra range. When silver was found in Nevada in 1859, and gold in Colorado in the 1860s, emigrants rushed in, leaving tight islands of "civilization" (saloons, brothels, newspaper offices, and railroad depots) in the wild. Then, after the Civil War, the pace of settlement picked up. Railroad and homestead, rancher and sheepman carved up the public domain all the way into the Rockies. Kansas, Nebraska, and Nevada won statehood in the 1860s, Colorado in the centennial year. In 1889–90, Republicans awarded themselves a dozen Senate seats by bringing in the Dakotas, Montana, Washington, Idaho, and Wyoming. Utah had people enough, but far too many wives per husband for the national government's taste; its admission to statehood took six years longer. By 1900, farm and railroad were making the frontier a memory; nearly one westerner in three lived in a city: just about the national average. As far as a traveler sampling the water, riding the streetcars, or examining the way government was set up could tell,

Denver was Des Moines with mountains—though it had a better zoo. When the shoot-'em-up cow town like Dodge City could boast of a roller-skating rink or a nationally famous cowboy band, talk of an American West seemed pretty nearly just that: talk.[4]

The frontier moved quickly across many different Wests. Some places fit the garden that promotional literature claimed this wilderness to be. Anyone grumbling about Iowa soil or California's central valley would have railed at Heaven as a letdown. But east of the Sierras and west of the Missouri, farmers would find the "unsettled" lands close to the old view of the West as a Great American Desert. Halfway through Kansas, west of the hundredth parallel, trees grew sparsely and rains came rarely. Much of the soil was infertile. Between the Dakotas and the Rockies, the high plains passed from the tall prairie grass to short grass, then to sagebrush and greasewood.[5]

At their worst, the Great Plains came closer to Purgatory than Paradise. When temperatures passed 110 degrees, even a light breeze turned wheat into husk and crisped the corn-blades into parchment. Inhabitants told of years so dry that trees followed the dogs around, and of a climate so scorching that wicked neighbors were buried in their overcoats, to make them feel warm in Hell. Howling chinooks could wipe out a foot of snow in a few hours without a drop of moisture melting into the soil. Those able to abide blizzards in April might find their crops devoured in July by clouds of grasshoppers and locusts. The rattle of insects landing in the grass sounded like hail. Juice from crushed bugs ran down the wagon tires in streams. Locusts were not finicky; they loved wheat, but had no prejudice against tobacco, window curtains, or bed covers. Sweat and grease gave savor to plow handles and wagon sideboards. States offered bounties for bushel baskets of locusts, but, as Westerners complained, one insect's funeral always called out at least two more for mourners.[6]

With wood so dear, settlers might first live in a sod hut. They used slabs of turf two by three feet for bricks, a buffalo hide for a door, and, maybe, issues of *Youth's Companion* for wallpaper, which served best if changed every spring. Proper construction could keep out wind and cold. Recipes heavy on salt could harden the floor; wall-to-wall rag carpets and ceilings constructed of old flour sacks kept feet cleaner and earthworms from falling into the soup. But a house of dirt was always a house of dirt. "There was running water in our sod house," one occupant joked. "It ran through the roof." Many wives must have yearned for the hardwoods of Illinois when gathering buffalo chips for fuel.[7]

Not all the Plains were as rugged as western Kansas, and pioneers could adjust to suit the worst surroundings. They discovered that properly seasoned sunflower stalks burned as well as firewood. The plant grew twelve cords to the acre—or so one salesman insisted. Where water could be found, or rivers ran, irrigation was possible. A lot of the desert was a *potential* garden, once ditches were dug, and the laws allowed farmers a steady supply of water running hundreds of miles from their own property. Across the high plains, cattlemen cut off from the watering holes made their own by drilling wells and bringing water to the surface with windmills. By the end of the 1890s, homesteaders were doing the same, and Nebraska teemed with "Go-Devils," "Battle-axes," "Mock Turbines," and "Merry-Go-Rounds," windmills of different makes that at least kept the kitchen garden green.[8]

Perhaps a better image for the West would have been a storehouse. Its real wealth lay in its natural resources: grassland fit for herds of cattle and sheep, minerals, and timber. As many as thirty-four million bison grazed the plains. "The country was one robe," a traveler summed up. Trains stopped for hours, waiting for buffalo to pass, and steamboats tied up along shore until beasts without number finished fording. For the Plains Indians, horse and firearm made the buffalo easy prey, indispensable to every aspect of their culture. They huddled in cloaks of hide, slept on beds of skin, or tanned it to make their tepees. The animal's hair made leggings, bags, and girdles and the bull's neck became the rawhide for Indian shields. The bone and horn were spliced together into bows and covered in buffalo sinew, which also made good bowstring. Boats, cradles, cages, spoons, waterbags, food, medicine, and religious regalia: the buffalo provided them all. Hides, whether bison, beaver, bear, or otter, were one commodity that Eastern traders could not get enough of. In return, they transformed Indian society with manufactured goods that tribes could not match: kettles, mirrors, Waterbury watches, repeating rifles, well-tempered knives, and whiskey. Had every Indian treaty been scrupulously kept and every white stayed east of St. Louis, the commerce of the prairies still would have changed the tribes almost unrecognizably from what they once had been.[9]

But those same broad prairies allowed sheep- and cattle-raising on the cheap. Across Texas ranged longhorns by the thousands, waiting for an enterpriser to rope and brand them. The longhorns were a bony, hardy breed. They could sniff water ten miles off (which was lucky, since they drank fifty gallons a day) and even ate the prickly pear, which gave them a strong, lively flavor. For thirty dollars a month, a cattleman could hire a ranch hand, and he could build an adobe corral from materials at hand. Starting in 1874, those who owned a domain broad enough could ring it with Joseph Glidden's twisted doublestrand barbed wire, a deterrent that the stupidest cow could appreciate and that the poorer homesteader could afford. Others saw no reason to buy grazing pasture. Government-owned land allowed free forage all year round. One reason why California changed from a cattle-raising state to a consumer of beef was the cost of buying land, when Plains-dwellers simply took it for their use.[10]

Across Minnesota and Wisconsin and still more from the Rockies westward stretched forests that were largely untouched. California had trees eighteen feet in diameter. Douglas firs rose a hundred feet without branching, twice as tall as the Eastern white pine. Two men would need a week to saw a single one down and cut it into usable pieces. No shingle could match the redwood for resistance to rot and weathering; Sitka spruce made ladders of unrivaled excellence, and hemlocks were ideal for furniture and flooring.

The Unsettling of the West

Gardens to be tilled, storehouses to be unlocked, the lands beyond the Mississippi opened the prospect of profit for many. But for whom? The question matters, for in the rawest physical sense, the opening of homes for Westerners and of natural resources for Easterners depended on the government's power to drive out the West's original inhabitants. It also taught a lesson that others in the Gilded Age would have to heed: those who fit themselves to changing conditions had the best chance of surviving on their own terms.

The West was open for settlement only after its original residents could be unsettled. All of it was occupied ground already. Back when Mexico's boundaries ran north of the Golden Gate, Hispanics herded sheep and ran cattle through the Southwest. Where whites had not already planted themselves, like islands in a sea of wilderness between the Sierras and western Kansas, natives had their realms.

Comanche and Cheyenne, Shawnee and Pawnee, Apache, Arikara, and Arapahoe: only outlanders or chroniclers would call them all Indians and leave it at that. For generations before white intruders arrived on the prairies, the native people had been paying for their nationhood in blood. By the mid-1700s, two European innovations had raised the price and the spoils. Out of the East came firearms, which were ever more powerful. Out of the Southwest came horses. Horses mattered more. Warriors could abandon the long bow, the big shield, the cumbersome armor of hide; they could now go on the attack and they could strike from farther away, faster, easier. Women in some tribes could now ride with the war parties and provide logistical support, or even fight in the second line of battle, raid base camps, and kill the wounded foeman. Systems of communication spread wide, with scouts riding a day ahead of the rest in open country.[11]

On the Great Plains by the mid-nineteenth century, a host of groups vied to rule or just to live: the Blackfoot Alliance near the foot of the Rockies; the Cree and Assiniboin in eastern Montana; the Mandan and Hidatsa of the Dakotas; and the Crow, so weakened by other tribes' depredations that its subjects had to make alliance with white traders and settlers to escape extermination. Most dreaded were the Comanches in the southern plains and north of them the Sioux, or Dakota nations. Fighting at least twenty-six other tribes in two centuries, they displaced the Omaha and the Ponca, the Pawnee, Arikara, Mandan, Crow, and Iowa, and came to dominate an area that stretched from the Great Lakes to the Black Hills.[12]

Tribes never spilled the kind of blood that Union and Confederate infantrymen shed at Shiloh, but a little bloodletting went a long way to keep ancient grievances alive. As Eastern settlers approached, some tribes invited them to help settle old scores. Many continued to think that way, even after the Civil War. Among the Great Father in Washington's worst failings, in their mind, was his reluctance to deliver on promised protection against other Indians. In 1870, a delegation of Arikaras called at the nation's capital. "The Sioux will never listen to the Great Father until the soldiers stick their bayonets in their ears and make them," Chief White Shield warned.[13]

How much louder that advice came from white newcomers, as disdainful of the Great Father's treaties as the Great Father himself proved to be, when it came to enforcing the promises in them! Their protest that farmers had a higher claim to land than hunters was blatantly self-interested. Their claim that "progress" dictated the death of tribal life, and, indeed, of the whole Indian race, was wishful thinking, that cloaked uglier sentiments. "The picture of a wild free Indian chasing the buffalo may suit some, but I like still life in art," humorist Bill Nye wrote. "I like the picture of a broad-shouldered, well-formed brave as he lies with his nerveless hand across a large hole in the pit of his stomach." Even so, white hatreds had real fears behind them. Easterners glamorized the noble brave as the innocent child. Western settlers could have told a very different if selective story, of natives carefree in taking white lives, delighting in the lingering agonies of their prisoners. Minnesota homesteaders might narrate the terrible August of 1862, when renegades broke from the reservation and butchered over 450 whites who never had done them harm—teachers and missionaries, women and babies included—because the government had failed to meet its latest installment for Indian lands bought and had tried to palm off rotten supplies. Thirty thousand inhabitants fled their homes. In twenty-three counties, hardly a white family remained. Were authorities the worse barbarians for arresting, trying, and condemning some three hundred warriors to death—and executing 38? One might well ask that of their hangman, three of his children killed, the rest still prisoners of the Sioux.[14]

Dishonors on that score were pretty much even. Nothing, not even later government restitution, could make defensible the attack that Colorado's hundred-day volunteers under Colonel John M. Chivington made on the Cheyennes at Sand Creek in 1864. Described by one acquaintance as "a crazy preacher who thinks he is Napoleon Bonaparte," Chivington had boasted at dinner parties of his dream to "be wading in gore!" Tribesmen who had sworn to keep the peace with their white neighbors paid for other Indians' offenses. Waving white flags, they were shot down. Over one hundred peaceable natives under federal protection, most of them women and children, were killed and scalped, their bodies ripped open with knives. The fresh scalps of whites found in the Indian camp were confiscated, too, but there were plenty more where those came from: the next year, Indians evened up the score on lonely farms across Colorado and Wyoming.[15]

The Frustration of Military Power

In the short run, the American military and the tribal warriors were more evenly matched than they appeared. General Grant hoped for a peacetime force of eighty thousand. Congress never gave him anything close. By 1874, the army had shrunken to twenty-five thousand, including commissary, engineers, ordnance, quartermasters, West Point dudes, and a host of dead, deserted, or discharged. "I have seen a captain go on parade with only his sergeant," an officer recalled, "the captain forming the front line and the sergeant the rear." All in all, as British journalist Rudyard Kipling sneered, it was "a dear little army," just big enough for survey work.[16]

Thirteen dollars a month in depreciated paper currency was hardly enough for a private to live on. Among the steadiest and readiest to reenlist were members of the black regiments, the "Buffalo Soldiers," as Indians called them (a name that came from the similarity they saw between the blacks' hair and the shaggy coat of the bison). Half of all recruits were foreign-born, over a fifth of them were natives of Ireland; as many as one-third of the soldiers deserted in a single year. Those who remained were lucky if they got any instruction in horsemanship and, with so little ammunition to spare, any practice at marksmanship. Many, as the artist Frederic Remington said of one black regiment, learned battle tactics in a school "where the fellows who were not quick at learning [were] dead."[17]

With superiors uncertain of how to handle the Indians and with wars flaring up as suddenly as brushfires, the army was always reacting to something already started, and coping with the wrong kind of war. It tried to keep the peace by dotting Indian country with some one hundred forts, barely manned and just good enough to collect news of trouble and send out a force to put a stop to incidents already over and done with. Indians could not match white regiments' discipline, organization, or firepower on the open field, but then, they rarely met the bluecoats on an open field. Speed and surprise were their strengths, not masterly rear-guard actions. In the desert where, as one observer complained, a person had to "climb for water and dig for wood," every fight with Apaches was an ambush, every white civilian a fair target.[18]

In the end, army firepower could not carry the day. Smart commanders like General George Crook would scrap the rulebook. Indian scouts and Indian tactics must be applied. In place of supply wagons, lumbering and burdened with fodder for the horses, the army must use pack mules able to cross just about anything and eat whatever was hardy enough to grow in the western wastes. By making war in winter on horses, crops, and wigwams, his forces just might prevent a bloody encounter thereafter. When the Sioux rose against intruders into their reservations in the Black Hills in 1876, Lieutenant-Colonel George Armstrong Custer got what was coming to him—not because he hated Indians (he rather admired them), but because he did everything wrong. He went into war in midsummer, when the Sioux were most mobile. Riding his Seventh Cavalry to Little Big Horn, he divided his troop's strength, ignored orders to wait for reinforcements to arrive before moving forward, and paid no attention to the advice of his Crow and Arikara scouts. They died with him.[19]

Victory over the Tribes Exacts a High Price

That they did tells something about one big reason that the army won the war in which Custer threw away his men's lives. As so often before, the tribal coalition that had begun the fight fell apart. Old grievances outweighed new realities. All the old enemies of the Sioux were against them, some of them with rifles in their hands. Inside the Sioux nation, tribes led by Red Cloud and Spotted Tail signed a separate peace. When the Cheyenne surrendered the following April, they helped the army themselves. So it would always be. In the 1880s, Crook led the army into the turbulent Southwest. Against the entire Apache nation, his fight would have been a daunting one. But Crook never faced a united front. He had to take on only two groups, the Mescaleros and one clan of the Chiricahua, led by Geronimo. Other Apaches shouldered guns and acted as Crook's scouts.[20]

Victory over the tribes did not come easily, nor swiftly. Strife in Minnesota and Colorado during the Civil War gave way to bloodshed in Kansas and Montana in the years just after. In the 1870s, when the government's "Peace Policy" was at its most humane, the Army brought peace of the most permanent kind to Modocs in California, Comanche in Oklahoma, and Cheyenne and Sioux in the Dakotas. Hardly had order been restored to the prairies than the Pacific Northwest was shaken by the Nez Perces' last-ditch effort to save their lands. Heavily outnumbered, Chief Joseph's warriors matched the army in tactics. Noncombatants went unharmed. There would be no women taken captive, no scalps waved in triumph. Warriors learned the enemy's insignias of rank, so that their shots could pick off officers and gunners. Unable to match a cavalry's firepower, they set brushfires and used the smoke to mask their own movements. The Nez Perces won every battle except the last.[21] After Geronimo's capture in the late 1880s, the Indian wars would end, but that was more than the army knew or believed, until the century's end.

Killing Them "Decently": From Nations to Wards of the State

Neither the army as a whole nor the government wanted to see the Indians wiped out. They wanted them contained, where the worst of white society could not contaminate and the best could not be butchered. Leaving the certain advance of "civilization" to deal with the tribes on its own terms would mean the certain death of everyone in them. Already by 1867, cholera, smallpox, syphilis, measles, and whiskey had killed tens of thousands for every warrior fallen in battle. By the 1870s, it seemed that concentrating the native tribes on reservations would give them a fighting chance of surviving long enough for them to adapt to the changed society around them. It would not be a pen where they were fed flour and beef, nor a captive market for traders flourishing handfuls of beads, but a school, a halfway house to citizenship. "If they cannot bear civilization," the *Nation* argued, "it will at least kill them decently."

Of the long view, more needs to be said, but the raw, plain fact was that, for the time being, the reservation was an internment camp to get the Indians out of the way. It was to lowland, malarial ground that Chief Joseph and his tribe were sent, not back to Oregon, as the authorities promised him on his surrender. Most of them perished of disease, one out of four in a few months, all six of Chief Joseph's children included. A hero even to many white settlers, Joseph would eventually get his people a better home in Washington, but not the fair lands on which he once had lived. "I think that, in his long career, Joseph cannot accuse the Government of the United States of one single act of justice," an army officer said of him. Year by year, the camps' bounds constricted, as white settlement came closer, and never were they allotted the better land of the West. By the time Grant's presidency ended in 1877, two territories took in the mass of nations: the Indian Territory between Kansas and Texas, and the western badlands of South Dakota. Five years before the 1889 land rush in which half of Oklahoma was opened up to a mob of whites, rushing in on the appointed day to lay claim to whatever they could lay their hands on, the Indian Territory there was already, as one wag put it, "merely a mental reservation."[22]

Some Indians fled rather than go into the captivity so philanthropically arranged for them. In 1878, the Cheyenne were ordered to Oklahoma. Hungry and promised food that never came, without buffalo to hunt and homesick, three hundred of them set out northward to join the Sioux on their reservations in the northern prairie. The army pursued them. Four times there were skirmishes, and still the Long March went on, until it reached Nebraska, with winter falling hard on the land. There, the larger part of the fugitives, mostly women and small children, were surrounded, disarmed, and housed in the empty barracks of Camp Robinson, not fifty miles from their goal. Forbidden to go on, ordered back to Indian Territory in weather that would mean almost certain death, locked in and kept from food or heat until they agreed to the move, the prisoners burned their furniture to keep warm, scraped frost from the windows for drink, and at last broke loose. Most of the fugitives were shot. Some were scalped. Of the 149 imprisoned, only seven were brought back alive.[23]

But what destroyed the Indian tribes far more effectively than the army was the commercial and industrial power of the East, which was able to pour settlement west in an ever-increasing flow, ever more conscious of the wealth of the West waiting to feed the mills and mints east of the Mississippi. Already, trade with whites had changed the whole shape of tribal society. Now settlers carved up the hunting grounds and emptied them of life. They brought the Indian population to its lowest point in 1890: 250,000 in all, perhaps 100,000 fewer than on the eve of the Civil War. By then, the only remnant travelers were likely to see were what the English writer Rudyard Kipling spotted at a depot: "bundles of rags that were pointed out as Red Indians."[24]

The Hispanics of the Southwest fared a little better. As American judges made clear, rancheros still held legal title to a little over thirteen million acres of California when the Mexican War ended. But a title did little good when squatters cut down the orchards, slaughtered the cattle, plowed the soil, and then, when ordered off the land, could demand pay for their "improvements," and when attorneys and court costs gobbled up whatever the ranchero had left over. Small ranchers in New Mexico survived by holding grazing lands in common. South of the Nueces, Texas Hispanics held estates as a family, rather than giving any one person a share to sell as he or she wished. But the cattle barons controlled the courts; the courts made private property the law of the land; and the original owners soon found that the more law there was, the less land they had left. By century's end, Anglos owned pretty much everything. The children of herders and skilled workers found themselves turned into migrant labor.[25]

Civilization's Great Plow: The Railway Locomotive

Across the Great Plains and into the Rocky Mountains, settlers flowed in the postwar years. Again, they came thickest where government land and railroad promotion took them. How did communities get built, an English visitor asked one speculator. "We commence building a line and send an engine with a barrel of lager beer ahead as far as it will go," the native told him. "Then we deposit the barrel somewhere in the prairie. A bar and some Germans gather around it, and soon there is a small colony, with a church and a schoolhouse. Meanwhile, we push our line ahead for five or six miles and repeat the beer-barrel business; and by the time the whole road is ready we have quite a nice little population."[26]

The task was nowhere near that easy. Companies sent out brochures and pamphlets by the thousands, from Portland to Prussia, to coax immigration west. They even renamed Edwinton, Dakota after Germany's "Iron Chancellor," and Bismarck it remains to this day. Kansas would "grow anything that any other country will grow and with less work," the Rock Island line assured prospective settlers. "Because it rains here more than in any other place and at just the right time." The only way to get a customer for one town's cemetery was to pick an inhabitant at random and shoot him, another promoter boasted. Scientist Ferdinand Vandiveer Hayden mustered a wide array of proofs to show that arid acres would turn to wetlands as soon as farmers took up residence—for "rain follows the plough."[27]

When Hill charged a $12.50 fare from St. Paul to his Montana lands, and the Union Pacific extended eleven years' credit and a 10 percent down payment on the lands it sold, when good farmland cost a mere three dollars an acre, would-be farmers found the lure irresistible. It *was* a lure for many, and not a snare. When an immigration agent for the Santa Fe Railroad invited Russian Mennonites to America, they had good reason to accept, just to escape persecution. Still, when they came, Kansas bloomed before their touch. The durum and turkey wheat seed they brought throve in the dry prairies; so did the Mennonites.[28]

"The railway locomotive is civilisation's great plough, after all," an English visitor wrote, as he passed over the prairie. "It strikes its five hundred and its thousand mile furrows, and the wilderness sprouts with smiling villages, swiftly to ripen into flourishing cities." Miners put Helena and Butte on the map, but the trunk lines made their growth jump and gave Helena the edge in the scramble to be Montana's capital. West of the Mississippi, where towns had not been planted already, the companies planted their depots ten miles apart and bought up the land around the stations, to sell. Small wonder that when Nebraska designed a seal, it included an engine and cars puffing towards the Rockies in the background.[29]

That the Northern Pacifics needed such extensive advertising to woo settlers and set prices so low did not attest to the West's unattractiveness, but to the appeal of its worst competitor, the federal government. How could a railroad firm charge high rates for frontier land when the federal government had millions more acres virtually to give away? In 1862, the Homestead Act had offered 160 acres for a ten-dollar filing fee to anyone prepared to occupy it for five years. The offer was too good to be true. For all the mythology of the Great Plains as a "safety valve" for city laborers, where any needy employee could take up ranching rather than revolution, free land came at a high cost: a would-be farmer needed money for seed, plow, animals, and enough food to subsist on until the first crop came in. On the treeless prairies, fencing alone might cost a thousand dollars.[30]

At its best, the Homestead Act offered a real chance to the poor children of midwestern farmers. It also enriched speculators out to strip the land of timber or coal, with the help of a crowd of front men, each claiming homestead rights. The Desert Land Act of 1877 passed over thousands of acres of grassland to cattlemen who promised to irrigate their individual 640 acres within three years—promises kept, perhaps, in one case out of twenty. Best of all was the Timber and Stone Act of 1878, which let settlers buy all the land they wanted for $2.50 an acre, as long as it was "unfit for cultivation."[31] Forest land worth $100 an acre went for a fortieth of its value; and mining companies bought 50,000 acres with resources beneath them worth millions for $14,000. Private enterprise in timber, coal, and cattle, obviously, were the bastard children of government policy.

The West the East Made

Everywhere, the influence of eastern enterprise showed itself in the development of the West. Maine loggers developed the Minnesota industry and opened up the Pacific coast's supply. The company town of Pope and Talbot looked like a New England town three thousand miles removed, full of workers talking with Down East accents. But then, the whole operation came from East Machias, Maine. Westerners used most of the barbed wire, but, from the start, Easterners made it. By 1883, one Illinois factory alone was turning out six hundred miles of it a day, and over the next twenty-five years, the price fell from $20 for each hundred pounds to $1.80.[32]

The West, in other words, was just the opposite of its dime-novel reputation as a self-sufficient land tamed by gunmen. For everything, from political leadership to prosperity, it depended on eastern desires, consumers, and corporations. What it needed, it had to buy from the East; what it made, it had to sell there. Its territorial governors came from the East and looked to Washington for their survival. Rancher, miner, and farmer made a living on the terms set by national law enforced by judges appointed from two thousand miles away. In such a world, the real hero was not the gunslinger. It was the promoter and developer. There, as in the East, the advantage lay with those with plenty of money behind them and good eastern contacts.

Beyond the Mississippi, it took big money to tap the forests properly. Trees that tall took teamwork, for one thing. They required logging crews of a dozen men, and specialized labor, with a boss logger to decide which tree to cut next and where it was to fall. With fir trees so high, the best place to cut must come some twenty feet above ground level, where less pitch had collected beneath the bark. Scaffolding and boards would rise like steps up the side of the tree. Redwood proved so brittle that loggers had to bed the ground with a "layout" made of soft boughs. Getting the tree down was comparatively easy. With rivers scarce and sawmills scattered far, and with trees too large for a horse and wagon to lug, logging might require a skidroad made from laying logs crossways. Even then, a 10,000-pound load (one tree) would need eight pair of oxen. Each log would need to have its ends tapered, so that it would not snag on things while being pulled. Where slopes were too steep for oxen, logging demanded costly machinery. This included the steam-driven "donkey engines," which were able to draw in steel cables that pulled logs from half a mile away, as well as little locomotives on narrow-gauge track to haul the timber; gang-saws; circular saws and bandsaws that allowed the cutting of hundreds of thousands of board-feet of timber a day; and the spindly wooden flumes, which could hurtle 40,000 board-feet of logs, shingles, or cordwood a day fifty miles distance, across hills and other ravines. None of these operations came cheaply. Western logging relied less on individual sawmills and small firms than on great ones, with plenty of capital. Often, these companies learned their trade in the East, for example, around the Great Lakes. Down the Pacific coastal range sprang company shantytowns, with space for a thousand workers. Roustabouts came from Canada and Europe to labor at a dollar a day, though they remained as seasonal employees, serving a few months and then moving on.[33]

Legend spoke of the Comstock Lode and the silver veins of the Sierras. In Colorado, gold was to be found and placer miners spread along a thousand miles of the Rockies south from British Columbia. Across Americans' memory plod hard-bitten prospectors, staking their claims. Actually, it took eastern capital and big money to make mining pay. With enough funds, hydraulic mining could bring veins to the surface by firing a high-pressure stream of water at them. Hillsides broke apart and the debris poured into long sluices that were then sifted through for minerals of value. Hard-rock mining lasted longer, but it took patience, time, and plenty of capital. Driving a shaft, and buying beams and posts to shore the tunnels, pumps to draw water out of the shaft, and hoists to carry the ore all required an outlay from the Pacific coast's cities and eastern banks.

The same held true of the cattle industry. In American popular fiction, the cowboy ranks with the desperado as the great symbol of western individualism, and the Chisholm Trail north into Kansas as an Abilene epic. The trail does deserve an honored place but in business history. Before it opened, Texas steers sold for three or four dollars apiece at home, scarcely a tenth of what Northern markets would pay. Owners drove herds to the Gulf ports, to Colorado mining towns, across Arkansas, even to California. But farmers to the east resented hosts of hooved locusts trampling over their crops, and stockmen along the way watched their own herds sicken from "Texas fever," a disease to which interlopers carried an immunity.[34] With Missouri and Arkansas shutting outsiders' cattle out by quarantine laws, ranchers needed a better outlet.

The Growth of the Cattle Industry

Then, in 1867, Joseph McCoy, backed by Kansas Pacific Railroad money, built a barn, a hotel, and a shipping yard in the dusty little village of Abilene and sent agents out to drum up business. That September, the first shipment, twenty carloads, started east. By New Year's, 35,000 head of cattle had passed that way and, within the next few years, ten million. Railroads could not find cars enough to carry them all, and turned them out to graze on Kansas land, where they fattened and sold for more than before. Abilene exploded with hardware stores, brothels, and saloons, and, on the other side of the tracks, frame houses and churches. McCoy became one of the wealthiest citizens, as well as mayor (Abilene's heyday lasted five years. The further west farmers pushed, the further west the trail had to run to keep clear of them; it ended in Dodge City, on the Atchison, Topeka & Santa Fe). Soon the cattle business was spreading northward to the Dakotas and the foothills of the Rockies. Where Indians once ran down buffalo, more domesticated livestock grazed. With pastures closer to the railheads, there was no need to use so tough and stringy a breed as the longhorn. Shorthorns and Herefords gave more and better beef and could be slaughtered sooner. With barbed wire fences to protect breeding stock from unwelcome attention, a rancher needed fewer hired hands to oversee the heard and could make a nice profit.[35]

As the profits became more apparent, as barbed wire and homesteaders began to close off the open range, cattlemen found themselves pressed to own the waterholes and grassland they needed. By the 1880s, some ranchers were borrowing from eastern banks or taking on eastern partners, many of whom did all their business by mail. Of 23 million head of cattle across the West, corporations held half. Offices in London and Kansas City handled the financing and hired managers at five thousand dollars a year to run things on location. The great "Beef Bonanza" grew on very different conditions than those just after the Civil War.[36] All the same, the cattle business had been just a business—pure and simple—from the first.

Cowboys were employees, working to supply eastern demand, though the work was unpredictable and left a lot to their initiative. Driving a herd up the Chisholm trail took grit especially. Just communicating between cowboys took hand signals over the thunder of hoofs and steers required constant attention. Given the least opportunity, they would wander astray, tumble over bluffs, fall afoul of wolves or rustlers, or panic. A stampede by night was every herder's nightmare. Anything could set it off, even the sight of a haystack after dark, and once begun, steers might trample their masters to death before stopping, and woe to the owners if several herds ran into each other! It took ten days for one luckless set of cowboys to sort out whose steers were whose. Cowboys did not sing or whistle because they were musical, nor just because they felt lonely (as many did), but as a sedative to a temperamental herd. Singing slogans off the back of coffee cans would do just as well. Prairie fires and storms, swollen rivers and mean horses could bring sudden death. No insurance company was run by fools big enough to sign up a wrangler.[37]

Their employers' fortunes went up and down with the national economy. When the federal government started cutting them out of the open range in 1885 and European demand fell, vast numbers of cattlemen were poised on the edge of ruin. The next two winters finished off all but the hardiest; for two years in a row, blizzards and harsh weather covered the Plains. Caught in the blast, cattle found themselves trapped by pasture fences, and froze to death along the barbed wire. They could neither paw through to what little grass remained beneath the drifts nor reach water. They panicked, stampeded, ran blind into the drifts or broke through the ice on water holes and drowned. A sickening vista greeted ranchers when they dug themselves out the following spring. Though perhaps no more than three in ten cattle over all had perished, it was said that travelers could walk from Missouri to Denver and never touch ground, simply by stepping from carcass to carcass.

The cattle industry survived, but a spectacle of such ruin forces another question on historians: was the rugged life worth the cost? Was the West as a garden of opportunity a mirage itself? Historians like to see it so. How many of them could have stood a year on the prairie frontier? It was a hard life. In winter, farm families found the snows cutting them off from all company, and the work just keeping the place going pretty much cut them off from society all the time. "Just born an' scrubbed an' suffered an' died," read the epitaph of one pioneer woman in a Hamlin Garland poem. Many like her could have said the same, though they lay without so much as a marker to keep their memory. For those who lay wife and child under a slab of sandstone with "Mary and Baby Good Bi" carved upon it, or sang hymns over a kinsman buried in a wagon box for lack of finished lumber, this frontier took a terrible toll. Some migrants went mad. Thousands more went broke. In Nebraska half of those who took a homestead lost it within five years. On the grasslands where, as one observer put it, "God had cleared the fields," bad weather and falling prices soon cleared the farmers. "What do I think about the joys of farmin'?" a Dakota farmer snapped. "What do I think about a hen's hind legs? I think there ain't no sech thing!"[38]

All these misfortunes may dim the great, dreadful accomplishment of a continent conquered and settled in seventy years. They cannot wipe that achievement out entirely. Many who came west stayed there, and were relatively content. Arid weather and remoteness made farming harder in Nebraska than New York, but as the towns spread out, they softened the daunting, isolated conditions that the first homesteaders had faced. Churches, societies, and, after 1896, rural free delivery, took at least some of the bleakness out of prairie life. Two million homestead claims were taken out before the century's end, and, with so much land bought from the government or private parties, they accounted for a minority of the West's newly made farmers, who tilled 430 million acres more than thirty years before. A country producing 211 million bushels of wheat just after the Civil War would enter the new century producing 599 million.[39]

The eastern demand for cattle made fortunes. George Littlefield, an impoverished southerner, made enough money to open his own bank and be chosen as regent of the University of Texas, though as he admitted, "The only practical knowledge I had gained in ranching is that a cow will have a calf." Actually, he and others like him did know something else: that big money could be made by driving other ranchers' cattle for a fee. By the mid-1870s, trailing-contractors moved just about every steer leaving Texas. For the risks involved, a dollar a day in season, as well as free food and lodging (if a bedroll under an open sky could be called that), seems poor pay for a cowboy. Still, it beat what most of them could have made on the southern farms they came from. For the one cowboy in five who was black, there were compensations not exclusively financial. Nowhere else off the frontier could they work side by side with white southerners for equal pay. A select few even made trail boss.[40]

But the whole idea of the West as a realm full of blasted hopes also misses the most obvious point: the East did not just make the West; it got rich off it. So did the world, and not just foreigners who immigrated. Europeans ate cheaper and better because of western cattle, sheep, and wheat. All through the 1870s and early 1880s, American grain fed an industrializing world, and would do so until fresh suppliers emerged in India, Africa, and Canada. Anthrax, which infected cattle overseas, gave American herders their high profit. English investment propped up the cattle boom.

From California and Nevada came half the gold mined in America; from Colorado and Montana, nearly two-thirds of the silver; from Missouri and Kansas, most of the zinc; from Colorado, Idaho, and Utah the vast majority of the lead; and from Montana and Michigan, four-fifths of the copper. Without the Mesabi iron ranges, and the abundance of natural resources that the West provided, the industrial revolution might have come more slowly, and at greater social cost. Southern ironmakers, with their own source of ore, might have been able to undersell northern competitors dependent on iron from overseas. As for Chicago, America's second city, its wealth depended on the West, and the West's way of life depended on the markets in Chicago. Farmers bought through the city's great mail-order houses, and ranchers grew livestock for the city to process. The wheat and corn of half a continent, the lumber of half a dozen states, the mortgages of a million farmers all depended on Chicago.[41]

A Culture of Waste

Abundant resources also raised a culture tolerant of waste. For all the warnings of explorer and geologist John Wesley Powell that eastern-style farming could not succeed long under western conditions, farmers west of the hundredth meridian kept using up water and applying their steel plows to drier soil, as if all the world was Iowa. Loggers cut timber as if there were no tomorrow, leaving behind clear-cut hillsides open to flood. Piles of slash and twig sparked terrific forest fires. One in Peshtigo, Wisconsin killed some fifteen hundred people in 1871, more than died when Chicago burned that same year. By the mid-1880s, too many cattle roamed the range. They ate the buffalo and grama grass beyond swift recovery, and left behind vegetation less nourishing. In 1870, a steer could get by on five acres of grassland on the Plains; ten years more, and overgrazing had raised the minimum to fifty on the southern range and ninety on the northern ones. The pressure on the land was one more reason why the hard weather of the mid-1880s took such a terrible toll on cattle herds. When the ranchers in Nevada's Great Basin overstocked their range, they met the same catastrophic end, losing three cows in four. Hydraulic mining washed whole mountainsides into the rivers, clogged waterways with gravel, and let loose floods that threw rocks into California's valleys, killing hundreds of acres of fruit orchards and inundating towns.[42] In Montana, the Anaconda Copper company ravaged everything to get the metal it sought. Whole streets in towns disappeared into the shafts drilled beneath.

Devastation turned cattle country to sheep pasture by the century's end; the sheep could live on plants that cows left behind. Basque, Mormon, Hispanic, and Scottish shepherds pressed far into cowboy territory. By 1900, Montana and Wyoming raised more sheep than cattle. Montana was first in the nation in terms of cattle production. Ranchers and herders blamed each other for soil stripped bare to blow away, and each was right. Where the "hoofed locusts" cropped mountain pastures, thistle and sheep fescue replaced the ground cover. In northern New Mexico, herders grazed a dry land so heavily that native grasses gave way to sagebrush, yarrow, and fleabane. Not even the sheep could eat those.[43]

Settlement changed the land in less dramatic ways. In 1875, only three trees grew in Tucson. Thirty years later, they numbered in the tens of thousands. Residents wanting their summer shade had imported chinaberry and mulberry and palms from Riverside, California. Easterners insisted on big front lawns, even if the water to keep them green drained rivers dry and killed woodlands along the streams' banks. No one actually planned to introduce English sparrows and starlings to Texas, but commerce brought them, driving out less pertinacious birds. The remaking of nature happened everywhere, of course. As New England farmers took to dairying, their fields bloomed with red clover grown from midwestern seed bought specially for improving the cows' diet.[44] Still, the transformation of the West was more dramatic and offers a far more cautionary tale about the price of "taming" the wilderness.

The Killing Fields: The Road to Wounded Knee

Return, then, to Buffalo Bill. The killing that earned him his nickname showed the exploitation of the West at its worst. Workmen laying the track needed food. Everything from bison tenderloins to tripe, tongue, and testicles made good eating. Hunters came, killing for sport, the more animals the better. Shooting from railroad cars as the Kansas Pacific rolled across the grasslands, travelers found a hundred miles of easy marks. With the introduction of a cheap new way to tan buffalo hides in 1872, the push was on. Enterprising killers could make hundreds of dollars a day, and for little more than the three seven-cent shells it took to fell each bison. Fertilizer manufacturers were willing to buy the bone for phosphates, and sugar refineries for carbon. One railroad lugged seven million tons of bones in a year and would have carried more, if it had had boxcars enough. Three years, and over 3.6 million buffalo had fallen on the southern Plains. By 1880, almost none were left. Out of Bismarck, trainloads of hides rolled east past hundreds of miles of rotting carcasses, their stench smothering whole counties. By 1884, the northern herds, too, were gone. The bare remnant, from which a slow recovery would come, belonged to Mary Goodnight, wife of one of the biggest cattle-ranchers in Texas, who raised and fostered a herd of her own.[45] When Congress authorized the buffalo nickel, the artist had to go to the Bronx Zoo to find one.

Uncontrolled, the enterprise and energy that had made the West was beginning to unmake it. Not until 1891 would the government take a hand in setting up forest reserves; not until the twentieth century would it start preserving the most picturesque wildness with national parks and landmarks, though a few far-sighted officials saw the need long before. Even they underestimated the damage already done to the garden, the cost of ransacking the storehouse. For whites, losing the buffalo was an aesthetic misfortune. For Plains Indian culture, it was the final sentence of death. "Nothing happened after that," a Crow warrior remarked. "We just lived. There were no more war parties, no capturing horses from the Piegan and the Sioux, no buffalo to hunt. There is nothing more to tell."[46]

But there was. It was the story of another West, a last promise unfulfilled, and a final example of good intentions gone wrong. There would be no hunting of the buffalo for the tribes of the Plains, not even if there had been buffalo to hunt. By 1890, the proud warriors had become wards of the state, fenced into reservations. Sanitation was poor, the schools were breeding grounds for disease, and they were overcrowded and poorly managed. Residents might enjoy all the discomforts of tenement life in the wide open spaces, with eight people living in a two-room dwelling. A government health service helped fight tuberculosis and trachoma, both of which were widespread among the Indian population. But authorities were never so energetic as when they set about trying to improve their wards, and improvement meant dropping the traditions that remained. William A. Jones, head of the Indian Office in the late 1890s, issued an order forbidding rations to any Indian who failed to cut his hair to the white man's length. Ceremonial dances must be done away with—and Indian feasts, themselves "simply subterfuges to cover degrading acts and to disguise immoral purposes."

The best example of uplift was what became a mainstay of Indian policy, the Dawes Severalty Act of 1887. To revive dying agricultural skills on the reservations, reformers prescribed a dose of private property. Every family head would become a homesteader on 160 acres, and every single male got 80. That left some 90 million of the 138 million acres of tribal land in government hands, to give white settlers, but it would help Indians, too, by forcing them to farm better with what they had. The proceeds from selling the surplus land would foster schools, to train Indians in citizenship and the skills they would need for blending into white society when the reservations were abolished. No more reservations meant no more corrupt Indian agents, no more grafting government supply contracts, no more pitiful dependency by a once proud people. Cut Indians off from their homes and heritage, and they would have no choice but to become civilized, fit for all the privileges of citizenship.[47]

The Dawes Act failed completely, as missionaries on the spot had warned that it would. Instead of reviving farming among the Indians, the law killed it. Before allotment, Sioux and Blackfeet hunters had taken up cattle raising. The new law parcelled out the open range into packets of land too puny for steers to sustain themselves. Not an acre was reserved for future generations; everyone believed that twenty years would see *fewer*, not *more*, Indians to inherit. Gradually, the promise of citizenship faded back into the argument that government knew what was best for its wards, and would guard them from themselves. States found ways of keeping Indians from the vote, and out of white classrooms. Instead of freeing the Indian from dependence on the government, the Dawes Act pauperized them.[48]

The schools were built, more than two hundred by the early 1900s, but there, too, the original promise turned hollow. Girls learned how to bake bread and arrange the slices on a plate "in a neat, attractive manner." Boys were taught the cruder manual skills; the Indian Office could foresee no future for them in a white world except as ditchdiggers, railroad hands, and lumberjacks. All students took "enough [history] to be good, patriotic citizens." (Columbus discovered, the Pilgrims landed, a golden spike was driven at Promontory Point, but no tribes appeared, even in a supporting role—for this was a course in *American* history.) After five years of agricultural learning, students reached the ultimate end in sophistication: they were taught how to plow a field! Not a single high school was built until 1921.[49]

A few Indians adjusted well enough. Quanah Parker, Comanche chief, fought until 1874 and then surrendered to be sent to western Oklahoma. Authorities found him so obliging that they gave him his own telephone and made him chief and judge for the tribal court. (He meted out the law better than he obeyed it—particularly the ban on polygamy. When the Indian Commissioner ordered him to get rid of all but one of his seven wives, Parker was quite willing—if the Commissioner agreed to pick out which six to dismiss. The matter was hastily dropped.) He would live to ride in Theodore Roosevelt's inaugural parade in 1905. But for most Indians, the reservations brought only degradation. Government concern, which was, at best, condescension, easily shaded into contempt. "The Indian is a child," Francis Leupp, head of the Indian Office, explained early in the new century. As "little wild creatures accustomed to live in the open air," Leupp's charges would be served better if, in place of schoolhouses, the government laid unwalled pavillions. And Leupp considered himself the Indians' protector.

The Dawes Act reflected good intentions; it was viewed as a Homestead Act for native Americans. Wounded Knee showed how meaningless those intentions were. Trouble had been brewing on the Sioux reservations of the Dakotas for some time. The Army was not to blame. The Indians' friends were, in their efforts to Americanize the Indians, providing them with livestock and farming tools and taking away another 9 million acres. Depriving them of the property, it was argued, was—like everything else done to them—really in their best interests. It would force them to farm

Consistency.
Joseph Keppler's 1891 cartoon attacks the butchery at Wounded Knee.

rather than hunt. Unfortunately, there was a catch: the land was worthless for farming. Dry, dusty, infertile, it grew nothing. The chiefs protested. No one listened.

In their despair, the Sioux turned to the comforts of a religious revival, and with the fervor of white camp-meetings. A self-proclaimed prophet appeared, preaching a doctrine half-Christian, half-pagan. Indians would rise again, if they but performed their Ghost Dance around the fire. A Messiah would appear and Christ would come again, with the Lord's vengeance in his hand, to drive white men into the sea. The buffalo would renew themselves, the tribal dead rising at the trumpet of Gabriel. Alarmed, Indian agents and the army sent out George Custer's old Seventh Cavalry, under General Nelson Miles, to prevent an outbreak. Fearful that Chief Sitting Bull might join the Ghost Dancers, white authorities acted sensibly: they sent Indians to take him into custody, the well-trained police force that Congress had created. Then the plan went horribly wrong. When Sitting Bull's followers tried to keep him from being arrested, there was a scuffle. Three policemen and eight of the resisters were killed. Sitting Bull himself was shot in the back of the head.

With the cavalry coming after them, the Ghost Dancers fled into the wilderness. They found their way blocked at Wounded Knee Creek. Once again, the army took precautions to forestall bloodshed, by putting on such a display of force that no one would dare resist. At first, it seemed to work. The tribe surrendered. But when more soldiers were brought in to disarm the Indians, trouble began. A Ghost Dancer assured his comrades that they had nothing to fear from the white man's artillery. Their rituals made them invulnerable. Tensions rose, and all at once a gun went off. With that, all hell broke loose. Soldiers opened fire, and from the hills, cannons roared out, killing white and Indian alike. Within minutes, some two hundred Indians and sixty soldiers lay dead. As the rest of the tribe fled, they were shot down. When the smoke cleared, bodies could be followed for two miles from the place where the action began. Virtually all were women and children.[50]

In that terrible moment, later generations would see the true West exposed, a land made by cultural genocide and conquest cloaked in cant about Manifest Destiny. But Wounded Knee no more represented the real meaning of the closing of the frontier than Buffalo Bill's show did. If anything, it offered a warning about the darker side of traits that all Gilded Age America shared: the emphasis on the preservation of order that justified federal troops being sent to guard the polls in the South; the bullying, righteous nationalism that found nobler outlets in the GAR; and the powerful sense of moral purpose, with absolute right counterposed against absolute wrong, that gave the temperance crusaders their resolve.

Chapter 6

Main Line to
E Pluribus Unum

"Her force turned the wheels of harvester and seeder a thousand miles distant in Iowa and Kansas," novelist Frank Norris wrote of Chicago:

> Her force spun the screws and propellors of innumerable squadrons of lake-steamers crowding the Sault Ste. Marie. For her and because of her, . . . all the Great Northwest roared with traffic and industry; sawmills screamed; factories, their smoke blackening the sky, clashed and flamed; wheels turned, pistons leaped in their cylinders; cog gripped cog, beltings clasped the drums of mammoth wheels; and converters of forges belched into the clouded air their tempest breath of molten steel.[1]

Norris was thinking of the city as empress, but the imagery fits a mighty machine as easily, stoked by the cheap labor of the millions who came from farms and foreign shores. What Norris had not mentioned, what he had taken for granted, was the wiring that made this and dozens of other city-engines do all those things: a wiring of steel rails laid down within two generations.

Railroads Lead Everywhere

Railroad building led to everything. Farmers could grow as much as they pleased; but their wheat would rot in the field without a quick way to market. Western North Carolina farmers had corn to sell at fifty cents a bushel and no buyers, protested one professor, while the eastern half of the state bought Illinois corn at three times the price. Until a railroad opened local markets, North Carolina would remain "a good place to come from."[2] Only when markets spread to every hamlet and from coast to coast would it pay industry to adopt machinery capable of producing goods for a nation of consumers. For the Kansas homesteader, life on the farm was more bearable because mail-order houses shipped the latest eastern goods to some depot within range of his buckboard. Did the South need to develop its coal and iron? Alabama first needed a cheap means of taking the raw materials out of the hills and the finished products away from the mills. Thanks to the railroads, Chattanooga became an ironmaking center, and was outdone in the 1890s by Birmingham, which rose from the open fields of northern Alabama after the war where two important rail lines crossed. Every town dreamed of becoming the next Birmingham, "Pittsburgh of the South." "This, sir, is a world railway," cried one citizen of LaGrange, Georgia, of a project carrying rail connections through to Columbus. "This is a railway which the God in Heaven seems to have marked out as the great line railroad between the Northern Lakes and the Gulf of Mexico . . . one of the grandest projects that has even been inaugurated."[3]

For all these reasons and more, railroads became the symbol for all the drive and enterprise of Gilded Age America. Even before the Civil War, states, counties, and towns all gave lands, subsidies, and protections of every sort just to get the track that would tap outlying trade. Peace rekindled the old passion across west and south. One line to Austin had to reach the city limits by a certain day to get aid. Seeing that this was going to be impossible, the city council met on the last day and pushed the municipal boundary out to where the track could reach it.[4] In all, state governments alone gave nearly 49 million acres. Texas handed out 8 million more than it had the right to give.

In 1862, Congress chartered two roads that together would link the Midwest with the West Coast. The Union Pacific (building west from Iowa) and Central Pacific (building east from California to meet it) got five "sections" of land (each a square mile) on either side of the track for each mile built and a thirty-year government loan. Two years later, a second route was chartered, running from Duluth to Puget Sound. The Northern Pacific got no loan, but was promised twenty sections per mile in the territories, and ten in the states (and in 1880, the government cut in half the Indian reservations around Yellowstone, which, by no coincidence, allowed the Northern Pacific quite a windfall; this was done by Rutherford B. Hayes's "reform" administration). The same bill doubled the original two Pacific roads' land grant: 12,800 acres per mile. Of five transcontinental lines completed by 1893, only the most northerly of all—James J. Hill's Great Northern—did it without aid.[5]

Land grants, generous though they were, actually brought in less revenue than critics imagined. It was commonly believed that 90 percent of Iowa and 75 percent of Michigan had been passed over to railroads; the real figures were 13 percent and 9 percent, respectively. Any populist orator knew that the federal government had "given" the first transcontinental roads a little over $64 million; he might not know that when the books were finally closed in 1899, over $63 million of the principal had been repaid, as well as nearly $105 million in interest.[6]

Desperate railroad men set down badly ballasted, ill-surveyed track, just to qualify for their grants, and later did the job right, at great cost. Even so, 40 million acres would end up forfeited. True, the railroads had taken title to 130.4 million acres of national domain by 1940; true, too, settlers in the Gilded Age were prepared to pay $14 an acre for the best Iowa land. But much of the desert West could not be sold at all. Most of that for the Northern Pacific, as General Sherman put it, was "as bad as God ever made, or any one could scare up this side of Africa." Offsetting the account, the government received special rates on carrying mail, government supplies, and troops that may have saved it as much as the railroads gained.[7]

If the companies were to stave off bankruptcy (and almost none of them did), they must sell settlers the land-grant domains, and at once; they must populate the West along their lines to create a traffic in passengers and freight that would make the roads prosper. That came easily if the route surveyed already had customers. Any "wild scheme to build a railroad from Nowhere to No-Man's-Land to No Place," like the Northern Pacific, was halfway into bankruptcy court before the ink dried on its charter. A smart railroad man like Hill built the Great Northern right the first time. To pay for it, he used the money that traffic was already bringing in from Minnesota's wheat-belt, itself peopled by Hill's railroad empire.[8]

Spanning the Continent

Around the first roads to the Pacific, Americans devised a legend as glowing, as lurid, as any in business history. Take Credit Mobilier, the contracting firm that the Union Pacific hired to build its road from Nebraska west. In effect, railroad directors hired themselves, paid out lavish prices for supplies and labor in government-guaranteed bonds, and collected the profit, as those bonds rose in price.[9] To make influential friends on Capitol Hill, Congressman Oakes Ames, Massachusetts shovelmaker and Union Pacific director, sold his colleagues Credit Mobilier stock for no money down, with the guarantee of dividends of several hundred percent. And what colleagues! The Speaker of the House, the chairmen of virtually every prominent committee, a future president, and a future vice president all took stock. Ames did not buy the House minority leader, James Brooks. As government director on the Union Pacific, Brooks made the other directors buy him. When the scandal broke, investigators accused Brooks of extortion, declared Ames a bribe-giver, and cleared everyone he supposedly had bribed. Soiled by the evidence, censured by the House, the two rogues hardly heard their consciences over the assurances of support from their constituents.[10]

Against that, set the heroic achievement of the Central and Union Pacific Railroads' real builders. With no bridge across the river at Council Bluffs, contractors had to ship their supplies up the Missouri during the three months it could be navigated. From there, it took ten thousand work animals to lug materials to the end of the track. They even had to haul water on the barren prairies. As for the Platte Valley's sparse cottonwood groves, the company stripped them clean. California's forests gave the Central Pacific all the ties and pilings it needed. For rolling stock and rails, though, it looked west, since ships carried it in, taking ten months around Cape Horn to the

Golden Gate and upriver to Sacramento. High altitudes forced the Central Pacific to protect thirty miles of track with snowsheds (40 million board-feet of them) and ten tunnels had to be cut through the last hundred-mile slope of the Sierras; a Scottish scientist helped by mixing up the first nitroglycerine in America.[11]

The engineers earned their fame, but the laborers who laid the eighteen hundred miles of track to San Francisco deserved the credit. On the Union Pacific, Irish immigrants and Civil War veterans were drilled like soldiers, not just for efficient track-laying, but to meet Indian attacks, Spencer rifles in hand. Lugging five-hundred-pound rails, driving some thirty spikes per rail, three blows a spike, and four hundred rails to the mile, a mile of building a day was pretty good work. In the last months of construction, Union Pacific workers were laying six to seven miles, dawn to dusk, and all for wages of four dollars a day or less. Living in shantytowns that moved as the roads advanced, feeding on buffalo meat, bacon, and beans from tin plates nailed to the tables, dipping out cupfuls from buckets of coffee, they ate fast and brawled joyously in the cities that followed the builders. (And "city" is no exaggeration. A typical one, Corinne, a "hell on wheels," contained nineteen drinking establishments and eighty "soiled doves.")[12]

On the Central Pacific, seven thousand Chinese "coolies" helped build the tracks through the Sierras. Lowering workers in wicker baskets from precipitous heights to carve ledges along the sheer face of the mountains, leaving their bones in unmarked graves wherever they died, the "Celestials," as they were known, baffled superintendents by their sobriety and suited Charles Crocker's contracting firm for their cheapness: $26 a month, without bed or board. Their only bad habits, from superiors' point of view, was their insistence on daily baths.

On May 10, 1869, when the Central Pacific and Union Pacific met at Promontory Summit in northern Utah, the whole country celebrated. There, the two railroad presidents swung silver mallets to drive gold and silver spikes into ties already drilled (they missed), engines from either side touched noses, and a telegraph wire linked from the last iron spike to both coasts sent a signal nationwide. New York's Trinity Church held a special service, bells rang in Philadelphia, Chicagoans assembled a seven-mile parade, and St. Louis set off the fire alarms.[13] There would be many such celebrations in the quarter-century to come, as four more transcontinental lines were completed.[14]

So heroic is the story of the transcontinentals that it may hide the more commonplace, day-to-day track-laying. At the end of the Civil War, some 35,000 miles were in place. But builders set down 75,000 in the 1880s alone, and companies ran 189,295 miles of line at century's end—with 49,685 more just for sidings and the railroad yard. In those years, a hodgepodge of railroads between the Mississippi and the eastern seaboard turned into a system, with trunk lines linking Chicago and St. Louis to Yankee commerce. Webs of steel meshed the farm belt north of the Ohio and made possible a steady flow of fresh fruit, vegetables, and milk from the countryside to every major metropolitan center. System building came more slowly south of the Potomac. Many of the smaller roads stumbled between poverty and receivership. Playing on initials, critics renamed the Houston East & West Texas (Hell Either Way Taken), and the Carolina & North Western (Can't & Never Will). Arkansas folklore told of the time a train robber held up the rickety Cotton Belt line, and got nothing but a tongue-lashing from the company president for having picked on so poor a firm (So advised, he left and held up the Iron Mountain instead). Population tripled from 1865 to 1916, but railroad mileage rose seven times over, freight ton-mileage thirty-five times, and gross railroad revenue twelve times.[15]

Railroads, New-Made

The tracks also kept getting better throughout the Gilded Age. Builders filled in the roads and laid culverts beneath them. As the trains grew heavier, bridges grew stronger; wooden piles gave way to stone masonry and steel. Engines became more formidable than ever. Changes in fuel and fireboxes allowed a stronger head of steam pressure, and more power to pull with. Freight cars had carried ten tons before; by 1900 they could bear four times as much.[16]

Four innovations mattered most. The most obvious was the gradual shift from iron rails to steel ones during the 1880s. Steel cost more, but it lasted five times as long—twenty years, in fact. Major Eli H. Janney, a Confederate veteran working at a dry-goods store, whittled out a model for an automatic coupler with his penknife, patented it, and arranged for its adoption by the Pennsylvania Railroad in the 1870s. In place of the hand-turned wheels that brakemen had to turn to stop each car, George Westinghouse developed an air-brake that would stop the whole train simultaneously. By the mid-1890s, over 410,000 cars and 27,700 engines employed the air-brake. Early in the next century came a last great change, the replacement of wooden passenger cars with steel-bodied ones, able to withstand derailment or collision.[17]

With the coming of the vestibule—the flexible tunnel between cars—a stroll down the length of the train required less heroic or acrobatic qualities than before, but passengers would have commented less on how much safer their ride was, than how much easier it was to bear. Four-legged passengers were also more comfortable because of the stock car, which was an innovation of the postwar era. Refrigerated cars were also put into use. One railroad executive's grumbles after riding on European lines revealed how far Americans had gone toward making heat, light, and bodily comfort standard features. "No heat except a foot-warmer, which is a fraud," he complained. "No light more than a good candle would give. No water, no urinal, no arsenal. All passengers on continental railways ought to be tested for pressure before starting out!" In America by 1890, candles had given way to kerosene lamps, then gaslight, and on the best eastern roads, electricity. Hot-water heaters, and after 1881, steam-heat from the locomotive itself, warmed travelers where dangerous woodstoves had reigned supreme. Thanks to George Pullman's parlor, dining, and sleeping cars, travelers enjoyed the comforts of home at speeds of forty miles an hour. Crowds of peddlers furnished anything they were missing, from Malaga grapes and caramels to the latest issue of *Harper's Weekly*.[18]

The railroads changed the landscape, and not just their own design. Promoters praised them for protecting exotic flowers in the mountains by opening wide, sunny thoroughfares and by raising the temperature, and for setting up electric currents that brought downpours to the dusty plains. (In fact, railroads rights of way cut through New England did bring all kinds of new plants: tumbleweed, western ragweed, black-eyed Susans, and Russian thistle.) It was said that no farmer in the grain belt lived beyond earshot of a railroad whistle, though this says more about where farmers chose to settle than where railroads chose to go: west of the Mississippi, the railroad usually got there first and brought the farmers after it.[19]

The Railroad Precipitates Regional Changes

Farmers in general changed, as well, in places where railroads gave them a chance at new markets. In relative isolation, the inhabitants of Bell County, Texas, raised wheat for their own flour until the railway arrived and drove local millers out of business; Charles A. Pillsbury of Minnesota supplied a better, cheaper product. But Texas growers could switch crops, now that they had a way of shipping cotton out. By 1890 Texas had surpassed Mississippi as the number-one cotton producer. Thanks to Hill's Great Northern, the center of the wheat belt moved from the Ohio valley into the Dakotas; railroad connections let Kansas and Nebraska outdo Ohio and Missouri for corn-growing.[20]

The railroads gave the cities commercial sway over more countryside than before; they also redistributed it between centers. Along the Union Pacific, towns grew where the company let them, and, if the line chose to build its depot elsewhere the towns vanished—or moved. There came a day when Cheyenne exploded in size. A train steamed into town carrying a town on its cars: frame-houses, boards, and furniture. "Gentlemen, here's Julesburg," a guard shouted. Where railroads stopped, Kansas City flourished; the thousand bypassed Ohio Cities went from prospective metropolises to ghost towns. Thanks to the railroads, Chicago became the gateway to the West, and then lost its supremacy in the wheat trade to Minneapolis and Milwaukee, while Atchison and Dodge City gave way to Kansas City as centers for the cattle drive.[21]

Needing freight to carry or just trying to save costs, railroads encouraged the development of western resources: cattle, coal, and timber, among other things. Every mile of track took 2,600 ties. By owning the forest, a company could supply itself and sell what was left. Until the 1880s, Mississippi lumbering clung to the riverbanks and the Gulf coast and remained primarily a seasonal trade. Then the Illinois Central started cutting the yellow pine inland and laid the tracks necessary to carry it to market year-round. Sawmills sprang up at every depot. Other railroads leased their forests to turpentine-distillers.[22] In the turpentine camps, black workers slashed the tree-bark for the "dip" that flowed out; stills processed it into turpentine, until the trees died from repeated gashing or the tinder-dry forest had burned down. Work was hard, life cheap, and prospects nil; among blacks, turpentine work was scarcely more respectable than convict labor, as much of it actually was.

Appalachian farmers had done logging on the side for years, but as railroads pushed into the mountains in the 1880s, lumber companies had a chance to carry timber out in large amounts. By the century's end, outside corporations held vast tracts of West Virginia woodland. Forty percent of the nation's lumber production came from the Appalachians by 1910: four million board-feet per year. Out near the Great Lakes, Frederick Weyerhauser parlayed rail connections into two timber empires, not one. He began as a sawmill employee, bought the business, and in time was selling boards coast to coast. In the 1890s, he looked further west to the Pacific coasts. James J. Hill of the Great Northern had millions of forest acres to sell and could always use the business Weyerhauser brought in. He sold the timber king a vast new domain. By 1910, Weyerhauser held two million acres and had hundreds of thousands more under lease.

The cheap lumber that afforded housing for so many therefore owed quite a debt to the railroads. On the other side of the calculation must be set the clear-cut slopes of the Blue Ridge, washed away with spring rains; the ravaged streambeds and watersheds; and the wreckage of bark, branch, and sawdust left to burn or clutter the landscape of Minnesota.[23]

Railroads did the same service for the coal country. Without a way to carry anthracite from the mine, factories would go unbuilt for lack of cheap fuel. Immense deposits lay unexploited in West Virginia and Kentucky until the tracks were laid from Pittsburgh. Small coal companies and great corporations wanting to own their own fuel supply moved into the mountains. Where they found no towns, they sent in gangs of carpenters, plasterers, and masons to build them. Compared to accommodations before, many mountain families found the monotonous dwellings of the company town, with their tarpaper roofs and raw wooden exteriors, a welcome change. Plastered walls, concrete sidewalks, and, in the larger towns, clinics and hospitals, brought a better way of living. But the mines scourged the land; the owners rigged the law to escape legal liability and issued broad-form deeds to get lucrative mineral rights for as little as fifty cents an acre. Poverty and exploitation make part of the bitter story of the mountains' development. But the cheap coal fueled an industrial revolution in the East, and helped cut the price of manufactured goods for consumers. In 1870, mines turned out less than 33 million tons, by 1900, they produced 240 million tons.[24]

Making a Mail-Order America

Ask the farmer how the railroad had changed his life, and, if he could do so without cursing, he would talk about the ways it affected what he sold. He might overlook how it changed what he bought, for so it had. In the harsh, lonely landscape of the prairies, no consumer items came, except by railroad. Two names stand out: Aaron Montgomery Ward and Richard Sears.

Ward led the way. Until the Civil War, businesses had sold their goods by mail, but usually stuck to one particular line of goods. Not Ward. Buying many items and in bulk, he could cut out the middleman and trim 40 percent off of the price. All he needed were sellers in bulk. The railroads provided them. In 1874, he issued a seventy-two-page catalogue of goods. Those beyond city limits could see what they wanted and order. Yearly, the catalogue grew. By the 1880s, it included a woodcut of leading items—though not, perhaps, all of the 10,000 products listed. Between Ward and the farmers a close communion of interest developed, strengthened by his guarantee of customer satisfaction or a full refund. So far did customers trust him that many wrote in asking his help selecting a mate. Ward begged off, but added that when a suitable match had been made, "we feel sure we could serve both you and her to good advantage."[25]

Sears carried the mail-order process still further. Earning his own way after his father's death, he became a telegrapher and then station agent along the Minneapolis & St. Louis. One day, the railroad dropped off a carton of gold-filled watches for the local jeweler. The jeweler refused to take them. Instead of sending them back, Sears sold them for four dollars apiece by mail order, and knew just the clientele who would snap up accurate timepieces: other station agents up and down the line. Having sold out the shipment, he ordered more and sold them. Sears knew a good thing when he saw it. He moved to Minneapolis to start up a watch company, sent out salesmen to peddle his wares along the railroads, and hired as a watch repairman a young man from Indiana, Alvah Curtis Roebuck. By 1899, Sears Roebuck had twenty-four different merchandising departments, from stoves to notions. Such a cornucopia required a mail-order catalogue to market its wares effectively. Sears wrote virtually all the copy himself, which became an increasingly heroic feat: "the Farmer's Bible" ran five hundred pages in 1895, and kept growing. By 1904, one million copies were being distributed every year; by 1907, there were three million. Finding it useful in the outhouse, not just the parlor, country folks took to the catalogue heartily. As one story went, a schoolboy was asked where the Ten Commandments came from. His answer came promptly: Sears Roebuck. That was where *everything* came from. But neither Sears nor Ward could have done anything without the cheap freight rates that railroad connections gave them.[26]

Shippers complained but, over all, rates were cheap and got cheaper. Competition made the freight charges drop faster than the price of farm goods, and they fell most sharply in the 1880s: nearly 70 percent in twenty years. Passengers paid less, too, and got more for their money.[27]

Railroads, then, did a tremendous service in turning the subsistence economy into a market economy and markets from local to national ones. They helped turn western trees into chairs from Chicago and Southern coal into steel from Pittsburgh. They helped shape a new industrial order, where the East benefited at the South's and West's expense. But one might also see the roads as setting the pattern for the industrial transformation of America in quite another way.

Big Business Comes to the Heartland

For if size is defined by costs and capital, the railroads were the first big business. Setting up a refinery cost only $10,000 just after the Civil War, and for $50,000, an oilman could build one of the largest in the land. Establishing his first large steel plant, Andrew Carnegie and his partners each put in only $20,000. That was precisely how much it cost to build one mile of railroad track, and in the 1870s, the Pennsylvania issued $78 million in securities just to expand and keep up the lines it already had.[28] Obviously, then, no factory cost as much to build as a line fifty miles long. One man could not find the money, nor even a partnership. It would take a thousand, ten thousand partners, stockholders each with a share in the capital. Given a number of such firms, promoters no longer could trust local bankers to take up all the shares. They would need to hawk their stock nationwide. A Philadelphia institution like Jay Cooke, his name synonymous with patriotism and sanctimony, could launch a national advertising campaign on his own for government bonds or Northern Pacific Railroad securities. Most companies had to find some other means of selling nationwide. That took a centralized market for shares: the stock exchange in its modern form. In March 1830, New York's traded as little as 31 shares a day. Not until 1869 did New York's specialized exchanges merge into one. Ten years later, it sold 700,000 shares in a single day, in 1886, a million. Almost all of them were railroad securities.[29]

Financial Changes Lead to a Modern Stock Exchange

On Wall Street and off, the companies got a special notoriety for issuing more shares than their property's assets could cover: "watering stock," as it was known (later folklore had it that the term originated with that Pecksniffian speculator, Daniel Drew, who, in his youth, as cattle-drover, used to water *his* stock just outside town and sell them before the less lasting part of their weight passed away).[30] A broker and his chums even dedicated a statue to "Commodore" Cornelius Vanderbilt with watering-pot in hand. This, of course, assumed that the amount of money that had gone into a firm should define its worth, and not how much the company could make—and Vanderbilt's New York railroads were able to earn a dividend of 8 percent even in the hard years after the Panic of 1873.[31]

But equally obvious, the new importance of shares changed the way raising capital took place. There would be new speculative techniques; traders would sell shares they did not yet own, for future delivery, gambling on the price changing over time to their advantage. By the 1850s, speculators were buying shares on margin: that is, they borrowed most of the money for a purchase, using their own money for only a fraction of the stock's purchase. Those ready to take risks that the New York Stock Exchange rules prohibited could wander down the street to "bucket shops," where, for a margin of 1 percent, they could buy even more shares. So many sales took place, and the price changed so quickly, that a telegraphic stock-ticker was needed for instant information; Wall Street was one of the first places to install telephones, so that investors could buy and sell without clogging up the exchange. So important were railroad stocks that in 1868 Henry Varnum Poor began issuing a yearly manual, giving the railroads' key financial facts (at least, those that the companies chose to tell); not until 1900 did John Moody complement it with his *Manual of Industrial Statistics* covering other securities.[32]

More important still, the railroads provided a model for what historians have called the "managerial revolution." The point is a natural one: large-scale enterprises need more coordination than small-scale ones, if only to promote efficiency. Railroads needed it most of all. They needed new accounting and statistical controls, and greater hierarchy. Owner and manager might be the same person in a country store. But with railroads requiring so much capital, the stockholders were the real owners. Collecting a few thousand investors to handle day-to-day decisions was out of the question, even if they had the special skills that such a business demanded. Therefore, a board of directors must govern the firm, leaving stockholders to pass on their work by yearly elections. Managers themselves could not handle all the tasks a railroad needed. There must be separate departments to raise and spend funds, with expert bookkeepers. A legal bureau must take on the paperwork and handle disputes; a purchasing department must buy all supplies; and engineers and technicians would need to be hired, who would work on salary, rather than for a share of the profits.[33]

With finances so complex, one set of books could not do justice. There must be a new, sophisticated means of accounting, with information gathered daily or weekly. A railroad that looked no further than the annual return would go broke in a hurry. If the managers were to set remunerative rates, they needed to know any number of things. How many passengers embarked at each station? Which depot loaded the most freight? Was the railroad's cargo mostly local or long-distance? What was shipped? Bookkeepers needed to find how far a company's operating revenue would pay off borrowed money, how quickly rolling stock and track depreciated, how much repairs would cost over the next few years, and what the present value of equipment was. There must be real cost accounting to find out not just whether one section of a road made a profit, but how it compared with others in the cost for carrying a ton of freight a mile. A large textile firm might have four or five sets of account books, and compile their records every six months. The Pennsylvania Railroad had 144 sets, thirty-three of them in the passenger department alone. It needed to go over the books every month.[34]

The consequences of the Railroad Age were awe-inspiring. Anyone looking at urban railroad stations would have imagined them as the palaces of the kings that an industrial revolution had enthroned. Union Station in St. Louis accommodated eighteen different railroads. After its completion, Grand Central Station in New York handled sixty-seven. But if the latter was big from necessity, it was opulent from caprice. The companies built it in French Baroque style, statue of Mercury (god of businessmen and thieves) included.[35]

In fact, the railroads were not so much monarchs as doubly beleaguered forces. On the one hand, the demands of capital had long since kept them from being commanders of their own fate. On the other, they found that the public was ready to forgive their abuses only through corporate infancy. A company placed on a solid financial footing would find its customers far less forbearing. Farmers and shippers never ranted against the railroads—until they got one.

Communities needing connections were far more charitable than those already tied to the national market. The most hated railroad man in America, for example, was the soft-spoken speculator Jay Gould. Those Americans who read *Chapters of Erie* could marvel at the financial jiggery-pokery by which he and Jim Fisk milked the Erie Railroad and then cheated "Commodore" Cornelius Vanderbilt of the rival New

Which Will Win?
The farmer battles the railroad monster in this 1873 cartoon.
In fact, it would take another fourteen years before there was
a "national authority" club to wield, and it would be
bureaucrats and shippers, not farmers, who wielded it. (New
York *Graphic*, August 14, 1873)

York Central when he tried to buy a controlling interest, by printing shares wholesale.
Four years after the "Erie War," Fisk died on the staircase of one of New York's finest
hotels, shot by his mistress's other lover. Within weeks Gould lost control of the Erie,
only to resurface at the head of Western Union, the Kansas Pacific Railroad, and, finally, the Union Pacific. "Jay Gould is making an inspection tour of his properties,"
a Missouri newspaper quipped. "He should have stopped at Jefferson City and taken
a look at our governor." One might imagine the people of Shreveport turning out
with tar and feathers when he came to town in 1887. Instead, they gave him a banquet. As long as "Mephistopheles" could build them another railroad, nothing else
mattered.[36]

Consolidation and Cooperation

But as the essential lines were completed, in state after state, the stream of aid
tapered off. Across the South, communities looked for legal means of repudiating their
public debt for railroad construction and found grounds aplenty, from technical in-

fractions and fiscal irregularities to lawmaking tainted with crisp wads of cash. Westward and southward the movement spread, to ban public aid in state constitutions or to set conditions for spending and taxing that no one could have met.[37]

With subsidies dwindling and construction costs soaring, railroads needed more cash than ever, both for building and for service on their debt. The trouble was in getting that cash. As mileage increased, companies found themselves fighting each other for customers. Getting lower rates every year, shippers loved the arrangement. Railroads hated it. Battling for traffic, they had to give in to big companies like Standard Oil that were looking for special bargain rates not open to their competitors: for example, a secret rebate on the published charge. Competition meant rate wars and instability, a meager revenue, and no cushion against hard times. Even the victors stood a good change of defaulting on their bonds and falling into receivership. What, then, was to be done?

The obvious answer was some form of horizontal combination: the uniting of firms doing the same kind of business. Conceivably, companies could do so through cooperation rather than consolidation. After all, on many matters, working together was essential from the beginning. If each company set its own code of signals, timetables, and track gauge without consulting the rest, chaos was sure to follow. With every town setting its time by the sun and setting its clock as it pleased, it was theoretically possible for a timetable to show its train leaving Town A for Town B ten minutes after it was scheduled to reach its destination. Noon in Chicago was 11:50 in St. Louis and 11:27 in Omaha. Illinois had twenty-seven local times, Wisconsin thirty-eight. Railroads did not standardize time until after the Civil War. Nor did they set a uniform gauge of track. Although there had been a standard width—4 feet 8½ inches, originally the distance between the wheels of the most common form of stagecoach— half of the nation's mileage was in something wider or narrower. As late as 1880, more than one mile in five on southern roads remained in some other gauge. Transferring freight from one line to another meant unloading and loading boxcars, or utilizing car hoists to lift the car from a truck of one gauge to that of another. Obviously, shippers and passengers would welcome railroad time and a uniform gauge.

A standard set of signals came the soonest, for obvious reasons: nobody liked train wrecks. By the 1870s, a closed electric track circuit had been developed to set the signals and a mechanical interlocking system had been established, so that signals and track switches had to match each other to operate. In November 1883, railroad companies split the country into four basic time zones. (Even then, Congress refused to sanction the practice officially until 1918, and an editor protested that he preferred to keep his watch on "God's time—not Vanderbilt's.")[38] Uniform track width took longest of all, but climaxed on June 1, 1886, with the switchover of the last 13,000 miles.

Setting standard railroad rates, however, excited hotter passions and pitted the industry's long-range advantage against individual companies' short-term gain. So, for all their efforts by 1890, owners could not agree on one uniform system for classifying types of freight or for determining each type's respective charge. Instead, they united on three. Capricious exceptions vitiated even these. Repeatedly, company presidents closeted themselves to divide up territory and agree on minimum rates. Usually the deal barely outlasted their parting handshakes. A few such pools did succeed, particularly in the South, and between lines piercing the plains from Chicago, but the process was rickety, to say the least.[39] And as the companies tried to underbid each other, railroad securities tumbled.

The alternative to a dozen minds with but a single thought was a single mind controlling all. So from the first, railroad owners tried to build territorial empires by laying down or buying up connections. More lines meant more customers on the books, and more chance for the company president to earn laurels as the Napoleon of finance. But it also made sense in the long view. The surest route to stable rates and a steady return lay in having a few companies do the job of hundreds.

If it could be done, that is. Until 1890, the task was as financially tricky as working out a lasting rate agreement. Southerners patched together a system, which went broke with the Panic of 1893. The Atchison, Topeka & Santa Fe bought other roads as if there were no tomorrow, raising its debt from $36.3 million to $158.89 million in four years and throwing its stock value from $140 to $20 a share. Then tomorrow came. Bond interest went unpaid, and the company went into receivership. Only in folklore did Gould rob his western trunklines into the poorhouse. He only spent them into the poorhouse by buying feeder routes that they couldn't afford. By 1893, a few railroad systems had come into existence, the rough outlines of those that twenty years later would dominate transport. For the time being, though, their ambitions had ruined them.[40]

With returns so uncertain and expansion so necessary, investment bankers became nearly indispensable. Only they could buy stock in the bulk that, say, the Pennsylvania Railroad would need to spread its system west of the Alleghenies and south of the Tidewater. Only they had foreign connections good enough to sell blocks of shares in Amsterdam and Paris easily. Necessary steps by railroad men thus carried them further from the control of the communities where projects had first begun, further from the local point of view that had put the prosperity of a Chattanooga or Port Royal ahead of bondholders' comfort or stockholders' security. Inevitable though accidents might be, would one trainman in eleven be injured yearly, and one in every 155 killed, if managers knew their employees as more than figures on an account book? When increasing grain charges of a penny a bushel between Buffalo and New York brought in $1.5 million, managers far from the wheatfields might shrug off any inconvenience this caused farmers they would never meet.[41] Rate setting that made sense to company officials trying to balance accounts between a hundred kinds of freight and a dozen roads, some competing and some not, looked perfectly absurd to farmers who wanted to pay as little as anybody else, and preferably less. For here a hundred pounds of tobacco cost 27 cents to travel forty-five miles between Bedford and Lynchburg, and only 46 cents more from Lynchburg to England![42]

The arrogance stung more than the remoteness. Here were "Robber Barons" like William Vanderbilt living like princes on the profits that small shippers paid them, and repaying their comfort with outbursts like his "The public be damned!" (Leave aside that Vanderbilt was tired and badgered; leave aside that he was explaining to reporters why he was adding an express service to his road, from which customers would benefit. For every Vanderbilt who said such words without meaning them, other railroad barons meant these things without saying them.) Small wonder that, to many westerners, robbing trains made Frank and Jesse James and their gang look like heroes. Everyone knew the story of how the robbers gave their earnings to a poor widow facing eviction. Legend had it that they examined passengers' hands, to make sure that none but "plug-hat gentlemen" were relieved of their cash. The Missouri House came close to the two-thirds vote needed to give the Jameses amnesty, while local residents warned the robbers when pursuers were near, and cheered to see railroad detectives gunned down. How typical of railroad methods that Jesse James should meet his end in 1882, shot in the back![43]

The Great Strike, 1877

Fittingly, the first great labor uprising, the Great Strike of 1877, began over a second round of wage cuts on eastern railroads. Employees wanted their pay restored, and walked out to get it. Quickly, the strike spread nationwide. Violence followed, plenty of it, and the worst came from the forces sent to keep order. In Pittsburgh, local militia units were dispatched to the yards. Many troopers joined the demonstrators. State troops fired on picketers, killing twenty and wounding hundreds. Only then did the crowd itself turn violent. Protestors wrecked several thousand railroad cars and over one hundred locomotives, destroyed every railroad building they could find, and seized the local armory and a telegraph office. In Chicago, over fifty workers died before militiamen's bullets. Before federal troops arrived to put authority on the side of the railroad managers, over a hundred people had been killed in Pennsylvania alone.[44]

Conservatives blamed the upheaval on agitators, communists, Greenbackers, and trade unionists, all of which, in their mind, were synonymous. In fact, the crowds that filled the streets included teenaged boys, millhands, and women. They were not warring on capitalism, but on monopoly, and their cause won friends outside of any working class. Wall Street brokers wished the strikers well, and Cincinnati businessmen told the press that they would pay higher freight rates gladly, if railroad employees got the benefit. Other workers had gone out on strike in various places: coopers, stevedores, coal stackers, and newsboys, among others. Order returned, but employers had had enough of a scare to make them cautious. There were no new wage cuts, and some lines restored old pay levels. Having wiped out the Trainmen's Union, railroad owners decided it best to let the other ones alone. Labor leaders would learn from 1877 that mob action could not stand up against a well-drilled military force. Victory depended on discipline and "a system of perfect national organization," say, a trade-union federation able to stand firm. Before the strike, only three brotherhoods enlisted railway workers. By 1900, there were sixteen. Even novelists took the crisis seriously, if only as an event dramatic enough to make the plot go. John Hay's *The Bread-Winners* actually made money.[45]

The Great Strike of 1877, then, was in its own way as significant an emblem of what had gone wrong with the Gilded Age as the driving of the golden spike at Promontory Point had been symbolic of the era's accomplishments. Even as he sent in the army, President Rutherford Hayes pondered the need for government action against the railroad barons, as well. Time only added to his uneasiness. "Shall the railroads govern the country, or shall the people govern the railroads?" he wrote in his diary from retirement. " . . . This is a government of the people, by the people, and for the people no longer. It is a government of corporations, by corporations, and for corporations."[46]

By that time, a rising chorus of those displaced or inconvenienced by the Railroad Age was taking on a coordinated and strident quality. Putting Californians' resentment of the Southern Pacific into pungent editorials, editor Ambrose Bierce described Collis Huntington, the railroad magnate, as "the surviving thirty-six of our modern Forty Thieves." Striking trainmen got a hero's welcome in some places and the benefit of the doubt in others. Two workers that had been arrested for obstructing track in the 1877 strike walked out of jail and into a carriage at the head of an enormous parade. The Plymouth brass band marched in front of them, mineworkers behind, and the whole county turned out to cheer. Out west, juries rushed to find some excuse to award damages to parties suing the railroads. Perhaps they only saw it as getting back some of the people's due.[47] Not by chance, the first serious attempt at business regulation began with the railroads, starting at the state level with the "Granger laws" of the Midwest in the 1870s, and then, in 1887 nationally, with the creation of the Interstate Commerce Commission. The first national corporations had laid down more than the framework for industrial growth. They had set off a national challenge and opened the way to a more powerful national state.

Chapter 7

Industrialism Unleashed

Railroad building was just one part of a sweeping transformation of American life in the Gilded Age. From the Civil War into the new century, the economy shifted hard towards industrial development. Manufacturing and transportation accounted for one job in four in 1860, and something over one in two in 1900. In the first year, manufactures had $2 billion in value; thirty years later, their value had risen to more than $9 billion. Iron ore production nearly quadrupled, from seven million long tons to twenty-seven million in just two decades. Adjusted to reflect the increased value of the dollar, the Gross National Product actually tripled.[1]

The Origins of Industrialization

It is important to see the industrial revolution as a process, and not as a series of events reaching some fulfillment. The transformation of production had begun long before the Civil War. It got its start when machine labor and mass production let factories spin yarn and weave cloth more cheaply than artisans could do it, and with Eli Whitney's discovery that machine tools could create interchangable parts, and a work process that divided up the task so that relatively unskilled workers could assemble the products that had called for a craftsman's touch before. By the early 1800s, there were textile mills along New England's streams; by 1860, interchangable parts had made it possible for factories to produce a watch that cost only a dollar, where half a century before the watchmaker charged fifty times as much. Nor was the industrial revolution complete in 1901, when the Gilded Age closed. It affected some places far more than others. Most manufacturing remained where it had been in 1860, in the great cities of the Midwest or close to the northeastern coast. For all the ballyhoo about a New South, Massachusetts still turned out four times as much in the way of cotton goods as South Carolina, and only three southern states made it into the top ten.[2] And a surprisingly large amount of what census takers counted as industry was only one step removed from the farm: curing tobacco, milling wheat, grinding corn, and butchering livestock.

Still, how different even those businesses had become in two generations! In the 1870s, a skilled hand could turn out three thousand cigarettes a day. Then James Bonsack devised a machine able to roll seventy thousand cigarettes in ten hours. Other inventors found a way to form a cigarette package and stuff the smokes inside it. In place of millstones, Minneapolis flour manufacturers tried a Swiss invention, chilled steel rollers that would keep the gluten in the wheat without discoloring it. Other devices shucked the husk from the hard spring grain. Together, the two changes converted the coarse, brown meal into white flour. Mills that made less than 300 barrels of flour a day in 1874 increased their output twenty times over in a dozen years. Machinery made mass production possible; a railroad network made mass distribution possible. Soon retailers nationwide were buying their flour from Minneapolis—3 million bushels in 1882, 7 million in 1890—and very likely from the Pillsbury brothers, among the first to apply the technology for flour making on mammoth scale. By the 1890s, the Pillsburys had gone beyond selling their flour to storekeepers by the barrel. They packaged it to be put on the store shelves, labeled with the Gold Medal brand.[3]

Clearly, inventions played a significant role in bringing about the shift from a shopkeeper economy to a factory-dominated one: only factories could house the many machines needed to do the job faster and on a larger scale, and only entrepreneurs with plenty of capital at their back could afford to buy the machines and start up in business at all. But the industrial revolution depended, as well, on two concepts, both of which kept production costs down: economies of scale—that is, by doing something bigger, one could do it cheaper—and division of labor. Together, the two principles could be merged to make a third, continuous flow.

Continuous flow saw its most literal application in the meat-packing business. By 1890, Bostonians might dine on beef raised in Texas, shipped in cattle cars from Kansas, and butchered in the packing houses of Philip Armour, Gustavus Swift, and others in Chicago. No longer was there the melee, where aproned workers with iron mallets broke the skull of whatever cow in the herd was nearest (half a dozen blows might do the trick, though fifteen was common). Now the cattle were run down a chute, sledged, and strung up on an assembly line. A continuous flow of carcasses moved from one worker to the next. As one economist put it, the animal had "been surveyed and laid off like a map." Each employee had one task, performed with numbing repetition: hoisting, say, seventy carcasses a minute, or cutting hogs' throats as they passed along the trolley line a hundred yards long. Rudyard Kipling caught the efficiency of butchering, amid the horror:

There was a flavor of farmyard in my nostrils and the shouting of a multitude in my ears. . . . Twelve men stood in two lines—six aside. Between them and overhead ran the railway of death. . . . Each man carried a knife, the sleeves of his shirt were cut off at the elbows, and from bosom to heel he was blood-red. . . . [Very nearly all the pigs ever bred in Wisconsin] had just been shot out of the mouth of the viaduct and huddled together in a large pen. Thence they were flicked persuasively, a few at the time, into a smaller chamber, and there a man fixed tackle on their hinder legs so that they rose in the air suspended from the railway of death. Oh! it was then they shrieked and called on their mothers and made promises of amendment, till the tackle-man punted them in their backs, and they slid head down into a brick-floored passage, very like a big kitchen sink that was blood-red. There awaited them a red man with a knife which he passed jauntily through their throats, and the full-voiced shriek became a sputter, and then a fall as of heavy tropical rain. . . . Then that first stuck swine dropped, still kicking, into a great vat of boiling water, and spoke no more words, . . . and presently came forth at the lower end of the vat and was heaved on the blades of a blunt paddle-wheel-thing which said, "Hough! Hough! Hough!" and skelped all the hair off him except what little a couple of men with knives could remove. Then he was again hitched by the heels to that said railway and passed down the line of the twelve men—each man with a knife—leaving with each man a certain amount of his individuality which was taken away in a wheelbarrow, and when he had reached the last man he was very beautiful to behold, but immensely unstuffed and limp.

When Union Stockyards held daily and passed for the slaughter 75,000 cattle and 300,000 hogs, livestock could be killed cheaply. They could be sold more cheaply, too.[4] The packers, unlike local slaughterhouses, used more than the 55 percent of a cow made into dressed beef. The blood made textile dye (Prussian blue)—the fats, oleomargarine—the hoofs, glue—the hair, stuffing for upholstery and mattresses. By the 1890s, Swift & Co. produced not just meat, but over 53 million pounds of lard and thirty thousand tons of fertilizer. As for pigs, packers found a use for everything but the squeal.[5]

National businesses, like Swift & Company, needed an expanded white-collar force. Here is the largest office in the world in 1901, the other side of Packingtown. (*Collier's*, 1901)

Andrew Carnegie, patron saint for the Age of Steel, taught the same lessons about industrialization and carried them a step further. Machinery, division of labor, and continuous flow helped him take first place among steelmakers. But so did administrative innovation.

Innovative Production Techniques Lead to Profits

As with slaughtering cattle, Carnegie realized, steel could be made more cheaply by making more of it, and making it every minute of the day, all year round. Thirty years saw the average annual output of a blast furnace rise from five thousand to sixty-five thousand tons. Running furnaces full time cost less than banking the fires and spending time and money to reheat them every morning. For the same reason, it made sense to keep pig iron molten in the Jones Mixer, rather than cooling it into bars and applying heat all over again later on when the converter was ready to turn it into steel. (This 250-ton thermos bottle was only one among many of "Captain" Bill Jones's inventions. Holding out for "a hell of a salary" when hired, the hard-driving Welshman got as much as the president of the United States, and was worth every penny of it. When the explosion of a blast furnace killed him in 1889, the steelmaker lost his most valuable capital investment.)[6]

Awed by the six-ton converters, the largest in the world, and their ability to make steel at rock-bottom prices, we may miss the way Carnegie's team reorganized the workplace to put them to their fullest use. Continuous flow took perfect coordination, every step of the way. Architects designed a factory with a floor plan that was ready-made for perpetual motion. Narrow-gauge railways bore materials through the plant. Other lines carried ore in and carried finished products out. The bars poured from the converter went straight onto molds on flatcar beds. Marveling at the efficiency, an English visitor remarked that he "would like to sit on an ingot for a week and watch the mill operate." "If you want an ingot cool enough to sit on," steelmaking pioneer Alexander Holley told him, "you'll have to send to England for it."[7]

The crackle of ledger pages makes poor background noise beside the roar of the machinery "breathing," but in accounting practices lay Carnegie's essential innovation to put his firm ahead of rivals. Hiring as his general manager an executive from the Pennsylvania Railroad who borrowed from the line's management techniques, he gave the steel plant an up-to-date accounting system, complete with the statistical tools to make immediate decisions. Every month (and, eventually, every day), Carnegie could scan the figures, count the costs, and compare them from one tally to the last, one division to the next. "We broke all records for making steel last week," one manager wired him. "Congratulations," Carnegie telegraphed back. "What about next week?" Armed with the figures, plowing profits back into capital investment, he poured out steel at an ever more prodigious rate, and at an ever smaller cost. The year he opened his first plant, it put out 21,674 tons of steel. Sixteen years later, Carnegie's output had risen twenty-five times over, to 536,838 tons. In 1873, it cost him $58 to manufacture one ton. By 1889, he sold it for $25, and still made two dollars of clear profit.[8]

New inventions and new means of production by themselves made possible the industrial revolution. They did not assure its success. The catch came in *consumption*. A revolution in selling and distribution had to go along with one in production. The hazards of the oil industry showed why.

The Oil Boom

For years, white settlers had known about petroleum, usually as an oozing tar that bubbled to the surface in place. The Aztecs turned the oozing tar into toothpaste and chewing gum, and Peruvians made oil into a reddish laxative that Spanish explorers swore by. Then, in the 1850s, a way was found to refine it into kerosene, a much cheaper source of illumination than whalers' spermaceti candles, and a lot less smoky and smelly than tallow. Burned in the new lamps with tall glass chimneys, so-called "coal oil" gave a brighter, cleaner light.[9] With buyers easy to find, all kerosene dealers needed was a steady supply.

Drillers of salt wells had brought oil to the surface with their salt water quite by accident; the Pennsylvania Rock Oil Company of Connecticut hit on the idea of doing so on purpose. It hired a dry-goods salesman, Edwin L. Drake, to try the experiment near Titusville, in northwestern Pennsylvania. Oil oozed into puddles on the surface there, so it seemed a good place to try, but two years of setbacks dulled the firm's enthusiasm. It finally decided to drop the whole idea. Before it could pass on the word to the men in the field, the drillers struck oil, more than Drake had containers for—though he used every washtub, whiskey barrel, and jar in sight. An oil boom was on.[10]

Not every well was a gusher. As one satire gibed,

> *Petroleum to the right of them,*
> *Rock oil to the left of them,*
> *Coal oil beneath them,*
> *Quietly slumbered.*
> *Stormed at with jeers and yells,*
> *Deeply they bored the wells,*
> *Down through the rocks of earth,*
> *Down to the mouth of hell*
> > *Bored the six hundred.*

But there was oil enough to spawn fleeting boom-towns, as raw as any western mining camp. "The whole place smells like a corps of soldiers when they have the diarrhoea," one visitor complained of Pithole, one such community.[11]

When the wells dried up, most of the towns turned into scrap lumber. But even where the oil reserves held out, as they did here and there in western Pennsylvania for the next thirty years, the boom towns meant no long-term boom. The area was awash in crude oil. A barrel sold for ten cents at the well, a gallon of refined oil sold for double that, and there were thirty-five gallons to a barrel. Even if one firm could buy up the whole oil country, it could not assure a stable price. Somewhere in America, another Drake would bring in a gusher. Either enough customers must be found to absorb the product or production itself had to be limited to assure a steady profit.

Creating and Supplying National Markets

Oil was an extreme case. Still, the basic lesson held. Businesses making goods for a national market needed to *create* that national market. Carnegie's fellow-Pittsburgher, Henry J. Heinz, showed how it could be done. A German brickmaker's son who began his career selling food from the family garden, Heinz borrowed money from his brothers to set up a horseradish bottling plant. The business failed, but Heinz knew he was on the right track.[12] Home refrigeration, even with the traditional icebox, remained as rudimentary as the refrigerated car in the mid-1870s. Fresh fruits and vegetables were plentiful in season, but, for eight to ten months a year, Americans lived largely on salt pork, corn meal, root vegetables, and bread. Only Floridians got a chance to eat grapefruit. Outside of California, oranges and lemons cost so much that children prized them as Christmas presents. The bland, unvarying diet of most Americans cried out for spices and relishes.[13] So Heinz found his way back into business as a bottler of condiments: chili and tomato sauces. From there, he expanded into a few prepared foods like baked beans with pork and canned peas.

Canning had been around since Napoleon's time, and bottled ketchup since the 1820s. Very likely a few Forty-niners carried seafood packed in Baltimore on their voyage to California. But as long as tinsmiths turned out 1,500 cans a day and canners had to spend so long processing food to make it safe for consumption, canning would remain a small-time business. Mark what a difference technology and the assembly line made! By 1883, one machine could solder pieces of tin-plate into the cylindrical sides of cans at 50 per minute. Another could close up both ends at 4,400 an hour. Calcium chloride sped up the boiling process and the pressure kettle gave makers more control over the temperature. Where factories could cook 2,500 cans a day, they now did 20,000 or more. Within thirty years, Heinz was canning sardines, sliced pineapples, tuna, and Bartlett pears at the rate of 150 cans a minute. Other inventions hulled peas and stripped kernels off of corncobs. Staff chemists found additives to keep food from spoiling in the can.[14]

Advertising a National Market

Heinz was the first to use the machines year-round, just as Campbell's Soup and Borden's Milk would be in their own industries—which was why they came to dominate the field and stayed there. He also found out how to use publicity to sell more. Even when he picked up the number "57" for the varieties of food his company sold in 1892, it was an underestimate. But the number stuck in the mind. So did the Heinz trademark, a little pickle with the company's name on it. Passengers sailing through the Golden Gate could see a "57" whitewashed ten feet high on the cliffs. ("My God!" one bewildered foreigner exclaimed, "they number the hills here!") On Broadway, Heinz put up one of the first outdoor electrical signs, a 1,200-bulb green pickle, which added to the electrical gallimaufry coming into existence on Times Square. At the Chicago World's Fair in 1893, the company handed out free watch charms shaped like pickles, spreading name recognition with tens of thousands of unwitting advertisers. And, of course, visitors to the Heinz factory got guided tours with free samples.[15]

Though Heinz advanced the advertising revolution, he did not create it. Credit for that really should go to the patent medicine makers. In the mid-1870s, they were joined by makers of soap, food, and new-fangled gadgets, and, twenty years later, by just about everybody else. The harder a product had to compete, the more likely it was to advertise—Swift's meats, or Proctor and Gamble's soaps—and this was truest when the label was just about all that set rival brands apart. But that label, with its unique brand name, counted for quite a lot, the moment a loyal constituency was built up. With proper advertising, and laws to protect trademarks, buyers would not buy just any cracker; they would insist on Uneeda Biscuit. Like the wailing baby in the advertisement, reaching for the elusive bar of Pear's Soap, they wouldn't be happy until they got that brand, and, no matter how much competitors advertised, Uneeda would have an assured market. So consumers could not escape the marketers, no matter how hard they tried—not when pennants boosted, billboards boasted, and barn walls, sidewalks, tree stumps, and even river bluffs, touted wares. After a day's travel in New Jersey, an English traveler concluded that the state belonged to "one Schenck," maker of pulmonic syrups and gargles.[16] In quite a different way, with their catalogues, Sears Roebuck and Montgomery Ward showed how publicity could build a constituency of consumers, coast to coast.

But if advertising helped make national markets, national markets prompted a change in advertising. Merchants might announce the arrival of a new line of goods in the daily, in a squib as unobtrusive as the news article it stood next to—or downright indistinguishable from it. "The Race Question is unsettled," one Southern item read, only to conclude, "But it is settled that Hood's Sarsaparilla leads all remedies." Aggressive sellers hit on the first tricks to catch the eye by printing the same line six hundred times in a row. After the Civil War, department stores like Macy's started throwing in stars or display type, breaking through column lines, and, eventually, using illustrated cuts. Starting in the 1880s, companies began turning to professional advertising agencies like J. Walter Thompson to sell their products. The agencies did such a good job that tourists sailing past the Rock of Gibraltar would complain at not seeing the Prudential Insurance name on its side. By the early 1900s, professional copywriters wrote the copy, ranging from catchy slogans ("You press the button; we do the rest") to jangling jingles, where Phoebe Snow rode the Road of Anthracite, no doubt straight to the cleanser Sapolio's Spotless Town. "Here is food for child or man," Campbell's Soup copy exulted,

> *And ages in betwix;*
> *It only takes one ten-cent can*
> *To make enough for six.*[17]

Newspapers could reach a local market, but for national impact, advertising would have to be placed in magazines. Religious weeklies opened their back pages, as did the mainstream monthlies, but by the 1890s, business had the best medium of all in the mass-circulation magazines that were aimed at the middle class, and those for women especially. What was good for advertisers proved a bonanza for the media. By 1919, advertising yielded over $2 billion. Freed from party-press subsidies, newspapers could rely on their advertisers more than their subscribers to keep them going. More ads meant more money for news coverage and more features that appealed to a wider audience meant more advertisers.[18]

The Persistent Problem of Competition

Thanks to the changes in manufacturing and marketing, factory size doubled in the 1870s and 1880s. And yet, bigness did not do away with competition. It may even have increased it. Local butchers had to match the prices of the dressed-beef trade. Country grocers found themselves challenged by the mail-order houses and the national brand names. "Who sympathized with you when your little girl was sick?" an Arkansas newspaper demanded. "Was it your home merchant, or was it Sears and Roebuck?" It was a nice argument, unless the customer happened to be black, in which case buying items from the home merchant that seemed above a Negro's proper place could be downright unhealthy—one reason that drummers, catalog in hand, fanned out across the Mississippi Delta in the 1890s. The cracker barrel, where customers had to scoop out handfuls, each soggier than the last, had never allowed grocers to stock more than one kind. One joke told of a shopper's protest at mice among the crackers. Impossible, the shopkeeper exclaimed: "the cat sleeps there every night." Now wholesalers had to compete with a variety of sealed boxes from the National Bis-

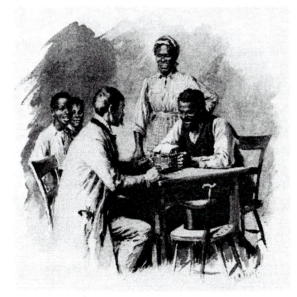

National markets meant national sales networks, like this typewriter "drummer" demonstrating the product at a Southern home in 1894. (*Scribner's*, April 1894)

cuit Company (Nabisco). Storekeepers who had made their food go farther by adding sand to the sugar, mahogany chips to the coffee, or plaster of paris to the flour now had to undersell goods equal in price and just possibly better in quality (though, until the Pure Food and Drug Act of 1906, the difference might be no more than a higher quality sawdust).[19]

So businessmen, big and small, felt mixed feelings about competition, depending on whether they were breaking into someone else's market or having their own invaded. Yet the search for stability and profits was an inescapable force. There were two ways in which it made business bigger: horizontal combination, which would control prices and output by owning all of one step in the process, and vertical combination, which would cut costs by owning every step.

Vertical and Horizontal Integration

Among the pioneers in vertical integration was Gustavus Swift, the Chicago meat packer. Packingtown could can or salt pork and sell it nationally but marketing fresh beef took a little longer. From their opening in 1865, the Union Stock Yards acted mostly as a way station, where cattle from the West could be corralled and then shipped east, to be slaughtered on the spot. Most of the cow was then discarded—though Swift had paid the freight on every pound of it. The solution was to kill the cattle in Chicago, ship nothing but the "dressed beef," and put the waste materials to use. In 1878, Swift's engineers adapted J. B. Sutherland's recent invention, the refrigerated railroad car, to this specialized use. Even then, the start-up costs for the new system were immense. The railroads, which owned loading docks and feeding stations along the routes, preferred to haul whole cattle. Swift & Co. was forced to build the refrigerator cars itself and pay special fees to the railroad for carrying them. It had to erect refrigerated warehouses to keep the meat in every major city where dressed beef was sent, and acquire the wagons to carry its product to local butcher shops. Yet by owning every step in the process, Swift gained far more than he had lost, and so did his rivals, when they made Swift's strategy their own. That was why by 1900, five meat packers dominated the interstate beef business.[20]

Any company that wanted to sell nationally tried at least some vertical integration. Breweries with a pasteurized product could ship their beer from Milwaukee to St. Paul for only fifteen cents, but who would buy it when local breweries already controlled the market? Cheap freight rates allowed the Schlitzes and Anheusers to set up a national chain of distributors, hire wholesalers, and open branch offices. When bartenders stuck by the local beer, the big producers took up the old British tradition: the "tied-house." Anyone wanting to set up saloonkeeping could get his back bar, mirror, glasses, even his cigar case, from the brewer on easy installments—but he had to push the producer's brand. At the same time, the brewers reached back down the production chain. Purchasing departments signed up growers to give them a steady supply of hops, malt, and barley. Other departments ran barrel-making plants. They even bought the forest to cut into barrel-staves.[21]

Refiners learned the same lessons. They, not the owners of the wells, were the big moneymakers during Drake's oil rush. The refining process was cheap, and the profits—$8 on every $13 barrel sold in national markets—were immense. New technology and the principles of continuous flow and scale economies cut production costs still more. A more intense heating process, with super-heated steam distillation and seamless iron stills, removed more from the crude. With a higher boiling point, the oil's molecular structure could be changed to increase refiners' yield by 20 percent. If oil flowed through faster, if the refineries produced more per day, the cost per gallon would fall from six cents to three cents. In the 1860s, the average refinery would turn out nine hundred barrels a week; by the 1870s, it could do a thousand barrels a day.[22]

But refiners soon found that they could make a greater profit still by cutting out the middlemen; they could accomplish this by building their own tank wagons to carry the oil, hiring coopers to make their own barrels, doing their own brokerage of foreign exchange, and setting up outlets for retail sales of the refined oil. In 1878, the refinery that owned its own tank car could save a penny a gallon per mile traveled. In two years, the car paid for itself. An oilcan fifteen cents cheaper than the firm could buy elsewhere saved $5 million per year, a barrel $1.25 cheaper brought savings of $4 million.

John D. Rockefeller and the "Oil Trust"

Still, as the oil-refining business showed, vertical consolidation had its limits. It was a clumsy means of controlling market prices and limiting output. Horizontal consolidation worked more efficiently. The pioneer in this method, and most notorious of all the so-called robber barons of the age, was John D. Rockefeller. Raised on the shabbier edge of the middle class, he should have learned rascality from his father, "Big Bill" Avery Rockefeller, an affable bigamist who traded in horses and quack cancer cures. "I cheat my boys every chance I get," he once boasted. "I want to make 'em sharp." As it happened, he imparted more solid lessons than getting wealth by stealth: never to go into debt, break a contract, nor leave a loan to anyone else outstanding once it was due, and always to get what was paid for.[23]

John became as sharp as morality permitted—and he did think himself a moral man. As a youth, he taught Bible classes, and late in life would declare, "God gave me my money." For books, politics, music, or drama, he had no interest at all. But making money did interest him mightily, and more in the gaining than in the keeping. Trained at a commercial college, finding a job as clerk for a commission house at four dollars a week, he proved so capable at his job that his salary increased nearly five times over in three years, and at age twenty he resigned to set up in business for himself.[24]

His name would go down as the wrecker of competitors. Under his control, the alliance of Cleveland refiners led by his own Standard Oil would expand to drive most of the independents out of business. In 1876, it took over twenty-four firms, in 1877 another thirty-five, in three years a hundred. Some methods were as crude as the oil they received. Railroads eager for Standard Oil's business were forced to kick back part of the rate they charged him—fifty cents a barrel on every two-dollar exaction—to keep Rockefeller's good will.

Rockefeller had mixed feelings about destroying rivals; the idea of rebates came from the railroads first, not from him. Sick of competing for the business of carrying petroleum, they made an alliance among themselves, split up the commerce, and rewarded the refiners who went along with the arranged pattern. All Rockefeller did was shift the initiative to the oil men, and loosen the system so that all who joined in the alliance had some say in how they ran their firms. Standard Oil would be a federation, not a monarchy, and Rockefeller would reign, not rule.[25]

Nor was the basic idea that unthinkably wrong. Competition was as wasteful as it was destructive. Firms selling their oil at a loss could outlast weaker rivals and have just enough strength left to crawl into bankruptcy court. Standard Oil itself attested to the advantage of cooperation. By speaking through one agent, Cleveland's businessmen could induce the railroads to give them a lower rate. What the oil industry needed was stability: prices that would ensure a good, steady profit from one year to the next, not so high that rival refineries would be set up to fill consumers' needs for less, not so low that the industry would fail to turn a dividend.

Vertical and horizontal consolidation fostered each other. Late in the 1870s, the producers of crude oil tried to buck the alliance of refiners and railroad companies by setting up the first long-distance pipelines. They, too, had learned the value of vertical integration; owning the wells and now the means of carrying Pennsylvania oil to the East Coast, they set up refineries of their own. The refiners aligned with Standard Oil had to build pipelines of their own, and not just to beat the new competition. Only belatedly did it dawn on them that the new technology would be cheaper than paying railroad rates, and that it would allow them to carry more oil on a more reliable schedule. But the innovation also caused its own problems. First, where was the money to come from? Second, what good were refineries in Cleveland if the oil in Pennsylvania was going to be shipped eastward anyway, for export overseas—as most of Standard Oil's product was? New refineries would need to be built, closer to the coast, and some of the old ones would need to be shut down or modernized. That would take central planning, and that meant a new legal fiction that could act in a handful of states without seeking a handful of charters or facing the taxes state governments put on any firm incorporated across the border.[26]

Rockefeller was aiming at coordination more than monopoly power in 1882, when Standard's legal counsel S. C. T. Dodd created the "trust," establishing a governing board for a federation of refiners. It was a spectacular achievement. The alliance consolidated its fifty-three refineries to twenty-two, and built three super-refineries. Wholesalers were bought out and taken over, as the trust went into marketing oil at home as well as abroad. The cost of refining oil fell drastically, to 1.5 cents a gallon and then to half a penny.

The story of consolidation and monopoly has an attractive juggernautish quality: competition assures winners and losers and, in the end, one winner alone. But Standard Oil showed how easily reports of a competitor's death could be exaggerated. Rockefeller did have real successes. In 1884, Standard Oil was refining 96,000 barrels a day. It controlled nearly four-fifths of all the refined oil in the country. But though it held a commanding position, and, in some parts of the country, was the sole supplier, Rockefeller never held an absolute national monopoly on production or re-fining. Firms cut out of kerosene sales found new markets in making lubricants, naptha, or paraffin waxes. Given time, they knew that Standard Oil would come to terms, for Rockefeller lacked the patience to sell at a loss for long. Take over com-petitors though he might, he could not take them all over. In 1884, a hundred other refineries were at work. They found their own railroad rebates and built their own pipelines.[27]

Nor could Standard Oil control the crude as it came from the ground, though Rockefeller forgot his early advice and tried that, too. He could come no closer to mo-nopoly than to own one barrel in four coming out of the ground. Something always got in the way—something, say, like the oil field under Spindletop in 1901.

Bursting from the ground of northern Texas came a gusher of unprecedented size. Every day, until it was capped, it poured out from 70,000 to 110,000 barrels of crude—a far cry from the average production of two barrels a day that eastern wells put out. By the end of the year, a new oil rush was on. There were discoveries of oil in Louisiana. By 1913, Oklahoma produced a fourth of the nation's supply. So many thousand firms were made and ruined that cynics christened the new field "Swindle-top," but out of Spindletop alone came Gulf, Texaco, and Magnolia (soon renamed Mobil).[28] Larger firms would need years to bring some measure of control and turn theirs into a profit-making venture, but Standard Oil never owned a big enough share to do the controlling.

There was a final lesson from Rockefeller's success, though it would take a later generation to discern it. An awareness of the market and of the latest technology could put a company on top. It could not keep it there, unless those in charge changed along with conditions. Rockefeller had grasped the possibilities of kerosene for illu-mination, but electric lights dimmed the potential sales of Standard Oil's chief prod-uct. Other firms saw what Rockefeller's did not, that new markets in oil for electrical generators or gasoline for automobiles could replace the old. By 1911, the indepen-dents would supply some 70 percent of all fuel oil, and nearly half of all lubricants. By 1924, Rockefeller's company controlled less than half the refining in the United States.[29]

As long as competition survived or could be revived, mass production and mass marketing would keep on bringing goods within the reach of more and more con-sumers. Prices fell faster than wages. Thanks to Standard Oil's "monopoly," whole-salers, who a generation before had paid a dollar for a gallon of kerosene, paid eight cents by 1885. They paid little more than a nickel a decade later. Using the waste prod-ucts from cattle let the meat trust prosper by charging a mere quarter-cent above cost on each pound of meat. Big breweries battled just as hard as small ones to grab the market but they never found a Rockefeller to lead them. They could charge eight dol-lars wholesale for a barrel of beer. Much good it did them; bartenders could get some-thing just as good for three dollars, and saloons were so plentiful that any owner ask-ing more than the slimmest margin of profit would go broke. But for the customer, the nickel beer and the free-lunch counter were among the Gilded Age's most unap-preciated marvels.[30]

What about clothing? Drawing on the designs of Walter Hunt, who was considered the father of the safety pin and a host of other gadgets, Elias Howe and Isaac Singer each developed an automatic sewing machine. Howe's invention increased the speed of sewing sevenfold. Singer's model allowed continuous stitching, though his real skill came as a promoter: by the century's end, three sewing machines in four worldwide were Singer products. In 1849, the device was so unusual that a circus put one in its sideshow and charged twelve-and-a-half cents admission to see it. Singer did demonstrations at fairs and carnivals. Before the war, only the poorest consumers, unable to afford anything costly or well fitted, bought "slops," as sailors called ready-mades. But when machines could do fancy trimmings, buttonholes, lock-stitches rather than the weak chain-stitches, the middle class could dress well without going to a tailor—and pay less for it. Sewing machines for shoes allowed readymades there, too. The McKay stitcher could fix soles on eighty pairs as quickly as a journeyman seamed one.[31]

A Revolution in Buying Habits Ushers in a New Era in Retail

A consumer culture was developing. At its heart lay the department store, where proprietors, buying in bulk, could sell for less, and sell just about everything in one place. Alexander T. Stewart led the way. An Irish immigrant who started with a shop selling lace, he ended up owning New York's Marble Dry-Goods Palace. It was actually made of cast iron; the "marble" exterior was painted on, but with its glass dome and steam-driven passenger elevator, it did seem like a consumers' palace, with floor-walkers as the attendant lords, serviceable, glad to be of use, and treasure rooms of merchandise on every floor. Unlike most shops, Stewart's wares were on display at fixed prices. Rowland H. Macy and John Wanamaker outdid the Palace. They provided soda fountains, lunchrooms, branch offices, and mail-order catalogues, as well. "Goods suitable for the millionaire," Macy's boasted, "at prices in reach of the millions."[32]

Chain stores would revolutionize buying in small towns the way department stores did the cities. The credit for that idea goes to George F. Gilman and George Huntington Hartford, whose Great American Tea Shop opened in 1859. Buying tea in bulk, they could sell it for thirty cents a pound—or seventy cents less than anybody else. Soon they were marketing spices and soap, coffee and condensed milk. Branch offices opened under a new name, the Great Atlantic & Pacific Tea Company. By the turn of the century, shoppers at their five hundred outlets seldom wondered what the A & P stood for as a name. They knew well enough what it stood for as a business: self-service, sale prices, charge accounts, and free delivery. By then, too, three hundred five-and-dime stores offered merchandise once carried only at the fanciest country "dry-goods" stores. For a nickel, the customer could get buttonhooks or safety pins, thimbles or soap. By pricing goods for just a penny less than the next full price (ninety-nine cents rather than a dollar), Frank Woolworth's chain stores also induced buyers to spend more.[33]

Out in the countryside, dry-goods stores multiplied. They might have a limited stock—"dry goods" such as napkins and spooled cotton thread along the shelves and counters to the right, groceries, cigars, and sundries to the left, kerosene and whiskey barrels at the back—but to customers for whom shoe-blacking paste, white sugar, ice in summertime, and bananas (the poor family's tropical fruit) were a novelty, the change was dramatic. Returning to his old neighborhood, a South Carolinian marveled to find two shops selling tea, where once people had done without. "These people had their smokeshops in the Northwest and their manure piles in the fertilizer factories," he wrote. Everywhere, country folk wanted more and made less for themselves. To get the money for store-bought goods, farm families had to put ever larger acreage into cash crops. Few regretted doing so. "They loved *things* the way only the very poor can," one Southerner remembered of his kin. "They would have thrown away their kerosene lamps for light bulbs in a second."[34]

For middle-class women, the consumer culture was doubly liberating. New products freed them from some drudgery and let them spend more time on other tasks. But it also gave them a new sphere in which they had power; for it was wives, not their husbands, who did the buying at department stores, and picked the products. At Wanamaker's or Woolworth's, their demand determined what goods the managers chose to sell. Retailers had to treat them with courtesy, or lose their trade to the shop around the corner. And, of course, for those who wandered past display windows and had time to banter with acquaintances and clerks, shopping was often the pleasantest part of the day.[35]

Competition's instabilities gave shoppers a good deal. So did a very different instability, one affecting the employees of this industrial revolution. The shift from iron to steel, for example, transformed workers' lives as much as it did the goods they made. Artisans needed a long apprenticeship, but enjoyed more control over their conditions when they achieved the rank of puddlers and molders. A puddler's work demanded stints of very hard, dangerous labor turning and working the molten iron in the refining furnace. Still, between "heats," he had regular rest periods, inseparable from the ironmaking process. He could sit, eat, chat, or even venture out to some nearby bar to refresh himself. Molders, who did the "ramming" and "pouring" of the iron had no such freedom to leave the foundry during their breaks, but at least they were given breathing spells.[36]

Steel changed all. Where the puddler could drive out carbon impurities from a hundredweight of iron in half an hour, the Bessemer converters could do the same for tons in twenty minutes. The molten iron simply flowed into the Bessemer as the vessel lay on its side. Air blown through the holes at the bottom of the converters set off a firestorm when the vessel was righted, but it burned off the impurities quickly, and prepared the iron for the additives that turned it into steel. As Bessemer converters, and, in the 1880s, open-hearth forges, replaced the puddler's furnace, they replaced the puddlers, too. Continuous flow meant continuous work, not the "heats" and pauses of ironmongering. There was no time out for lunch nor for rest. Instead of running all day, factories ran all day and all night, Sundays included. Competition forced managers to save wherever they could, and that meant keeping labor costs down. So instead of more workers manning the machines at the old schedule for wages and hours, existing employees had to stay longer. They were expected seven days a week, and twelve hours a day. Every other week, day and night shifts changed places in the "long turn." A worker on the day-shift stayed through the night, and kept his new hours until the next "long turn." For some tasks, the laborer worked from six to six; puddlers began at two.[37]

Industrialization and competition, clearly, each worked in contradictory, disturbing ways. Americans ate better and worse for having cheap white flour, free from all the impurities and most of the vitamins in the old, coarse kind; the change from cornmeal may well explain why pellagra swept the rural South in the new century.[38] More, perhaps, than the Civil War, mass production and marketing, and railroad and communications networks turned a Union of states into a nation, with a common culture. At the same time, it made new divisions, widening the gap in ways of life between rich and poor, skilled and unskilled, industrial worker and farmer. The competition that fostered innovation and a cheap abundance of goods drove down wages, as well as prices. The cooperation that brought stability to the marketplace actually broke down local monopolies, but it also allowed businesses the power to ignore the very competitive forces that made the system so creative.

Not surprisingly, Americans felt mixed feelings about this spanking new world. A southern family might pride itself on living in a house of mill-planed boards and using that marvelous novelty that cheap timber now allowed, toilet paper—even as the children ran around in stockings that mother had knit. A businessman like John T. Woodside of South Carolina could point to the cottonseed mill and textile factory he had made, and still lament the self-sufficient, localized world of his youth. "Neighbors in those days were sure enough neighbors," he wrote. "They would lend you anything they had. How changed things are now in this age of commercialism[;] you could scarcely borrow a chicken much less a mule."[39]

Industrialization, then, raised anew the problem of the Age: how to adapt to a changing world without sacrificing the values of the past. What might be given up, so that the essence of what made America blest among nations might be kept? How to square the commonweal with individual aspiration, ambition with idealism, old republican virtues with the profit motive?

Chapter 8

The Unhuddled Masses

America could not escape from the world but there were times when it seemed that the world was escaping to America. As the century's last decade began, 42 percent of New York City's people were foreign-born, as were 41 percent of Chicago's, and 37 percent of Minneapolis's. More than one Minnesotan in three was born abroad, 29 percent of Massachusetts residents, and 22 percent of Illinois's. By 1910, one American in seven was of foreign birth. It was not surprising that the Statue of Liberty standing in New York's harbor should have been, from its completion in 1886, less a symbol of the open society than of the open door, nor that even those who were immigrants themselves should feel misgivings over their perception of the door as being too widely ajar. "Give me your tired, your poor," read Emma Lazarus's poem inscribed on the base of the statue,

> *Your huddled masses yearning to breathe free,*
> *The wretched refuse of your teeming shore;*
> *Send the homeless, tempest tost to me,*
> *I life my hand beside the golden door.*[1]

The "wretched refuse" themselves might have appreciated the sentiment more than the description, even from a poet only six weeks in this country.

Why They Came

Two things made this great migration unsettling to those already here. The first was its size. Between 1877 and 1890, more than 6.3 million people immigrated to America, and between 1900 and 1906, nearly as many again. In forty years, fully 23 million Europeans came across the seas.[2] The second was the newcomers' place of origin. Until 1896, most of the immigrants either shared the English language or Protestant religion of those already here. Out of the British Isles they came, out of Germany and Scandinavia. The so-called "Old Immigration" kept coming, but after 1880, their ranks were mixed with a breed more alien in language and religion: laborers from southern Italy, as well as refugees from the empires of Turkey and Russia that stretched from the Baltic to the Black Sea and westward to the Aegean. Many of the "New Immigration" were Jewish or Eastern Orthodox. Even the Catholics of Lithuania and Poland practiced their faith in ways unfamiliar to the clergy already here. In 1880, immigrants from southern and eastern Europe numbered less than a quarter of a million; in the thirty years that followed, 8.4 million more of them emigrated. By 1907, they counted for five of every six who came.

Why did they come? For many, an intensifying bigotry at home made them look abroad for refuge. The nationalism uniting Germany and Italy in the midcentury affected the great Russian empire in quite a different way. There, the czars presided over "Russification," to impose one culture on a multitude of subject peoples. In the Polish provinces, Russian authorities attacked the Catholic church, on the steppes, the Mennonites, but everywhere they gave special attention to the Jews. Lawbooks bulged with restrictions on their rights: 650, by one count. Mobs sacked the Jewish *shtetls*, raped the women, killed the children, burned the temples of Israel, and shredded the word of the Lord. While the pogrom raged, police simply watched. Afterwards, they might escort the rioters to the next ghetto to continue their work. Czarist officials wrote and published as fact the Protocols of the Elders of Zion, a supposed Jewish blueprint for world conquest. Two years of violence left some thousand Jews killed and many more wounded. The message was plain: the Russian empire had no place for keepers of the faith.[3]

New nations needed armies. They did more than recruit—they drafted. When the conscription officer's knock on the door could mean twenty-five years' service in Russia, twelve in Austria-Hungary, residents had the strongest incentives to run for their lives.[4]

At the same time, new freedoms made emigration more possible than before. Until 1860, the empires of southern and eastern Europe, and the Far East, forbade their subjects to leave. The birth of Italy brought the death of restrictive laws down the peninsula. In 1867, the Austro-Hungarian authorities loosened the bonds, and with the Russo-Turkish War of 1877, the Turks lost their grip on most of the Balkans, and the gates lay open to them.

Want uprooted the settled peasants of Europe, a want, curiously enough, brought about because, in so many ways, life at home had never been better. More children than ever lived past their infancy. But more people meant less land for the father to divide among his sons and less food on the table. Between 1860 and 1910, population in eastern central Europe grew more than 75 percent. Farmland did not increase anywhere near as much. If work was to be found for all, some must be ready to go wherever else in the world it was being offered.[5]

For consumers, the industrial revolution had brought a new plenty, but it plunged many producers into crisis. Grain from Kansas could undersell the produce of Italy, even in Calabria.[6] The landlord of central Europe found that with the latest threshers and reapers, he could do the work of a dozen tenant families, at a fraction of the cost. Why leave them on the land at all? When steam-driven engines in Boston could turn out shoes so cheaply, Kiev's Jewish cobbler might have trouble finding buyers.

Old ties loosened less because of hardship than from a new sense of possibilities. Before, a peasant might endure anything, convinced that suffering was the lot of man and work simply a duty ordained by God. It was too much to expect that labor would lead to landownership or savings, or a rise in social class. With the industrial revolution and the end of serfdom in central Europe, the situation changed. Now, bettering oneself *did* seem possible.[7] Especially for those already on the move seeking work, that sense of possibilities must have been particularly strong. If a day's journey would turn up a job with a better income to it than anything the local village could provide, what could a week's journey produce—or two week's, to the New World? That know-how to which Americans contributed so much, that capitalism which Americans liked to see as their special way of thinking, both uprooted the Europeans and set them on the road.

Neighbors and kinsmen already settled in the New World sent the irresistible word home. "Here the food is overflowing," a Norwegian immigrant wrote friends used to the frugal board, "and we get to drink as much sweet milk as we desire; when the milk becomes sour, it is thrown out to the pigs." With work, a family might own land. The breadwinner might possess a suit, or even two, and store-bought furniture. To a Hungarian girl fresh from a little village, one of New York's most amazing sights was the children everywhere, "with *shoes and stockings on!*" At home, such luxuries were put on for holidays only. Once the migration began, it perpetuated itself. Letters, as Italians put it, forged a chain across the Atlantic, tugging whole lines of residents from one particular village. Without the chain, the passion to rush to America might touch a community little or not at all—especially since letters so often held prepaid tickets. Where the chain led, the villagers went. That was why Sicilians from Santo Stefano di Quisquina ended up in Tampa, Florida, and those from Melilli found quarters in Middletown, Connecticut.[8]

Thus far, the immigrants' story seems to fit cherished legend. So it does, but with two limits. Those who sought to better themselves went all over the place, and not just to the United States, and quite a few came, not as settlers but as sojourners, or even as commuters.

Inside Europe, movement stirred up communities where no one dreamed of crossing the seas. As farmers' prospects diminished, at least one resident in three in the area between Hungary, Croatia, and Poland found home or work away from the home village. From western Galicia, over 60,000 inhabitants made a yearly migration to the Ukraine to harvest the grain in 1890, and by 1900, it would be 100,000. Masons from the outlands took jobs in Budapest and tinkers roved from town to town looking for work. Moving once, however short the distance, a peasant was likelier to move again, and farther, if need be. By the 1880s, Italians were flocking to Argentina and Brazil for temporary work. Not until the next decade did many of them try their fortunes in North America.[9]

Quite a few who crossed the seas never meant to stay. Many who left America meant to return at a later date. Italy's "birds of passage" left when they had earned money enough to make the venture worthwhile: enough for a dowry, say, or to buy a certain number of cows. They were less unusual than historians once imagined. While the Japanese came to the mainland of the United States as families, the first wave of Chinese was mostly made up of single men, intending to prosper and return to their kinfolk across the Pacific. Nearly three Slovaks in every five who came to Pittsburgh around 1900 went home again. They had answered ads in the Slovak press for temporary jobs, and had taken them because they *were* temporary. When a fact-finding commission interviewed Italian passengers leaving America in 1907, it found that well over two-thirds planned on returning.[10]

How They Came

Bright legends surround the newcomers' motives for coming; darker ones cloud the circumstances of their arrival. Certainly it was no easy coming, nor easy crossing, and the earlier an outlander came, the harder the trip. Especially for those planning a permanent move, leaving home meant heartbreak. Husbands left families behind, while they got established in their new home. Orthodox Jews knew that they would find it harder to practice their faith in a bustling New World. "You who will not break a thread on the Sabbath now will eat swine in America," a neighbor warned one Russian girl.[11]

A traveler from beyond the Elbe would need to make his or her way to the Baltic ports. Their belongings tied in a sheet, traveling in boxcars, packed like cattle, immigrants would board ships that treated them no better than livestock. For thirty-five dollars, passengers could embark on ten to fifteen days of pure hell in steerage with two thousand others. Seasickness, hunger, misery, and filth were their lot. Two bathrooms, "dirty, sticky and disagreeable," served them all. They washed in cold sea water with no soap; they slept on berths of iron with mattresses of straw. Few ships served kosher food for the Orthodox Jews. One family got by on hot water with some brandy and sugar, and the bread it brought on board. Each passenger got the cheapest fare the liner could get away with: about sixty cents' worth per day, supplemented with goods the crew sold at outrageous prices.[12]

Companionship and hope may have kept spirits up, but there must have been deep fear as well. One in five would arrive in America only to be sent home again. If they came to New York after 1892, they would land at Ellis Island and face a day of pretty callous handling. The federal inspectors and doctors were neither cruel nor ignorant, but they were underpaid, overworked, and had no time to spare on courtesies. Before the immigrant left the ship, he or she got a number. Herded into a vast hall, the immigrant would stand in one line, then another. The first doctor would look for the most obvious ailments and mark each patient in chalk. A second expert looked for contagious diseases. A third doctor pulled the eyelash back to scan the eye. Examiners versed in foreign languages peppered the immigrants with questions. Had they jail records? Had they money? Did relatives expect them? Had they signed up for a job here already? If the immigrants gave the right answers—and to admit to a job waiting was the wrong one, since contract labor was forbidden by law—the New World opened before them at the other end of the ferries that ran—twenty-four hours a day—from Ellis Island to New York.[13]

Those with a fixed destination could buy railroad tickets to nearly anywhere. Portuguese fishermen settled along Cape Cod; Basque herders took to the mountain West. Northern European farm families found homes in the Dakotas, and a few French and Irish trickled into the South, but most newcomers had a city as their destination. To many of them, all places must have looked equally strange, not just in custom but in name. Some knew no more than a word they had heard from friends and written down, to show to ticket agents as unfamiliar with Croat as the immigrants were with English: Linkinbra (Lincoln, Nebraska), Pillsburs (Pittsburgh).

"My Disappointment Was Unspeakable": Harsh Realities

To those who came intending to stay, the New World did prove a hard, demanding land, and the promise one paid in clipped coin. Those raised in villages must have found city life a harsh adjustment. "My disappointment was unspeakable," a Galician later recalled of his arrival at Johnstown: "squalid and ugly, with those congested shabby houses, blackened with soot from the factory chimneys—this was the America I saw." The smell alone was an unwelcome novelty, enough, as a New Yorker said, "to knock you down." Urban space was too valuable to allot much of it to working-class apartments; there were sure to be too many wedged into too small an area. So in the poorer section of town, one might find four, five, even six-story walkups, the "block of flats" accommodating dozens of families. Overcrowding could be overwhelming. Along Cherry Street in New York, experts estimated the population at 5.6 per apartment. In Boston's North End, where Italians lived in squalor, three or four shared a bed. Neither there nor elsewhere was there privacy to be found. Naturally, with epidemics carried so easily, the death rates in the tenements were appalling. At their worst, New York's slums had a mortality rate 80 percent higher than the national average of 20 per thousand. For slum children, it was 136 per thousand. In Chicago, one child in two died before reaching a fifth birthday. Parts of New York City were known as "lung blocks" because of the sweatshops and tuberculosis that were rampant.

Immigrants were welcomed as cheap labor and used against each other. Each new wave served as strikebreakers against the wave before. So many foreigners came that, in some industries, they drove the wages down below the level of subsistence. A semiskilled worker in the garment trade made fifteen dollars a week in 1883, and less than half that in 1885. Women earned as little as three dollars. The unskilled suffered most of the occupational death and injury, and newcomers stood a better chance of finding jobs in the unskilled labor force than did the skilled. As a result, the roster of those killed on the job in Steelton in 1907 read like the rolls of an eastern European village: Tesak, Pajolic, Stifko, Szep, Susic. "Before I came to America," an Italian joke ran, "I was told that the streets were paved with gold. When I got here, I found out three things. First, the streets were not paved with gold. Second, they were not paved at all. Third, they expected me to pave them."[15]

America required adjustments. Parents and children, wives and husbands, ended years of separation to discover themselves strangers. Occasionally, marriages dissolved, sometimes in divorce and sometimes with no more than another notice in one immigrant paper's "Gallery of Vanished Men." Peasants accustomed to barter found themselves at a loss in stores where prices were fixed. Those wanting to honor the Jewish Sabbath usually could not find jobs that gave them Saturdays off. Religious life that had centered on the synagogue now shifted to the home, with greater obligations on family members to keep the faith. "The whole American life was strange to me," one woman lamented. From knowing everything back at school in Russia, she had come to a place where everyone understood more than she. "All the wrong side up," immigrants grumbled. "The children are fathers to their fathers. The fathers children to their children."[16]

Under the circumstances, it would not have been surprising had many of the immigrants gone home in despair, and not just as commuters having earned their pay. Some did. Would he emigrate from Ireland again, given the chance, someone asked a miner in the Pennsylvania coal fields. Bitter words flew back: "I would buy a ticket for hell rather than here." Yet most immigrants who came planning to stay did so, and not simply because, like the Russian Jews, there was nothing to go back to. Hardship or no, America offered a chance. The more modest the newcomer's dreams, the more likely they were to be fulfilled. A Swedish farmhand just after the Civil War could make thirty cents a day at home. For the same work, he might make seventy cents in Minnesota, and in harvest season, four dollars. Hungarians and Slovaks compared their modest gains—an acre or two of land, "city" food and readymade clothing—to the comforts of home and were well content. "We had very little," a Pole remembered, "but there was more of this bread here than there, and something on this bread, too." Even the wooden floor of a tenement beat the dirt floor of a shanty. Newcomers knew poverty, not famine. If those left behind had any doubt, they found conviction in a second migration, the migration of money into central Europe. In 1906, the postmaster of Centinje saw thirty thousand dollars in money orders pass through his hands. Other immigrants simply stuffed cash into the envelopes; nearly forty million dollars passed back to Croatia in twelve years.[17]

Hopes lived in part because the Old World heritage survived. Only for the first wave of immigrants from any country was America wholly strange. After that, they found some semblance of their native land again, established in America. Let a Pole come to Milwaukee in 1890 and he could find neighborhoods in the southwest end of town where, as one unfriendly observer remarked, one could see "no names but those that end with a sneeze."[18] Jews coming to the Lower East Side found tenements, dirt, noise, and poverty. But the ghetto also offered a place where others spoke the old language, worshiped in the familiar way, ate the customary foods, drank the same intoxicants as across the seas. Here at least was a refuge from the gibes of Gentiles and their least likable customs.

A New World on Old World Terms

Some newcomers did their best to fit into the culture in which they found themselves; the English found adjustment all the more painless because so many Americans had a yen to be English themselves, and not just writers and painters like Henry James and James McNeil Whistler. For the others, immigrant communities eased the transition. Instead of shedding their culture, the foreign-born pioneers had rebuilt it. Polish-Americans began founding mutual-aid societies and gymnastics clubs almost as soon as they arrived. Swedes who settled near their compatriots found fraternal orders like the Svea Society, singing groups like the Freja Society or the Svenska Gleeklubben. They might subscribe to *Svenska Amerikanaran*, or any of twelve hundred papers published in their own language. Jews from eastern Europe might attend a Yiddish theater. Twenty-five cents let in a whole family and plays ranged from old classics to modern adaptations of *King Lear*.[19]

So, in the short run, the melting pot only melted here and there. It did not make America one society, or even give all immigrants a sense of a culture in common. Anglos might understand that the Cubans and Spaniards in Tampa shared little beyond language. Over four centuries, the two societies had diverged in customs and politics. Italian shopkeepers knew that the coffee blend they sold to Spaniards no Cuban would stomach, and many a newcomer from Sicily owed his job on the cigar-maker's bench to a Spanish employer's distaste for Cuban troublemakers. But the native-born must have been baffled to see some Spaniards form a Centro Espanol and others a Centro Asturiano, or the darker-skinned Cubans abandoning the Circulo Cubano to set up the more exclusive Union Marti-Maceo.[20]

Instead of dropping old customs, newcomers adapted them. Sicilian wives had helped in the fields during harvest season in Italy; in upstate New York they migrated to the canneries during the busy period, and worked alongside their children putting up fruits and vegetables. Russian women skilled in dressmaking and tailoring could not open shops in New York, but they could enter the needle trades.[21]

Many immigrants strove to stay as they had been. Even so, change began as soon as they left home. Indeed, two kinds of change, not one, made immigrants over simultaneously. On the one hand, the new land made them identify themselves with the nation or culture from which they had come, rather than something smaller. Hitherto, many Europeans had never identified themselves beyond their village or region. Italians called it *canalismo*, that distrust of anyone beyond the range of the sound pealing from the local campanile's bells. Native-born Americans never imagined that there were three distinct dialects of Slovak, nor that costumes differed from town to town,

The advertisement for lager beer, aimed at German-Americans. (Library of Congress)

but Slovaks knew. Some Americans had no notion that they *were* Slovaks, as such. Italians coming to St. Louis still saw themselves as Catanesi or Caggionesi. Towns west of Milan had quarreled over religious shrines and grazing rights, and grudges came across the Atlantic with the baggage of their sons. Sicilians almost always married other Sicilians, though they might extend their tolerance far enough to wed someone from some other province of Sicily. Swedes and Hungarians acted the same way.[22]

Localism gave way only slowly to nationalism, and nationalism lingered strongly enough to keep those of the same religion from making common cause. While English speakers from county Cork shouted themselves hoarse for Irish nationalism, their Gaelic-speaking compatriots, who identified themselves by the town in which they were born, wondered what all the fuss was about. Bringing all those of Irish ancestry together for a St. Patrick's Day parade took some work, but it was nothing compared to the Knights of Columbus's attempt to make Columbus Day a Catholic holiday. They failed completely. Irish and French Canadians balked at giving an Italian that kind of recognition, while Italians saw him as a national hero, not a religious one. Even when "uptown Jews" stretched out a hand of welcome (as they did after recovering from culture shock), it was not always taken gratefully by a people proud of the Russian Jewish community they had left behind. "We are not *schnorrers!*" one newcomer exclaimed, in response to German offers of charity, "and we want to take care of our own."[23]

Americanization

Yet even as the transformation from localism to nationalism took place, immigrants were Americanizing, sometimes without being aware of it. The first signs were the most obvious. Immigration officials, unable to spell the names given to them, made Wahlgrens into Greens, Lapiscarellas into Carrells. To fit in, foreigners adapted their names as well. Francesco became Frank, Rivka Ruth. Making an Old World name into its English equivalent (for example, Piccolo into Little) was no great step, but some immigrants went further, as a Cincinnati shop sign attested: "Kelley and Ryan, Italian bakers."[24]

Over time, even those who resisted the loss of their native tongue found it slipping from them, or changing. As early as 1860, for example, Italians in America had created a distinct idiom. To their former countrymen it sounded like the mother tongue corrupted, to their new-found compatriots, it seemed to be a gibberish of American words with Italian structure and sound. It was neither. It was creative, occasionally humorous, and practical. English words took an Italian flavor: beefsteak into *bistecca*, Quaker into *Quacquero*. Some words showed up wherever Italians settled, like *Orriope* (make haste), readymade for a country where everything was done fast. But America bred not one universal "Italgish" so much as a series of local ones. In New York, the Yiddish idiom and Irish-American pronunciations made Italian words sound like new. Only a New Yorker would be able to translate *Toidavenne*: who else referred to T'oid Avenue?[25]

Immigrants sometimes discovered how far they had gone from their roots only when they returned home. Kinfolk scratched their heads at the pronunciations, not to mention the novelties that the New World had made in vocabulary. Sicilian children would dog a returnee's footsteps, just for the laugh he would give them when he opened his mouth to speak Italian.[26]

The newcomers to America *had* to change. The land itself required it, and American capitalism—with its glistening shops, its consumer culture, its celebration of technology—transformed foreigners as inexorably as it did the country's native sons. Scandinavian loggers headed for Minnesota's forests, while her farmers headed for the state's pastureland. But the hardscrabble life on Scandinavian mountain farms gave newcomers no preparation for the prairie. Everything differed, said one newcomer, except the fleas. Back home, farmers grew cabbages, not corn, barley, or wheat. Penniless Scandinavians hired themselves out to Yankee farmers at a pittance, not just to raise the down payment on land, but to learn American methods for growing an American crop. Wives may have been equal partners in making a living back in Norway, but with the adoption of American machinery, tasks once done by women, such as haying, became a manly prerogative. So did milking and tending the animals, to the disgust of husbands, many of whom had difficulties keeping the milk from going out of the udder and up their sleeves. If women resented losing the privilege of serving as field hands or being restricted to more middle-class and motherly tasks, they kept complaints to themselves. Jewish wives, accustomed to working while their husbands pursued scholarship in Old World communities, found themselves ready and able to work—and their husbands ever more determined to keep them at home like American wives (even if this meant sewing and pressing piecework around the kitchen table rather than earning a wage in the factory).[27]

Even the most commonplace tasks were made anew. Everything from cooking to cleaning changed when peasants moved from farmhouses to tenements. Windows and wood floors were there to be washed; instead of taking food out of the garden, there were trips to the market. There was no root cellar, no storage space for foods in the city. Milk, bread, and virtually everything else had to be bought every day.[28]

Many customs stopped at the water's edge. When Swedish Lutherans left the old country, they cut themselves off from a state that paid their church's way and picked its pastor. Now the congregation handled both tasks. Saddled with new responsibilities, it took on new powers. Women got the vote in parish meetings, and raised their voices to give the faith that austere moral cast so lacking back in Europe. No longer was the pastor's word law, nor his judgments accepted without a murmur. And new traditions arose as old ones faded, like the gift giving at Chanukah on the Lower East Side, or Holy Week at Lindsborg, in central Kansas. When four hundred singers—men in black, women in pink and white—performed Handel's "Messiah" oratorio in 1900, they drew ten thousand listeners. Yet the custom dated back only twenty years, and parishioners were so unprepared at the start that they had to import their soloists and orchestra from Illinois.[29]

Americanization must keep going on, if the foreign-born wanted to advance in the society around them. The only questions were, how much, and on whose terms? From within the immigrant community itself came the pressure to learn enough about the land of their adoption to get along. Mothers set in the old ways wanted their daughters to learn American habits. Some parents even forbade the children to bring home any books but those in English. Institutions helped families assimilate on their own terms. Jews on the Lower East Side of New York turned to Isidor Straus's Educational Alliance. They could take classes in English, or attend lectures on American government taught in Yiddish. If they read the Yiddish press, they might study the features on the geography, education, and government of the United States. From 1897 on, the New York *Tageblatt* provided a page in English that translated the most difficult words into Yiddish equivalents. Yet the forces resisting immediate change were strong, and as long as immigrant communities had thriving institutions, they added to the resistance. A Yiddish newspaper and a Yiddish theater helped keep separate those people not eager to fit in on the terms that their fellow believers "uptown" had arranged. Differences over how far to change the traditional rituals to adapt to city life gave rise to Conservative and Reformed branches of Judaism, just as it splintered Swedish Lutherans. But perhaps the greatest encouragement toward keeping separate from America was the "golden door" that Emma Lazarus immortalized. For most foreigners, it stood wide open. Immigrants knew they could go home, and many planned to do so. Newcomers kept coming. As long as those conditions held, Old World customs would be worth holding onto, and would get a constant refreshing from the latest arrivals. Just possibly, full assimilation would never have happened without immigration restriction.[30]

But if America changed the immigrants, they changed it, too, and not just because they drove wages down and supplied the cheap labor that rapid industrialization required. Many brought skills ready for use: Lancashire textile workers, Russian stone masons, German pharmacists, French watchmakers, and Italian jewelry workers. For any city dweller, the immigrant experience was as close as the nearest delicatessen. Nobody had to be told where spaghetti, pumpernickel, or borscht came from, though most people would never have credited the Germans with potato salad. When Americans early in the new century sat down at a Steinway piano to play one of the bright tunes of Victor Herbert, they little thought that a German immigrant had created the first, and an Irishman the second.[31]

Enemies Within the Gates?

Immigration changed Americans' lives for the better in many ways, and for the worse in some, but on any terms, change added more disturbance to a world already being transformed by the machine makers and money getters. As natives of the old Protestant stock saw it, the republic needed more than a common set of laws. It depended on a shared cultural heritage: widely held values and an understanding of American traditions. With neither language, religion, nor blood in common, a nation of immigrants would turn into a federation of ethnic enclaves, just made for strife and demagoguery. By the mid-1880s, dark fears were being voiced. "Crime and ignorance and superstition" seemed to land by the boatload—the "dregs of all foreign countries." Businessmen blamed labor violence on newcomers; workers blamed them for low wages. Prejudice dogged all newcomers from beyond the British Isles. Some of it was gentle stereotyping: Italians all ate macaroni, had dark eyes, hot passions, and an inextinguishable love for song. But the stereotypes got darker very quickly as the number of Italians increased. Stiletto—vendetta—brigand—Mafia—such words summed up the entire culture to those who kept the real newcomer at arm's distance. Ignorance could be seen as stupidity. One joke explained why all Italians were called Tony: because when they got to this country, their caps always had a card in them to guide them to their destination, labeled "To NY."[32]

A new, more virulent streak of anti-Semitism surfaced, but showed itself mostly as contempt. Catholics, by contrast, inspired terror. To Protestants, the religion conjured images of tyranny and persecution across the ages, and of voters marching in lockstep to the tune that the Pope played in Rome. Tale-mongers spread whoppers, all of which found believers: that 72 percent of all desertions in the Civil War were Catholic, for example. The Inquisition already had set up its courts and black-hooded judges in America, one author warned. "For the present it 'tolerates'; it will burn whenever it will be safe to burn." Starting in 1887, the American Protective Association claimed a million members by the mid-1890s. Across the Midwest, it harassed Catholics as far as it dared. Members promised never to hire Catholic employees or join them on a picket line. Crowds stoned Catholic picnickers, petitioners forced school boards to fire Catholic teachers. Phony documents circulated, pretending to be Papal decrees setting the time for worshippers to rise up and kill their Protestant neighbors. So tense were relations in Toledo that the mayor bought Winchester rifles with which to arm Protestants.[33]

Fear of foreigners set second-generation immigrants against the newer arrivals, and against each other. The very Catholic religion that Irish and Italians shared split them apart, right down to their taste in cathedral architecture. As the two immigrant groups vied for day-laborers' jobs, antagonism turned to open war, brawls in the streets, and fistfights in the alleys. Italian chestnut vendors were driven out of business, and the "dago" or "wop" who passed through the doors of an Irish-American saloon was just asking for it. German Jews greeted the first Russian Jews with distrust, even contempt, and dubbed them "kikes," because so many of their names ended in -ky or -ki. "What can we do with those wild Asiatics?" the *American Hebrew* asked.[34]

Not every prejudice turns into a pogrom, and the nativism that stigmatized did not destroy foreigners. One Russian Jew remembered first seeing Manhattan decked in Christmas lights, and felt nothing but wonder. Here was a Christian's holiday, "and people were going in the streets and nothing happening and you didn't have to be afraid. And nobody told you that you killed their God." Still, the sting was there, in the cartoons of shrugging Jewish old-clothes dealers, planning to burn their business for the insurance, or wearing noses big enough to carry in a wheelbarrow.[35]

"Kearneyfornia": The Sandlotters' Revolt

Where race entered into it, xenophobia took on a special ugliness. With the completion of the transcontinental railroad in 1869, foundries and firms on the Pacific coast found themselves shoved to the wall by eastern products. Farmers, miners, and teamsters blamed the Central Pacific for robbing them, but took it out on the cheap Chinese labor that the railroad employed. Memorials flew east, begging for anti-immigration laws, but already some Californians were applying more direct means against the "moon eyed Pig faced Monsters." In 1871, Los Angeles mobs raced through Chinatown, smashing windows, ransacking homes for loot, and stabbing or shooting whatever residents they could find. "We have clubbed them, stoned them, burned their houses and murdered some of them, yet they refuse to be converted," the Rev. Henry Ward Beecher commented acidly. "I do not know any way, except to blow them up with nitroglycerin, if we are ever to get them to Heaven."[36]

The Panic of 1873 carried resentments into the political mainstream. Gathering in sandlots for violent rallies, San Francisco laborers founded a Workingmen's Party. Its leader, Dennis Kearney, an Irish-born sailor who had found prosperity in the draying business, knew a good issue when he saw it. What the state needed, Kearney declared, was "a little judicious hanging" to teach monopolists a lesson and rid America of the cheap Chinese labor they used to oppress honest workingmen. His followers preferred to put reform into a new state constitution. The "Sand-Lot Revolt" carried city elections and spread statewide. Joining the pack, the two major parties wrote a new constitution that Kearney's followers could live with. California banned special charters and set up a railroad commission and a state board to reform taxation. It guaranteed a six-month school term and enacted the eight-hour day on public works projects. But alongside the reforms, the document declared Chinese residents ineligible to vote and forbade them public employment. Municipalities were empowered to send them packing, force them into select neighborhoods, or keep them from holding fishing licenses and privileged jobs.[37]

Congress felt the heat. In 1879, it closed the doors on the Chinese. President Hayes vetoed the bill as a violation of treaty obligations—and then allowed his diplomats to renegotiate the treaty to allow exclusion in all but name. Three years later, another president signed a bill barring Chinese laborers for ten years. It was renewed in

1892 and made perpetual ten years after that. Under other legislation, Chinese residents had to furnish a certificate proving themselves eligible to stay. They could not get bail if arrested and could be deported without criminal trial. The number of Chinese dwindled, from 101,000 down to 85,000. In one notorious case, a merchant dying in Chinatown summoned his wife and children, who ran a branch store in British Columbia. When they reached San Francisco, customs officers refused to let them land. By the time authorities in Washington reversed the decision, the merchant was dead. A military guard accompanied the family to the funeral, to make sure that after services were done they would go right back on board ship.[38]

Not until the twentieth century would nativists muster the strength to bar the gates to Europe's New Immigration, as well, but the shift was perceptible. Genteel Boston Brahmins founded the Immigration Restriction League and petitioned Congress for action. Already in 1882 the law shut out paupers and convicts. In 1885 it added contract labor to the list. Only a presidential veto kept it from requiring applicants to pass a literacy test in 1897, and states made restrictions on alien land ownership.[39]

End, then, not with Emma Lazarus, but with a native poet, Thomas Bailey Aldrich. Not for him the lifted hand beside the golden door:

Wide open and unguarded stand our gates,
And through them presses a wild motley throng—
Men from the Volga and the Tartar steppes,
Featureless figures of the Hoang-Ho,
Malayan, Scythian, Teuton, Kelt, and Slav,
Flying the Old World's poverty and scorn;
These bringing with them unknown gods and rites,
Those tiger passions, here to stretch their claws.
In street and alley what strange tongues are loud,
Accents of menace alien to our air,
Voices that once the Tower of Babel knew!

O, Liberty, white Goddess! is it well
To leave the gates unguarded?

. . .

Have a care
Lest from thy brow the clustered stars be torn
And trampled in the dust. For so of old
The thronging Goth and Vandal trampled Rome,
And where the temples of the Caesars stood
The lean wolf unmolested made her lair.[40]

Chapter 9

Opportunity?

Any close study of America's elite in the late nineteenth century makes one suspect that the rich could afford anything except good taste. One well-to-do man gave a banquet to his pet dog, and presented it with a $15,000 collar set in diamonds. Not that the hunger and unemployment across town went entirely unnoticed: in the hungry 1890s, "poverty socials" became the latest fad. Millionaires showed up in paupers' dress—the more rags and tatters, the better. Guests dined on wooden plates, covered their laps with napkins made from old newspapers and sipped their beer from tin cans: total cost, $14,000.[1]

For that the indulgent rich got the editorial scorching they deserved, but the doctrine of self-advancement that Americans espoused gives them a faint defense. Evoked in pulpit, paper, and the dime novels of Horatio Alger, the rags-to-riches myth constituted a secular gospel, the Gospel of Success.

Andrew Carnegie, the greatest of steelmakers, was that Gospel made flesh. Born in a tile-roofed cottage in Dumferline, Scotland, his father a weaver who went broke and came to America on borrowed money to die of overwork, Carnegie started out as a bobbin-boy in a textile mill at $1.20 a week. In time he rose from messenger to telegraph operator, clerk on the Pennsylvania Railroad, and before long, division superintendent. Investing wisely, he had enough money to set up a little ironworks by the time he was thirty. It made rails, and his old business contacts now made a small fortune into a large one. From there, the rest was history.

Social Darwinism

Or, rather, the rest was political economy. By the late 1870s, scholars and economists had fashioned a world-view that combined the laws of supply and demand with the law of fang and claw. From the publication of *Origin of Species* in 1859, Charles Darwin's theories of how living forms had evolved had attracted a wide audience. Ministers found ways to square his theories with a strict interpretation of Scriptures, social scientists applied his conclusions to the making of civilization. Competition explained which life forms endured. It followed that competition could explain progress in society itself. Foremost among those interpreters was Herbert Spencer, the English scholar. In ten thick volumes of analysis during the 1860s, he applied Darwin to the social institutions around him. Just as with the thousand primordial forms that antedated the cow or the horse of Spencer's own day, mankind contained individuals of differing capacities. The ablest would succeed. The weak and reckless would fail. And that survival of the fittest was all to the good. Unhampered, the natural process of elimination meant progress.[2]

Unhampered: there lay the difficulty. Human beings, through their governments, simply would not let the process alone. They violated two essential laws, said Spencer, "the law of equal freedom," which let any man do as he pleased as long as he hindered the freedom of no one else, and "the law of conduct and consequence," which let the unfit find their place on the garbage heap of history—or on the garbage heap of the city dump, as the case might be. Society was too complex for any official to understand; the side effects of any action too broad for any bureaucrat to predict. If the state financed schooling, poor families would have that much more incentive to raise children, who might turn out to be as worthless as their parents. Using government to quarantine or vaccinate meddled with the natural order. It saved "those of the lowest development." Any man not smart enough or successful enough to take care of his own health had no business living in the first place. The least government was the best, essentially a police court to keep order and punish crime, but nothing more.[3]

Few Americans went as far as Spencer. They appreciated both public schools and good drainage. But Spencer's books sold well here. So much in his teachings seemed so American: the confidence that technology would bring progress and that there was a natural, even a supernatural order in the world; the well-founded distrust of politicians to do anything right, beyond elect themselves; and the enduring republican faith, dating back to Thomas Jefferson's day, that the widest possible personal liberty was good for man or institution. Weekly, E. L. Godkin's *Nation* applied Spencer's Social Darwinism to the evils of American politics. For Southern planters, it was not so far a stretch from the idea that blood and a sense of honor set them above poor whites to the notion that success favored those strong in character.[4] Spencer's disciples ran virtually every economics department of consequence in the land. William Graham Sumner, professor of political science at Yale, stood foremost. Championing competition as the great regulator of economic life, Sumner argued for the certainty of success for those with the right qualities. Government action, whether in forbidding goods made by convict labor, interfering in strikes on either side, or in setting work conditions, only made a mess of the natural process.[5]

Work and Win: The Success Myth

By implication, Sumner's thinking left all credit for achievement to the individual at the top, and made his accomplishments the reward of obedience to the Supreme Law of life. Ministers lauded the money-getters. "You cannot help wanting to possess," a Presbyterian divine assured rich parishioners; "to want to possess is the finger mark of your divine origin." At the same time, Social Darwinism numbed twinging consciences. If anyone could succeed who was fit to do so, then those who failed had only themselves to blame.[6]

The self-serving quality of businessmen singing praises to a doctrine that let them keep all they made and trample whoever got in their way makes an easy target. But what is one to make of Booker T. Washington? His faith in the success myth was genuine. It was founded on his own experience. Born a slave, trained at Hampton Institute, he took the daunting task of heading a newly chartered black college in Tuskegee. There, students would raise the buildings themselves. They made it from bricks they shaped from the tawny clay of Alabama and fired in a kiln of their own creating. Three times the kiln was completed, only to fail. Washington pawned his gold watch to pay for a fourth, and this one succeeded. It made brick enough for class-

Booker T. Washington. (Emmett J. Scott and Lyman B. Stone, *Booker T. Washington: Builder of a Civilization* [New York: Doubleday, Page & Co., 1917], frontispiece)

room buildings and more for sale. By 1907, there were eighty-six buildings, nearly all of them raised by the students. At Washington's death in 1915, Tuskegee was world famous. Women and men learned how to raise chickens, turkeys, cattle, and bees— one hundred hives of which stood on a sunny slope just behind the poultry house. Students learned little Latin, but plenty of artisan skills. All, as one white remarked, learned "to work by working."[7]

Asked if he had seen the school, one visitor exclaimed, "School! I have seen Booker T. Washington's city." It had become exactly that, and the source of opportunity for the black community all around it. Experts taught farmers how to get five hundred pounds of cotton to the acre where before they raised two hundred. A dispensary provided medical care for anyone needing attention. A building and loan association helped build houses, and a ministers' night school augmented the learning of black country clergy. When the German government wanted to raise cotton in one of its African colonies, it sent to Tuskegee for experts.

Washington's confidence in people's ability to raise themselves shaped his action. A like faith made Gilded Age Americans build vocational schools for workers, night schools for immigrants, and agricultural colleges for would-be farmers. The same could be said for the one philanthropy of Andrew Carnegie's that got the most attention, the endowment of library buildings. By 1926, there were 2,811 of them in the United States alone, from Lexington, Kentucky, to Castleton, Vermont. Each one was a monument to Carnegie's belief that people should escape poverty not through charity but by raising themselves. Give anyone the chance to learn, and he might open the library doors out on a world unlimited in its promise.[8]

Tuskegee should remind us of something else that is often overlooked: the gospel of self-improvement was based on the idea that not just brains but moral character determined who rose and who fell. And more: it assumed that moral character itself could be shaped, and would turn out best when a person learned to depend on himself. Washington believed that only by taking control of their own destiny and making a living for themselves could blacks gain the self-respect and respect of whites on which any legal equality had to stand. Personal responsibility was the first, necessary step toward moral and material advance.

Yet tough questions keep intruding on the case for Social Darwinism: how far did Gilded Age America reward work with success? Did the conditions on which Sumner's theories rested really apply in the first place? Were the social costs of Social Darwinism affordable?

America did furnish plenty of success stories, though mighty few Carnegies. If Booker T. Washington remained a hero to black southerners lifelong, it was because for so many of them, self-help *did* mean improvement. Every year, the Tuskegee Negro Conference showed proof in various ways that hard work brought rewards. There, for example, sat representatives from the Farmers' Improvement Society of Texas. By setting up a cooperative and buying supplies in wholesale amounts, they freed black farmers from debt. The money left over built schoolhouses and fixed roads in their communities. Soon frame houses stood where shanties had been, with picket fences and rose bushes by the front door. Members' wives formed the Woman's Barnyard

Auxiliary and taught themselves how to raise pigs and chickens for sale. Nobody would get rich marketing butter and cheese, but they lived better than any of them would have dreamed possible a generation before.[9]

Who Rose?

People rose, then. Poor people prospered. There were more professionals, more skilled workers every year. If statistics could be believed, working-class Americans had more money to save and more to spend at the end of the Gilded Age than at its beginning. They ate twice as much meat and fish as their English counterparts, and nearly four times as many vegetables and fruits. Yet where two-thirds of the European worker's pay check went for food, the percentage in America fell in a quarter century to somewhere between one-third and one-half. Women in the white-collar work force put by enough to open savings accounts; in some city banks, they outnumbered male depositors.[10]

Still, the vision of "progress" takes some very serious qualification. From 1860 to 1890, real wages went up, and they rose most during the 1880s. By 1900, the "average worker" in manufacturing made $435 a year, a record high, and with living costs falling, his dollars bought more. For a nickel in the late Gilded Age, for example, you could buy a decent lunch from the local bar, a dozen roses, or a Manhattan passenger's fare on the Staten Island ferry. Even so, a factory worker's wages could barely buy subsistence. An urban family of four earning $506 in 1877 just barely crossed the poverty line. Forty percent of unskilled workers made less, some of them much less.[11]

What made the figure misleading was how many exceptions there were to the "average." Skilled labor got the bulk of the benefits, in an economy increasingly geared to unskilled occupations. Where women working in an office made $660 a year and school teachers $450, millhands made $260. Men made 75 percent more than women doing the same work and 250 percent more than children did. Southern workers earned only 70 percent of that which those in the Northeast made. However much movement might take place around the edges, the country began the Gilded Age with a permanent lower class and a permanent upper class. In 1889, seven-tenths of the national wealth belonged to one three-hundredth of the people. Generally, it was estimated that seven-eighths of all families controlled only one-eighth of the national wealth.[12]

Social Darwinism's simplicities come into plain view by a glance at Horatio Alger, the author so often identified with the doctrine's coarser form. Earning no more than $250 plus royalties (which he rarely got) for a serial, he wrote more than 140 of them, but hard work only carried him from modest circumstances to dire poverty. Success came too late. Only after he died in 1899 did his books really sell well.

The bestsellers had Alger's words; and yet they were not really Alger's books. Publishers had streamlined the narratives into tales of adventure and success. They had cut out the moralizing. A minister's son, himself driven from the pulpit for showing too much familiarity with some of the boys in the congregation, Alger was not teaching readers how to do well only, but how to do good. His heroes sought "respectability," middle-class virtues, not wealth without end. And when good boys rose, they got by with a little help from their friends. Hard work mattered, but so did pluck and luck. When the banker's daughter fell into the river, the hero would be there to save her and win a better job as his reward. Fate giving virtue its due? A mere stroke of good fortune? Whichever one it was, the laws of the market had little to do with it.[13]

In his fantasy world, Alger came closer to the truth than Professor Sumner did. Rising depended on circumstances. "The on'y way I iver expict to make a cint is to have it left to me be a rich relation," the fictional bartender Martin Dooley commented ruefully, "an' I'm th' pluthycrat of me family; or to stub me toe on a gambler's roll or stop a runaway horse f'r Pierpont Morgan. An' th' horse mustn't be runnin' too fast. He must be jus' goin' to stop, on'y Morgan don't know it, havin' fainted." Yet, in a sense, Social Darwinism was not really a proven failure. As long as individuals started life's race on unequal terms, Spencer's doctrines remained untested, and class, race, culture, and gender skewed the prospects of success for the vast majority of citizens before they set their hands to toil.

Far from being fluid, class lines were distinct. The worlds different classes inhabited were more separate than in the past. Except when passing each other on Broadway, rich and poor never mingled. The children of the affluent went to the academies and then college; the miners' children went no further than the public grade schools, if they went at all. When the wealthy socialized, they did it in the exclusive comfort of their clubs. When they worshiped, it was at select churches of their own endowing. At the First Presbyterian in Wilkes-Barre, for example, the price of a pew amounted to more than a year's wages for most miners.

In Pennsylvania's coal country, the Slavs defined success as owning their own homes. A house ten feet high and twenty-five feet square, without yards, indoor plumbing, nor even painted sides, might seem a modest enough goal, but to afford it, wife, husband, and children would have to work a half-dozen years. Even then, they could spend no more than $2.86 a month per person at the store for food and supplies. Cereals, starches, cabbage, and cheap pork—these constituted their entire diet. As long as it took three incomes just to afford a house, schooling was a luxury few unskilled workers could afford to give their children. But that closed the next generation off from the talents management positions required. By contrast, the children of professionals and skilled workers found white-collar employment within their reach. Education, genteel manners, middle-class values, all opened office doors to them, and a growing industrial order meant an expanded bureaucracy, with desks, paperwork, and sales positions for thousands. Unskilled workers generally stayed that way. Even then, those able to keep their jobs saw their lot improve, but many were forced to move on, half of them leaving every two years.[14]

The more privileged a person's beginnings, the further he could rise. Among the leading industrialists in the 1870s, no more than one in twelve had begun among labor's ranks, and most of them from the skilled artisans. In Pennsylvania's coal country, wide-open opportunity might have brought new men to the top. Instead, the financial elite groomed its sons as successors. Established Wilkes-Barre businessmen opened the new mines, for they had the wherewithal to explore for fresh coal deposits and buy the ground. Marrying into money was the best way they knew to double their income.[15]

Beyond class barriers, culture and background defined where one began and limited one's success in going beyond that. A simple familiarity with American ways and the American language was one reason that the native-born had a better chance of succeeding than the foreigners. Prejudice was another. To rise to the very top, or even to the middle class, it helped to be Protestant and northern European. Irish might patronize Josephine McCluskey's millinery, but the very name drove Anglo-Saxons away—until she rechristened herself "Miss Delavenue." To be an Irishman was to be a hod-carrier, and by 1900 the Irish were losing ground even in skilled trades that they had dominated before the Civil War. Other groups had still less chance. The farther east or south of central Europe a person's origin, the more intensely the bigotry defined what job they or their American-born children were good for.[16]

At the bottom of the heap among Europeans were the many cultures between the Baltic and Black Seas, usually classed as Slavs. Cast into the least skilled and dirtiest work, they went where stereotype declared them fittest—and stayed there. In the mills of Steelton, foremen at the open hearths were nearly always Irishmen, workers at the blast furnace Serbs, toilers at the open hearth Croats. The grueling labor at the back of the furnaces were so much the province of Hungarians that the large ore shovels took the name "Hunky banjos."[17]

Racial Prejudice Presents Overwhelming Obstacles

Compared to race prejudice, nativism was mild. By 1917, two hundred thousand southern blacks owned their own farms. Scott Bond, a former slave who went from tenant farmer to Arkansas landholder, told the secret of his success: "I worked from can't to can't—from 'can't see in the morning' till 'can't see at night.'" Within the ghetto, lawyers, doctors, realtors, and shopkeepers could make a living from clientele of their own color. They formed their own business associations and exclusive clubs. Blacks owned 51 banks—49 more than in 1900; 25,000 shops rather than 10,000, and a thousand undertakers' parlors. The old black aristocracy, based on free ancestry, light complexion, and education, found itself crowded by newcomers whose money had carried them up among the privileged few.[18]

But the founding of Nashville's One Cent Savings Bank & Trust Co. in 1904 exposed Jim Crow's limits, not just the achievement of black enterprise: it was the city's first Negro-owned fiduciary institution in thirty years. Unless he lived in a city like Atlanta, the black businessman rarely earned more than a competency in the ghetto, and none at all in the world beyond. Indeed, the barriers against black improvement rose higher as the industrial revolution proceeded. Electrician, tinsmith, paperhanger: the more specialized the line of work and the newer the kind of job, the less chance for a Negro. Trade unions drew the color line in taking apprentices, much less members. Occupations once open to all, like railroad fireman, barber or headwaiter at a high-class establishment, closed tight. No matter how able their reporting skills, black journalists found few white big-city newspapers willing to hire them, any more than a Negro preacher would find a white congregation or a Negro lawyer a white client. Even those blacks catering to a white clientele—barbers, say—did so only by excluding black patrons.[19]

Especially in the South, the new barriers were part of a deliberate policy to grind blacks down below where their natural talents might put them. In 1889, the Shreveport *Daily Caucasian* urged turning custom into official white policy. Blacks being less than human, they must be driven from the "easy job," like bootblack, porter, clerk, or cook. Whites who hired them for decent work should feel the consequences. The "Shreveport Plan" did not need enacting; white society had gone far towards putting it into effect already. "We are kindly disposed to the negro race," a Louisianian protested some years later, "wherever and whenever they properly demean themselves." Even so successful a farmer as Scott Bond knew better than to advertise his good fortune to whites, who felt that no Negro should get above his station. Among blacks, he spoke perfect English; among whites, the dialect they expected. When a Northerner addressed him as "Mr. Bond," he was appalled. "In de fus' place you know you don' mean it," the farmer explained "And if you does you can't afford to call niggers 'mister' in dis part of de country." "Cross-eyed nigger" would do for him, or at most "Unc Scott."[20]

Gender Inequality in the Workplace

It was nearly as unthinkable that any important spot would fall to a woman, whatever her background, breeding, or attainments. To be sure, opportunity had widened. In trades catering to women exclusively (dressmaking, say, or millinery), women could go from apprentice to proprietor and eke out a precarious living, though being their own boss seemed like compensation enough for many. Corporate America hired far more female workers than before, and not just for factory work. Between 1870 and 1900, the number of saleswomen in chain and department stores rose from several dozen to over 142,000. In the next twenty years, it would double. Once the exclusive preserve of well-schooled men, business offices found that with new machines like the typewriter and with the subdivision of tasks, they could hire any woman who had taken a commercial course in high school. By 1900, women made up over a third of all clerical workers, by 1920, more than half.[21]

Yet women's advance came only within the most narrow limits. Conventional wisdom still pronounced the home woman's natural place, and that homily applied to her wage-earning, as well. Piecework, sewing garments or assembling paper flowers around one's own table took just as long and paid as pitifully as factory work, but it was easier to get. Because rearing children was seen as mother's work, it followed that they would make the best schoolteachers or nursemaids. Household chores went along with other wifely duties; they were free to hire themselves out as maids or as washerwomen in the commercial laundries that set up in every city after 1870. Even jobs that had belonged to men were reexplained as "women's work" when the gender barrier was broken: because the tasks were light, or because dainty fingers were better suited to typewriter keys, or because a sex used to plying thread and needle had a natural gift for running the treadle sewing machines.[22]

Whatever the occupation, the employee could rely on a few constants. First, the

Making White Goods.
Some department stores manufactured their own products. As the
illustration makes clear, employers saw sewing as "women's work"
and hired no others. (*Scribner's*, January 1897)

job had little or no room for advancement. Typists might rise to head the typing pool, but never into the rank of junior executives. Second, the pay was lower than men made. Third, it was assumed that when the employee married, she would go back to the home where she belonged—which, until 1890, was the case about 96 percent of the time.[23]

Even among the professional careers, the road to success did not run very far. Professions tied to the mother's nurturing role were most open: social and welfare work, for example. But professional societies kept women from advancing into the most prestigious disciplines, and, indeed, took over the turf for themselves. The number of trained nurses increased seven times over between 1900 and 1910, but not of woman doctors; leading medical schools set up quotas to limit admissions to 5 percent. Every small town had a woman for librarian. Every major research collection was headed by a man.[24]

The magnificent transformation of the economy in the Gilded Age, then, started with a privileged few to reap the benefits, and never wiped out the disparity. "The rich are growing richer," the Commissioner of Labor insisted at the century's end, "many more people than formerly are growing rich, and the poor are growing better off."[25] Statistically, he may have been right, but the improvement of the underclasses seemed to inch along, while the mansions of Newport gleamed, ever more palatial, ever more self-indulgent from one year to the next. Within walking distance of the lordly brownstone flats of "the 400," the cream of New York City society, a traveler might come upon the shanties of the poor. The contrast of condition had always been a common sight, but industrialization made it seem more intense: the ragged children bathed in the glow of department store display windows, stocked with more consumer goods than ever before—for those able to pay. For too many Americans, the Gilded Age was an Age of Iron: hard, crude, and, to the unfortunate multitudes, of crushing weight.

Children born to poverty faced a good chance of never living to escape it. A baby born in a working-class neighborhood had two to three times the chance of dying in infancy that one born in the middle class did. Known as the "summer complaints" because they rose when hot weather turned foul waters and filthy streets into pestholes, diarrhea and gastroenteritis accounted for one death in three. Buried under stones inscribed with no other heading than "infant" or "baby," their passing unnoticed in the public press, they left behind a grief among the parents that was one of the incalculable prices of poverty.[26]

Sentimental lithographs might cast old age in a wistful glow, but "Silver Threads among the Gold" rang less true to those who had gone through life seeing precious little of either gold or silver. For them, the popular song "Over the Hill to the Poor-House" fit better. Those who lost a husband lost an income and were among the most desperately poor. For lack of support, they might have to surrender their children to the local orphanage. "For a few days everybody is sorry for you; after that you're just another widow," one of them counseled another in a novel of the day. "And a widow—there are a hundred widows. Widows are nothing."[27]

Anyone uttering the old homily, "We are all alike in the grave," obviously never visited a cemetery. There, poverty and wealth showed themselves for generations to come, with the rich lying side by side in family plots set down in the graveyard's most desirable neighborhoods, and the poor lodged in single graves placed on the outskirts. That was if they were lucky. Workers unable to pay their own way into the ground ended up crowded into potter's field. From the mausoleums of the rich, the ghosts of employers might well have been able to spot the headstones of some of their workers, but not of all: the poorest had nothing to mark where they lay.[28]

One could see the same in the difference between the housing of the working class and the middle class. From the paintings of John Singer Sargent and others shines an affluence and comfort, full of confidence and stability. But no painters took on the slums in the 1870s and 1880s. There, they would spy very different sights. The first thing a casual visitor noticed in tenements varied. It might be the darkness of unlit halls, "like the black mouth of a mine shaft," as one inspector commented. More likely, it would be the stench. "Imagine dense fumes of frying fat and boiling vegetables," another caller urged his readers. ". . . Fancy that these are blown inward until they meet another body of dead air left by two or four adults, eight to sixteen children who have slept there for eight hours . . . deep foul bedclothes . . . also waiting for a chance to catch the least particle of fresh air . . . and you have somewhat of an idea of a tenement hall." Light and air were equally scarce commodities. Some families got both from the central air shaft, polluted with the smells of cooking and whatever garbage had been thrown in there. On the lower floors, there might be one toilet in the hallway for the entire family's use. On the upper floors, there would be nothing. Should the building contain a rear courtyard, the inhabitants might have recourse to the "school sink," a board with seat-holes cut out, suitable for laying over a trench in the ground that in theory was flushed out every day by the tenement management. Poor neighborhoods had less police and fire protection, less sanitation and sewage treatment. Stores sold their goods at a higher price. Parks were more needed, and harder to find. Crime, congestion, and cholera were the only things that residents could find more easily than people elsewhere.

Poverty in the Gilded Age stares at us from the eyes of the subjects of Jacob Riis's photographs or from those of Lewis Hine's street children. That is, it was a city phenomenon. In fact, as in our own day, the poor were everywhere, often hidden from the photographer or the casual visitor by being tucked away in isolated sharecropper's shanties or hardscrabble farms in northern New England. Others among the impoverished moved too constantly to leave a clear likeness.

Itinerants as a Fixture of the American Landscape

To the middle class, the army of itinerants were all alike, tramps who would rather scrounge than work and rather drink than do either, graduates of the prisons likely to be employed at no other institution thereafter. In fact, even among the desperate men, huddled in their "jungles" in the waste areas near railroad yards, lines of class might persist, with "bums" below and "hobos" on top.[29]

For some artisans, wandering was part of the craft. Among cigar makers, carpenters, hatters, and iron molders, the unions even set up traveling cards to let them join locals wherever they landed and help them find jobs. Many of the so-called hobos served as seasonal labor, doing everything from harvesting wheat to sweating in the lumber camps and shearing the sheep herds west of the Rockies. More often, however, it was the unskilled who took to the roads, and their condition was far more desperate. When employers had to cut back their work force, many eliminated the young, unmarried men first. Like Terence V. Powderly, later mayor of Scranton and head of the Knights of Labor, they might trudge along the railroad ties two hundred miles and more, stopping at every machine shop and farm to ask for a job.[30]

The search for work might take them as far as Central America, where, as one itinerant wrote his fellows, "Turtles are plenty; we get mock turtle, turtle soup, turtle hash, turtle steaks, turtle pie, turtle boiled, baked and fried, turtle's eggs and turtle egg cake, turtle fritters, turtle tripe, and some turtle dishes I have not found a name for to date." All in all, an itinerant's life did not read like that of footloose ne'er-do-wells in romance novels. "One year ago I was an industrious, respectable head of a family," a wayfarer wrote.

> My family are now a thousand miles away, scattered and broken up. They and I hardly hope to meet again. The world is a desert to us. I have no friend. I have no roof to live under, no table to eat at, no clothes to distinguish me from thieves. Yet I am not a thief. I have nothing. I am welcomed by no human being; and I am at the mercy of the lowest; yet I do not feel as if I honestly take a pair of shoes or a coat without the owner's consent.[31]

When they were lucky, tramps found an open boxcar to take shelter in, with something to grab that could be eaten or sold, but railroad companies made that a risky practice. Hired goons patrolling the freight yards could be tougher than any hobo. Necessity therefore made many tramps risk death by riding outside of freight cars, on the brake rods beneath or the couplers between, or even by holding onto the machinery between the wheels. However they did it at the turn of the century, usually some ten thousand traveled the lines each night. They could be found in flophouses, the filthy makeshifts set up in warehouses and run-down hotels. There, vagrants might find sleeping quarters for a nickel. Their rooms were cubicles subdivided with cardboard or chickenwire, their washing facilities a bowl and towel shared by all. Everywhere lice and fleas crawled, and everything—straw mattresses, halls, floors—reeked with the stink of urine.[32]

"Life's a failure for ninety-nine percent of us," a farmer cried out in one of Hamlin Garland's rural novels. To a small, articulate minority, the divide between rich and poor brought a powerful revulsion against the whole basis for Social Darwinism. "The hundred or so boys actually born stark naked in log cabins half a century or more ago . . . and who have been cast to the surface of the ever-restless political sea, struck oil, married a competence, wrecked a railroad, swindled an orphan or stolen a valuable idea from a confiding inventor, are offered in evidence," fumed a Texas insurgent:

> Think of preaching economy to a man who is striving to pay house-rent, feed and clothe a family on $5 a week—and half the time out of work!—of telling the wretch who toils for 50 cents *per diem* that he should "live well within his means and lay up something for a rainy day!' I sometimes wonder that the workingmen don't grow weary of being hectored by these wooden-heads and shut off their wind.[33]

Was this, then, the promised end? Was it not possible that a system which allowed some to rise to high and others to fall so low, would destroy itself?

Progress and Poverty

Some Americans thought so. Among them was Ignatius Donnelly, who spent the last half of his life battling for lost radical causes and against the railroad monopolists of Minnesota that in youth he had served as a paid lobbyist. His novel, *Caesar's Column*, painted a harrowing tale of capitalism crashing down, and bringing all free institutions with it. Other observers were less bloody-minded, but as despairing. Troubled by injustice, Henry George, the most celebrated and reviled social critic of his day, turned to Edward W. Youmans, a social philosopher and editor of *Popular Science Monthly*. What could be done to improve matters? Youmans threw up his hands. "Nothing!" he exclaimed. ". . . It's all a matter of evolution. . . . Perhaps in four or five thousand years evolution may have carried men beyond this state of things. But we can do nothing."[34]

Answers so fatalistic have never gone down well—not in societies as dynamic and restless as America's, and certainly not with the man who posed Youmans the question. Raised in a middling, pious Philadelphia household before the war, Henry George worked at plenty of things, and lectured himself on the need to save and study as diligently as any Horatio Alger hero. But whether it was a delivery boy, typesetter, sailor, clothes-wringer salesman, or gold digger in California, toil returned a miserable reward. When he proposed, he had no more than the fifty cents in his pocket; when he married, someone had to lend him the suit. Then, in the first years of America's second century, he found his calling as a social prophet. Wrapped in a saffron robe, writing late into the night in his shabby San Francisco home, he indicted a society gone wrong. "The present century has been marked by a prodigious increase in wealth-producing power," he wrote:

> We plow new fields, we open new mines, we found new cities; we drive back the Indian and exterminate the buffalo; we girdle the land with iron roads and lace the air with telegraph wires; we add knowledge to knowledge, and utilize invention after invention; we build schools and endow colleges; yet it becomes no easier for the masses of our people to make a living. On the contrary, it is becoming harder. . . . As liveried carriages appear, so do barefooted children.[35]

When free land gave out, opportunity perished. With it went the hope, character, and resourcefulness of the American people. Thus rang out the tocsin of warning in *Progress and Poverty*, when it appeared in 1879. It made George into a celebrated figure (but not, as it happened, a rich man. He gave more copies of the book away than he sold, and pirated editions flourished. To the day he died, he stayed in debt.).

And yet, the way out of the problem that George proposed was so very simple. Socialism was the last thing he had in mind (he had voted Democratic in 1876, and would again). For national and state governments, he nursed only suspicion. They were too far from the people's will, too cavalier with American liberties. *Progress and Poverty* did not summon workers to the barricades. It was aimed at the middle class, to get them to act before plutocracy made barricades unavoidable. Clear thinking now could prevent a revolution later. The enemy was simple: it was rent. The land was not landowners', but God's. Its benefits belonged to all, and were monopolized by a few. Labor and capital—both were controlled by rent:

> Every blow of the hammer, every stroke of the pick, every thrust of the shuttle, every throb of the steam engine, pay it tribute. It levies upon the earnings of the men who, deep under ground, risk their lives, and of those who over white surges hang to reeling masts; . . . it robs the shivering of warmth; the hungry, of food; the sick, of medicine; the anxious, of peace. It debases, and embrutes, and embitters.

Simple problem, simple solution: let landowners keep title, but let local government tax away the profit they took from rent and the increased value of the land. Enact this, the single tax, and all other taxes could be lifted (which, considering how little government cost in those days, was the one point no critic would dispute). Land monopolists would have to restore their unused acreage to the open market. At the new low prices, factory-hands could afford to turn into farmers. With a smaller labor pool, employers no longer could drive wages down. Workers would get their due, vice and crime would evaporate, and the idle would find useful work to do.[36]

All this sounds like economic rubbish. But George deserved his admirers on more general grounds. Turning to the tradition of Thomas Jefferson and Andrew Jackson, where ending special privilege mattered more than government programs, where open opportunity and a classless society went hand in hand, he used the past to mark the way to a more humane future. Talking economics, George insisted that the best society was not one governed by the market, but one determined by the spirit of Christian morality. Fusing economics and ethics, he struck at the root of Social Darwinism. People were not consigned to misery or raised to wealth by their abilities, *Progress and Poverty* insisted. Society helped make them what they were, and society, if changed, could give them the chance to evolve in different directions.[37]

Actually, most successful executives found little time for pondering over cosmological philosophy at all. Those who chronicled their own success were surprisingly unwilling to credit their rise to the ruthless law of competition. On the contrary, they seized on the traditional virtues: piety, self-denial, hard work, and thrift. Trust, not drive, was as important a quality for success in the world of investment bankers as it was in the shops Horatio Alger described. It had to be, in a profession where one's name meant everything.

Challenges to Social Darwinism

That railroad president who longed for a school in political economy that would harden men's hearts, had he reflected on matters more, might have wondered whether Social Darwinism was more likely to soften brains. Free competition worked to shippers' advantages by giving them low prices, but it killed most railroad enterprises by affording them a low return. It meant poor service, poor roadbeds, and a rich graveyard of victims from railroad accidents. Indeed, the real rule for railroads was, as one expert put it, survival of the *unfittest:* a company thrown into bankruptcy could operate more cheaply under a receiver than its solvent competitor, which still had to pay interest on its bonds and dividends on stock.[38]

"Before Spencer, all for me had been darkness," Carnegie insisted, "after him, all had become light—and right." But when he endowed a library, or funded world peace, or provided scholarships to those who were worthy, the steelmaker was holding out a hand to those who strove. No strict Social Darwinist would approve. Carnegie saw nothing wrong with laws protecting or outlawing women and children on the job, or setting the eight-hour day for workers.

In fact, he knew no other way it could be done. "Organized capital can beat organized labor," he reminded an interviewer in 1891—a year before his own mills at Homestead proved that point in a concrete, not to say bloody, fashion. As for the idea that there was a genetic link to success, Carnegie would have none of it. The great men of society, he was sure, would come from the families of the poor and not from those of the rich, the winners in Social Darwinism's struggles. Brilliance appeared out of nowhere, like "a wild flower found in the woods all by itself." Carnegie, in short, was perfectly willing to endorse Spencer as long as he did not have to understand him. (Spencer himself might have felt uncomfortable about having Carnegie for an admirer. Visiting Pittsburgh at the millionaire's behest in 1882, he was appalled at the steel mills and told his host, "Six months' residence here would justify suicide." They disagreed about everything, from the need for social legislation to the philosophical way to accept misfortune. Spencer could not have appreciated Carnegie's reply to the complaints of an unappreciative public, that abuse was simply a backhanded testimonial to greatness. "I could wish that you had been imprisoned, tortured on the rack," Carnegie assured his hero. "This would have been no greater reward than is your due.")[39]

In 1883, Social Darwinism met its first serious scholarly challenge with the appearance of Lester Ward's *Dynamic Sociology*. Ward posed a question about Social Darwinism's very basis, its analogy between evolution in the natural world and in society. Did human beings really want to imitate Nature? Progress there was not efficient—quite the opposite. The very term "natural selection" implied that most life was created, only to die out, *unselected*. Everywhere, Nature had to depend on immense wastes of its energies, just to keep things as they were. An octopus laid fifty thousand eggs to assure a single survivor. A codfish hatched a million progeny so that two of them would make it. Let academics talk about society advancing by natural selection. Farmers knew better. They pulled weeds from their cornfields, rather than open the ground to free competition. Horticulture and cattle breeding diverted nature from the path marked for it by Darwinian evolution; but was progress impeded by a world with cereals, fruit trees, and an immense variety of dogs?

Society must learn Darwin's lessons right. As long as it left progress to untrammeled competition, the fittest might survive at the expense of humanity in general. They would waste its coal, exhaust its soil, ravage its forests, and squander its human capital. Things did not have to be that way. "Survival of the fittest" sounded all very well, but it begged the question, *fittest for what?* Drop a whale in the Sahara dessert or a camel in the Atlantic Ocean, and the change in conditions would change them from survivors to goners. In society, too, a change in environment might mean a change in individuals' chances of living decently. Human beings could do what the whale and camel could not. They could change that environment, and should have no fears about doing so. Government was not necessarily inefficient, Ward reminded readers. Schools, post offices, tax and customs collectors, fire departments, even the geological survey, did tasks once handled by private enterprise and did them better.[40]

The lesson that the usefulness of a principle or a quality might depend on its surroundings offered the final irony about Social Darwinism. Instead of supporting things as they were, it could sustain a revolution to make institutions over. A new society could breed a new American. In a more conservative sense, the philosophy put tradition to the test: did it fit present circumstances? Was it relevant any longer? It was in such a vein that the Massachusetts jurist, Oliver Wendell Holmes, Jr., published *The Common Law* in 1881. "The life of the law has not been logic; it has been experience," he wrote. ". . .The law embodies the story of a nation's development through many centuries, and it cannot be dealt with as if it contained only the axioms and corollaries of a book of mathematics." Understanding the past would set judges free to apply legal principles with an eye to conditions in their own day.[41]

Chapter 10

More? Labor's Revolutionary Tradition

Those who wanted to see how industrialism was changing America for the better in 1876 could walk through Machinery Hall in Philadelphia. But anyone reading the daily papers would have glimpsed its more disturbing effects. In Jersey City, the steelworks cut wages by 20 percent and in New York, jobless Irish longshoremen bloodied Italian strikebreakers. A reporter visiting the cotton mills at Fall River spotted a fourteen-year-old girl with "wan cheeks and a dejected look" carrying a dinner-pail to the factory door. Her younger brother labored inside for six dollars a month, the family's sole income. "Mother worked in the mill and supported Johnny and me until her eyesight failed and then I went to work," she told the newspaperman. "I worked too hard and ran six looms, and so I was obliged to give up . . . and my little brother took my place. I fear I will never be able to help mother any more, and I don't know what will become of us."[1]

Admittedly, the centennial year was one of unusual hardship. By 1878, the economic depression that had fallen over America after the panic of 1873 was beginning to lift. Everyday Americans did better in the decade that followed. Yet even in the best times, industrialism took a terrible toll on those least able to defend their own interests, a working class that defined itself as everything *but* a working class.

Labor's Loss of Control

How well a laborer did in the Gilded Age depended on pay and training, and that depended on how many others could do the same job. Skilled workers got along best, because they were hard to replace. That gave them some say in setting their own wages and hours. A home and a savings account lay within reach. If they were married men, their wives stayed home and their children had a chance at schooling; there was no need for more than one wage earner to keep food on the table. Unskilled laborers, carders in the cotton mill who earned $1.08 a day, say, or seamstresses in Milwaukee "glad to get" $.75 for sewing a dozen shirts, outnumbered skilled ones heavily.[2] They were more easily replaced, more dependent on what management chose to give them, less able to make do without two incomes. Children left school after the first few grades to enter the work force. Lowest of all were the transients, lucky to find work enough to keep them from beggary. When work was plentiful, they did whatever came their way. When it was not, they relied on the poorhouse and the soup kitchen.

What workers earned made a difference in how they lived, but they also distinguished themselves from each other by what job they did. Seamstresses in their apartments and saleswomen in department stores took very different training. Coal miners did dirty, deadly, exhausting work, for pay often little better than a millhand's, but took pride in the job they did. A good miner needed to know enough masonry to drill rock, enough about drainage and carpentry to shore up the tunnel that he dug; what toiler above ground had such versatile skills?[3]

Yet, in the end, all artisans held in common advantages that set them above other wage earners. They were not commodities to be bought and dispensed with at will, but free Americans, with some say about their working conditions. The tools a miner used were his own. So were the hours he worked, as long as he filled his daily quota. Paid on the piecework principle, the skilled cigar maker could adjust his own pay and hours by how many cigars he chose to make. Whether he came to work at seven or eight or nine was his business; how late he stayed, no boss could tell him. If a funeral, a picnic, even a baseball game called, the hat maker felt free to drop his tools and go. Most skilled workers made more than cigar makers, and hat finishers. But no price could be put on an artisan's status, on the pride that made the cigar maker stroll to work in coat, tie, and hat like a gentleman. Higher wages might tempt him to other employment, but often he came back again, ready to take a pay cut for the power over his own life. "Once a cigar maker, always a cigar maker," as the saying went, might have applied equally to other ill-paid artisans.[4]

Dignity, discretion, and, often, good pay: the values artisans cherished had given work its meaning and fit with a radicalism dating back to the Revolution. Instead of foreign ideas dividing society along class lines, the most articulate spokesmen for labor had reminded their followers of the heritage for which their ancestors had taken up arms, of an independent people, as free on the cobbler's bench as on the town common, with rights equal to anyone else's. The republican philosophy was so simple, so compelling, so well rooted in the tradition of American individualism, that it would take another revolution to unsettle it.

By the end of the Civil War, that revolution was already under way and gathering strength. Still, old ways survived well into the next century. Among workers in machine shops, the need for skilled labor persisted. No tyro off the street could make a boiler. For tasks involving hand tools, where workers could still afford to own them, the industrial revolution changed habits hardly at all. Carpenters, plasterers, and bricklayers continued to build houses and get their pay much the way they had before.[5]

In absolute terms, there were more artisans in 1900 than there had been in 1860. They just mattered less, as a proportion of the work force and in how important they were to the making of goods that Gilded Age America needed. Mass production and continuous flow—the very terms meant that the artisan was giving way to the assembly line, and the product made by a series of machines, each of which was beyond the means of the individual worker. No longer owning his tools, he no longer owned his time nor himself. The division of labor that machines involved meant that the range of skills needed for a job narrowed from a dozen to one, the training from years to days, and the worker's own indispensability to his employer from much to little. Where once four skilled craftsmen made a chair, now a dozen less highly trained specialists—sawyers, joiners, gluers, and varnishers, to name a few—replaced them. In place of the wretchedly paid seamstress, firms hired wretchedly paid sewing machine operators, or farmed out specific tasks in the making of clothing to sweatshops, where, for ten to eighteen hours a day, an entire family would earn its twenty dollars per week in piecework.[6]

The economic transformation meant not only that good pay was harder to get. It was also harder to keep. Yearly wages did rise between 1860 and 1890, but unskilled workers counted themselves lucky if they got a full year's work. Some firms paid workers in "scrip," company money redeemable only at company-run stores, where goods sold at higher prices than usual.[7] Garment workers paid rent on the sewing machines they ran, and were responsible for repairs. Other factories penalized workers with fines, some of which were created specifically as wage-reducing devices.

Low wages meant hunger, misery, and a crushing insecurity. Where the "aristocracy of labor" could afford homes with a parlor, a piano, and a few of the trappings of middle-class life, those less fortunate could afford neither education nor savings accounts, much less burial insurance.

That assumed, of course, that employees would reach an old age. Often, they didn't. As industrial demand for coal rose, so did the number of men dying underground. "Fire-damp," the methane gas that gathered in pockets along the manways, ignited at the spark from a miner's lamp with instant fatal effects. Where the mine was very dry and coal-dust particles thick in the air, an open flame could set off an explosion, as it did at Avondale in 1869. There, a column of flame rushed through the ventilator shaft, destroyed the hoists, and trapped the miners. Not one of the 108 men lived to breathe open air again. Less spectacular but more steadily murderous were other accidents: they cost two lives every three days in the anthracite fields and maimed countless others. Falls from roofs were the worst. As soft slate and rock tumbled down, bodies would be flattened. Comrades could only pick them up for burial by scraping them off the ground with a shovel. For those who lived, injury was almost inevitable, and certainly so along the chutes, 150 feet long, that fed the coal into the breaker. There, "breaker boys" sat picking out slate and refuse rock as it passed. A worker was sure to cut his hands regularly. That was called "redtop," and it was said that the boys' path home could be traced across the snow by the drops of blood along the way. Others died, in peak season as much as one a day.[8]

The shift to the mass production of steel magnified the risk in that industry. Some departments were so hot that workers had to wear wooden-soled shoes, and water sizzled as it struck the floor-plates like butter on a griddle. Even without an accident, stokers and roughers worked at temperatures near 128 degrees. But accidents were commonplace. With liquid stock hanging at the top of a furnace a sudden pitch downward might burst it and kill everyone within range. As metal streaming into the converter hit the edge of the mold, a deadly rain of iron would spray, burning whomever it touched. In one year—a good year—accidents in Pittsburgh cost 195 steelworkers and ironworkers their lives. Guards on power saws, well-lit hallways, enclosures for passenger elevators, fire escapes and sprinkler systems would certainly have made factories much safer. The technology existed to save lives. Only the will was lacking. Coal mines ran without fans to cut down on fire-damp, without escape routes for emergencies, without first-aid stations. Employers actually forbade "breaker boys" to wear gloves. Bare fingers were surer to catch the slate. Company responsibilities were narrowed to removing the body from the mine, shoving it into a "black maria," driving it to the miner's house, and depositing it on the front porch.[9]

Workers' compensation had to thread its way through a thicket of law, with the employer protected three times over. If an occupation had known dangers, the management could defend itself on the grounds that the employee "assumed the risk." If the employer could tie the injury to another worker's negligence, the "fellow servant" rule freed the firm from liability. "Contributory negligence" was the third legal defense. The injured party could not collect without proving blamelessness beyond challenge. For all these reasons, the worker ran short on legal protection. The millhand at Homestead could read his own possible fate in the cripples that sat begging at the factory gate with signs around their necks: "I am injured and blind—my eyes were destroyed by hot steel."

As the concentration of capital into employers' hands changed the relationship of master to servant, it left the old republican ideals of the artisans an empty shell. In the days of the smithy's forge and weaver's hand loom, employer and employee had a rough equality. They could settle their grievances as individual to individual. A man newly hired did have some real "freedom of contract," and the wage he got was one generally acceptable to both. But when an applicant for a job brought neither skills nor tools to the enterprise, he had no bargaining power at all. When jobs were hard to find and men equally fit for the labor were easily available, the terms of employment were all at the owner's command. They were all the more so because of the restrictions an employer could put on workers with whom he contracted. The law permitted him to force them to "yellow-dog contracts," where the employee must swear never to strike or join a union. It allowed the blacklist, by which anyone earning a businessman's displeasure could be assured unemployment throughout the firms in that industry henceforth. And it permitted the hiring of strikebreakers to replace the workers who struck because of their conditions.

So much power almost invited arrogance and abuse, in the name of business efficiency. Spurning negotiations with his men, an ironmonger explained that it was "for the master to do the thinking." A hardware manufacturer insisted that the employee be kept on long hours for his own good: "too much leisure is a detriment to his welfare." Long experience on the job actually became a liability in industries where brawn counted. Without a promotion or pension, many skilled workers graduated into middle age and into the pool of unskilled labor at the same time.[10]

To fit the demands of the machine, industrial labor had to take on machinelike dependability; to suit the marketing revolution, employees had to be redesigned themselves. Consider the railroads: could they leave their employees to show up when they pleased, or engineers to run trains the way cigar makers made cigars, with pay at so much per trip? Passengers would not appreciate a system where an engineer got his quota out of the way by running the Thursday and Friday trains on Wednesday and then taking the rest of the week off. With trains sharing tracks and coordinating with one another, a line that ran the two o'clock express at four stood an increased chance of hitting the three o'clock coal train, or leaving passengers stranded between connections.

Proper coordination demanded rule books. At first, a one-page sheet with a timetable on the back satisfied railroads' needs. By 1870, the companies issued hundred-page manuals bound in leather, along with a pledge to sign, affirming that the employee had read it through. Every few weeks, handouts would amend and add to the rules. Who did what was made explicit, and duties went beyond loading baggage to take in good manners to passengers and obedience to superiors. An employee could be fired for grumbling or covering up others' misconduct. He lived where the company said, wore the kind of watch it decreed, and regulated it as rules set down. Rule books also spelled out how one-sided the responsibilities were. As some said plainly, the employee could not expect compensation for sickness or disability, even when the job was to blame.[11]

Railroads led the way, but other businesses found good financial reasons for adopting rule books and special training themselves. Because department stores catered to the middle class, sales depended on high-toned employees, taught to dress in a subdued, middle-class fashion and to speak in middle-class grammar. Lists of "Store Don'ts" circulated. A factory could not afford the independence of craftsmen who did business when they pleased. So men stood at the factory gates to check off the time when employees entered or locked the doors when the workday had begun, so that latecomers would have to wait until lunchtime to begin their tasks—for a half-day's pay. By the 1890s, mills were installing time clocks and making workers punch in. It was among the degradations that offended employees the most. They made "one feel more like a member of a goat herd than a human being," one department-store saleswoman complained.[12]

Not all employers were ruthless and remote. Small firms persisted alongside the giant ones. The pit boss of the Loyal Hanna Coal Mine fired miners for having missed work to attend the funeral of a child crushed to death on the job, where others might excuse that kind of absence or show up at the graveside themselves.[13] Still, the general trend of the Gilded Age was unmistakable. The search for profit left workers without protection. The law of supply and demand assured more goods and cheaper. It did not guarantee safer and better conditions in the workplace. The Gilded Age saw skilled and unskilled labor draw further apart in work experience, in their satisfaction with American society, in pay scales and control of their own lives. It saw the division between workers within a single industry, as the tasks they held in common dwindled. It saw the division between labor and capital, as the tools and terms of employment became more exclusively the possession of the employer, and as administrative structures separated the capitalist further from the work experience that his employees faced every day.

Workers did not accept their lot easily. Needing to make a minimum number of sales per day, saleswomen would do what was required, and not much beyond it; making more than "a good book" would only reflect badly on fellow employees not doing as well that day. Management might order them to wear black, but they refused to wear uniforms, and battled hard against stores' buying their clothing for them. After years of struggle, employers had to give in, just as they did on their efforts to keep shopgirls from using their idle time to socialize. In no employment was the subjugation of personal life so complete as with house servants, one million strong in 1870, and the difference in rank sharpened over the next generation. Master or mistress decreed their uniform and their manners, expected their attentions from waking-hour to past bedtime, and separated their living quarters to "below stairs" or back rooms. Only one power lay beyond the employer: keeping them. Domestics changed jobs often, not to better themselves, but to show themselves free women still.[14]

The Rebirth of American Trade Unions

These were small victories. Larger ones would come only if organized power met organized capital. To do that, workers must discover a common interest. They must act collectively, either as members of a craft or as a class. There were two ways to do it. City laborers had tried both in the 1830s. Briefly, they had set up working-men's parties to advance a program and had built trade unions to control wages. Neither had lasted. Loyalty to the two main parties had crippled the first, and hard times had wiped out the second. Still, in the 1860s, organizers were ready to try again, but with a few changes. If there were going to be national markets, there had to be national unions, and in the decade after the war, eighteen of them appeared. In 1866, representatives of twenty different trades gathered in Philadelphia to form the National Labor Union, which had the potential to become a federation of unions and the rallying point for wage earners.[15]

If anybody could have turned that potential into reality, it would have been William Sylvis, head of the iron-puddlers' union and NLU president from 1868 on. Sylvis was a fervent Methodist, well steeped in the republican tradition. In his mind, he foresaw an industrial America where cooperative enterprises might make every worker self-employed, and a labor movement open not just to white men, but to women and blacks. Trade unions could not restore the old independence by themselves. Government must help. Instead of bankers with special charters issuing their notes, the "people's money"—U. S. greenbacks—should circulate, and the more the better: a money supply too big for bankers to control would cut interest rates and raise wages. Such a reform program required a party of and for workers.[16]

Sylvis's dreams came to nothing. He died in 1869, before he could give the NLU's leaders anything more than a moral authority, but already the federation had fallen out of trades-unionists' hands into those of middle-class reformers, with less interest in bread-and-butter issues than broad social change. The more the NLU worked to set up its own party, the less the unions wanted anything to do with it. Its attempt to nominate a presidential candidate turned into a joke when the nominee refused to run. Local workingmen's movements fielded parties in a few states. They ended up with nothing more than political sweet talk. Standing alone, without a larger organization or political backing, the national unions weathered good times and broke in bad. With the Panic of 1873, most of them perished.[17]

The Cause of One Is the Cause of All: Knights of Labor

Sylvis had been onto something, though, and when a new alternative arose, it built on his vision of a "great brotherhood" of workers, committed to long- and short-term reforms, a combination of union and political party. Founded among the Philadelphia garment cutters by Uriah S. Stephens, the Knights of Labor soon discarded both Stephens and the secret mumbo-jumbo of a fraternal order. By 1879, it had set up what Sylvis never managed, a federation of crafts with real power among the leaders. That it did so at all was due to Terence V. Powderly, new Grand Master of the Knights and for fourteen years the most famous, respected labor leader in the nation.

With his pince-nez, long, gaunt face, and genteel manners, Powderly might have been mistaken for a schoolteacher. Based on his career, his moral pieties, and his teetotaling habits, he might have been mistaken for a middle-class preacher. His father had risen from coal miner to mine owner and would sit on Carbondale's first city council. Powderly himself became mayor of Scranton. But the Grand Master knew deprivation firsthand. He had seen his father fall back to the status of a common laborer and had himself been forced to leave school at age 13 to work on the railroad. As a practicing machinist, he knew something of an artisan's pride in his craft. "I hate the word 'class' and would drive it from the English language if I could," he would say later on. Instead, Americans must define themselves in the best republican tradition, as producers and nonproducers. On one side stood farmers, craftsmen, housewives, and sharecroppers. On the other stood those who got rich on others' toil: speculators, lawyers, and, of course, politicians.[18]

Powderly grasped something essential in the discontent over the new industrial order. Workers were not objecting to the rich having grown rich. They did resent how monopoly and large-scale capitalism had narrowed the right to rise to a privileged few, and robbed the rest of their control over their fate. The republic of the Founders, based on equal rights, stood endangered by a system that, as one Knight charged, crushed "the manhood out of sovereign citizens." Not Karl Marx, but the Declaration of Independence and the Bible offered the guidelines for what America must be. The Knights fought for dignity and independence, not just wealth.[19]

Restoring old virtues would take new means. Like Sylvis, the Knights supported trade unions as a way of putting pressure on the employers, and like him they wanted cooperative enterprises, banking reform, greenbacks rather than national bank notes, and an end to the partnership between government and monopoly that had given business so many advantages. But they also called for a wider public role on behalf of the toiling classes. Only legislation could make factory work healthy and safe every-where. Public ownership of telegraph lines and railroads could give all monopoly's advantages without leaving it in the selfish hands of the few.[20]

The vision had a wide appeal and by the early 1880s, Powderly's organizing tal-ents were paying off. In three years, membership grew fourfold. Farmer and factory hand, middle class and working class, met in common assembly and pledged them-selves to help evolve the wage-earning system into a cooperative one. Between 50,000 and 150,000 women joined: shoe-stitchers and carpet-weavers, waitresses, school-teachers, and domestic help. In the South, one Knight in three was black, and though they marched separately in the parades and formed their own locals, the organization welcomed them. Factory workers appealed to the Knights, and the Knights ended up as leaders of strikes they had neither begun nor approved of, and as negotiators of set-tlements. Torchlight parades, rallies, and petitioning campaigns all showed the Knights' appeal by 1886. They won elections and marshaled the force to make Con-gress end Chinese immigration in 1882 and contract labor in 1885.[21]

By 1886, with the Knights 750,000 strong, larger victories seemed mere months away. Instead, the movement collapsed. The very breadth of its appeal gave it a mem-bership wanting very different things. When businessmen or politicians joined an as-sembly, they were as verbally supportive of Powderly's general program as they were hostile to any specific action here and now. Trade-union members wanted the eight-hour day, but came to distrust the more utopian schemes; Socialists liked the long-term goals, but disliked the trade unions. As for evangelical Protestants, they grew ever more uneasy alongside German radicals, who made their eight-hour parade on Easter Sunday, and waved banners reading, "No God, No Master."[22]

The more the workers rushed into the Knights, the more the strains in the or-ganization showed. By 1884, the rank and file were much more militant on labor is-sues than the national leadership. Labor parties battled for office, and not always with Powderly's blessing. Workers struck for higher wages, but without his support. A spirit of cooperation could never grow if worker and capitalist confronted each other, and the Knights could not endure, if they must throw their wealth and power into fights they were almost sure to lose.[23]

In opposing strikes and supporting peaceable boycotts, the grand master seems more out of touch than he actually was. Outside of the big corporations, many work-ers identified with their employers. That was truest in small towns. There, master and servant knew each other as neighbors and went to church together. Unions were not so far from the fraternal orders and self-improvement societies that they once had been, unequipped for a long, hard fight and uncomfortable about picking one. With

Terence V. Powderly is introduced at the Knights of Labor's annual meeting in 1886. The picture offers a perfect balance: a black Knight on one side, and General Robert E. Lee's son on the other. (Library of Congress)

employees so easy to replace and so fearful for their jobs, they had to treat a strike as a last resort. The middle class could make the cause of one the cause of all by refusing to buy products made by exploiting labor. Its members could not join a labor walkout, and cooled quickly to any cause that threatened the peace—as strikes had a way of doing. When fellow workers refused to walk off the job, they were threatened, sometimes beaten. Clashes with police, arson, and vandalism grew more common as strikes wore on, and with them the "respectable" classes' commitment to keeping public order would harden. For all these reasons, when states started setting up the machinery to make arbitration possible in the 1880s, not just ministers and businessmen, but many labor leaders, as well, welcomed the move.[24]

Had the Knights grown more slowly, more of the workers in its ranks might have shared Powderly's caution. Instead, the jump in membership and a few dazzling strike successes swept away doubts. Those wanting "eight hours for work, eight hours for sleep, eight hours for what we will" could not wait, and saw no reason to do so. In the whole Knights' program, the eight-hour day seemed the item easiest to get and the one most likely to change workers' lives instantly. It might even solve the problem of too many workers and too few jobs: when the employed cut back on their workday, employers would have to hire more people just to get as much done. Instead of the regular annual layoffs that so many workers suffered from, the eight-hour day would spread labor evenly across the year. Comfort, security, and a proof of the people's power to set the terms for the new industrial order—what reform could do so much? By 1886, the time seemed ripe. Momentum in the workplace seemed to be with the Knights. Cooperation and negotiation could win over some employers, but others would stand fast without tougher methods. So in Alabama, miners walked out when their employers hired Italian labor; employees in Durham, North Carolina, left the job to protest the scantily clad women on the cigarette cases; and across the South, other Knights struck to demand more money and the eight-hour day. By mid-April, employers by the hundreds were giving in, rather than risk the strikes set for May Day.[25]

Then came May 1st itself, and workers turned out to parade and show their full strength. Some 300,000 workers in 13,000 firms stayed away from their jobs. Open-air rallies inspired crowds, sometimes in English, sometimes in German, Polish, or Czech. Down Michigan Avenue, 80,000 Chicagoans marched, arm in arm and singing, while rooftops on either side bristled with Winchester rifles that were wielded by Pinkertons and citizen volunteers. Respectable people everywhere expected trouble. A few radicals hoped for revolution. Neither happened. May Day was more a holiday than a day of reckoning, and most employees reported for work the next day. But there were plenty of exceptions. Freight stopped moving in railroad yards, laundries and sweatshops closed down, and Cincinnati streetcar workers refused to run the transit lines.[26]

Alarmed, Powderly and the general executive board scrambled to get back in control of a runaway movement. On May 4th, they ordered railroad workers to end their walkout against Jay Gould's railroad system in the Southwest, a strike that was already lost, and had turned into a make-or-break test of the Knights' power. Within days, the national organization had changed its bylaws to make strikes virtually impossible. It ordered Chicago butchers and New York dockworkers back on the job. Violence in the streets and cross-purposes among the Knights drained the force out of the eight-hour-day movement. Some strikes won their demands, but the big ones, like those on Gould's railroad, ended in defeat. By autumn, the Knights' goals seemed farther away than ever. Employers went to court for injunctions against boycotters and staged lockouts to replace union employees. Where they could drive white and black Southerners apart, they did so. White strikers were arrested, black ones beaten and killed.[27]

Powderly may have meant to save the movement. He sped it to its death instead. "The trouble with the whole army of the discontented is that they are tired of churning so long and seeing no sign of butter," grumbled one labor paper. "Agitation, education, organization, is all very fine at the first go off, but what is the prospect? When will these dreams of ours materialize? . . . The point of contest is will the butter come? Can it be we are churning skim milk?" With the dashing of immediate hopes, members rediscovered their differences. Trade unions and middle-class reformers, Socialists and artisan republicans squabbled about ends and means. Among the industrial workers who had only recently come to the Knights, Powderly's caution looked like a double-cross. When he gave labor parties a cautious support, they blamed him for defeat. By year's end, many local assemblies had emptied. There were only 220,000 Knights in early 1888, and less than half that two years later. A movement that had begun in the cities evaporated there, lingering only in the hinterlands where temperance and reform mattered and trade unions had no following.[28]

Business Unionism: The AFL

With irregular employment a fact of life, with immigration from Europe and the countryside affording business a steady supply of unskilled labor, a working-class movement would have to base itself on other principles than the grass-roots politics and old-fashioned republicanism of the Knights. Instead of putting energy into changing the new industrial system, workers must look to their own immediate interests. Trade unions gave them the muscle to do so, but only if organized nationally, and if different trades joined a federation with enough power at the top to get respect. That would take tighter control than Powderly's Knights and help that gave workers a reason for sticking with the union and federation both. An organization that could hold out benefits for every day—rather than in moments of crisis—and the means for tiding strikers over from the central treasury would bind its membership fast. They would have to pay higher dues than Knights did, but what they got would give them security and a sense of solidarity both.

The driving force for change came from two leaders of the Cigar Maker's International Union, Adolph Strasser and Samuel Gompers. Born in a crowded tenement in London's East End, Gompers knew poverty as clearly as Powderly had. Still a boy, he came to America to escape starvation and just barely succeeded in the slums of New York where Bohemians who were desperate for work earned a pittance making the cheapest cigars in sweatshop conditions. Not surprisingly, Gompers took to the writings of Marx and Engels. From them, he learned that only the workers could help themselves, and only through organization. An eight-hour day would come when the threat of a strike forced employers to give it, not when Congress passed a law mixing cant and loopholes.[29]

Under Gompers and Strasser, the Cigar Makers' International Union showed how far a strong organization could ease working conditions. Its $150,000 strike fund did more to deter trouble from employers than twenty speeches about the iron heel of capitalism. When a cigar maker died, the organization took care of the family; if his wife or mother died, it chipped in $40 for burial costs. When cigar workers went on the road looking for work, the first place they went for help in a new town was the union secretary. At the local they could find clean towels, bleaching soap, brushes, and combs. When they moved on, the local provided a loan to tide them over, advice on rooming houses, a list of job openings, and a "meal ticket" for a free dinner.

These were bread-and-butter matters. But in other respects, "business unionism," as it came to be known, dealt with the same problems that had so troubled the Knights: the dignity of the worker and the loss of control over production. Thanks to the CMIU, no supervisor could give an employee a public tongue-lashing. He had to pass on his grievance to the shop collector, who would take care of matters more discreetly. Whether work rules were reasonable, what quality of work was acceptable, the union decided. If a worker had to be dismissed, it took place as work ended on Saturday, rather than when he came in on Monday.[30]

"Business unionism" drew on tradition as liberally as had the Knights. Strasser and Gompers accepted trade-union custom in basing their organization on crafts, rather than on whole industries or neighborhoods. Skilled workers who could not be easily replaced had always had the best chance of winning their demands, and the unions that lasted had always been those that offered benefits. Most of them, indeed, had offered little more than fraternity and a little insurance. That would remain at the heart of their appeal for years to come. Nor did Gompers rule out political action. Members could lobby and vote as they pleased. Gompers, like Powderly, had voted the Greenback-Labor ticket himself, and he kept a sentimental affection for Socialism much longer than he admitted. The real difference was in how much politics became a sideshow for "business unionism." A long-term political agenda with justice for all mattered less than a fairer deal for union members here and now.[31]

Already by mid-1886, the trade unions had had enough of Powderly's Knights. In December, they made the schism official, by founding the American Federation of Labor and putting Gompers at the head. (The hostility was one Powderly returned. "Mr. Gompers never came near me only when he was drunk," he declared, "and *I will not transact business with a drunkard at any time or place.*") As Powderly's forces dwindled, Gompers's grew, not dramatically, but with a steady regularity. During the hard 1890s, the AFL actually added to its membership. It did better still as prosperity returned. With 548,000 members at the start of the new century, it peaked with 1.7 million in 1904.[32]

From Brotherhood to Business: Growth and Change in the Labor Unions

With so much money to handle and so many locals to coordinate, a national union took a well-organized bureaucracy and an increasingly centralized authority. Except for one year, Gompers headed the AFL until his death in 1924. There would have been nothing wrong, necessarily, with one-man rule, had it been done democratically, which it wasn't. As president, Gompers controlled the Federation treasury and opened it to whatever groups he pleased—which meant, in effect, whatever groups pleased him. The *American Federationist* spoke his line alone. Any delegate could speak at an AFL convention, but no measure could pass without going through a committee Gompers chose. If delegates caught him napping and did manage to get through a policy that the president found distasteful, he usually could ignore it. What was true at the top was true in the craft-unions themselves. Leaders did not worry about what the rank and file said in convention: they simply never called a convention. The cigar makers had none for sixteen years, and tobacco workers had to go to court in 1939 to make the leaders call their first in that century. The organization gave workers more of a voice on their jobs, but the bureaucracy muffled or silenced that voice in how the organization was run. The first generation of labor leaders, with their shared hardships and their memories of wandering with the tramps, passed away. Gone, too, were the disheveled sack-coats and straggling mustaches; by World War I, Gompers himself sported a diamond cravat pin, while the head of the United Mine Workers had switched from a black, soft-felt hat to a silk derby.[33]

Unions, in effect, had gone from being a brotherhood to being a business. The language of labor organization at the start of the Gilded Age had been very different. It put the image of fraternity, of democracy, foremost. They were the *Knights* of St. Crispin, the *Sons* of Vulcan, the Industrial *Brotherhood*. The secret rituals and rites of Stephens had some meaning, after all. And, like other brotherhoods, they dedicated themselves not simply to the protection of one another, but to their moral uplift and improvement. Powderly's distaste for drink made him a fit spokesman. Though the old language outlasted the century, by the mid-1890s, it was being replaced with another, the union as an enterprise—up to date, prosperous, efficient—and well run by those fittest to command.[34]

Hard-headedness in advancing members' self-interest had been central to the AFL's appeal all along, and that fight the leaders ultimately came to see as their own exclusive province, not to be shared in by union organizations outside its ranks nor by government authorities. As trades-union members made their benefits a selling point, they wanted no competition from state capitals nor from Washington. Gompers might back compulsory education, city ownership of streetcar lines, women's right to vote, factory inspections, and a ban on goods made by convicts but he and the AFL fought relentlessly against laws to regulate men's hours and wages, to guarantee old-age pensions, or to force business to arbitrate.[35]

In doing so, the AFL denied help to the vast majority of American workers for whom it could do nothing, and for whom it had no intention of doing anything. Craft unions wanted nothing to do with blacks, recent immigrants, or the unskilled in general. Instead of organizing women, labor leaders pronounced them unorganizable because the weaker sex lacked the willpower to stand firm in a strike. Only in 1892 did the AFL hire its first woman organizer, Mary Kenney, and it let her go after five months—choosing no successor until 1908. (Mary Kenney would keep up the fight; in 1903, she helped found the National Women's Trade Union League, which, in time, helped organize the garment workers of New York.) In fact, as the women Knights had shown, they could outdo the men in grit. Kenney organized forty different unions, many of which endured for years. But there was no getting around the numbers. In 1900, only 3.3 percent of all women working in industry had a union to represent them, and that proportion was cut by more than half over the next ten years.[36]

Instead of expanding its ambitions as membership increased, the AFL became ever more cautious. In the 1880s, Gompers himself had not differed all that much from Powderly regarding the need to unionize women. He favored using a general strike to win the eight-hour day and looked to the day when unions based on craft would merge into industrywide organizations. To the century's end, he still expressed hopes of organizing the unskilled workers, as well as the skilled—someday. Rightly, he warned his colleagues that if "common humanity" did not push them to unionize black workers, "self-interest should": the bosses would only turn Negroes into strike-breakers and use the color line to break down organized labor. Almost alone, he managed to keep machinists and blacksmiths out of the AFL for adopting Jim Crow rules. On all those issues, Federation members voted him down or experience destroyed his hopes.[37]

The Lessons of Homestead, 1892

No event was more chastening than the Homestead strike in July 1892, and the destruction of the Amalgamated Association of Iron and Steel Workers, a constituent member of the AFL. Until 1892, Andrew Carnegie kept on good terms with his employees at Homestead. But public relations were one thing and profits another. He and Henry Clay Frick, the company chairman, saw no way to drive profits up without driving the craft union out. While Carnegie hid in Scotland, Frick wielded a free hand. When he started a lockout in departments where union men were strongest, all the employees, skilled and unskilled, left their jobs. Frick hired a private army from the Pinkerton National Detective Agency to protect the new employees he meant to hire in place of the old. On July 6th, as the bargeloads of guards approached the plant up the Monongahela River, Homesteaders grabbed guns, hoes, and sticks from picket fences to fight them off. All day the battle raged. When the Pinkertons surrendered, they fell into the hands of townspeople, by now shouting for vengeance. All told, sixteen people died that day. Within the week, Pennsylvania had sent eight thousand militiamen to break the strike, and Homestead reopened. The strikers lost their jobs and their homes. The Amalgamated lingered, hapless and well nigh memberless for eleven years more. "Oh, that Homestead blunder," Carnegie wrote, when he came home again, "—but it's fading as all events do & we are at work selling steel one pound for a half penny."[38]

The Homestead catastrophe offered a brutal lesson in the AFL's limits against a major corporation. The Federation could do little more than watch. Its effort over the past three years to compel companies to accept the eight-hour day had failed. In the late 1880s, workers won most strikes. By the early 1890s, management had the edge. As long as immigration from the countryside and from abroad came unchecked into the industrial cities, unskilled employees could easily be replaced. Organizing industrywide unions was a doomed enterprise. Supporting them through a strike would bankrupt the AFL, only for results no better than at Homestead. So the trade unions tendered sympathy to strikers outside the federation, as well as advice, help, and even a little money, but ventured no farther.[39]

If "business unionism" was an advance for labor, it fell far short of the promise that Powderly's Knights had held forth, of a society transformed. Yet the grand failures and halfway successes were more akin than they seemed. Both of them were based on the belief that power must be returned to where it belonged, among the producing mass of Americans. It was a belief that reverberated far beyond the unions themselves and belied the whole idea of a working class with interests separate from everyone else's.

All through the Gilded Age, laborers on strike discovered how many friends they had. When longshoremen struck for forty cents an hour, squads of policemen had to escort strikebreakers to the wharves, with children hurling stones at them all the way. Cigar-store owners rallied behind the cigar-maker's union when it struck in 1877. Shopkeepers refused to serve strikebreaking militiamen; local businessmen aided miners evicted from company towns and helped build new housing for them. Public opinion did not always go with the union against management. Strikes are inconvenient things, and towns whose prosperity relied on an industry often identified their fortunes with the managers. But there were plenty of towns like Homestead.[40]

It was not capital alone that defeated Powderly and checked Gompers, nor a failure of vision. The very energy and flow of a Gilded-Age America did it—most of all the surging tide of foreigners and countryfolk into the cities. Ready to take work on any terms, they made every advance for labor a precarious one. A crowd of jobless outside the gates was the strongest possible discouragement for agitation, even complaint, by those lucky enough to have a job. Because so many of the immigrants meant to go home again once they had made a competence, they felt little interest in the long-term benefits of belonging to a trade union or in the particulars of the republican tradition.

A Clash of Movement Cultures

They could, however, feel an interest in the culture they had left behind. Here may be the most important explanation for the failure of America to develop a working class that saw itself as one. For people to see themselves as an economic class, they must put their position ahead of their heritage or even their craft: workers first, not Irish or Germans or Catholics or weavers or Democrats. The poverty, the indignity of being subordinate, the grievance of getting too small a share of the profits might give laborers a shared sense of experience, even if their tasks were as different as those of a seamstress and an iron puddler. They might live as neighbors, and as neighbors they might trudge to the same job at the same hour. They might share a social life: picnics, concerts, and amateur theatricals. Finally, all might share in the same politics, champion the same values, and hurrah for the same slate of candidates. Together, all of these would create a common experience extending far beyond the workplace, a "movement culture."

Yet none of them came naturally, especially in the bigger cities. There, workers might live close to each other and alone, barely knowing their neighbors. Newcomers from different coasts might send their children to different schools, show up for the parades of rival parties, and drink at different saloons. Unions and labor parties could create a "movement culture," with effort. For a while, in the mid-1880s in some cities, the Knights actually succeeded. But it could never compete with the other "movement cultures," which were better established and more vibrant: the political culture that Republicans and Democrats had spent thirty years developing, with its hoopla and sense of tradition; the middle-class culture that department stores, advertising, and mass-circulation magazines celebrated as both the ideal and the norm for all

Americans; and, richer than any, the immigrant cultures, from German-language schools to Polish athletics societies and Jewish benevolent associations, which gave those staying briefly in the New World some semblance of the Old.

The richness, the variety of American culture in the Gilded Age could not wipe out a working-class sensibility. It simply hindered its growth every step of the way. The very openness of society did more than the Pinkertons or Social Darwinism to make labor's struggle a hopeless one. Rather than deploring how little Powderly and Gompers achieved, it is very much a wonder that they accomplished so much.

Chapter 11

Anarchy with Police

Haymarket Square, 1886

In early May 1886, things went terribly wrong in Chicago. A year before, strikers at Cyrus McCormick's reaper factory had rolled back a pay cut. Their victory lasted until the following February, when McCormick imposed a lockout and hired a new, nonunion force. With Pinkertons and police protecting the strikebreakers, bitter clashes along the picket line became a daily event. On May third, a rally on behalf of striking lumber-shovers turned into an attack on McCormick's new employees. As rocks rained down on the police, patrolmen set upon the protesters with clubs, then revolvers. Two strikers died. Many more were wounded.[1]

Instantly, the German anarchists of the International Working People's Association moved into action. Puny in numbers, fire-breathing in language, already the terror of Chicago's middle class, and exasperated by workers' failure to realize May Day's revolutionary potential, they called a protest rally for Haymarket Square. "Annihilate the beasts in human form who call themselves rulers!" a leaflet in German cried. "Revenge!" echoed the English version. "Workingmen to Arms!!!"

Gathering guns, fashioning bombs, a few militant anarchists readied for Armageddon, but those who showed up for the rally came to hurl nothing worse than bloodcurdling threats for the future and appeals to good conduct for the present. The crowd, a disappointing three thousand, listened politely. Burly Carter Harrison, Chicago's mayor, showed up, rightly confident that nobody would do him harm. By

Someone hurls the bomb at Haymarket, 1886. There are only two things wrong with the picture: nobody in the crowd shot back at the police, and Samuel Fielden was not rabble-rousing when the explosion occurred. (*Harper's Weekly*, 1886)

the time the last harangue began, Harrison had strolled home to bed. So had all but three hundred people. It was then, with lowering skies and rain about to break up the meeting that the police moved in. "We are peaceable," Samuel Fielden, the orator, protested. Just as he said that, from somewhere in the crowd, a bomb flew. It exploded in the front rank of the police, killing one instantly, and mortally wounding seven more. With that, police opened fire indiscriminately, into the crowd, into each other. Sixty patrolmen were wounded. With bullets flying, the crowd broke and ran. Protestors were shot, trampled, crushed. Seven or eight died, and dozens more were wounded.

"NOW IT IS BLOOD!" one headline shrieked. Across the country, newspapers pronounced the incident the result of "Dynamarchist" conspiracy, played up the bomb, and overlooked the fact that the police had done their share of killing. From reading the New York *Tribune*, one might imagine that a blood-crazed mob had set upon the police, "and, holding its ground, poured volley after volley into the midst of the officers." With a panicked public clamoring for action, Chicago authorities raided socialist offices and halls, arrested hundreds, and indicted eight leading anarchists for having set on the bomb-thrower. None of them threw the bomb. If any of them knew who had, the prosecution failed to show it. The best the state's attorney could do was insist that the perpetrator, whoever he was, must have been an anarchist, inspired by years of inflammatory language from the defendants. Before a packed jury kept in line by a bullying, bigoted judge, the prosecution led perjured witnesses through their paces. On the tables were spread an array of bombs, shells, and dynamiting caps; it scarcely mattered that none of them could be traced to the defendants.[2]

Jurors brought in murder convictions all around and seven death sentences. Shocked by the miscarriage of justice, even some of those who had cried for blood a year before joined the drive for clemency. Ministers, bankers, workers, and railroad presidents signed petitions and sent wires to the governor. On just one Sunday, working men in London gathered sixteen thousand signatures. Under Illinois law, the governor could commute no sentence unless the condemned prisoner asked for mercy. Two did. Both got life sentences. Helped by a friend outside, one prisoner used dynamite to destroy himself in his cell. Spurning mercy when justice was their due, unprepared to renounce the legitimacy of violence, the rest went to their deaths.[3]

Six years later, a new man sat in the Illinois governor's mansion. John Peter Altgeld was ambitious, able, a property-holder of some standing. He also had committed himself to look into the case again, whatever the consequences. Reviewing the trial record, convinced that the procedures had been outrageously unfair, he issued pardons to the three survivors and got the natural reward for courage: the abuse generally reserved for anarchists. To the end of his days, he would appear in cartoons, pistol or torch in hand, his head covered with the red cap of a revolutionary.[4]

The Haymarket catastrophe captured American disorder at its worst, and laid bare fears close to the surface of public life. That made the incident special—not unique; for the violence could be found everywhere, and with it the sense of things just about to fall apart.

An Epidemic of Violence

Popular history blames much of the Gilded Age's disorder on the rawness of the West. In dime-novel and yellow journalism, bandits reigned supreme. There was, for example, William Bonney, a young man with a cheery disposition, who took to herding sheep in Arizona and working as a ranch hand. When he was seventeen, he killed a blacksmith in a quarrel. He later boasted of taking twenty-one lives (nine is likelier). Whatever the truth of it, Billy the Kid won a lasting reputation. A year after being gunned down in 1881, he lived on in eight different novels.[5] Alongside the mythic outlaw stood the mythic gunfighter with a badge. Wild Bill Hickock insisted that he had killed over a hundred men, while Bat Masterson, an Indian fighter and army scout who settled down as sheriff in Dodge City, took the credit for having killed one man for each year of his life. So great was Masterson's reputation that, in time, he hardly had to draw his gun at all. Luckier than Hickock, who was shot from behind at the poker table while holding aces and eights (the "dead man's hand" from then on), Masterson lived to turn sportswriter for a New York newspaper.[6]

Bat and Billy made good copy, nothing more. Much more significant was the way that rival political and economic groups across the West used violence to settle disputes. Cattle barons, owners of small ranches, and homesteaders vied for water rights, while families repaid scores with all the persistence of kinfolk in Icelandic sagas. In Arizona, for example, the Grahams and Tewkesburys for six years waged what would be christened the "Pleasant Valley War." It ended only when the combatants had finished each other off to the last man. Cowboys cleared the range of sheep by rim-rocking, that is, by driving flocks before them off bluffs and cliffs: those in front stampeded over the edge, pressed by the sheep behind.[7]

Even though the crime rate as a whole was falling in many eastern cities, the pressures of urban growth, ethnic rivalry, and lagging police services made the problem seem worse than before. Long before the Haymarket bombing, Chicago had earned a special reputation for lawlessness. No area could beat the "Bloody Maxwell" neighborhood of the twenty-second precinct. So loosely did the ordinary laws apply there that when one gangster was arrested, he protested indignantly, "You can't do anything to me. I only shot a cop! Anybody's got a right to shoot a cop!" In 1871, New York City contained at least thirty thousand professional thieves, and many of them had no scruples about shedding blood. One gang actually published a price list for its services: a nose and jaw broken for ten dollars, both eyes blackened for four, ears chewed off for fifteen dollars, and a more permanent solution applied for one hundred dollars or more. For homicide, however, southern cities held prior claim at the turn of the century. Memphis had a murder rate nearly seven times the national average.[8]

For all the talk of crime bosses and hired thugs, Gilded Age violence, like charity, usually began at home: between neighbors, husband and wife, parents and children. Barroom brawls on weekends and spouse abuse during the week were the likeliest flareups among the city working class. Most husbands did not beat their wives, but those who did often saw nothing to apologize for. As some of them argued, a man had the right to use his property the way he pleased.[9]

From where did the contagion of American violence come? Nativists blamed the alien hordes, unfit for American institutions. Such fears found one particularly shrill voice in *Our Country*, a bestseller from the time of its appearance in 1885. Its author, Reverend Josiah Strong, secretary to the American Home Missionary Society, described the immigrant-swollen cities, those "tainted spots in the body-politic," as breeding grounds for anarchy and destruction, riots, bomb-throwing, even revolution. New Orleans residents blamed lawlessness on the so-called Black Hand, the Mafia. Some such organization did exist, as anyone in the Italian neighborhood could attest. There, in twenty years, bullies with sawed-off shotguns assassinated some seventy inhabitants who stood in their way, shook down shopkeepers, and served as something of an unofficial government. By 1890, they had launched a full-scale war on the wealthy Povenzano family and its dockside businesses. As the dispute raged, someone shot Hennessy, the chief of police. He lived long enough to say who had done it: "Dagoes!" There were nineteen indictments. A jury acquitted or came to a disagreement on every defendant. Was justice served? Possibly. The victim had many enemies, including the relatives of the late chief of detectives, whom Hennessy had killed some years before. But how much easier it was to credit the verdict to bribes doled out by the Mafia![10]

Indigents as Society's Scapegoats

Taking class more seriously than culture, panicky editors saw the homeless as the most obvious sign of social breakdown. Utter the word "tramp," a social scientist remarked in 1877, and the image arose of

a lazy, shiftless, sauntering or swaggering, ill-conditioned, irreclaimable, incorrigible, cowardly, utterly depraved savage. . . . He will outrage an unprotected female, or rob a defenseless child, or burn an isolated barn, or girdle fruit trees, or wreck a railway train, or set fire to a railway bridge, or murder a cripple, or pilfer an umbrella, with equal indifference, if reasonably sure of equal impunity.

In time, the tramp would become a staple of humor-magazine jokes, with "Weary Willie" and "Nervy Nat" committing mayhem and dodging responsibilities with inexhaustible cheek. When movies came along, Charlie Chaplin's "Little Tramp" would be a still later and far more likeable version of the caricature. But in the 1870s, responses to vagabondage were much more savage. "A wrecked freight car invariably means a dead tramp," a St. Louis paper remarked. "It's an expensive but effective way of getting rid of a very undesirable class of nuisances." The Minneapolis *Tribune* lauded local farmers' murder of two tramps as the first step to "fertilize the land with their dead bodies," a trustier deterrent even than the Chicago *Tribune*'s suggestion to housewives to lace their handouts with arsenic.[11]

With increasing frequency, too, propertied Americans placed the danger of disorder on the anarchists and communists that they came to imagine in their midst. As late as the 1870s, communism had conjured up nothing more atrocious than the free-love colony at Oneida, or the cooperative communities of utopian dreamers, where gentle idealists sought to fashion a new world free from materialism. Then, in 1871, events in Paris gave the term new, terrifying meaning. In forming a commune to govern themselves, a group of Parisians had not been trying to remake the world. Within weeks, the French army retook the city and started running firing squads round the clock to get rid of troublemakers. But the imagery that wild propaganda gave the commune lingered long after the shooting stopped. Communism now stood for the destruction of all property rights, the rule of ne'er-do-wells and thieves, the butchery of bishops and the desecration of churches, the dissolution of the marriage bond, the arsonist's torch, and the terrorist's bomb. Actually, the few Americans who embraced Marxist ideals were more likely to wave a banner than a bomb. The 1877 railroad strikes were far from revolution, and the forces of order did most of the killing, but level-headed conservatives saw the commune arising in their midst. Every disruption could be traced to tramps or communists, master-detective Allan Pinkerton insisted. "Every act of lawlessness that was done was committed by them."[12]

Much of the breakdown of order Americans worried about was of a kind that truncheons and pistols could not prevent. "The French commune rears its head in Cincinnati," screamed one newspaper, after German citizens rallied to allow music concerts and beer selling on Sunday. Such hysteria was not as silly as it sounds now.[13] In a time of technological revolution, people clung to familiar institutions all the more passionately, because they offered a fixed point of reference in a changing world. Yet ministers, polemicists, and trade unionists all declared that the old ways were in danger. The threatened past might be the craftsman's republic of free and equal men, or the English-speaking Protestant commonwealth, small-town values, or white supremacy. Still, the threat was there, and a very plausible one it seemed, in a country where change was the only constant. Groping for means of keeping order, whether it meant crowd control or fixing upstart groups in "their place," took on a commanding importance.

What, then, could be done to change the pathology from which disorder grew? The most obvious step was to forestall danger with force, as police did at Tompkins Square in New York City in 1874. Laborers were given a permit to rally. The night before their meeting, it was revoked, but no one bothered to inform them, not even the police sent to watch the protestors. Only after a crowd had gathered did authorities order it to disperse. Police moved in at once. Mounted officers rode into the masses, clubbing everyone in their way. Those who were the most poorly dressed received special attention.[14]

Less noticeably, but with equal severity, the law moved against the vagrants. Starting in New Jersey in 1876, "tramp acts" made it a crime for workers without visible means of support to move from one place to the next. Any tramp who kindled a fire on a highway or came into a yard uninvited in Ohio earned himself three years in prison. Civil rights belonged to stable members of society; where vagrants were concerned, judges could leap from legal reasoning to hysterical abuse to justify heavy penalties. The tramp was "a public enemy," the Ohio Supreme Court insisted, in defending prison terms for those having no fixed abode, "a thief, a robber, often a murderer, and always a nuisance."[15]

At their worst, the laws were used against blacks needed for field labor in the South, hobos during wheat-harvest season in Kansas, and striking workers everywhere; without proof of a job, they could be locked up for thirty to ninety days or contracted out to a landowner to work off their sentence. Mechanics, engineers, sailors, and cooks all took to the road and ended up in jail. Perhaps one arrest in ten in Buffalo, New York, was done under the tramp act: 2,110 in 1891 alone. Author Jack London found his wandering ways took him before a judge and onto a chain gang. It was to the advantage of police to enforce the tramp acts to the utmost. Often their salaries were based on how many prisoners the jails held and how many meals had to be provided; the more inmates, then, the better. Occasionally, bums were enticed into town with promises of women, liquor, cigarettes, even cash—and given bread and water and the prison lockstep to learn instead. A cook lost his job and left town, seeking another employer. The first town he got to jailed him. So did the next, and the next. "Only the rich can get justice," muckraker Henry Demarest Lloyd charged; "only the poor cannot escape it."[16]

Punishments for crime stiffened, as well. Throughout the Gilded Age, communities applied themselves to increasing the sophistication of the machinery for keeping order. During the nineteenth century, the entire criminal justice system was remade, from prisons to policemen to parole. Constabulary duty was expanded, professionalized, and divided into its separate functions. It had to be. New York City was not New Rochelle. With population expanding, with crowds of strangers swelling the size of the towns, neighborhoods could not protect themselves. Citywide police departments were needed. By the 1880s, patrolmen were bearing firearms. In the years that followed, duties other than fighting crime were peeled away. At the start of the Gilded Age, for example, policemen handled everything, from preventing child abuse to providing cheap lodgings for tramps. As with everything else, specialization became the rule. Other groups, such as the New York Society for the Prevention of

Cruelty to Children, handled matters relating to the exploiting of children. In 1877, it returned 25 lost children, in 1897, 2,810.[17]

Efforts to control the disorder in American life went beyond the application of policeman's clubs and suppression of the "dangerous classes." Self-control became one of the driving forces in middle-class life. It could be seen in conductor Theodore Thomas's campaign to turn concert audiences from rowdy participants into courteous listeners, always punctual and meekly accepting whatever musical program their betters selected; it showed itself in the Knights of Labor's commitment to temperance; it explained the stream of etiquette books and child-rearing manuals, setting down rules of deportment and discouraging displays of public emotion.[18]

More disturbingly, by putting such an emphasis on the need for stability in American life, those with power in society used the law to fix it more firmly in their hands, or at least to slow the pace of changes that might bring about a greater equality.

The Conservative Chill Touches Women's Rights Crusaders

The chilling effect was unmistakeable when it came to reforms that seemed to threaten the traditional family, especially the husband's prerogatives. Before the Civil War, divorce laws had loosened. A court could end a marriage with a simple decree, and the grounds multiplied to more than four hundred. From all over the Northeast, wives flocked to the Connecticut "divorce mills," and, in one joke, a conductor bawled out to train passengers, "Indiana, next stop! Ten minutes for dining, five for divorce!" Feminists such as Elizabeth Cady Stanton and Susan B. Anthony would have liked to ease the process even further; it was their belief that until marriage became a partnership of equals, unhappy wives needed all the chances for escape that they could get. A few radicals like Victoria Woodhull, "the Bewitching Broker of Wall Street," even compared marriage with slavery. Woodhull had emancipated herself with a divorce and remarriage, and was so open-minded that she shared her house with both husbands simultaneously. Feminism, as she saw it, would legalize prostitution and encourage free love. Spiritualism and suffrage alike inspired her vision for the woman's rights movement. "We mean treason, we mean secession," she exclaimed, in a speech to fellow activists. "We are plotting revolution; we will overthrow this bogus republic and plant a government of righteousness in its stead."[19]

Friends like these did the women's movement worse damage than enemies. By the mid-1870s, feminists were scrambling for cover. Even Stanton and Anthony dropped the divorce issue, and the more conservative advocates in the American Woman Suffrage Association framed the case for women's suffrage on how it would make the family stronger. Within a decade, the laws began to limit the number of grounds required for divorce. Reformers were not really trying to strengthen women's subjection to men. If anything, their belief in feminine frailty made them readier to help wives escape from unkind husbands. Courts gazed with friendlier eyes than before on wives' right to a separation for mental cruelty: this might involve the husband's telling dirty stories in front of neighbors or his frigid indifference. Divorce rates went up sharply, especially at the century's end. But all the changes had a conservative purpose: to keep true marriage, with all its obligations, from being broken without good cause, and to leave it to judges to decide whether separation was warranted. That aim went hand in hand with judges' readiness to decide which parent had child custody. Only nine states gave husband and wife equal rights of guardianship. Elsewhere, the probate judge played Solomon. "His power outrivals that of kings," one judge wrote,

> *Your children, when you prove unfit,*
> *Are whisked away by sovereign writ.*
> *In short, it may truly be said,*
> *He has you living, he has you dead.*
> *The moral is, as on you trudge,*
> *Propitiate the Probate Judge.*[20]

The conservative impulse did not simply oppress women. It protected them, because it assumed them weak enough by nature to need protecting. There were harsh exceptions. North Carolina's Supreme Court waved away "trifling cases," where the flogging that a husband administered his wife left no permanent injury. But most courts saw themselves as guardians for the "frailer sex." Wife beating, no matter what size the stick, broke the law in most places, and the laws got tougher. Maryland and Delaware actually brought back the whipping post as punishment for spousal abuse— and used it. Until the 1880s, most states set the age for women to consent to sexual intercourse at ten years old (Delaware thought seven old enough). Laws like that virtually invited seduction and rape. Reforms raised the minimum age to fourteen or higher.[21]

Yet the protective impulse also assumed that women were less capable of handling their affairs than men. Gilded Age manners saw womanly reputation as so frail a thing that it demanded chaperones on every public occasion, including visits to the theater. Crossing the street, the able-bodied lady must rely on the arm of the sturdy policeman, and if she dared write a letter to the editor of the local newspaper, it must be couched in the language of one naturally shy about intruding on matters outside of her proper sphere. Over time, laws did chip away the common law rule that "husband and wife are one person, and that one is the husband." Before the Gilded Age ended, a wife had gained broad powers to lend and borrow, to control property she brought into marriage or acquired after it. Even so, state laws doled out rights in skimping amounts. Many states forbade wives to go into business for themselves, administer estates, or even act as guardian over their own children. A husband who shot his wife's lover had a good chance of acquittal and even applause for showing such manly honor. But as the New York *Herald* put it, "What would be chivalry in a husband is murder in a wife." Women were likelier to be convicted, unless they convinced the jury that they were out of their heads at the time. Juries bought it readily: doctors agreed that the frailer sex was mentally unstable at the best of times, hysterical and impulsive.[22]

The Perpetuation of Racial Inequality from 1887–1900

No group felt the tightening of control more than blacks, and in the mid-1880s, the imposition grew considerably stronger. Before then, to be sure, conditions were far from equal. Free Negroes had worked, lived, and prospered only where the laws permitted them in prewar years. Theaters and shows had no separate section for them; they were cut out entirely. After the war, conservatives tried to apply the old code to the newly freed. Rather than allow blacks to come into city parks, Savannah officials closed them. Republicans put civil rights laws on the books that were instantly ignored, and provided for "equal" accommodations rather than shared ones. Streetcars were an exception, but from railroads to steamboats, blacks usually found themselves paying first-class fares for second-class service. Even where laws did not force separation, custom usually did. Blacks went to their own saloons, billiard parlors, churches, and schools. Nashville boasted a colored skating rink, Montgomery set up colored fairgrounds. Cities built separate cemeteries and parks. Which park belonged to which race might not be stated openly, but everyone knew. Usually, brothels drew the color line; in Atlanta, black whores and white did business on separate blocks.[23]

So custom dictated, until the 1880s. But around 1887, custom no longer seemed enough. Race prejudice was taking a keener edge in the Deep South. Thomas Dixon, Jr., reflected the change at its most extreme. A tormented man, good at nearly everything he tried and unwilling to carry any of them through, Dixon found fame with a novel he wrote in answer to the folksy comic blacks of the *Uncle Tom* stage show. In his novel, Negroes were not children—they were beasts. Learning or the vote just made them more dangerous. They killed their unwanted children, settled lovers' quarrels with an axe, raped blonde eleven-year olds, and took over public office. When the publisher Walter Hines Page got the manuscript, he found himself captivated—so captivated, in fact, that while reading it on his way to work, he was knocked over by a cab. Page simply picked himself up and started reading where he had left off. Needless to say, Dixon got a contract for his book. When *The Leopard's Spots* came out in 1902, it sold a million copies. Dixon's *The Clansman* came soon after and did just as brisk a business. Eventually, the two would turn into a sellout drama, adapted from stage to screen by D. W. Griffith in the first great American feature picture, *Birth of a Nation*.[24]

By 1910, language like Dixon's was common, and not just in the cotton South. Southern newspapers trumpeted every "outrage" any black man was reported to have committed, and their readers believed every single story. Black women were sluts, the editors of one respected northern weekly explained. Naturally, when mothers were of "such easy virtue, their sons can hardly be checked in their most unmanageable crime"—though the magazine thought that burning the accused alive might help. Scholarly authority up North backed up the white supremacists. Professor Nathaniel Shaler of Harvard ascribed blacks' civilized qualities to imitation of their masters; now set free from white restraints, they were reverting to the savages they had once been. Francis Wilcox, chief statistician of the U.S. Census, had figures to show that black crime was soaring, and University of Pennsylvania zoology professor Edward D. Cope showed why. Sutures in the skull promoted intelligence, he explained. Those in whites grew lifelong, those in blacks until around age fourteen. To Professor Cope, America's duty was clear. It must deport every black in the country.[25]

Actions spoke uglier than words. Lynching had happened in slave days, but not so commonly. Then the victim ranked as too valuable a piece of property to waste at a rope's end. By the 1880s, lynchings were increasing. They were most common in

**The VIRGIN MARY and the CHILD CHRIST .
Could the Child Christ possibly be of the same flesh as the Negro?**

By the early 1900s, when *The Black a Beast* appeared with illustrations like this one, prejudice had reached its worst point in forty years. (*The Black a Beast*, 1903)

the Black Belt, along the Gulf coast and in the sparsely settled uplands of the Old Southwest where cotton grew. In these areas, the black population was rising steeply and there was precious little legal machinery. But incidents happened everywhere. In Memphis, four blacks lost their lives for starting a grocery store in competition with the white one. In Kentucky, a black was hanged on the courthouse steps for allegedly encouraging a white boy to steal. Blacks just passing through were especially vulnerable, and those accused of "outraging" white women the most surely doomed. Let death come in a manner "so horrible that the memory of the deed will linger in that neighborhood for a hundred years," a Florida editor urged readers.[26]

Lynching even took on the trappings of a formal ceremony. It was most likely to happen in July, after much planning, and with a well-disciplined crowd, led by "worthy" and "prominent" citizens, who found no trouble in getting officers to hand over their prisoner. Men would do the actual killing, but women and children were welcome to watch. Some people might bring picnic lunches, others brought cameras to catch the victim's last moments or a gramophone machine to pick up his screams. These could go on quite a while longer than the three minutes available on a wax cylinder. The victim might be hanged, but not always, and this punishment was least likely when the charge was rape. Lynching therefore grew more elaborate, with emasculation before death and degradation of the remains after. One of the worst took place in Georgia in 1899, when Sam Hose was accused of murdering a farmer and raping his wife. Whites advertised their intention to seize and burn him the following Sunday. Two thousand people showed up. Railroads ran special trains, carrying crowds on excursion fares in from Atlanta. Hose was chained to a pine tree and castrated. Then, as a newspaper reported gleefully, "the fun began." He was doused in kerosene, set ablaze, and, before the remains had cooled, was parceled out for souvenirs. One participant carried a slice of Hose's heart to give the governor. The governor may have been shocked, but not half so much as when blacks called on him to protest the lynching. Their distress, he could only conclude, was due to race prejudice.[27]

One could think of any number of reasons for white society's reaction and Deep South alarmists: hard times down on the farm, or white yeoman fearing competition from black sharecroppers and resenting a process that was degrading them to the status of tenants, too. A few incidents gave fears of integration some grounding. Southern courts had begun ruling that a first-class ticket entitled anyone, whatever his or her race, to a first-class seat in a railroad car. Only a few companies put on separate cars. "You can't make a g—d— cent out of it," one executive explained, in refusing to segregate passengers.[28] But much of the pressure for Jim Crow seems to have arisen with the coming of age of generations from both races born since the war. Blacks trained in deference by years of slavery were passing away. So were memories of the savage lesson in politics the Redeemers had taught them. Whatever the reasons, by 1890 the cotton South was suffering a massive anxiety attack.

First came the laws ordering separation on railroad cars; in four years, eight states had acted. Then came railroad stations and streetcars. One by one, the prohibitions piled up. After 1900, they came thick and fast: ferryboats, steamboats, zoos, jails, chain gangs. Cities established zones where blacks must live, and, like Nashville, separate graveyards where they must lie thereafter, a mere wall away from white sepulchres. Atlanta even arranged for every court to have separate Bibles for witnesses to swear on. Downtown, the Prudential Insurance building had two passenger elevators, but blacks were restricted to the lift nearby, labeled, "For Negroes and other large packages." But at least that was better than the city zoo and libraries, none of which admitted blacks on any terms. Where court failed to act, mobs sometimes dispensed a justice of their own, rampaging through railroad cars to throw off "respectable colored ladies and leading colored men" traveling in the first-class cars.[29]

The Atlanta Compromise

In a conservative time, reform itself would need conservative raiment. In the women's suffrage movement, many advocates gave up trying to claim equal rights, and stressed the virtue that went with true womanhood. Frail as she was, woman needed the vote for her protection, but her femininity would bring morality to men's politics. By making their own separate institutions, by extending "woman's place," activists could find work of importance to do, without challenging men's control.[30] So it was, too, with Booker T. Washington, when he rose before a crowd at the Atlanta Cotton States and International Exposition in 1895. Like any other southerner, he assured his listeners, the Negro wanted no outside intervention, even on his own behalf. The South must settle its race problem its own way. Facts were facts. Whatever Reconstruction promised, whites remained unwilling to share government with any other race. Prejudice could not be wished away. Instead, Washington offered what would come to be called his "Atlanta Compromise." Rather than strive hopelessly to win the empty advantage that politics afforded, let blacks turn their energies to making their own lives better. "No race can prosper till it learns that there is as much dignity in tilling a field as in writing a poem," Washington pleaded. Hard work and education would give the Negro property and bring him closer to equality than voting ever could. Facing a sturdy, conservative black propertied class, white prejudice would melt away. As one reporter paraphrased it, "Get yourself right, and the world will be all right."[31]

Promising acquiescence rather than agitation, embracing the values of the New South, Washington leaped instantly to the acknowledged leadership of American blacks. Black southerners spoke reverently of "Uncle Booker"; white businessmen applauded a philosophy so safe—so apparently reasonable—and opened their checkbooks for Tuskegee Institute. Presidents consulted Washington before choosing blacks for office and welcomed his corrections on advance copies of their annual message, where "the Negro question" came up.[32]

Then and later, more militant blacks accused Washington of selling out rights already given for empty promises of fair treatment. By the early 1900s, they had found a spokesman. William E. B. Du Bois was northern-born and educated at Fisk, Harvard, and the University of Berlin. With such a background, it was only natural that he would find the humiliating retreat that accommodation demanded an especially galling one. A first-rate scholar, he taught at Atlanta University to widespread acclaim. But his color barred him from the world beyond the school except on Jim Crow terms. When his infant son died, Du Bois cried out with "the awful gladness in my heart. . . . No bitter meanness now shall sicken his baby heart till it die a living death, no taunt shall madden his happy boyhood. . . . Well sped, my boy, before the world had dubbed your ambition insolence, had held your ideals unattainable, and taught you to cringe and bow. Better far this nameless void . . . than a sea of sorrow for you." Twice Tuskagee offered Du Bois a position; twice he refused it. When he published *The Souls of Black Folk* in 1903, he threw down an open challenge to Washington's doctrines. Instead of acceptance, blacks must agitate, protest, and resist.

But where, in the end, could this lead? When segregation came to Savannah's streetcars in 1906, blacks refused to ride them. The boycott cost the companies $50,000. Nashville blacks raised the money for steam autobuses of their own, rather than submit. When the Southern Bank in that city built separate tellers' windows, black depositors took their savings elsewhere. But the boycott broke, just as it would in Atlanta, Augusta, and Rome; the autobuses could not handle the city's steep hills nor the steep tax authorities levied on them. Jim Crow laws stayed on the books, and the separate windows remained in the bank. Using white sources to make her case, black Mississippian Ida Wells-Barnett documented the mob violence against blacks and refuted the apologists who blamed it on black ravishers. But the price of speaking out was high: in 1892, a mob smashed up her newspaper office and drove her out of the South. A black nationalist like Robert Charles of New Orleans might fight for his life, as he did when the police came to his rooms to arrest him for a scuffle with a patrolman one evening in 1900. He shot the police captain as the latter broke through the door, and he then escaped. "If one negro can hold 20,000 at bay, what can 10,000 negroes do?" a Boston admirer would marvel later. But Charles was killed in the end. So were nearly a dozen blacks who just happened to be in the wrong place when white mobs careened through the streets, demanding vengeance.[33]

"I am not deceived," Washington told listeners wearily in 1911. "I do not overlook the wrongs that often perplex and embarrass us in this country." Against the unfairness in school funding, the discrimination north and south, and the lynch mobs, he spoke as militantly as Du Bois himself. Quietly, behind the scenes, Washington helped press court challenges against Jim Crow. His faith in self-help was genuine, certainly, but his Atlanta Compromise was based as much on the realization that, with most of the money, scholarly sophistry, mass media, and guns on the other side, accommodation seemed like the best of many bad alternatives for black southerners. Washington's was the counsel of despair as much as hope, and the hope looked increasingly hollow set alongside the front-page stories of racial violence.[34]

Vigilanteism

Where matters of race and ethnicity were concerned, however, the South was an extreme example, not a unique one. The "white-cap" movement, with hooded night riders applying violence against minority groups, began in Indiana in 1887. Soon it had spread as far as California. Hispanic ranchers and herders joined it against their rich white competitors who had seized most of the public range. Anglos in southern Texas applied the lash and arsonist's torch to Mexican property; whites in the Panhandle turned its methods against blacks.

That same tolerance for violence meant that in the West and South, vigilante action was apologized for, even honored. The worst case took place in New Orleans after the acquittal of the Italian defendants. When a mob of 20,000 assembled at Beauregard Square, the prison guards fled and the warden saved his building by opening the cell doors. The defendants never made it out of the building. The crowds broke in and shot down eleven of them, then propped their bodies against a wall as a public display. There should have been an outcry, and so there was—in Italy. A grand jury refused to indict the mob's ringleaders, while the jurors that had acquitted the victims lost their jobs and were run out of town.[35]

Vigilante movements gave themselves legal cover out West. Generally, vigilanteism was a somewhat more exclusive practice than lynching, through the largest vigilance committee had thousands of members, and the medium-sized groups had several hundred. But the leaders of society ran the show, and gave their special attention to those in the lowest caste of western life. Vigilance movements functioned under a body of self-made law. Some even wrote constitutions, sworn to by all participants. The accused might actually get a formal trial and a chance to defend himself from charges. Some victims actually were acquitted or let off with a beating, but in fifty years 511 people lost their lives. Closely related to vigilanteism were the private armies of the range—stock owners' organizations and Homesteaders' Protective

Associations—many of them chartered by the state. Some of them hired lawyers. Others employed regiments of gunmen. Stockmen might call their hirelings "cattle detectives" or "stock inspectors," but their inspections never needed repeating. They would ride down bands of rustlers, kill them all, and depart.[36]

As the police professionalized, vigilanteism lost its moral authority out West and the Deep South's violence set that section apart more distinctly, but the underlying American impulse remained, to impose an order that seemed ever further out of reach. However ironically, the spokesmen for conservatism and order became spokesmen for the use of force, even violence, to solve the disputes in society. "If the club of the policeman, knocking out the brains of the rioter, will answer," said the *Independent* in 1877, "then well and good. But if it does not, . . . then bullets and bayonets, canister and grape . . . constitute the one remedy. . . . Napoleon was right when he said that the way to deal with a mob was to exterminate it."[37]

Law at the End of a Nightstick

If "New York's finest" had a hero, it would have been Alexander S. Williams, a police captain whose courage and strength made him the star of many a citywide parade. He earned his pay, and, as inquiries into police corruption later revealed, quite a bit more as well. He also earned his nickname; for "Clubber" took pride in seeing to it that any thief, vagrant, foreigner, or striker he brought in was indelibly marked. After fifteen years on the force, he had had 358 complaints lodged against him and been fined 224 times for brutality. Then he was promoted. And why not? Others shared his belief that there was "more law at the end of a policeman's nightstick than in a decision of the Supreme Court."[38]

For too many Americans, personal and moral authority *were* something ultimately proven by the use of force. The romanticization of the Civil War, the doctrine of "survival of the fittest," the working-class idea that manliness included the readiness to repay an insult with a fist, all did their share to sanctify violence. That Indians lost against soldiers, or that city "rabble" gave way before militiamen, became one more proof of who was better than whom. This kind of thinking was not the whole story of the Gilded Age, by any means. Alongside it, set the peacemakers and missionaries, boards of arbitration, and churchgoers; against the pattern of lynch mob violence that characterized Georgia, set the energy with which sheriffs and local communities in Virginia prevented it from happening. Still, the disorder and the search for control were too glaring to overlook.

What, then, did they say about "progress" itself? The question preyed on no mind more than that of America's favorite humorist, Samuel Langhorne Clemens, or "Mark Twain," as he signed himself. A master of the western vernacular, Twain's comic world, where a cheating miner could win the frog-jumping contest by filling his rival's frog with buckshot, had already taken on streaks of darkness by the time he wrote *Tom Sawyer* in 1874. Mingled with the sunny larks of boyhood along the Mississippi were melodramatic adventures involving murder and betrayal. Ten years more, and *Huckleberry Finn* would give the same setting a grimmer tone. Floating down the river, the main character is fleeing from a brute of a father, but not into an idyllic world. Instead, Huck is a witness to a South of bigotry, slavery, lynch-mobbing, and a "code of honor" based on bloodletting. Even the comic rapscallions pretending to be a long-lost Duke and the French Dauphin end up tarred and feathered.

And worse was to follow. Twain began *A Connecticut Yankee in King Arthur's Court* as farce, where Hank Morgan, having got the worst of a "misunderstanding conducted with crowbars," wakes in sixth-century England. Before long, Yankee know-how and modern gadgets are playing the merry deuce with a world rotten with chivalry and smothered in superstition. Hank saves himself from execution one time by "causing" an eclipse of the sun, and gets rescued on another occasion by a host of knights on bicycles. The high-spirited adventure stayed in the final version. So did the satire. But the whole tone had changed before the last chapter into a carnival of mass destruction. With electrified wire fences and Gatling guns, Hank and his faithful few mow down twenty-five thousand knights. "Land, what a sight!" the narrator exulted. "We were enclosed in three walls of dead men." "Imprisoned" was a better word: the victors dared not leave their machine-made fortress, and were sure to die if they stayed among the putrefying corpses. And they did die—every one of them.

Hank Morgan never grasped the moral, but Twain made it plain: between the barbarism of Old England and the civilization of New England, there was not a particle of real difference, where the use of violence was concerned. "The march of civilization" that Hank led carried him in a full circle. What prospect, then, that the future would ever show progress over the past, except in its ability to destroy? In their emphasis on the need for bloodletting as the means of bringing a kinder, nobler world, the Chicago anarchists may have been more American than they supposed.

Chapter 12

Salvation Armies: Self-Help and Virtue's Legions

One hot summer day in 1894, a white North Carolina woman decided to take her children out for an amusement. A minister was baptizing converts in the creek. "This was a stylish occasion," she wrote her husband, off in Congress, "and the preacher, a tall fine looking negro, was dressed in a long black robe fitted at the waist and with a black cap on and looked like a R. C. priest." Fifteen blacks, robed in white with white caps, came for immersion. Bessie Henderson found it "quite picturesque when they entered the water, but the African nature had to assert itself in spite of *robes*. They clapped hands, shrieked, clasped the preacher and were generally idiotic. I am glad to have seen it once."[1]

Henderson's entertainment was the Baptist's defining moment in life. We may imagine that Social Darwinism dominated American thought throughout the Gilded Age. It didn't. Far more often than historians would let us believe, people took their cues from God than Godkin.

Take away religion from most history textbooks, and scarcely a line would be lost. Take it away from a history of the Gilded Age, and the times lose their meaning. Foreigners noticed at once how many churches, cathedrals, and synagogues there were. The 1870 census counted 72,000. At least half of a largely Protestant America worshiped on Sundays, prayed through the rest of the week, and glimpsed the hand of the Lord always. "It was God who sent you children, made the potatoes turn out well, put the blight on the orchard trees, and caused the roan mare to sicken and die," one Christian would remember.[2]

Americans Express Their Faith

American religion came in as many varieties as its people at the start of the Gilded Age. Four million Roman Catholics attended some four thousand churches and chapels, most of them in northern cities or southern Louisiana. In Utah, Mormons had virtually built a nation-state around the Great Salt Lake. Minor sects, among them the Mennonites, Amish, and Shakers, had built communities of their own, unstained by an outer world's corruptions. Within the great Protestant mass, denominations vied for converts. "I was so amused when you asked if Mr. C. was a Baptist," one lady wrote another, "—*no indeed* I never would have married him if such had been the case, and I am truly thankful he is an Episcopalian." But other Protestants, figuring one kind of preaching as good as another, would show up for whatever church took their fancy that week. New England Congregationalists went to churches that their great-grandparents had built. They heard crisp sermons under "wooden steeples, whose white painted sides," an observer remarked, "sparkle in the bright sunlight uncommonly like marble." Villages in the Appalachians, unable to afford a minister, might gather to hear the Methodist circuit rider, who showed up every other Sabbath and preached to as many as six congregations. Or worshipers could attend camp meetings just after the harvest, and spend as many as a few weeks hearing three meetings a day. Pious folks wallowed in hellfire exhortation there, while less easily stirred types brought the fixings for a picnic and "a few days of love-making in the woods."[3]

As ever, true believers lamented about piety gone soft. "People don't go to church as they should," a North Carolinian wrote, "and I am fearful somebody will wake up at the judgment disappointed." Country ministers had the most to complain about. Besides appealing to backsliders, they might have to dig their own potatoes, butcher a hog, and even hammer together a coffin for the person at whose funeral they would be reading the service. With such poor pay, and with so few others in the community to provide leadership, the black minister found himself even more hard-pressed. As a Southern Baptist put it, he had to act as "a horse doctor, weather prophet, must attend the living, bury the dead, tell the farmer when to plant, act as a bondsman for all his people." And in what coin were their efforts repaid? "In this section churches, which once flourished, have been disbanded," a newspaper in Alabama's Black Belt reported, "and the buildings from which the Holy Word has been expounded by eloquent men . . . are now the homes of goats and hogs and bats."[4]

In fact, the great story in Protestantism since the Civil War was one of growth, particularly among three million former slaves. Even before the fighting stopped, an army of ministers rushed south to bring them the Gospel. Northern missionaries from the African Methodist Episcopal and African Methodist Episcopal Zion Church led the way, but they could not match the Baptists' influence. By 1890, black Baptists outnumbered AME members four to one. Altogether, by 1903, three million black communicants of all faiths attended some twenty-six thousand churches. All the denominations published newspapers and magazines and sent missionaries of their own to uplift the people of Africa, England, and Latin America. "Within his own parish he is practically priest and pope," an observer wrote of the black minister.[5]

Religion gave Americans more than salvation. As blacks emigrated into northern cities, their churches became the center of community activity, with girls' clubs and recreation centers. Some ran mutual benefit societies, offering life insurance policies and sick-pay. Their ministers were both moral and political guides. For many women, church activities opened up possibilities that the rest of public life denied them. Often, they outnumbered men—except, of course, in the pulpit and in church government. Men ran church finances and attended regional conferences as delegates; as deacons or elders, they enforced gospel discipline, and in some denominations, enforced the scriptural injunction against women so much as speaking in church meeting. But a revival generally swept up women first. Their religious spirit drew in husbands and children soon after. Out of the churches came benevolent associations and missionary societies, many of them formed and run by women. As for the Sunday schools, they belonged to women, and gave them a forum for expressing their own views of what Christianity meant.[6]

What Christianity meant, first and foremost, was the guidance of behavior in life and the saving of souls. Throughout the Gilded Age, this would be church's main aim, and, for many of them, its only aim. Yet so forceful an institution could not help being swept up in the moral problems of the day—of vice, poverty, and uncontrolled social change. Religion, after all, only began with Sabbath services. True faith had to affect one's whole behavior. It must confront tempting sins: the traveling circus, where female costumes "hesitated to begin and ended almost immediately," the use of tobacco, known to cause "many cases of emasculation," and the "disgusting craze" for roller skating, a devilish device for undermining self-respect. Church members who swore, drank, or played cards stood less of a chance of coming before the congregation for punishment than they had before the war. Still, it often happened, and in small towns, getting "turned out of the church" brought a social disgrace few sinners could bear for long. But the conscience that religion fashioned could be depended on to enforce morals, as it did with one Louisiana widow coaxed into selling her cow on Sunday. "May our merciful Father in Heaven pardon me for this desecration of his holy day!" she wrote in her diary, after reflecting on her act. She even tried to return the purchaser's money.[7]

Reforming personal behavior was the church's responsibility. But what about reforming the ills of society as well? On this, there was no agreement. A belief in individual responsibility both strengthened and challenged Social Darwinism's case for leaving individuals to make their own destinies. When disorder broke out, ministers could take as conservative a line on social problems as Herbert Spencer himself. Some of them condemned strikes. Other deplored the eight-hour day. Yet Social Darwinism and religious teaching did not really sit well together. If Spencer was right, self-interest was the one true source of civilization's advance. Implicitly, Social Darwinism confused the idea of people being better off with the concept of people becoming better. Flinging aside a sermon that showed how faith in the Gospels explained every great "success" from Pittsburgh to Packingtown, one Christian spotted the blasphemy: it would make the property-poor Christ "the conspicuous failure of history."[8]

Instead of self-interest being morally right, ministers argued, whatever was morally right ultimately was in humanity's self-interest. One's first responsibility was not to oneself, but to God and to others. Indeed, among the pietists, strongest in the evangelical Protestant denominations, a virtual command lay on right-thinking people to change the world to fit the will of the Lord, and at once. Because religion with them was a matter of faith, rather than ritual, anyone could be saved by making the personal effort to take God's grace. But if anyone could be saved, it followed that *all* could be saved. A sinful world could be purged of evil, and what could be must be: those possessed of the Lord's word had a duty to bring the world as close to Christ's kingdom on earth as they could. "It is the duty of the minister of the Gospel to preach on every side of political life," Reverend Beecher thundered in 1862. "I do not say that he *may*; I say that he *must*. That man is not a shepherd to his flock who fails to teach that flock how to apply moral truth to every phase of ordinary practical duty."[9] Such a duty showed itself in two broad ways: the desire to help the unfortunate and to cleanse society of vice.

Historians have been dismissive of Gilded Age philanthropy, and especially of that by the "Robber Barons." Some of them see it as a fad, others as an attempt to foist high European culture on America, with the rich as the tastemakers. J. Pierpont Morgan, Wall Street's greatest banker in the late nineteenth century, was an original patron for the Metropolitan Museum of Art and the American Museum of Natural History. Modeled on England's Rugby, the prep school at Groton stood on land his money helped buy.[10]

Yet elitism fails to tell the whole story. Elite institutions did not replace the pleasures of the middling sort; they supplemented them. Nor did magnates simply play patrons of the arts. Morgan put over $1 million into a new building for the New York Lying-In Hospital, an institution caring for pregnant women unable to afford prenatal care or food. Rockefeller bankrolled the University of Chicago in its early years. By 1900, he had found other causes: settlement houses, the Children's Aid Society, the New York Association for Improving the Condition of the Poor, and the Charity Organization Society. His money sustained the national campaign against child labor and for cleaning up the slums. As for Carnegie, he gave in retirement as relentlessly as he had earned before: money for seven thousand church organs, for medical care for the blind, for black colleges in the South, and to set up the beginnings of a retirement-pension system for teachers, which existed nearly a century later. Before he died in 1919, there was a Carnegie Institute in Pittsburgh, a Carnegie Institution in Washington, a Carnegie Hero Fund, an endowment for international peace, and a $135-million trust to spread knowledge and understanding.[11]

Carnegie, of course, was most known for the libraries. It was, in a sense, only seed money. Communities had to fill the shelves and keep the libraries going. "D'ye know what a libry is?" the fictional bartender Dooley quizzed his favorite customer.

> I suppose ye think it's a place where a man can go, haul down wan iv his fav'rite authors fr'm th' shelf, an' take a nap in it. That's not a Carnaygie libry. A Carnaygie libry is a large brown-stone, impenethrible buildin' with th' name iv th' maker blown on th' dure. Libry, fr'm th' Greek wurruds, libus, a book, an' ary, sildom—sildom a book. A Carnaygie libry is archytechoor, not litrachoor.[12]

But the gift was a real one. The shelves filled, and, whatever Carnegie's intention, millions benefited.

Beginning with ironmonger Peter Cooper's Union in 1859, businessmen funded polytechnic institutes and endowed professorships in engineering and practical mechanics. Philanthropists put out the money to make Radcliffe a Harvard for women and brewer Matthew Vassar gave women a college entirely their own. If Johns Hopkins became one of the first universities to accept applicants regardless of sex, the credit belonged to Mary Garrett, who made that a condition in endowment from her husband's estate.[13]

What inspired the Robber Barons? In some cases, they hoped to salvage their reputations or salve their consciences, but not always. Rockefeller started giving when he started getting. By the end of the 1870s, he was donating tens of thousands of dollars yearly to newsboys' homes, fresh air farms, and black aspirants to the ministry. Carnegie began his career already convinced that whoever died rich, died disgraced.[14] The explanation may really be so simple that we overlook it: moral responsibility, like the ambition to succeed, knew no class lines.

Scientific Philanthropy

The stale odor of sanctimony and the chill of scientific efficiency hang around the organized do-gooders of the age. Postwar charity relied upon scientific method as well as Christian love. During the Civil War, private agencies had discovered that to help the soldiers took more than gush or good intentions. Organization, coordination, and businesslike methods were essential. Clara Barton learned that lesson well. Born in Massachusetts on Christmas Day, she found her calling not in the schoolroom or the Patent Office, but in nursing the sick and comforting the dying in the Civil War. No matter how much aid she was sent, there was more that needed doing. "I carried [the supplies], and with my own hands wrapped them about the mangled, bleeding forms, or fed them to the thirsting famished soldiers just brought from the field of blood and strife," she wrote her friends. ". . .Today I am empty handed, and hourly expecting tidings of another battle. From all I gather, it must come soon, and . . . I have only my empty hands. *Can you help fill them again for me?*"[15]

Her hands were never empty again. Traveling to Switzerland in 1869, she met with officials of the International Committee of the Red Cross. Impressed by its principles, she was even more awed at its efficiency in the Franco-Prussian War, which broke out the following year: "no mistakes, no needless suffering, no starving, no lack of care, no waste, no confusion, but order, plenty, cleanliness and comfort wherever that little flag made its way." Drought, plague, and flood claimed victims year in, year out. Chicago burned in 1871 and 1874, Boston in 1872. Aid had poured in, but always in a haphazard way. Some giving necessarily had been wasted. All that could be changed, with preparation and coordination, and when Barton founded the American Red Cross in 1882, it provided both.[16]

Others shared her commitment to scientific philanthropy. In 1863, Massachusetts set the pattern for other commonwealths with a state board of charities, controlling help to all misfortunates, from the blind to deaf-mutes to paupers. There and elsewhere, boards visited correctional institutions, collected statistics, and published reports exposing conditions. In that sense, they made help to the needy not just more businesslike, but more humane. They took on the practice of letting out the care of paupers to the lowest bidder. In some states they took children and lunatics out of the poorhouses to find them more generous accommodations. Still, scientific philanthropy had a steely edge. Efficiency meant cutting out help to the "incorrigibles." There must be no soup kitchens serving food to all comers, no handouts to derelicts or lazybones. Help must go only to those in established institutions. "We must reform those mild, well-meaning, tender-hearted, sweet-voiced criminals who insist on indulging in indiscriminate charity," one reformer declared.[17]

Philanthropists did have a point. If there was not enough help for all, it made sense to allot money where most worthy. Without businesslike methods and tough-mindedness, this could not be done. But the chariness of the charitable also grew from assumptions about poor people. The religious belief that poverty often stemmed from sin (self-indulgence or sloth, most likely) added to the suspicion that alms might be given in vain. That, after all, is what the common phrase, "poor but honest," in fairy-stories was suggesting—that the two qualities usually went separate ways. If condition and character connected, logic dictated that making the beneficiary self-supporting would take moral uplift, and not just a chance at a job. The poor must be shown their own faults and taught to cure them, as a step out of the slums. "Do not say that a piece of bread, an old coat, a pair of cast-off shoes, a hat of archaic pattern, can do no harm," the dean of Yale's law school warned. " . . . For he who has discovered how to live, without labor, on the labor of other people, is on the direct road to . . . graduating from the pauper class into the criminal class."[18]

At its most severe, philanthropy looked like police work. Secular and religious philanthropists alike sent the "friendly visitor" (middle-class women, mostly) to the poor, partly a spy into the merits of the supplicant and partly a preacher providing "moral oversight for the soul." The caller's prosperity would be as good as a sermon. It would show how an upright character brought all the rewards in this world, as well as those in the next. Where industrial leaders ran a charity society, they put their energies into controlling the work-habits of the unemployed.[19]

The mix of science and sanctimony did not elicit universal applause. One poet lashed out at

> *The organized charity scrimped and iced*
> *In the name of a cautious, statistical Christ.*

If the Good Samaritan had shared the new charity, Reverend Lyman Abbott commented, he would not have rescued and tended the man set upon by thieves. "He would have hurried on to Jerusalem and organized a society for the relief of sick and wounded travelers, with a president, vice-president, treasurer, half a dozen secretaries, a board of managers, and a collecting agent in every district of Palestine."[20]

Perhaps, though, what mattered was not just how help was given, but that Americans gave it. When the Sea Islands off the Carolina coast were hit with a hurricane in 1893, the Red Cross did more than coordinate the aid that poured in. It set to work helping the inhabitants plant and fend for themselves. A thousand bushels of Irish potatoes were bought. Local ladies cut them up for seed; families planted them and raised a substantial crop. Sewing circles mended and prepared the cast-off clothing sent to unfortunates. A million feet of pine lumber was shipped downriver and placed on the landings at the islands; each man was then required to build his own house, with a garden as well. Not only did $30,000 end up feeding 30,000 people for a year. By the time the Red Cross closed up operations, the sufferers had raised more food than they could eat or sell. The black communities not only recovered. They did so with pride in their own efforts. A half dozen years later, when a hurricane devastated Galveston, the Sea Islanders came together and, poor though they were, collected $397 to send west, " 'cause dey suffers like we did, and de Red Cross is dar."[21]

Help for those in need came in every form, not just the scientific kind. Responding to a famine in India, Americans between Kansas City and Chicago donated 20,000 bushels of corn, and the Rock Island railroad hauled it for free. Women's groups in Philadelphia and Boston set up day nurseries and kindergartens for working families. New York had its Children's Aid Society, with a summer camp and a farm school for slumdwellers, and a Girl's Vacation Society to send young women upstate for several weeks' rest. With what little they had, Cleveland's black women founded a home for the aged poor, and Bostonians of all races donated reading material to the Lend a Hand Book Mission, to send thousands of volumes yearly to black churches and schools across the South.[23]

However much libraries, art galleries, fresh-air funds, music halls, and Sunday afternoon concerts softened the harshness of Gilded Age society, they did not change the basics. The poor stayed poor, the privileged kept their advantages, and the slums remained the horrors they had always been. Yet the tug of moral responsibility persisted throughout the age, as strong as the smugness of Social Darwinism. For many southern girls, the Young Woman's Christian Temperance Union of the South set spirits free and gave their idle hands endless tasks: supporting lunch houses and rest cottages for factory women, carrying solace to prisons and poorhouses, forming hygiene clubs, and setting up drinking fountains in the cities. It was in works, and not in faith alone, one member boasted, that they meant "to carry the philosophy of Jesus Christ into politics, . . . to cause morality to become the rock-bed of our national life and brotherhood the ozone of its atmosphere."[23]

The City as a Social Threat

The quickening pace of social change only gave an urgency to the moral forces in the Protestant countryside. Looking citywards, many Americans felt anxiety, even alarm. The homespun virtues of small towns seemed to be in danger.[24]

Anyone who ventured into a city could see depravities galore. Consider, for example, prostitution: Chicago had two hundred brothels just after the Civil War, plus a host of women who had gone into business for themselves. At least two thousand women plied their trade there every night. The business could be as high-toned as the Everleigh Club in Chicago with its gold-colored bathtubs and marble-inlaid beds. More middle-class establishments charged a dollar or two for a trick. Then there were the "cribs," unadorned, harrowing tenement houses, where some 250 prostitutes did their business in rooms only slightly bigger than closets. Visitors to Chinatown in San Francisco could find thirteen-year olds, their faces painted in India ink and Chinese vermilion, leaning out of casement windows to invite customers in. Many cities gave up trying to wipe out prostitution. They simply restricted it to special "red-light districts:" Guy Town in Austin, San Francisco's Barbary Coast, and the glamorous, notorious Storyville in New Orleans.[25]

One hardly needed to be a blue-nose to feel offense at a business institution that turned women into commodities and made money from adultery. Prostitution paid $40,000 a year for protection from police harassment in Kansas City. One New York brothel's "john book" showed that police made up a third of all customers. One prostitute in eleven took her own life. The trade made abortions, alcoholism, and drug abuse probable, and somewhere between one-half and three-fourths of the women contracted veneral disease.[26]

Or what of the saloon? There were plenty of reasons besides moral ones for controlling the sale of alcohol. Doctors asserted that a few cocktails turned the drinker's blood to water and burned the skin off the inside of the throat, and that by speeding up the heart beat to abnormal levels, the first glass of whiskey would compel another and another, just to prevent cardiac arrest. Every year, Prohibitionists warned, the liquor traffic destroyed half a million homes and left twice that many children "worse than orphaned." Prostitution, poverty, violence, and political corruption all could be traced back to the saloons.[27]

The city had plenty of other snares. Instead of the old-fashioned minstrel show mocking Negro pretensions, working-class audiences patronized the burlesque shows, where bold women sported their allure in tights and skimpy dresses and flaunted their sexuality. With a little work, one could find pornographic literature with such suggestive titles as *Only a Boy*, *A Night in a Moorish Harem*, and *The Lascivious London Beauty*. More discreet readers could drop by the barbershop and thrill to the sex and sensational crimes, cheaply printed and luridly illustrated on the pink paper of the *Police Gazette*. Gambling hells, cockfighting pits, and confidence men throve in the city. So did a whole working-class culture, where the Sabbath mattered most as a day of pleasure.[28]

What was to be done? Reformers offered many solutions. If the unchurched would not come to Christ, evangelicals decided, He must come to them. Tract societies spread the word among recent immigrants and Monday newspapers published a digest of Sunday's best sermons.[29] The Young Men's Christian Association established branches in every big city. More successful still was the Salvation Army, the self-proclaimed "Church of the Poor," which doled out food and faith simultaneously. Building soup kitchens, day nurseries, and homes for prostitutes, it sent out "slum brigades" to reclaim the streets for Christ, and collected a goodly following. A few established churches made themselves community centers. The "institutional church," as it was known, still held choir practice and converted sinners, but it drew the young with basketball courts and boys' clubs. All these efforts helped church attendance and eased the lives of the poor. They did little to reform the city's habits. Evangelist Dwight Moody got vast crowds at his revivals. Unfortunately, most of them were already professed Christians. Immigrants and infidels stayed home.[30]

Looking for the causes of depravity, some city planners found one in the chaos and squalor of the unplanned metropolis. When warehouses, brothels, and open sewers predominated, there was no way for citizens to raise their minds above the everyday. Change the environment, and those who lived in it might change as well. Give them parks instead of poolrooms, public dance halls instead of lewd "concert-saloons," and they would take the moral entertainment over the immoral. Give them a city of grand boulevards and vistas, monumental public buildings, and they would take enough pride in it to wear their citizenship as an honor, not to be soiled by a vote for wicked men.[31]

Such a dream inspired one of the most famous architects of his day, Daniel H. Burnham. In his city plan for Chicago in 1909, which the civic fathers adopted bits of, he built a city of dreams, where order and broad thoroughfares replaced ramshackle expansion, and where great parks broke up the sordid monotony of tenement and business district. At the center the city hall towered, big enough to spy from the suburbs. Already, Burnham had tried out his ideals in the last great exposition of the nineteenth century, the Chicago World's Fair. There, his "White City" offered a vision for what urban life might be like at its best, in a combination of Parisian (or, at any rate, plaster of Parisian) Beaux-Arts with classic columns evoking ancient Rome. Order and beauty merged. "The damage wrought by the World's Fair," Louis Sullivan wrote savagely, "will last for half a century. . . . It has penetrated deep into the constitution of the American mind, effecting there lesions significant of dementia."[32]

Some designers saw monuments as the means of inspiring a new sense of duty. Cities raised innumerable statues. They built fountains and laid out squares to make in an instant the grandeur that two millennia had given European cities. The "dangerous classes" gave it a chilly reception. After all, when an improvement was laid out, planners did not knock down the mansions of the rich, but the tenements of the poor. When Nashville residents proposed a "delightful park," in 1888, they favored putting it where the squalid "Black Bottom" stood. No one asked what would happen to the residents.[33]

Moral Reform

But reforming Americans' behavior did not need to wait on reforming their hearts and minds. It couldn't. Bartenders did not take the pledge, even if a few of their customers did. New drinkers replaced the old. Laws could not change the hearts of men, but they could clean the moral atmosphere to make it easier for sinners to redeem their souls. Coercive government would not take liberty away so much as enhance it, by freeing people from temptation and dependence on vicious habits. "Liberty is not license," one pietist summed up: "*it is the right to do right.*" To the argument that a people should be free to do as they pleased with their property and spare time, temperance reformers agreed—as long as that freedom did not injure others, the way whiskey-selling did. "Can any man in his senses believe that it is the right of any man to drink that which will cause him to commit crime?"[34]

Moral reformers concentrated on many causes, not just one. As one of New York's self-appointed censors for forty years, Anthony Comstock put all his 210 pounds of muscle and bone and all the ardor in his soul into the fight on smut. He formed the New York Society for the Suppression of Vice and used it to enforce statues that the police neglected. When Congress passed a law against sending pornography through the mail in 1873, the Post Office picked Comstock as special agent, a natural choice. Nothing suggestive escaped his wrath: the classics of Balzac, Flaubert, the indecencies of Ovid, Voltaire, and Aristophanes, and the homoerotic poetry of Walt Whitman. His emissaries raided art studios to confiscate nude statues. If Comstock could have had his way, boxing and football would have been against the law, as exciters of violent passions. Boston had its Watch and Ward, run by the genteel of Beacon Hill, and most towns adopted similar vigilance societies. Because of "Comstockery," censors banned Mark Twain's *Huckleberry Finn* as impure, and Stephen Crane was forced to publish *Maggie: A Girl of the Streets* privately under an assumed name.[35]

Prostitution was harder to eliminate. New Orleans tried licensing brothels. Other cities put them under health regulations and ordered regular medical checkups for the prostitutes. Regulation worked in Europe, but reformers were appalled and

SUMMER-RESORT PIETY.

WHAT THE SACRED SEASIDE IS COMING TO.

Summer-Resort Piety.
Anthony Comstock would have approved. (*Puck*, 1883)

ended the experiment before it could show results. Beyond that, they were not able to go. The red-light districts survived into the twentieth century, when a larger coalition, strengthened by women's rights crusaders and widespread publicity about veneral disease, made headway.

Legislatures dominated by rural districts could do more against the desecration of the Protestant Sabbath. What resulted was a crazy-quilt of specific bans. New York made it illegal to sell milk, bread, or eggs, but permitted the retailing of meat and fish; when automobiles appeared at the end of the century, new statues allowed the sale of gas, oil, and tires, but forbade the buying of tire-jacks or antifreeze. Laws elsewhere forbade social visiting on Sunday, the operation of cheese factories, the running of mail-trains.[36]

Frances Willard and the Temperance Movement

None of these campaigns stirred the controversy and made as dramatic a change in habits as the fight to limit or outlaw the sale of alcohol. A host of groups pressed the cause: the Cadets of Temperance, the Catholic Total Abstinence Union, and the National League for the Suppression of the Liquor Traffic. The Women's Christian Temperance Union, though, would become the driving force among them all. It took as its emblem the white ribbon of purity. It published temperance songs for the Band of Hope, children converted to the cause and trained to challenge their drinking parents with water-tight argument. The WCTU Division of Prison and Jail Work visited inmates at convict labor camps and penitentiaries to pass out tracts, lesson books, and bouquets of flowers, tied with a white ribbon and carrying a Scriptural text. The WCTU's training school prepared missionaries and its committees gathered evidence from science and the Scriptures to hurl at the drinking classes.[37]

At their head marched Frances Willard, dean at Northwestern University and WCTU president for nearly twenty years. Before she joined the cause, the "Uncrowned Queen of American Womanhood" had been a rather diffident temperance advocate who saw the cause as a means of advancing her real interest, the women's movement. Her priorities changed quickly. A must at conventions, she kept order with a gavel made from the bung-starter of a closed down saloon. By the 1890s, she had turned the WCTU into one of the top lobbying forces in America. In time her likeness stood in the Capitol's Hall of Statuary, the first woman so honored.[38]

White Protestants and small-town residents led the way on temperance, but they found lots of allies. Catholic Sunday-school classes learned the same warnings about alcohol's effects that Protestant ones did. They even read the same WCTU *Envelope Leaflets*. The Father Mathew Societies could count thousands of Irish-Americans that it had brought round. So widely did the temperance appeal spread that the WCTU had to print its literature in sixteen languages.[39] Even black and white churches worked together for a time, and black colleges helped in the fight on Atlanta's gin joints. Then, as Jim Crow thought hardened, the southern Prohibitionists advanced their cause by race-baiting: the saloon must be closed down to prevent Negroes firing their spirits for rape. By 1907, Birmingham Dries, supporters of Prohibition, played

Frances Willard, head of the WCTU.
(Library of Congress)

up "PICTURES OF NUDE WOMEN ON BOTTLES OF WHISKEY SOLD TO THE NEGROES."[40]

A movement that broad had a good chance of carrying the day. Under the leadership of Governor John P. St. John, Kansas began the process in 1880 with a Prohibition amendment. By 1889, half a dozen states were bone dry. This might seem a poor showing, especially since three states would backtrack in the decade to come, but there was another way of looking at it. State constitutions might remain with the Wets; the Dries kept winning locally. When the Arkansas legislature beat a Prohibition amendment, 62 of the 74 counties voted to close their saloons anyway. Elsewhere, states limited the selling of liquor by requiring high license fees, forbidding sales within five hundred feet of a public park, and closing saloons on Sunday.[41]

Reformers cast the fight as one of the godly against the rumsellers. In fact, the Prohibition struggle showed just how divided the godly were on the question of making people good by law. Against the pietists stood what some historians have called the liturgist faiths: many Catholics, Jews, Episcopalians, and German Lutherans to name a few. They, too, took morality seriously. What set them apart was their skepticism that the world *could* be perfected, or that it was a Protestant state's business to try. If sinners shunned temptation because they feared the law rather than the Lord, were they any closer to salvation? What made the state a better judge of moral conduct than the church? What kept a Protestant-run government from defining good and evil to suit beliefs that other faiths did not share? Drinking was a case in point. Catholic and Protestant might agree that carousing was ill-advised, even immoral. Making it a sin to take a drink at all was another matter. Pietists could see the need for Sabbatarian laws. Open the parks, libraries, museums, or the Chicago World's Fair on Sunday, and irreligion would fester. But workers resented laws that kept them from enjoying their one day of rest; Jews saw no reason to shut down for a Christian's holy day, after honoring their own the day before; and Catholic immigrants used to the "Continental Sunday" did not feel themselves the worse for taking communion in the morning and lager beer in the afternoon.[42]

Behind the moral attitudes, non-Protestants sensed something uglier in the pietists' crusade, a war against all cultures different from their own. Too many temperance advocates let their real feelings slip. "Servile tools of this Romish priesthood plant their saloons upon every street corner, and locate their beer gardens under the very shadows of Protestant houses of worship, and use the enormous profits to fill the treasury of this foreign church," one of them raged. The WCTU might claim that it welcomed help from women neither native-born nor Protestant. But it also backed laws to keep out "the scum of the Old World." By the 1890s, it was blaming immigration for seven saloonkeepers in eight.[43]

The whole pietist agenda was rather like the debate topic that Mrs. Willard once suggested, "that the differences between Harvard and Yale be settled by arbitration, without resort to football." It seemed an attack on an urban culture that reformers detested more than they understood. City-dwellers could list some good reasons for appreciating the saloon. It gave the working class one of the few pleasures within its means: a few hours of relaxation and socializing among friends. For the price of a nickel beer, a worker could usually fill himself on the free lunch that the saloonkeeper's wife set out on the counter: hard-boiled eggs, onions, radishes, sandwiches, and soup. In most towns, the only watering trough stood before the saloon door. Parks had no urinals; saloons did. For the poor, the bar offered a cheap boardinghouse, warmth on cold nights, and companionship. Slumdwellers could escape the congestion of overcrowded flats, and very likely the drinks they bought beat tap water in both flavor and safety.[44]

An Urban Culture

Immorality did indeed flourish in the city, but then, everything did. If "hayseeds" wanted to see a display of the latest consumer products or ride a merry-go-round, they had to wait for the annual county fair. City slickers could browse in a department store any time they wanted, or hop a streetcar down to the amusement park. By 1905, New Yorkers were flocking to the two parks on Coney Island, where twenty-five cents bought them twenty-five rides. Working-class families made two or three outings there every year. For those unable to afford the Human Toboggan and the Leap-Frog Railway, a nickel let them in to watch at the crowds and see one million electric lights go on at dusk. Instead of the traveling show with its tired cast bluffing their way through Shakespeare, city audiences could attend a musical comedy. Working men could take in the burlesque and variety shows, while middling families enjoyed the cleaner pleasures of vaudeville. For a few nickels, customers got acrobatics, song recitals, and animal acts, building up to the "wow finish."[45]

Not just vulgarity but high culture bloomed in the cities. There in the Gilded

Age the first great symphony orchestras found patrons and attracted German conductors like Leopold Damrosch and Theodore Thomas. New York led the way in the 1870s; under Thomas's guidance, Boston and Chicago followed soon after. Where but in a big city like Chicago could music lovers find eight thousand contributors to build a new concert hall? Where else could Thomas have found the financing to let him play music from Richard Wagner's *Tristan*, without coddling the audience by putting wedding marches and "Turkey in the Straw" on the program as well? By 1880, Boston, Washington, and Chicago had all founded major art galleries, though New York's Metropolitan Museum of Art, begun in 1871, remained foremost. Guided for a quarter century by Luigi di Cesnola, an imperious veteran of Italy's revolution, the Met collected masterpieces from Etruscan vases to paintings by Vermeer and Winslow Homer.[46]

Opportunity might be stinted, but where was it more open than in the cities? There, an immigrant like Harry Houdini, the escape artist, or Al Jolson, the singer, could ride vaudeville to stardom. So did Bert Williams, a top act for thirty years and one of the Ziegfeld Follies' biggest comedy hits. (No other black entertainer drew so large a white audience, though it never actually saw him—only the shabby dress suit, white gloves, melancholy look, and burnt-cork coating in which he appeared on stage. "Bert Williams is the funniest man I ever saw," his friend W. C. Fields would comment, "and the saddest man I ever knew.") As prizefighters and ballplayers, laboring men could make a tenuous living and win a fame impossible anywhere else. Small towns had the peace of mind but cities had the jobs. Not all the moralizing warnings about city vices could keep farmers' children from going there, as they did by the millions.

Some reformers learned to live with the city, especially those who tried living in it, like the missionaries of the settlement-house movement. Toynbee Hall, in London's East End, offered the model for teaching slum inhabitants good Christian values with a middle-class flavor. In 1886, New Yorkers opened the first in America. Ten years later, there were seventy-four settlement houses nationwide and, a generation later, over four hundred. The most famous were New York's Henry Street House, founded by Lillian Wald, and Hull House, founded in 1889 in Chicago by Jane Addams and Ellen Gates Starr. Young women, mostly college educated and Protestant, many of them with classroom experience, came to teach. There, immigrants came to learn English and citizenship skills. Settlement house workers set up debate societies and lecture series, taught slum mothers the importance of bathing and sanitation, trained them in manual skills to compete in the job market, and ran kindergartens and day-care centers for the children of working parents. Soon an art gallery joined Hull House's main dormitory, then a coffeehouse, a gymnasium, and a nursery.

Some reformers became apt pupils themselves. To their surprise, they found the immigrant women not so different from themselves—their culture something not to be replaced, but to be supplemented. Instead of giving their people what they *ought* to have, they gave them what they needed and wanted. Milwaukee's settlement house began simply as an agency to collect the clothes of the poor, to carry to the homes of the rich for mending. With the 1890s, the purpose shifted. By the end of the decade, it was offering manual training, night school, public baths, and a circulating library.

It taught Hebrew and emphasized the common religious heritage of Russian and German Jews. By no accident, Hull House looked nothing like Toynbee Hall. Instead of the exclusive architecture, modeled on university quadrangles, the Chicago settlement house opened outward onto the street.[47]

Ranging themselves against a growing, many-cultured America, on the other hand, moral reformers were waging a hopeless fight. City pleasures, working-class enjoyments, might be tamed. They could not be done away with. Prohibition was one such hard-won fight, if ever won it was. Unable to get whiskey, thirsty Kansans guzzled patent medicines, many over 50 proof. Lydia Pinkham's Vegetable Compound was more than 18 percent alcohol, and there were plenty more: Prickly Ash Bitters, Paine's Celery Compound, and Boschee's German Syrup. Women visited doctors more often than men, but men apparently visited the pharmacist far more regularly than women, though one of the latter, in requesting alcohol, either made a sudden recovery or changed her mind when she crossed out "rheumatism" to insert "putting up pickles" as her reason. How well the laws were enforced depended entirely on how strongly the neighbors felt. A town was safe, as long as it could claim as one inhabitant did of his, "We have more cranks to the acre and more spies, than any other city in the State." Liquor consumption fell. Even critics of Prohibition did not dare suggest that Kansas consumed more than a quarter as much as before the amendment. Still, enforcement remained patchy.[48]

The harder the Protestants struggled against "vices," the more bitter the quarrel of immigrant and native, pietist and liturgist became. By embracing temperance reform, women's groups may have won support for their being allowed the vote that no appeal to equal rights could have given them. They certainly added to the fervor in opposition to it. As long as women's suffrage would help Protestants impose their morality on America, immigrants and city bosses wanted no part of it.[49]

The cultural wars of the Gilded Age were a natural response to a changing America. Both sides fought for traditional values, and both claimed themselves the best custodians of morality. What may matter most, however, is the fact that these issues mattered so much. The struggle between competing cultures may reflect better on the era than it seemed at its ugliest, for here stood a society with enough diversity to prevent any battle for a single orthodoxy from ending in total victory, and enough vitality to keep the struggle to improve American life an unending one.

Chapter 13

"What Are We Here For?"

"The Palmy Days of Politics"

Meeting in convention in 1880, Republicans did not take long considering a proposal to take partisanship out of government appointments. Up rose a Texas delegate. "What are we here for?" he shouted. "I mean that members of the Republican party are entitled to office, and if we are victorious we will have office."[1]

Thanks to blunt talk like his, the Gilded Age conjures up visions of politics at its worst. A fair case might be made for just the opposite. Politics was the biggest participatory and spectator sport of the Gilded Age, and, because different states put their own elections in different months—Ohio, Pennsylvania, and Indiana in October, Maine and Vermont in September, Kentucky and North Carolina in August, Connecticut in April—there was just about always something to watch. Readers cared enough to pore over seven columns of political speeches, plastered across the front pages of newspapers, which were short in length and long on partisan sentiments. Most towns outside the South had two newspapers at least, and cities like Detroit might have eight. Chicago had eighteen. Naturally, Democrats and Republicans each had an "organ," grinding out the news to its own distinct tune. To believe the reporters' accounts, one's own side held nothing but "monster rallies," while the other attended "fizzles" and "funerals." At the masthead flew the party banner and the approved ticket; below, editorials hectored readers to register, turn out, watch for spurious tickets, and, when the votes were in to see why their own side had won, no matter what the returns said.[2]

Political cartoonists entered into a Golden Age. Setting the pattern for a generation of artists was Thomas Nast of *Harper's Weekly.* He invented the Republican elephant and the Tammany tiger, popularized the Democratic donkey, and put chin-whiskers on Uncle Sam, though children loved him most for his roly-poly Santa Clauses, the model artists would imitate from then on. When Horace Greeley ran for president in 1872, Nast's attacks were so brutal that the victim complained that he didn't know whether he was running for the presidency or the penitentiary. As the Civil War issues that gave Nast a national fame faded, gentler artists took his place. Publishing three full-color cartoons weekly, poking fun at ministers, magnates, and minorities, two great humor magazines made a joke of society, but took their politics seriously. *Puck* leaned Democratic, *Judge* became a Republican powerhouse.[3]

To those politically engaged, results mattered with a passionate intensity. "Free trade makes cheap labor," a Republican cried; "cheap labor is degraded labor; degraded labor makes tramps; tramps make criminals; criminals make Democrats." But it is essential to see that campaigns were not just a way of dealing with issues. They were fun. Showing up to parade or to vote became a social occasion in small communities. At its liveliest, a campaign was to an election what Mardi Gras was to Ash Wednesday. Partisans marched and yelled down the boulevards. They waved torches and garish banners, sang parodies of Civil War marching tunes, wore costumes, and listened to endless speeches. What was a little rain on their parade? "It proves we are no fair-weather democrats," one soggy participant cried. "We don't care for mud or rain or pneumonia."[4]

Americans came, they saw, and, if they were male, they voted. In the 1880s, over 80 percent of northerners eligible to vote did so. A really gripping campaign—like that in 1896—raised turnout in some states above 95 percent. Most voters were unshakeable Republicans or Democrats. Usually the minor parties (Greenback, Labor, or Prohibition, for example) took one voter in twenty, if that. Pure, independent voters, switching from one major party to the other, were less common still. Changes depended on the newly enfranchised more than converts. Those sore over their own party's candidates simply stayed home.[5]

Though few places east of the Rockies gave them the vote, women did more than stand on the sidelines. They passed around the petitions for moral legislation, attended the political rallies, and, in some places, instructed newly naturalized immigrants in the intricacies of voter registration. As long as the moral health of children depended on the school system and on building parks, the Women's Municipal League had a vested interest in helping reformers win New York away from Tammany Hall's Democratic machine, and women everywhere joined in getting out the vote in school board elections. The League raised $10,000 among women for the reform ticket in 1897, passed out circulars, and called seventy-five mass meetings; against them, Tammany had to call out ladies of its own. Wives who cared about certain issues could sway husbands who didn't; that was why, by 1900, the major party committees had women's departments preparing special material. Hiring women to speak at mass meetings that year was only right. As reporters noted, many times the men in the audience were outnumbered.[6]

Big-City Machines Dominate Political Power

Politics was a sport anyone could play. Still, as in others, professionals had built-in advantages. They ran the machinery, raised the cash, chose the issues, and took the offices, from Senate seats to post-office clerkships. Party poll-watchers policed the voting-places, and the organizations printed up the ballots, with their own slate standing alone. Illiterate voters knew how they were voting: the neighborhood party organizer told them. In any case, a good printed slip would have a Democratic rooster or a Republican eagle on top. Voters still could "scratch" candidates they disliked from the ballot. Casting a split ticket was much harder, unless some disgruntled faction passed out slips of its own. When necessary, the "floaters," who hung around the polls waiting to be bought for one side, took a five-dollar gold piece in one hand and the right kind of ballot in the other.

But did good politics amount to good government? Did it not, instead, result in mediocrity and misrule? Two stereotypes dominate our impression of Gilded Age leaders: the frock-coated bloviator, tongue wagging fine-sounding nonsense, and the cigar-chomping boss, that master of fund-raising and organization. Both represent politics without policy, power without purpose. One of them smothers democracy, the other makes a joke of it.

Both types existed. By the 1870s, many of the idealists who had led the Republican party before the Civil War had been muscled aside by bloody-shirt orators and tough political kingpins with well-disciplined troops behind them: the "Stalwarts," like ruthless Senator Oliver P. Morton of Indiana, paralyzed from the waist down (due, said his enemies, to unspeakable sexual frolics in his youth),[7] fierce, swarthy "Black Jack" Logan, whose power stretched beyond his Illinois constituents to every GAR post, and crafty old Simon Cameron of Pennsylvania, who defined an honest man as one who, once bought, stayed bought. As they died or retired in the late 1870s, a new breed of boss emerged, more manager than corsair. Matthew S. Quay of Pennsylvania, an organization man with a drooping eyelid and unsleeping resolve, was said to know how to stay mum in fifteen languages. Let a lawmaker cross him, and the boss turned to his files, "Quay's Coffins," which were full of fatal revelations.[8]

Nowhere has folklore found government of and by the people in shorter supply than in the cities. The urban boss that fixed the stereotype was William M. Tweed, who ran New York's powerful Tammany Hall machine just after the Civil War. His ring could bring voters to the polls, or buy ones already there. Friendly judges naturalized immigrants wholesale. Professional witnesses swore to the good moral character of seven hundred people a day and still had time to steal gold watches and diamond rings. "The ballots made no result," Tweed later boasted; "the counters made the result." The robbers ran the courts to suit themselves, with receivers and legal referees plundering corporations and dividing with the judges. Petty politicians cashed in on city jobs. The greediest were known as the "paint-eaters," prepared to strip the walls down to the laths. Contractors kicked back 65 percent of what the city paid them to the innermost ring, but they padded their bills enough to make it worthwhile. One carpenter charged $360,747.61 for a month's work on the new courthouse, and Andrew Garvey, "the Prince of Plasterers," extracted $2.8 million, only $20,000 of which could have been honestly spent. Estimates of the ring's take ranged from $200 million upward.[9]

Thieving and tyranny, however, tell only one part of the story. Bosses generally found holding onto power a very tricky business. The stronger a governor's powers were, the more he was likely to cross the boss and get away with it. Sometimes Tammany Hall made mayors, but the mayors usually made themselves: they took a top rank in New York's business community. Quite a number of them had every gentlemanly quality except gratitude. Tweed's glory days lasted less than a decade and ended in a thumping defeat in 1871. Within a year Tammany had expelled him, within two years he was on trial, and within four years he had fled the country. A quarter-century later, less lurid scandals drove Tammany boss Richard Croker out of America for good. Luckier than Tweed, he escaped a prison cell and died quite the English gent. One of his horses even won the Derby.[10]

A smart boss couldn't boss. He had to pay close attention to underlings and challengers. Big-city machines often worked more like coalitions, where rival factions and neighborhood associations vied for influence. If the boss gave them what they wanted, they delivered the votes. If he neglected them, they knifed his ticket at the polls or drove him out. Canny operators like Thomas C. Platt, the "Easy Boss" of New York at the turn of the century, did not drive the state Republican organization. He nudged it—or drifted just in front of it. Come the Sabbath, he would gather his lieutenants together at the Fifth Avenue Hotel for what became known as "Platt's Sunday School," not so much to give orders as to take advice.[11]

That went for interests outside the party, too. A successful boss had to show himself a pretty honest broker, trusted to give every important interest a hearing. Otherwise, funds and votes would dwindle. At the same time, the crowd of interests that forced the boss to act as broker made him seem vital, even to some among the high-toned business classes, if government was to function at all. As a young reporter, Lincoln Steffens got a civics lesson when he asked Croker why a boss was needed, "when we've got a mayor and a council and—" "That's why," Croker interrupted. "It's because there's a mayor *and* a council *and* judges *and*—a hundred other men to deal with. . . . A business man wants to do business with one man, and one who is always there to remember and carry out the—business."[12]

He had a point. State, county, and municipal governments had grown into a tangle of overlapping authorities. Cities had no powers that they could call their own. The state had chartered them and could change the provisions as it pleased. It could fire the mayor, abolish the police department, or decide where streetcar lines would run. "Ripper bills" tore powers from the city when they were abused, as, for example, when voters elected candidates from the wrong party. Inside the city, different departments might cover the same responsibilities, aldermen and mayor warring over prerogatives. Boss-run government overcame the confusion.

Theoretically, at least, machine rule betrayed democratic institutions to give people the benefits democracy was meant to provide. For the working class, city government showed itself not in the man at the top, but the man around the corner, the local agent of the machine. "I think . . . that there's got to be in every ward somebody that any bloke can come to—no matter what he's done—and get help," Boston politico Martin Lomasney explained. "Help, you understand; none of your law and your justice, but help." That could mean a job on the payroll for a friend, lodgings for the homeless, contributions to pay for the rent of families in danger of eviction. And the local representative of the machine never missed a wedding nor a funeral.

In Manhattan's working-class wards at the turn of the century, who did more for women than Tammany's "Big Bill" Devery? Every day, "Devery's Deaconesses" canvassed the city, looking for needy families to supply with meat, milk, and shoes. A host of doctors hustled down the streets, looking for sick babies, and trained nurses came to tend the more serious cases. With two steamers, three vaudeville troupes, four brass bands, five barges, six bagpipers and a glee club of striking coal miners, Devery invited working women on a one-day holiday trip up the river. For the children, there was "a Himalaya of ice cream"; for the babies, three thousand nursing bottles; for the mothers, five hundred heads of cabbage and five thousand pounds of corned beef. No wonder mothers named their newborns after him! (And Devery, ever the gallant, showed up for the christening, and sent the family a five-dollar coupon, good at the local furniture dealer's.)[13]

But as reformers could have pointed out, in all the bigger ways machines did not serve the people—only the people that counted. What made an interest legitimate for Tammany Hall was how much cash or how many votes it could deliver, not whether it had general support and certainly not whether it was right. All the technicalities of law that prevented men from carrying on a business as they liked could be circumvented with a friend in power: zoning restrictions, health and safety regulations—even jail sentences for murder. For a pay-off, the machine shielded those from whom the poor themselves could have used protection: loan sharks, fences, quacks, and racetrack fixers. "Big Bill" may have been generous, but he could afford it: he had made a million dollars on a six-thousand dollar salary as police chief. It was pretty obvious where his money came from and just as obvious why he spent it so freely. An election was approaching and, as he pointed out, "Take care of the wimmen first off, and they'll lead the men to the right votin' ticket at the primaries."[14]

A growing city needed someone to build bridges, roads, and gas mains. A boss gave the construction work to his chums. He could award the contracts for garbage collection, or decide which banks would get the privilege of selling municipal bond issues and taking a commission. In return, the machine received contributions to win elections with. Arrangements like that gave Detroit streets paved in cedar blocks that floated off in an April shower and caught fire in dry weather when cigar butts were dropped on them. Dirty politics and dirty water were natural companions.[15]

The machine shortchanged the poor twice over. It bought their loyalty in petty cash, raised by handing out licenses for the privilege to exploit the city-dweller, and it bestowed small favors, while resisting any reform that would rile economically powerful contributors. So tenement-dwellers got a Christmas goose, while the slumlord escaped visits from the city board of health and the transit company was given a monopoly on trolley lines and was allowed to charge workers one-fifth of their daily wage just to get to and from work. As long as a Democratic boss ran Baltimore, the black Republicans in the slums of "Pigtown" got nothing. Their neighborhoods broken up by brickyards, lumber yards, and open sewers, residents could not call on charity services or street cleaners: there were none. "[Foul] streets, foul people, in foul tenements filled with foul air," a reporter wrote; "that's 'Pigtown.'"[16]

The real drawback to organization politics was not how it thwarted democratic process. It was how it used the process to make politics so local, so immediate in its purposes, that a larger outlook and a sense of the public interest became hard to translate into law. Government worked very well as a goody machine, rewarding friends rather than remedying abuses. But party organizations had no incentive for making departments run smoothly or offering long-term programs that required their own constituents to sacrifice for the benefit of all. Most of all, the strength of local machines added to the weakness of the federal government. Nowhere were these faults plainer than in the spoils system on which organized politics fed.

The spoils system had been around since the founding of Jamestown in the early 1600s. Given the choice between doling out offices to their foes and friends, leaders always preferred friends. Still, it was not until the 1830s that federal service grew large enough for hirings and firings to become a national issue. That was when Senator William Marcy of New York gave the process its name, by hailing "the idea that 'to the victor belong the spoils.'" More tactful defenders made regular purges sound like democracy in action. By making the bureaucracy in their own image, the parties would be forced to take full responsibility for their actions. Coming "fresh from the people," officeholders would be far more responsive to what the American people wanted. Before long, even a change from one Democratic president to another brought the wholesale slaughter of party faithful, to make room for others. "I may have said, 'to the victor belong the spoils,'" Marcy grumbled in 1857; "I certainly never justified plundering your own camp!" Another thirty years, and presidents were spending four to six hours a day, just listening to would-be public servants make their appeals—and, it must be added, resenting the time lost.[17]

As federal employment expanded and government revenues went up, so did the range of favors available for the party faithful. By 1865, there were 53,000 government positions, by 1885, over 130,000. Postmasters used their offices to fund partisan newspapers or to keep opposition journals from passing through the mails. Contracts to build, repair, or deliver, to carry the mails or publish the nation's laws, all went to the government's friends.

The spoils system did not just reward individuals. It enriched the parties, all of them insatiable, and for good reason. Party presses usually could not pay their way out of subscriptions and advertisements. They needed subsidies. There had to be money for hiring convention halls and paying speakers' traveling expenses. Parades, banners, handbills, uniforms, and printing up the ballots cost money. Party regulars might subscribe some of the money, Wall Street bankers and railroad men now and then contributed too, and candidates bled freely. But the spoils system gave "ins" a definite financial edge. They simply assessed the appointees. Of course collectors insisted that the contribution was "voluntary." So it was, in the way a mugging was a voluntary donation. At first, the 1876 law forbidding the assessment of federal employees only made things worse. Jobholders risked jail by paying and dismissal by refusing. State leaders and ward heelers also made their exactions. Altogether, they might consume six percent of the officer's paycheck.[18]

The spoils system was no more a guarantee of bad government than boss rule was. Historians like John Lothrop Motley and poets like James Russell Lowell got the English mission and some appointees served with such distinction that they became career diplomats. The trouble was, ability was often a fringe benefit. Usually the Navy Department belonged to a politician from some Atlantic state—Connecticut, say, or New Jersey. When an Indiana hack got the Cabinet post, the story went round of how, on his first tour of a warship, he tapped the deck with his cane, started in astonishment and cried, "Why, the durn thing's hollow!" Because Philadelphia's mayor chose all policemen, every new administration meant a clean sweep of patrolmen, to make way for hungry partisans with just brains enough to swing a club and not enough to distinguish against whom they swung it.[19]

In theory, at least, the spoils system, like organization politics, meant government by the people, through the party they chose. In effect, it meant government by the party organizations, who got out the vote for their side. Appointment was as exclusive as any aristocracy; a man had to have thrown his energies into partisan frays and with the right clique in the party. And what had been true about the illusion in the bosses' power was true of presidents'. Officially, they commanded a vast army of appointees. In practice, they depended on local politicians for advice on whom to pick and whom to dismiss. Patronage did not make President Ulysses S. Grant an emperor. It made him a broker between party factions. If he wanted his nominees confirmed, he had to oblige senators, congressmen, and, most of all, the Republican party that elected him.

The more complex the government's functions grew, the more refined its needs became and the more the spoils system hindered public business. It was costly, cumbersome, and often corrupt. How could it help being so? When parties relied on offices for their own funds, ill-paid employees had new reasons to make their jobs pay better. To avoid trouble, legitimate as well as illegitimate business paid New York patrolmen tribute. In some cities, the rates were fixed: pushcart peddlers paid $15 a week, bootblacks 75 cents, merchants $10 a month for setting up stalls on the public sidewalk. For anyone hoping to pound a beat, then, the expected $250 contribution to Tammany Hall seemed a bargain.[20]

Liberal Reform and the Case for Civil Service Reform

Against so base a system, a swelling chorus of criticism rose after the Civil War. Those left out of the pickings or mulcted on the politicians' behalf shouted loudest— merchants, say, paying tribute just to get their goods through the tangle of custom-house red tape—but so did more selfless types, soon to be known as the Mugwumps because, as one joke had it, they sat on the political fence, their mug on one side and wump on the other. If so, it was from independence, not indecisiveness. City-dwellers, more often than not professionals with a college education, or even a pedigree back to the Pilgrim Fathers, they let no party do the thinking for them. Instead, they heeded the great journals of opinion, among which were *Harper's Weekly*, edited by the first head of the Civil Service Commission, white-whiskered, delicate George William Curtis, and *The Nation*, under the keen, jaundiced management of Edwin L. Godkin. They were good-government men (and, a little later in the century, women): the "goo-goos," as cynics derided them, or liberal reformers, as historians call them.[21]

It is hard to warm to such upright figures, free from likable vices and full of te-dious virtues. One suspects that Godkin's idea of a good time was to sit inside pen-ning a cutting article on the menace of the mob. The issues that excited them may even look dull in retrospect: a dollar backed in gold, a government run by bureaucrats, a scientific reduction of the tariff. Elitists, who often saw no farther than the wharfs and counting-houses of eastern cities, disdainful of all organized groups, from big business to labor unions, they cherished order and good manners. They did not want a more democratic government; they wanted a better one, run by experts and pro-fessionals like themselves.[22]

Still, liberal reform meant more than this. It was a young New York state as-semblyman, Theodore Roosevelt, ferreting out the extortion and blackmail in city of-fices, offering reform bills, and setting up a city reform club that he withdrew from soon after, so that it could keep a proper distance from professional politicians—and George William Curtis, Republican delegate to the national convention, appalled at the attempt to bind him to support for a nominee whose honesty he doubted, ex-claiming, "An honest man I came to this convention, and please God, an honest man I will go!" Courage, contempt for expediency, and a sense of public duty stand high among the virtues of any age.[23]

The Mugwumps never doubted that they were right, but then, about the spoils system they *were* right. There were plenty of insider advantages, but the spoils system may have been the worst. It degraded whatever government did. Instead, reformers wanted laws choosing officeholders based on merit and protecting them from a purge, the moment the opposition took power. England had tried it. The New York Post Of-fice had, too, and so had the Interior Department. It worked. There should be com-petitive examinations and an end to assessments.

Oddly, the merit system advanced farther and faster in the supposedly boss-ridden northern cities, not because the Mugwumps were strongest there, but because local government mattered so much more in people's lives than the national one did. Businessmen, taxpayers, and party professionals all had good pocketbook reasons for wanting to make parts of the system work efficiently. Since the Civil War, states had been setting up metropolitan police commissions, and not just to put the spoils in other hands. From Boston to Brooklyn, that seemed the only way to get saloons closed on Sundays. By the 1880s, independent boards managed other city functions: school boards, park commissions, sinking-fund commissions, and trustees to run the library system. The appointees were not experts themselves, but neither were they politicians. They came from the independently wealthy elite of merchants, bankers, and business executives. Many kept office until they died.[24]

Even where cities ruled themselves and bosses called the shots, the merit system grew, for practical reasons. Cities needed experts in areas that politicians knew nothing about, or dared not meddle in. A Tweed could still give Health Department jobs to hacks. Put on the stand and asked what he knew about hygiene, one Tammany appointee confessed that the department was fresh out, but would be getting more soon. But as professionals banded together, appointments like those became harder to do without causing a ruckus. It made sense that practiced physicians run municipal hospitals, or that trained civil engineers design the projects that gave the "b'hoys" so much construction work. Some departments offered such a meager payoff that they were not worth exploiting. How much graft could a schoolteacher or librarian rake in? Needing talent and not seeing a "take," the spoils system let professionals run the parks, libraries, and classrooms to suit themselves.[25]

Professionalism even invaded the spoils system's cherished provinces. Before the Civil War, volunteer companies raced to the scene of every fire and fought their rivals for the chance of putting it out. Half a century later, cities had put firefighters on the payroll—and under civil service rules. Some cities kept on choosing lawyers or Civil War generals to run their police departments. But in Milwaukee and Washington, professionals remade the system. There were even twinges of change in Boss Croker's New York.[26]

To the Pendleton Act, 1871–1883

Yet if the cities showed the possibilities of the merit system, the national government exposed its limits. Partisanship was too strong to yield easily, especially when civil service reform would shift power from the state machines to Washington, from Congress to the executive branch, and from elected officials to unbudging bureaucrats.

Early hopes flickered, now bright, now dim. Under President Ulysses S. Grant, Quakers and Protestant ministers took the place that grafting hacks had held in the Indian bureau. In 1871, Congress set up the Civil Service Commission to prepare guidelines for a separation of officeholding and politicking, and Grant put George William Curtis in charge. But it was hard not to suspect that Grant, whatever his lip service to reform, neither understood it nor appreciated it very much. Within two years, Curtis quit in despair. Another year, and the House stopped funds for civil service reform. Grant dropped the idea.[27]

Within months of Rutherford Hayes's inauguration in 1877, reformers sensed a change. Hayes certainly was a good man, as visibly good as the White House had had since Lincoln. The billiard table gave way to potted plants. At presidential banquets, wine lists vanished, for so had the wine cellar. Desperate guests risked "Lemonade Lucy" Hayes's annoyance by smuggling their own liquor bottles in under their coats, and soon crowds learned to sample the oranges at the fruit table, spiked with what at least tasted like rum.[28] Sundays, the Hayes family gathered around the piano to sing psalms; on good days, the Cabinet joined in, and Carl Schurz, Secretary of the Interior, did the accompaniment.[29]

Hayes showed his good intentions from the moment he announced his Cabinet. He chose a maverick Democrat from Tennessee as postmaster-general and patronage-broker across the South. John Sherman may have been an old political pro and Senate insider, but "the Ohio Icicle" had the efficiency the Treasury Department needed. As for Schurz, he *was* liberal reform, so restive with corruption that he had launched the bolt from the party five years before that had run Horace Greeley for President. "I doubt my own convictions when Carl Schurz argues against them," a partisan confessed. Now he took on the contractors, timber cutters, and Indian agents with a special doggedness. Within months, the president had published new rules for government workers, in order to bar them from the worst forms of political meddling. The regulations would have been even better if enforced. The administration had lapses enough, admittedly. In the South, spoils were passed out in the same old way and for the same old purposes. Western mail contracts went to big-time grafters with political pull, some of whom would face indictments before long. Still, Hayes gave the country its cleanest civil service in years.[30]

He also made the right kind of enemies: the Stalwart Republicans around Grant, and the most prominent of them in particular, Roscoe Conkling, New York's senior senator. Looks did not just deceive in Conkling's case. They dazzled. Everything about him seemed exotic, from the green trousers to the Hyperion curl dangling over his brow. He even wrote in purple ink. An affair with Kate Chase Sprague, daughter of the chief justice and wife of Rhode Island's boozing junior senator, ended abruptly the day her husband returned home with a shotgun over his arm to chase Conkling off the premises, dignity intact to the end. But there was nothing exotic about "Lord Roscoe's" political skills, including a mastery of invective. "He can speak daggers," a woman wrote, "and poisoned daggers at that." The daggers he fashioned for reformers were among his sharpest. "They forget that parties are not built up by deportment, or by ladies' magazines or gush," he sneered. Rather, they were built by keeping places like the New York custom house in the hands of Conkling's machine. As the biggest dispensary of jobs and the government's single largest source of revenue, it could not be left in unfriendly hands. When Hayes nominated replacements for Conkling's three leading henchmen there, he got his way. But just as significantly, it took him two years to get it. Senators were so tender about their privilege of having the final word on who should be appointed in their states that they refused confirmation the first time around.[31]

Hayes's boldness, then, was heartening, but worrisome. In the end, everything had rested on his good intentions and iron will, not on law. Congressmen had no intention of giving up their power to grant favors. Progress towards civil service reform had been made only because the man in the White House would have it so. What if his successor had no such scruple? Was there a single good appointee safe from dismissal, a single executive order that could not be revoked?

That was what made the presidential nomination in 1880 so vital. For Conkling and Stalwarts like him—"Black Jack" Logan, the Camerons, lascivious Matt Carpenter of Wisconsin—the retirement of Hayes must mean a restoration. They wanted Grant one last time. The war hero, just back from a trip around the world and three years of banquets, welcomed with parades (in one, the ice company carried a gigantic bust of him, carved from solid ice), was willing to take a third term; he had nothing else to do. When the convention met, Conkling had all but rounded up a majority. Proudly he told the delegates,

> *When asked what state he hails from,*
> *Our sole reply shall be,*
> *He comes from Appomattox*
> *And its famous apple-tree*

Grant did not prevail, not because the party was wedded to reform, so much as because other candidates had ambitions of their own. Most of the holdouts supported James G. Blaine of Maine, among whose many names were "the Plumed Knight" and "the Magnetic Man," but never "the Incorruptible." In the end, the Stalwarts' enemies rallied around Congressman James A. Garfield of Ohio, and, to please New York's Stalwarts, gave the second spot to Chester Alan Arthur. An elegant, mutton-chopped man about town with no diffidence about squeezing every honest penny from official position, Arthur's career had reached a sort of climax when Hayes fired him as Collector of the Port of New York in 1877.[32]

Garfield was bright—a hard-working, constructive congressman with more savvy at framing and passing bills than any presidential candidate in two generations. He meant well. Every now and then he had dabbled in reform, just as he did in corruption, developing some immunity to both. Promising to reward merit *and* deserving Republicans, trading on his birth in a log cabin and his shoulder straps won in battle, he met the two requirements put on a nineteenth-century presidential candidate: to keep off the front page and salve the injured egos of other party leaders. Smarting from his defeat, Conkling was inclined not to lift a finger on the ticket's behalf. Promised a free hand in New York, he ended up lifting his voice on the platform. A midcampaign switch in issues from the bloody shirt to the tariff did wonders in fundraising on Wall Street. So did Garfield's promise to let the railroad managers nix any Supreme Court prospect. Standard Oil helped Republicans in some states; the Greenbackers, radical enemies of the "Money Power," helped in others. Some seventy thousand dollars went to buy unpledged voters in Indiana. Prosperity's return may have helped the ticket most of all, with Republicans able to point to the full dinner pail or the empty head of the Democratic candidate, General Winfield Scott Hancock. The Republicans squeaked into the White House, and their margin on Capitol Hill was paper-thin. Still, that sufficed, and nobody but Garfield could have managed it.[33]

Then the trouble began. From the moment Garfield entered office, the spoilsmen were beating down his doors and breaking in on his meals. Rather than let a petitioner down, he once confessed, he would prefer running an icehouse in Hell. He sent Lew Wallace to Turkey as a diplomat to soak in the local color for a sequel to *Ben Hur.* (Wallace never wrote it.) Worse still, the new president picked a fight with Conkling when he put Blaine into his Cabinet. The "Plumed Knight" was, as his enemies put it, a sky-rockety sort of man, just the kind of demagogue *not* to make secretary of state. Ever since he had compared Conkling to a dunghill, the two men had been implacable foes; now Blaine had the means to drive the New Yorker from politics. Conkling wanted a New Yorker in the Treasury and a friend in the Custom House. He thought his campaign efforts deserved it. Instead, New York had to settle for the Post Office, and the Collector of the Port lost his job to an enemy of the New York machine. Conkling stormed; he bullied; he got nowhere. By May, with his machine further dismantled daily, Conkling saw certain defeat ahead. If fall he must, he would go on his own spectacular terms. He quit the Senate and forced his junior colleague, Thomas Platt, to stalk out with him. (Sixteen years later, "Me Too" Platt would be back, firmly in control of party machinery.)[34]

Given time in office, Garfield might have broken from Blaine's clutch, but time ran out that summer. While Garfield was hurrying to catch the train to his class reunion, Charles Guiteau, an office seeker whose fevered brain included the delusion that he was rightful heir to the English throne, fired a shot into Garfield's back. "I am a Stalwart," he shouted, "and now Arthur is President." Not quite: it took Garfield two months to die. Americans mourned, and for themselves as much as for Garfield.

A Harmless Explosion.
Roscoe Conkling goes out of the Senate with a bang; Tom Platt goes out with a whimper. Vice President Chet Arthur goggles, and Democrats caper around joyously; with those two senators gone, they now had a majority. (*Puck,* 1881)

"Chet Arthur!" men were heard to murmur. "Good God!" Blaine was out of the Cabinet by Christmas. When Conkling was tendered a spot on the Supreme Court, no one should have been surprised—certainly not half as much as when Conkling refused it. What did surprise them was how presidential Arthur turned out to be over all. He refused to put himself on display, even for patronage hounds. "Madam, I may be president of the United States," he told one caller who quizzed him about his drinking, "but my private life is nobody's damned business." The new chief executive redecorated the White House in Tiffany glass and gold wallpaper, set workers to whitewashing the exterior, fashioned himself a coat of arms, and designed a presidential flag. Even on fishing trips, he affected a dandy's style in dress, courtliness, coaches, and languor. Guests at state banquets appreciated the French cooking, and especially enjoyed the wine.[35] When Arthur vetoed a pork-barrel bill, reformers applauded. Vetoing a measure closing off Chinese immigration for the next twenty years took even more courage. (Congress overrode the first and passed a ten-year version of the second.)

Most astonishingly, this creature of spoils politics did nothing to thwart civil service reform. Only a catastrophe like Garfield's murder in the spoils system's name could have brought the Mugwumps' cause back to life; then, when the Republicans lost the House in the off-year elections, the pressure for sweeping legislation became irresistible. Suddenly, partisanship worked in favor of reform rather than against it. Ohio Democrat "Gentleman George" Pendleton offered a measure that both parties would appreciate, outlawing assessments, making the Civil Service Commission permanent, and putting the merit system into practice for 14,000 officeholders. Anything that cut Republican funds suited Democrats, while Republicans had a good reason to spare their appointees from dismissal. Very likely the Democrats would win the White House in 1884. The fewer heads they could knock off, the better. So Pendleton's measure passed easily. Each party, as one supporter joked, was trying to cheat the other, and both would succeed.[36]

The Pendleton Act merely offered the down payment for full-fledged civil service reform. Much remained undone, even at the century's end. So quickly did the federal government grow that spoilsmen had 32,000 more jobs to fill in 1900 than they had in 1883. The Internal Revenue Service was still a party perk. So were most of the post offices; so was just about every patronage job outside the big cities. The parties continued to set the terms within which a merit system was allowed to continue. Departments, not the Civil Service Commission, oversaw tests and promotions. When a vacancy came up, they never forgot who their friends were. Naturally, most of the spoils jobs in the country were below the federal level. States hardly bestirred themselves to write Pendleton Acts of their own.[37]

Yet it was no small feat to impose standards for half the postmasters and most of the customs officers in the country. Better still, the bill had a kicker to it that made partisanship a continuing agent of reform. Any president could expand the merit system on his own. Most welcomed the chance; they hated a system that let congressmen hold an administration program hostage until jobs were doled out and filled the corridors of the White House with office beggars every day for hours on end. Naturally, too, when an executive yielded power, he wanted to shield his friends. Now, with an executive order, he could do just that. In 1883, one office in ten was covered—by 1900, two in five. A professional, largely nonpartisan bureaucracy would take two generations to develop, but the foundation was laid. As partisans jeered:

> *We shall see some queer mutations*
> *And improvements not a few;.*
> *Firemen now must know equations*
> *And be up on Euclid, too.*
> *Practical we are, not narrow—*
> *Here the proof of that appears:*
> *Men who wheel the nimble barrow*
> *Must be civil engineers!*[38]

The shift to a more professionally trained bureaucracy went far beyond civil service reform and the cities. To avail themselves of expert knowledge, state legislatures set up bureaus of labor statistics and passed the responsibility for railroad regulation to appointed commissions. Between 1865 and 1910, a House of Representatives "fresh from the people" turned into one where experienced members returned for term after term, and earned chairmanships by their seniority. Committees multiplied and specialized. Even the press gallery went professional.[39]

The Move toward Bureaucracy

No government able to redress society's wrongs was possible without public trust. That took officers who knew their job and owed their loyalty to the state, and not the boss. Let the cholera epidemic of 1892 speak in bureaucracy's defense. Thriving on stagnant pools and filth, carried by flies, milk, and fruit washed in infected waters, *vibro cholerae* could kill apparently healthy people overnight. When it ran through Hamburg, eight thousand died. But before it could reach America, city agencies had leaped into action. Inspection teams put incoming ships under quarantine. The Board of Health divided the slums into districts and prepared for an outbreak. The outbreak came, but few people died. Could Tweed's minions have done as well?[40]

Still, the move towards bureaucracy came at a price, both to Americans in general and to the party system in particular. What public life gained in efficiency, it lost in democracy. When the Capitol correspondents set standards for membership in the press gallery, for example, they cut out not just lobbyists and moonlighting clerks, but women and blacks. The highest and most complicated government offices would be closed to all but those with training for the job.

But where, in the end, would that course take policy making? So intently did the most inflexible Mugwumps concentrate on making government honest and efficient, that they gave little thought to its use. They welcomed the creation of state bureaus of labor statistics as good in themselves. Workers, by contrast, saw them as means to an end. The information gathered might expose poor factory conditions and stir the middle class to act on labor's behalf. Instead, many agencies turned out like Rhode Island's, shrunken to a sinecure, overseeing statisticians who saw themselves as bean-counters, not agitators. Bureaus like his, the first national commissioner insisted, were never meant to "solve social and industrial problems."[41]

Standing apart from the sordid deal making and appeals to personal advantage that the bosses used so well, Mugwumps were doomed to short-term successes and long-term failure. Elected mayor of Brooklyn in 1881, Seth Low did everything that silk-stocking taxpayers and Protestant ministers could have asked. He cut payrolls, salaries, and the city debt. Streetcar franchises went on the basis of merit. Patrolmen took out after prostitutes and gamblers. Low's government was pure, chaste, and sterile. In 1883, "Boss" Hugh McLaughlin's machine swept back into power. The lesson was one that some Mugwumps would never learn: New York made Seth Low its mayor in 1901, and even with his new, bigger realm, he kept ruling it in the same small ways. Two years later, he was out for good. "You will not get far on the Bowery with the cost-unit system and low taxes," a journalist summed up. The way to win was to make municipal government "as human, as kindly, as jolly as Tammany Hall."[42]

Civil service reform and professionalization did not overthrow the partisan tradition. It did loosen the parties' hold on administration and force them to change the way they engaged in politics. As one of the stronger, more selfish reasons for taking part in politics vanished, some of the fervor evaporated, too. So did the ready cash that assessments had provided. Political organizations had to look elsewhere to make up the difference and found a cash cow in American business. In 1888, Matt Quay took charge of the Republican presidential campaign and put on paper the way of thinking that partisans on both sides were making their Gospel. The organization must "put the manufacturers of Pennsylvania under the fire and fry all the fat out of them," he wrote. Quay could do it, too, but favors like that came with pricetags attached.

With spoils dwindling, both the need to raise money and to bring out the vote shoved the two parties to offer something more concrete than Civil War sentiments and appeals to old loyalties. They had to offer a program that would promise legislative action on their constituents' behalf. What power partisanship relinquished in setting the agenda, special interest would take up. It was the final irony that the party system Mugwumps had hoped to eliminate would be founded on "business principles" long before the government itself.

Chapter 14

The Myth of Laissez-Unfaire

Do-Nothing Government?

Americans talked of laissez-faire as if it were a national monopoly and a cure-all, but statute books spoke louder than words. Every year, Congress legislated more. In the 1870s, over 37,000 bills were introduced; in the 1880s, this figure surpassed 81,000. On the state level by 1900, there were 20 fish commissions, 25 railroad commissions, 25 bureaus of labor, over 30 boards of public health, and no end of boards of public education and inspectors of different sorts. Nearly all of them had appeared since 1860.

Bosses in the North and bayonets in the South had shaken faith in government power just after the Civil War. Later observers complained about legislatures "sandwiched through and through with railroad lawyers." "The Politician is my shepherd," went one parody,

> I shall not want. He leadeth me into the saloon for my vote's sake. He filleth my pockets with five-cent cigars and my beer-glass runneth over. He inquireth concerning the health of my family even to the fourth generation. Yea, though I walk through the mud and rain to vote for him, and shout myself hoarse, when he is elected, he straightway forgetteth me. Yea, though I meet him in his own office, he knoweth me not. Surely the wool has been pulled over my eyes all the days of my life.[1]

The more remote the government, the greater the suspicion that public power would exert itself only for the sake of private privilege. By the 1890s, people spoke of the Senate as "the Millionaire's Club." Nevada sent its silver-mine nabobs, California a railroad baron, Montana a copper magnate. Elsewhere in the Capitol, the crowd of paid lobbyists and hungry congressmen left many with the same impression that San Francisco editor Ambrose Bierce gave in one of his fables:

> A statesman who attended a meeting of a Chamber of Commerce rose to speak, but was objected to, on the ground that he had nothing to do with commerce.
> "Mr. Chairman," said an Aged Member, rising, "I conceive that the objection is not well taken. The gentleman's connection with commerce is close and intimate. He is a commodity."[2]

At times, it seemed as though probity was a quality as precious as rubies, and nearly as scarce, even in the Redeemers' South. Conservatives had vowed to turn the Republican rascals out, and so they did—to make room for fresh rascals. In Georgia, Kentucky, Tennessee, Virginia, and Alabama, the state treasurers emptied the vaults to invest in Mexican silver mines, cotton futures, and their own bank accounts.[3]

Yet there was no getting around it. Even in the South, government power fell only to rise again, at least on paper. The necessity lay as close as Sunday dinner. When food providers battled each other for their margin of profit, they skimped on cleanliness or quality. Local dairies saved money by feeding their kine on "swill," the cast-off dregs of nearby breweries. "Swill milk" was so low in butterfat that it looked blue, coming from the cow, and to fix the color, dairymen poured in plenty of chalk dust. (Farmers played the game the other way around. They sold milk that was one part cow to three parts pump water.) Without outside controls, buyers might sicken and babies dependent on fresh, clean milk might die. Government intervened with state inspectors and pure-milk ordinances, a few of which were almost worth the paper they were printed on. St. Louis even outlawed skimmed milk.[4] And food was only one issue involving the life or death of innocents. Where citizens' health or safety were at stake, common law gave governments a broad police power. (That included citizens' moral health; lawmakers could close down opium dens, gambling joints, and liquor retailers; certain states did away with prizefighters and football; Iowa even stopped the sale of cigarettes.)[5]

Moreover, the demand for public action came from all over. Symbol of Republican independence though he was, no one farmer could hold back a horde of locusts or bar his farm to Russian thistle seed that was blown across the prairies, choking out the wheat. "The sidewalks run between hedges of it," a reporter complained. "The chinks of the sidewalks are fringed with it, the yards and vacant lots are matted with it." Eventually, market forces might drive the makers of third-rate fertilizer out of business. But by then bad selections would have put the farmer out of business, too. State government had to help, with state chemists to evaluate fertilizers, subsidies to train professional entomologists, and taxes to relieve the thistle's worst victims.[6]

Laissez-faire suited employers only where labor was concerned. "I say the legislature has no right to encroach upon me as to whether I shall employ men eight hours or ten or fifteen," said Henry V. Rothschild, a clothing manufacturer. But without courts to enforce contracts, deals were meaningless. Without patent protection, no Edison would bother to invent. No play, no book, could earn foreign writers a cent in royalties without legal sanction. Self-interest itself dictated a federal trademark law in 1881, and an international copyright law a decade later.[7]

The Many Constituencies for Active Government

Money talked pretty loudly in getting its way from government, though never in one voice. When regulators set freight rates, grain shippers and railroad tycoons had very different ideas of what charge was fair, for example. Still, any group able to rally votes behind it could at least get a hearing. The Department of Agriculture serves as a monument to farmers' power. Established in 1862, raised to Cabinet rank in 1889, it quickly expanded to fit the varying needs of different farm interests: from animal husbandry to ornithology. It inspected livestock brought from overseas, wrote quarantine regulations for everything from hog cholera to sheep scab, graded meat at slaughterhouses, and tested vaccines. Distributed free and by the hundreds of thousands, the Department's *Yearbook* sent out reams of useful information. So did agricultural experiment stations set up with federal money: they sent out 445 annual reports and bulletins to half a million subscribers.[8]

Where labor unions were strongest, politicians listened to them, too. Witness David Bennett Hill, New York's notorious governor in the late 1880s. "If Hill had been brought up in Texas, I reckon he'd a' killed a dozen men by now," one admirer commented. A machine politician, proudly partisan, contemptuous of those who would reform the spoils, saloons, or suffrage, Hill knew how to spout the Democratic catchwords about self-reliance, but he was the last man to perish for a principle, not when there were plenty of workingmen ready to listen to spokesmen from the United Labor Party.[9]

New York City's mayoral race in 1886 drove the risk home. Henry George had offered to run as labor's candidate, if thirty thousand workers would promise to back him. He got thirty-four thousand pledges, wrote his own platform, and ran on it. Little had conservatives dreamed that there were so many "Anarchists and Socialists and Strikers and Deadbeats of every description," among them forty Catholic priests, a bishop, author William Dean Howells, and former President Hayes. George gave the Democrats a run for their money, even in Tammany country. Coalitions like his— Irish nationalists, socialists, trades unions, and middle-class reformers—were born to fracture, and George's did, but major parties took no chances. They must beat him at his own game. From then on, every platform had something to suit labor leaders in it.[10]

By no coincidence, a month before the 1886 mayoral election, Governor Hill commuted the sentence of some Knights jailed for leading a boycott. Nor did it just happen that he pushed for laws to end stock watering, incorporate trade unions, and provide arbitration for labor disputes. He actually got a long list of measures on the books, including ones regulating labor and tenement conditions, turning Saturday afternoon into a half-holiday, and creating Labor Day. In fact, nearly every statute book north of the Ohio showed the mainstream parties' bid for the labor vote. In ten years, over 1,600 laws affecting labor were enacted, and most of them, controlling health and safety, passed court challenge.[11]

Action only started at the water's edge. As much as four-fifths of the cotton crop crossed the Atlantic for sale, and more than half of all tobacco. Even companies doing well at home looked overseas to do better. Cedar from the Pacific coast went into coffins in China and timber propping up Australia's gold mines came from half a world away. The roast beef of old England itself stood a good chance of coming from the Great Plains. Indeed, as one brochure pointed out late in the century. "Armour's corned beef cans mark the desert and Nile routes to Khartoum; you will find them on the banks of the Amazon, the Ganges, and the Volga."[12]

Businesses could open foreign markets on their own. When the makers of agricultural machinery wanted to open Russian markets, they hired as their salesmen the very people that antisemitism had driven out; Jewish immigrants not only knew the language, they understood how American machinery worked, and could explain it. By the early 1900s, thousands of tons of reapers and harvesters were unloaded every year at Odessa and carried all the way into Central Asia, sometimes on camel back. Enterprisers traded new lamps for old in Baghdad, made sacred scarab charms for Egyptian customers, sowed Russia with Dakota wheat seed, and outfitted India with cast-iron Krishna statues. Still, business welcomed government help. Starting with Secretary of State William Evarts in 1877, monthly consular reports were written to advise businessmen of where to sell their goods. At every international exhibition, America displayed its wares. Especially in Mexico, the Caribbean, and along the west coast of South America, American diplomacy promoted American markets. Evarts's successor, James G. Blaine, made a specialty of Latin American relationships; his own successor, Frederick T. Frelinghuysen, concentrated on Samoa and Hawaii. But both went out of their way to protect firms' advantages abroad. So when the London *Times* quoted an ill-informed consul's report of a farmer fallen ill from trichinosis after eating American sausages—"worms in his flesh by the millions, being scraped and squeezed from the pores of his skin . . . creeping through his flesh and literally eating up his substance"—a sensation turned into an international quarrel. Using health concerns as an excuse for protecting their own swineherds, Italy, France, and even Turkey shut out American salt pork, and Germany did the same for pork, salt or fresh. American officials waged a desperate fight to open the markets again.[13]

Even those denied full citizenship could change the laws. Women petitioned, lobbied, gathered signatures, and organized to bring pressure on government. As long as they could defend what they did as a blow for home and family, they got a friendly hearing. Disgusted by spitting on the streetcars, the Ladies' Health Protective Association of New York brought police action. Soon they were scrutinizing bakeshop conditions and closing down slaughtering pens downtown. At some schools, students choked on the smell of manure from stables next door and teachers were drowned out in the cackle of nearby poultry pens. Ending both was women's work. The Chicago Woman's Club had sufficient clout to get woman doctors for the county insane asylum and to set up free kindergartens.[14]

The Selective Nature of Government Action

And yet, a list of the laws would be as deceptive a guide to government action as laissez-faire slogans were. Government promised more than it performed. Some promises were part of a political con game from the first. What a group's gains meant depended on the economic clout of interests affected. In general, corporations could rely on more faithful protection than consumers, farmers got more than factory hands, property more than people. At least in outward show, Governor Hill's program brought New York miles closer to social justice. But how little change came from so much law! New York might demand that employers pay wages every week in one session, only to exempt railroad workers in another, or add new occupations to those to which its maximum-hours laws did not apply. Limits on how long women and children could work became meaningless, when the state failed to provide machinery for enforcement at all.[15]

Why should this have surprised anyone? When political parties made the legislation, they kept an eye out for votes and money. Actual regulation made enemies. By contrast, laws that codified good intentions, however hollow, and programs that did people favors or bestowed offices and contracts, made friends. So the programs carried out most faithfully were those that put deserving partisans to work.

What Cities Did—And Didn't

This may explain why city government showed so many concrete achievements—literally. Those achievements critics missed; there were so many ugly things to see elsewhere. Something certainly was wrong when the mayor of New York appointed as local school trustee a man one year dead, and then belittled his mistake by arguing that the selection scarcely mattered: that ward had no schools.[16] Perhaps tongue in cheek, an 1884 guidebook to New Orleans urged visitors to go into the ninth ward for fishing and duck shooting: the neighborhood was "as unknown as the centre of Africa." Many cities lagged on installing water filtration systems. Out of Philadelphia taps flowed a liquid with a taste that one connoisseur likened to "a solution of gum boots and coal tar," and a British wayfarer, discovering what looked like a glass of weak buttermilk by his plate in a St. Louis restaurant, was astonished to find that this was the "fresh water" he had just ordered! (From then on, he made do with St. Louis champagne, which, he admitted, beat plenty of the French brands.) To do street cleaning properly would have taken an army of sweepers. A thousand horses, after all, dropped five hundred gallons of urine and ten tons of dung on pavements every eight hours, and even a small city had many thousand. Except for the "white wings," New York City's disciplined sanitation corps in the mid-1890s, no city even tried to afford efficient clean-up costs. Foreigners found American paving more atrocious than any in the world—when they found it at all.[17] Granite made city life deafening with the clop of horses. Not until the century's end did asphalt catch on, though cities did lay it first where reducing noise mattered most: around hospitals, churches, and schools. Even then, the streets belonged to lunchwagons, waffle sellers, pushcarts, streetcar lines, and commercial wagons, rather than to the pedestrians.[18] Commerce mattered, whatever the congestion.

Indictments like that of police reporter Jacob Riis helped New York City put through a tough new housing code, compelling future tenements to have fire escapes, flush toilets, and rooms of a decent size, with windows, transoms, and ventilators. All it took was enforcement, which was hit or miss. There were too few police, firemen, or health inspectors, especially in poorer neighborhoods. When innovations like gas or electricity came to the city, business districts got the amenities long before the slums, and black areas got them last of all. With seventeen white playgrounds already built, Birmingham's black children got their first in 1914, with $300 a year in city money for its upkeep out of a playground budget of $15,375.[19]

The drawbacks of city services and the misery of millions obscures very real accomplishments. For all the feebleness, say, of Nashville's Board of Health, for all it *could* have done, it still managed to cut the death rate in half over a fifteen-year period. City water may have been pure poison, but Americans could get a lot more of it than Europeans had. Thanks to metropolitan building programs, aqueducts piped one hundred gallons a day per resident to New Yorkers, and half as much again to Philadelphians. There was more water for tubs and toilets, enough for tenement dwellers to afford what in Berlin or Manchester would have been a luxury. So abundantly did cities provide it that outlying suburbs were ready to merge with them, in return for a share. Gas lamps gave Old World cities a quaint, golden glow, but for light and convenience, they could not compare with the electric lights that Cleveland raised around its public square in 1879, nor the brightness of Times Square when New York followed. American cities led the world in the construction of public libraries and schools. Nearly all came into being during the Gilded Age. No other country could boast such advances in free public education beyond grade school, nor such a wealth of teaching aids as blackboards, charts, maps, and even pianos. Boston had 1,100 acres of park, and in New York's Central Park, gardeners planted up to five million trees, shrubs, and vines in its first ten years.[20]

In almost every case, the city did best when rich, poor, and middle class alike stood to gain. An efficient fire department would save the insurance underwriters from bankruptcy, but they could call on the whole community to back up their demands. Whether Mrs. O'Leary's cow kicked over the lamp that started the Chicago fire in 1871 or not, everyone who went through it knew that the fire was an equal-opportunity destroyer, spreading beyond the Irish shantytowns to the business district itself. (And, if a further lesson were needed, Chicago's business district burned down again three years later; this time the cow had an alibi.) But there were plenty of reasons why programs that required construction did best of all. Taxpayers were willing to pay more for tangible results. What could be more tangible than Chicago's advance in the quarter-century after 1870 from 61 miles of improved street to 1,007? Electrical lighting and good sewers added to property values. Party organizations liked any reform that would allow them to hand out contracts to construction companies and providers of brick and asphalt. Bankers welcomed any improvement that allowed them to market municipal bonds, which in the hard years after 1893 did better than just about any other.[21]

Even when government action had more severe limits than in the cities, three main points remain in its defense. First, the states *were* doing more, and they were venturing into areas they had never gone into before. Second, intervention, however modest, provided a basis for more ambitious action later on. Third, the problems of coordinating state policies made national action only a matter of time.

Railroad Regulation

Railroad regulation showed that unmistakably. Though two New England states had set up a commission before the war, the credit for a lasting, precedent-setting agency goes to Massachusetts, and especially to its founder, Charles Francis Adams, Jr. Himself a peculiar mixture of aristocrat and businessman, Adams had all the sense of public duty that made his family so widely admired and so rarely elected. He fought at Gettysburg and Antietam (or, at any rate, fell asleep on the field while the battles were going on). As a postwar specialist in railroad administration, he reached a surprising conclusion. Since competition wrecked railroads and monopoly allowed them to mulct their customers, the public interest needed some outside influence to make the market work fairly: government must step in. Adams was not urging public ownership. Like all Adamses, he despised politicians (family members excepted). State-owned railroads—and a few still existed in 1869—were just plum trees for spoilsmen to shake. At the same time, regulatory laws made day-to-day would end up with administration as hodgepodge as a party platform. But if the state chose commissioners versed in railroad finance and operations, they would be able to judge whether the companies were asking fair rates or a pirate's ransom.[22]

In 1869, Massachusetts took Adams's advice. It chose three commissioners: Adams, a corrupt businessman, and "the damndest fool I have met lately." With no staff, procedural machinery, or powers of enforcement, the board could only give advice. It suggested proper rates to the companies; then questionnaires checked on whether rates had changed in fact. Even on matters of safety, the board shunned dictation. It drew up a set of standard rules on air brakes and electric signals, but did not order them adopted.[23]

Mark, then, the advance by 1897! Twenty-eight states had commissions. While those in the Northeast resembled that of Massachusetts, other states took the Illinois model, which could set maximum rates. As Adams put it, westerners made commissions into constables. In the early 1870s, the upper Midwest put through the so-called Granger laws, setting rates by legislative fiat. (As it happened, the Grange had little to do with any such measures; in Iowa and Illinois, they stood with the railroads against the radicals.) Sometimes the constables were like many of New York's finest: on the take or asleep on the beat. The companies certainly had plenty of say in any policy that got made. They filled the press with self-puffery, employed lobbyists, helped elect their lawyers to the Senate, let officials in on special real-estate deals, scattered free passes to every prominent figure who asked (countless legions). But regulators still made trouble for railroad managers, and even a "weak" commission was likely to go through a body-building program eventually.[24]

Whose Jurisdiction? The Blurred Boundaries of City and State Regulations

Finally, state regulation only made national action more acceptable. From the first, the Supreme Court beamed on the constable commissions. It even let states set rates for companies with charters that specifically spared them from such regulation. After all, the common law required reasonable rates, and the legislature had the right to decide just what "reasonable" was. Setting rates on interstate shipments was different. That was a federal responsibility only, said the Court in 1886. Already, two years before, both parties had endorsed a national regulatory commission. Early in 1887, one of them became law. The Interstate Commerce Act set up an independent agency to investigate abuses and prosecute those who committed them. It forbade rate discrimination, banned pools, and gave the Interstate Commerce Commission power to decide whether rates were fair and uniform.[25]

Federal regulation did appeal to some railroad executives, in principle. Better to have one master than nearly forty, each with its own vagaries. If railroads could not get together in a pool and cooperate on their own, a bill turning the government into compulsory matchmaker was worth a try.[26] But *a* bill is not the same as *the* bill. Railroad men screamed highway robbery. They objected to the clause on pools, but far more to the ones requiring the same rates per mile for long-haul and short-haul traffic. They watched in alarm as states took the federal law as a model for fortifying their own commissions' powers. "I believe I would just about as soon own chips, wet stones and dogs as an investment in Railroad stocks," one business executive fumed.[27]

The Interstate Commerce Commission that followed was not a stacked agency, by any means. As far as the clause forbidding pools permitted, it worked to create the stable rates without which railroad companies would cut each others' throats and their own. But it did a pretty poor job of it. Small shippers had nothing to complain about: regulators helped cut short-haul rates twice between 1887 and 1893. But all rates fell, and with them the railroads.[28] An appreciative Congress added to the commission's powers, allowed it to compel testimony before it, and gave it new safety laws to enforce.

"If the Interstate Commerce Commission were worth buying, the railroads would try to buy it," a commissioner grumbled in 1900. This was, in fact, an overstatement. The ICC made progress in setting up a uniform classification of rates. By drawing on state commissions for information, it compiled more reliable statistical weaponry than any lesser agency could, and provided a forum for coordinating individual states' efforts to bring the railroads to heel. Neither Janney's automatic coupling device nor Westinghouse's air brake would have become standard equipment without the ICC, for railroad owners were slow to accept new technology where profit was not attached (which was why passenger cars had the brakes installed by the late 1870s, and freight cars took several decades longer). "Do you pretend to tell me that you could stop trains with wind?" "Commodore" Vanderbilt snarled, when Westinghouse tried to promote his invention. "I'll give you to understand, young man, that I am too busy to have any time taken up in talking to a damned fool." When only one car stopped by hand brake could make air brakes useless from one end of the train to the other, and when trains shared each other's cars so promiscuously that a fifty-car train might have the rolling stock of twenty companies hitched on, the air brake was money thrown away, until some outside authority forced it on all railroads equally. So the real credit belongs to Lorenzo S. Coffin, once a Union chaplain and a member of Iowa's railroad commission in the 1880s. A master of publicity and pressure, he pushed through a bill to install automatic couplers and air brakes on every car rolling into the state, and in 1893, got Congress to require it nationwide. Backed by the railroad brakemen's unions, the ICC turned the law into action. Six years later, the number of employees killed or injured in coupling cars had been halved, to the monstrously unacceptable figure of seven thousand a year.[29]

By then, however, the ICC's weaknesses in rate making had become so glaring that railroads themselves agreed on the need for its overhaul. The original act had not specifically said that once the ICC found what a fair rate was, it could make companies adopt it, whatever was intended. The James J. Hills never got a judiciary they could trust completely. One reason that they got Congress to open federal courts to their appeals just after the Civil War was the uncertain reception that the state bench provided. Even in the 1890s, railroad men were twice as likely to lose an appeal to the high court as win it. But in three vital particulars, federal courts made a real difference. The first involved cases where railroad workers were hurt or killed on the job. Federal judges led the way in freeing the companies from responsibility, under the "fellow-servant" rule. Second, federal decisions changed bankruptcy procedures to give railroad managers greater power at the expense of bondholders and stockholders. As a result, railroad empires went broke—they didn't break up, and creditors had to absorb the cost when outstanding debts were "adjusted." But of course national railroad systems were more likely to care about satisfying their long-haul customers than heeding local shippers' complaints. Third, jurists like Stephen J. Field took a leading role in breaking down regulatory power. Rate setting, conservatives argued, deprived the corporations of their property. That could be done constitutionally, but only with safeguards for due process, safeguards that no legislative action could assure.[30]

Who, then, could decide what made a rate fair? First, the Court gave judges the right to do so, as well as the ICC. Railroad companies discovered that while regulators could clip rates in theory, legal appeals could overturn any decision or delay action eternally. In 1897, the justices cut the ICC out entirely in the *Maximum Freight Rate* case. That same year, the Court threw out the grounds that state and national commissioners had used to regulate discrimination between long-haul and short-haul rates. To railroad companies' dismay, it also wiped out their exercise of discretion to oversee rate stabilizing agreements. Not just a "pool"—firms dividing up traffic or profits among themselves—but any agreement on classification, switching service, rates, terminal and storage charges, or interchange of cars—violated the Sherman Anti-Trust Act, a majority declared.[31] That left hardly a wrack behind.

The Supreme Court and Regulation

The way the Supreme Court marred railroad regulation may be the best, ironic testimonial to how far governments fell from laissez-faire in the Gilded Age. All through the last third of the century, judges were expanding their own powers to match the advance in those of governors, legislators, and congressmen. Initially, they left lawmakers alone. Tradition gave tremendous latitude to the police power, and jurists liked to give elected officials the benefit of the doubt. Every so often, there would be a rumble from the bench about how the police power had its limits, and woe to the authority who crossed them, but those limits usually stood somewhere else, rather farther off than anything the states happened to be doing.[32]

By the last decade of the century, that was changing. Up to 1864, the Supreme Court had struck down a federal law only twice. In the next ten years, it did so ten times. State laws in record numbers failed to meet constitutional requirements, and state courts became still more aggressive: in New York against a statute forbidding a cigar making in the tenements, in Massachusetts against a ban on employers' levying fines for damage done on the job. Most ominous was the way jurists began to use the doctrine of liberty of contract to thwart labor legislation. Assuming workers really *were* free agents, able to choose a job and have a say in a contract's conditions, what right had the state to keep them from working a seven-day week? or to keep women out of the mines?[33]

Already the Supreme Court was harkening to business's argument that government intervention in business deprived firms of their property without due process of law. Of course, the bench would have to broaden what due process meant and who it protected. Corporations would need to be covered, just as individuals were. By the 1890s, both changes had happened. Even progressive justices were stressing the limits on the states' police power. Before the century had ended, the bench had fashioned the concept of "substantive due process." In practical effect that meant that the court had the right to decide not just whether a measure was constitutional, but whether it was fair. The court could set standards and procedures that had to be met.[34]

In 1905, the Supreme Court took up a New York statute limiting bakers to a ten-hour day. Joseph Lochner, owner of a bakery in Utica, broke the law twice. He appealed his fine. Maximum hours legislation, his lawyer argued, denied an employee the right to work extra time, even when he wanted to do so. By five to four, the Court agreed. It brought forth the sharp dissent of Justice Oliver Wendell Holmes. Reminding his brethren that citizens' liberty to do as they liked had always been subject to limits (truant officers, say, or postal laws, or taxes), he struck at the heart of the philosophy of judicial activism, that courts had the right to second-guess legislators on what economic theory to base their laws on. "The Fourteenth Amendment," Holmes reminded, "does not enact Mr. Herbert Spencer's *Social Statics*."[35]

There are two points essential to see in this revolution. With all the court decisions, regulation and legislation continued. If anything, it quickened—even in the months just after *Lochner.* In state after state, legislatures closed the "fellow servant" loophole that courts had helped to open. Soon Congress was following suit. Railroads faced more oversight, not less, on everything from crossing gates to the stoves that warmed the cars. "Every legislative season in every State in this country of free speech and equal rights is the winter of discontent and fear to the directors of all great corporate interests," grumbled one corporate journal.[36]

Lawmaking continued because the courts let it go on. Most statutes escaped review, and those challenged usually escaped unharmed. The police power still covered an imperial demesne. *Lochner* itself would have turned out differently, if the justices had been convinced that ten hours on the job was all that employees' health could stand. Three years later, Louis Brandeis made the case better, in defense of an Oregon law keeping women from working more than a ten-hour day in any industry. This time the Supreme Court bought the argument. In 1917, by five to three, it even upheld a law extending the same limit to the hours that men worked, bakers included.[37]

Legislation continued because of the responsiveness of both parties to pressure-group politics, and this responsiveness may have been what saved them from going the way of the Whigs and Federalists. As long as Republicans and Democrats would make concessions, third parties served more as a protest and a goad to action than as a real alternative.

That flexibility explains much of the failure of the Knights of Labor to build a workingmen's party that would last. In the mid-1880s, that goal seemed possible, not just in Henry George's New York, but in Richmond, Virginia, and Rutland, Vermont. The Knights made a black miner mayor of an Ohio town and a bank janitor mayor of Waterloo, Ohio. Two Knights from the South won seats in the House in 1886, and everywhere aldermen, legislators, and congressmen won after pledging their loyalty to the workingmen.[38]

The minor party never got beyond its promising beginning. The destruction of the Knights' unions and Powderly's lack of support weakened them. As factions quarreled, an unlikely coalition became an impossible one. Still, what may have delivered the *coup de grace* was the timidity of the elected Knights and the nerve of the major parties. City officials elected by workingmen backed the eight-hour day for municipal workers. They forced railroads to pay wages at least every two weeks and spent more on schools and water lines than before. Any Republican or Democrat could offer a program as meaningful. That is just what they did, though, in reforms that proved more symbol than substance. The most militant Knights might not be coaxed back into the major parties, but enough workingmen would be to keep the political system in the same old sets of hands.[39]

The system's flexibility let it survive outsiders' challenge. It also sped on the trend towards government being used as a grab bag for special interests, farmers and workers included. The broker-state was just coming into being. It was most visible at the city level, least so at the national; that fit in well with the assumptions of Gilded Age America, that the government closest to the people should have the most responsibility. Still, the models for federal policy to follow, and the precedents for Congressional action, were being made. Already, in many respects, American government by 1890 had become the cop on the beat, keeping the public peace and honest dealing, and the traffic cop, directing commercial traffic to make the economy run smoothly.

Chapter 15

Tariff Wars in the Billion-Dollar Country, 1884–1890

"The purification of politics is an iridescent dream," Kansas Senator John J. Ingalls sneered to a reporter in 1890. " . . . The Decalogue and the Golden Rule have no place in a political campaign. The object is success. To defeat the antagonist and expel the party in power is the purpose."[1] Ingalls had a point. To the politically engaged, politics *was* war, its very language bristling with bellicose images. When the campaign clubs marched, they boasted such names as "Zouaves," "Minute men," "Continentals," "Phalanxes," "Legions," and "Hussars."[2]

What did all the political scramble amount to, in the end? Cynics then and later described Republican and Democrat as two bottles, both brightly labeled and both bone-dry. "Platforms ain't made to stand on; they're made to get in on," a congressman pointed out. Certainly the generic politician spouted endless drivel, but most voters had grown-up reasons for voting Republican or Democrat. Party differences rooted themselves in the issue of what government power was meant to do. At state level and below, where government affected people's lives the most, politics took on its bitterest quality. Matters of personal behavior—drinking, keeping the Sabbath holy, appreciating the right religion and accepting the right American heritage—were spilling into politics more and more as city habits and Old World customs took hold.[3]

For both parties, the past played godfather to the present. Republicans stood on their heroic war record. They were the saviors of the Union, the defenders of black southerners' right to vote Republican, though the first no longer needed saving and the second elicited big talk and puny actions. Still, on matters from Indians to internal improvements, Republicans did offer a more hospitable refuge for people with faith in the active, creative uses of government power than did Democrats. The impulse to uplift, to reform, to make the nation in the Protestant North's image still ran like a golden thread through the Grand Old Party. That was why the temperance movement held such appeal for so many of the rank and file. Democrats might protest one minister defining the split as one setting them, "the party of iniquity," against "the party of God, the party of Jesus Christ," but they knew what he was talking about. Only in Democratic states did dueling persist. Only there did the chain gang and convict lease substitute for the penitentiary. Woman's suffrage found its few male friends among Republicans. Democratic states lagged in making education compulsory, or even possible—which, Republicans gibed, was why the voters there remained Democrats.[4]

The party of moral ideas confronted the party of ancient ideals. Between 1876 and 1892, Democrats either won or came within a hair of winning every presidential election. In two, they could argue fairly that they had been cheated out of victory, and in a third, liberal applications of "soap," as vote-buying money was called, had turned the odds against them. Of course, a Democratic definition of a fair election was one where their side did the only stealing. A really honest election in the South would have changed the results drastically. "Sing a song of shot guns," one poet jeered,

> *Pocketful of knives,*
> *Four-and-twenty black men,*
> *Running for their lives;*
> *When the polls are open,*
> *Shut the niggers' mouth,*
> *Isn't that a bully way*
> *To make a Solid South?*[5]

The party program did have a wide appeal, nonetheless. Nursing the most obstructive ideas of Jefferson and Jackson, quite a few Democrats made their careers one long objection. They hated to see the national government do a job that the states could fail to do just as readily. America must be as its citizens, not their rulers, made it. Republican ideas of progress meant keeping certain groups from doing as they liked and helping others to gorge themselves at consumers' expense. Republicanism meant a partnership between government and business: bounties to ship owners, land grants to railroads, legal privileges for national banks.

> *Know ye the land where the radical vulture*
> *Is the emblem of satraps who rule its fair soil?*
> *Where all is protected except agriculture,*
> *Where Labor is free—to pay taxes and toil;*
>
> *. . . .*
>
> *Where the bondholder sits on his throne like a vampire*
> *And cuts off his coupon untax'd at his ease,*

While the soldier who fought thro' flood, field and fire,
Is taxed for the steel-bands screwed on at his knees;

    . . . .

Up with the Eagle and Down with the Vulture!
Make these your vows and each day renew them—
For Free Trade, Equal Taxes, and Free Agriculture,
For God's blessing on them, and E Pluribus Unum![6]

For half a century their watchword had been "equal rights to all, special privileges to none." Whether for Catholic or consumer, then ideal still rang true. Democrats, in that sense, made themselves the spokesmen for the dispossessed and the outsider.

Tariff Issues Help Define Party Affiliation

When these dividing lines are clear, then one of the apparent mysteries of the Gilded Age makes sense: the rise of the tariff issue as "a thing of duty and a jaw forever." By the 1880s, exacting import duties served two increasingly contradictory ends. The government needed money; special interests wanted protection (and just about everybody was a special interest). The Morrill "War Tariff" of 1861 had given both. War ended, but the duties persisted, even after government expenses fell and the debt was well on its way to being paid off. In 1880, the average rate was 42.6 percent; responding to pressures to reduce it in 1883, Congress revised the schedules . . . to 47.1 percent! By then, the real argument was not how to pay for government, but how to shield American businesses from foreign competition. The tariff had turned into a political patchwork, where, as one Texan complained, the duty on books and the lack of one on playing cards meant "free poker and a taxed Bible."[7]

To later generations, the bitterness of temper with which partisans clashed over duties on wool and wine seems incredible. But care they did. To many a Republican, the friends of free trade were downright un-American, the catspaws of English manufacturers, duped by propagandists paid in British gold. To many a Democrat, the tariff was robbery, nothing less. "A tariff with *incidental protection*," thundered the Reverend Henry Ward Beecher, "is like beefsteak with *incidental strichynine*."[8]

In fitting present problems to past traditions, the issue could hardly have been bettered. Republicans made the Morrill Tariff one more reaffirmation of that nationalism for which they stood, one more proof of how government could act positively. Class lines melted away under the warm beams of Protection: the same tariff that kept manufacturers in business put more money in employees' pay packets. Free trade meant cheaper coats, but cheap coats meant cheap men, because it would take wage cuts to compete with an English make. The G.O.P. had protected the Union and the Negro from rebels once. It shielded the family from rumsellers and Roman Catholics now—and the breadwinner from pauper labor, too.[9] To Democrats, on the other hand, the tariff was just one more example of government helping the moneyed classes against competitors and consumers. With three-quarters of all exports being farm goods, cotton foremost, and after that breadstuffs, pork, beef, and butter,

The Bosses of the Senate.
Keppler's cartoon referred specifically to the forces behind the high tariff. John J. Ingalls is the spectacled man standing up in the second row. (*Puck,* 1889)

many a farmer found his foreign markets shut off because foreigners would not buy where they could not sell. "They don't promise the poor protection from the cold," radical Henry George charged; "it is protection from coal."[10]

Every economic interest had a strong opinion on the tariff. Manufacturers who needed raw materials from abroad wanted them duty-free; merchants sought rates light enough to quicken the flow of imports and exports. Cheap ore from overseas would nourish ironmongers along the Atlantic coast and rile their Pittsburgh competitors, blessed already as they were with an inexpensive domestic supply nearby. Farmers shouted against the tariff on machinery and factory goods, but, where they raised sheep, bleated for protection for raw wool. In 1880, Democratic presidential candidate Winfield Scott Hancock had been made a laughingstock for declaring the tariff "a local question." But Hancock was right. No Democratic congressman wanted free trade for goods made in his district. Tariff legislation was a grab-bag of duties, because a majority in either house took a grab-bag of interests.[11]

An issue so likely to bring trouble inside the parties, ironically, had a ready-made appeal. Republicans and Democrats both coveted each other's votes. The tariff issue was just the weapon to carry along on a raiding party. Southern businessmen might go Republican for their own "infant industries' " sake. Kansas farmers and New England Yankees could be shaken from their Republican moorings by persuading them that tariff reform meant money in their pockets.[12]

So the issue combined principle, pocketbook, and partisan feelings in ways that made it nearly irresistible. It became more so in the 1880s because the tariff protected the country to the verge of fiscal crisis. It hauled in more money than the Treasury knew what to do with. Businesses complained. With so much cash locked in government vaults, credit had grown tight and might set off a panic and depression, as it had in 1873. Cutting rates might slash the revenue. So would boosting them to prohibitive levels. Unable to compete any longer for American customers, foreigners would hardly think it worthwhile to pay customs duties at all. John Bull would have to find markets elsewhere.

The Presidential Election of 1884

Curiously, the tariff came into its own as an issue in the shower of mud that passed for an election in 1884. Fatally stricken with Bright's disease, President Arthur made token efforts at winning renomination, but he was no match for the "Blainiacs." That spring, Republican delegates shouted James G. Blaine's nomination through. Mugwumps just shouted. They remembered how fifteen years before the then-Speaker had done favors for the Little Rock & Fort Smith Railroad, and then used it to strong-arm the company into giving him a special deal. When the Democrats took the House in 1875, they began a score of investigations. One of them netted Blaine. At first, the former Speaker denied everything. Then a disgruntled bookkeeper, James Mulligan, appeared before the subcommittee to testify, carrying a packet of Blaine's own incriminating letters to Mulligan's former employer. With his ruin nearly certain, Blaine went to Mulligan's room and cozened the letters from him. The following Monday, before investigators could brand him thief as well as crook, he strode to the Speaker's platform to defend his name and his right to keep his private letters confidential. "I am not ashamed to show the letters," he shouted. "Thank God Almighty! I am not ashamed to show them." Out of his coat he drew the packet. "There they are. There is the very original package. And with some sense of humiliation, . . . I invite the confidence of 44,000,000 of my fellow-countrymen while I read those letters from this desk." In cold print, Blaine's letters had a sinister look, but the performance swept away doubts among his listeners and among all Republicans wanting to believe in him.[13]

Eight years had passed, but liberal reformers had not forgotten. For them, Blaine was the "Tattooed Man" of *Puck's* devastating cartoon, his sins indelibly marked, his candidacy "a conspiracy of jobbers to seize on the Treasury." They even toyed with the idea of supporting a Democrat—or, rather, one particular Democrat. Elected governor of New York in 1882, when Republicans committed political suicide, Grover Cleveland had taken on the Tammany Hall machine and two-bit jobbery in his own party. That, to Mugwumps, showed the kind of spirit public officials ought to have. As one defender cried, "We love him for the enemies he has made."[14]

Among those enemies, however, were some Buffalo clergymen. A few weeks after Cleveland's nomination, local papers brought forth "A TERRIBLE TALE." Ten years before, the nominee had entered an illicit affair with Maria Halpin, a young widow. Out of their union came an illegitimate son, soon taken from the mother's care and committed to an orphanage. The story made sensational reading. Only Cleveland's well-publicized honesty saved him. "Whatever you do, tell the truth," he told campaign managers. Ministers came calling and got the whole story. The bachelor nominee had indeed had a liaison with Halpin. So had many men—married ones. But Cleveland took full responsibility, legal and financial.[15]

Leave aside the ability of both candidates, the inventive mind of Blaine and the courage of Cleveland, as partisans did, and the race might seem nothing better than a choice between a corruptionist and a debauchee. Dirt flew. Democrats marched the streets chanting the choice passages from one of Blaine's incriminating notes: "Burn! Burn! Burn this letter!" Republicans sang: "Ma! Ma! Where is my pa?" ("Gone to the White House, ha! ha! ha!" Democrats responded—after the election.) Yet voters kept their eyes on the plain issues all the time. As long as the Prohibition and Labor candidates stirring up voters about real wrongs, the two major parties had to address those matters somehow. By stressing family values, Blaine could appeal to the Protestant churchgoers who might otherwise vote for John P. St. John and he could appeal to Irish Catholics, too. With the Maria Halpin story, Republicans also made a bid for women's support, as a way of reaching the men in their lives. Blaine never liked sex-scandal politics. He pushed the tariff issue for all it was worth. For the first time since the war, that—not the "bloody shirt"—gave Republicans their main selling point. In Ohio, tariff talk might bring back temperance-minded sheep farmers fearful of duty-free wool. In Virginia, even in Tennessee, it might just crack the Solid South. In every factory town, it made the perfect answer to the cry that Blaine was bought by the "monopolists." And Blaine never forgot the Irish, usually heavily Democratic. Let them see that a high tariff would strike a blow at England, and they might vote Republican. The tariff as a protector of prosperity and good wages was hard to sell that year, with pay cuts and mill closings, and harder still because Democrats kept changing the subject. Still, Republicans came unexpectedly close. In the end, victory or defeat rested on New York.

Blaine needed every vote he could get there, Stalwarts included. Improbable legend has it that agents called at former senator Roscoe Conkling's law office. Would he speak on Blaine's behalf? For Conkling, it was like a dream come true. "Gentlemen, you have been misinformed," he told his guests. "I have given up criminal law." (But not, apparently, criminal prosecution. Republicans recognized a familiar hand in letters to the press blistering their candidate.) Playing the character issue for all it was worth, Republicans arranged for a gathering of ministers to call on Blaine at the Fifth Avenue Hotel. Unfortunately, the testimonial fell to Dr. Samuel Burchard, whom the candidate would later christen "an ass in the shape of a preacher." "We are Republicans," he told the candidate, "and don't propose to leave our party and identify ourselves with the party whose antecedents have been rum, Romanism and rebellion." Broadcast far and wide before Blaine could disavow it, that phrase drove a wedge right through the moral coalition that Republicans had worked so hard to fashion. Irish Catholics about to leave the Democratic party had one more reason to hesitate. Soon after, Blaine attended a banquet at Delmonico's to scare millionaire guests with the free-trade bogey-man. The following morning, New York City workingmen read the whole story in one devastating front-page cartoon in the New York *World*. There sat "Belshazzar Blaine and the Money Kings," cheek by jowl with the sinister monopolist Jay Gould and William ("the public be d——d") Vanderbilt. In the foreground, a ragged family begged for scraps. Most important, Republicans upstate voted the Prohibition ticket and cost Blaine the lead he needed there. A South made solid by the usual bullying and election rigging and a thousand-vote majority in New York gave Democrats the electoral college for the first time in twenty-eight years. They sang:

> *Hurrah for Maria! Hurrah for the kid!*
> *I voted for Grover, and damned glad I did!*[16]

Cleveland Tries So Hard to Do Right

They could have chosen worse, or for that matter, less. Reportedly, one southerner shaking his hand burst out, "I've voted for lots of Presidents in my time, but I ain't never seen one before. Well, you're a whopper!" Cleveland weighed 260 pounds, and never did much to change it. Exercise bored him. Even his outdoor sports, duck-shooting and fishing, let him stay in one spot for long spells of time. What energy and force there was in that mighty frame went into official work, which was incessant and painstaking. He answered his own telephone and his own conscience, a no-nonsense Presbyterian conscience. A White House wedding to Frances Folsom, his law partner's daughter, mellowed him a little and was among the most popular things he ever did. Patent medicines put the First Lady's face on their circulars and swore that her attractiveness came from eating arsenic every day. As much in compliment to her as in disparagement of him, one critic exclaimed, "I detest him so much that I don't even think his wife is beautiful." Still, Cleveland stayed pretty rough-hewn, enjoying nothing more fancy than whiskey and cigars with his chums and dinner with the servants. His prose had as little polish as his personality. The only phrase that he would be famous for—"Public office is a public trust"—was a newspaperman's invention.[17]

Cleveland's bluntness gave him a peculiar appeal. Many would have followed him to the end of the earth—or to the end of their political careers, which is where Cleveland led some of them. "What is the use of being elected or re-elected," he once burst out, "unless you stand for something?" That something, liberals exclaimed, was the ideal of placing public service above partisan and special interests. "I have tried so hard to do right," he would murmur as he lay dying in 1908, and no one who knew him well could have doubted it, however much they disagreed with his sense of where his duty lay. One downcast spoilsman left Washington for North Carolina empty-handed. "There was one long, loud, deep growl among our Democratic friends all the way," he raged—the sweetest testimonial to Cleveland's commitment to reform any Mugwump could ask. It was a refreshing change when the administration took out after the grafters fattening on navy contracts (and would have been still more refreshing if the firm they pilloried had actually been guilty). Other presidents vetoed pork barrel schemes. None till now dared set his hand against pension swindles.[18]

Later, he would appear to his critics as the most negative of reformers. When droughts swept Texas and Congress appropriated $10,000 to help victims buy new seed, the president vetoed it, explaining that "though the people should support the government, the Government should not support the people." But in two years as governor, he had helped push through a civil service reform law, signed a measure ending the use of convict labor, got a law to force examination of every bank's books once a year, and protected Niagara Falls by making it into a park. Under Cleveland's presidency, the Justice Department challenged railroad land grants and extracted eighty-one million acres from corporate hands. No longer was the Union Pacific allowed to lag in paying its debt to the government. National forest reserves doubled. Where Arthur's administration added four new vessels to the fleet, Cleveland's added thirty.[19] More impressively, and with an eye on all the political benefits that might come the Democrats' way, he took on the tariff, "mother of trusts." In the fall of 1887, he sent a special message to Congress, making a powerful argument for revenue reform.

What came out was not exactly reform. In the House, Roger Q. Mills of Texas brought a bill from committee, which, Republicans thundered, was outrageously free-trade. In reality, serious cuts fell on raw materials that manufacturers were glad to get more cheaply: hemp, salt, wool, flax, lumber, coal, and copper ore. Where southern Democratic interests were involved—Louisiana sugar, South Carolina rice, cotton goods—the rates changed hardly at all. The cuts in duties on textiles, iron and steel, and the surplus itself were more symbolic than real. So frank an attempt to catch votes might as well have been written on flypaper—or wastepaper, since there was no chance of a Republican Senate passing it. Cleveland did not press the point. Having urged the tariff issue, he then left it severely alone, and even tried to water down resolutions in its favor as they came out of the national convention.[20]

The 1888 "Campaign of Education"

More than any other, 1888's was a "campaign of education," though quite a lot fit well with the hoopla. Protectionists mailed pamphlets by the thousands to western farmers. But they also taught parrots to squawk, "tariff is a tax" to make the Democratic slogan sound ridiculous. Democrats marched through New York waving rattles in mock sympathy for those "infant industries" still needing coddling, and cheered for Buffalo Bill, who rode alongside them in a yellow dogcart. Issues mixed claptrap and statistic promiscuously. The Mills bill, Cleveland's opponents charged, was one last Confederate raid to wreck the North or to open the way for a British invasion of trade goods that would beggar the working classes. Pretending to be Charles Murchison, a Briton in exile, one Charles Osgoodby wrote to the British ambassador, Lord Lionel Sackville-West, for advice on how to vote. The ambassador took the bait. He sent back the reply that, however the president might twist the lion's tail that fall (and Cleveland had done just that by calling for the power to retaliate against Canadian trade), it was all playacting. After the election, things would be different. England's interests were better served by keeping Republicans out. When the correspondence hit the press in late October, the ruckus was tremendous. Crowds chanted, "Sack, sack, Sackville-

West," and within the week, the president had forced the British government to do just that. When he presided over a parade down Broadway, Cleveland stood alongside the green-clad mother of Charles Parnell, the leader of Ireland's home-rule campaign in Parliament. It was too late. "They have given Sir Sackville the shake," an Ohio senator told listeners, "and now all that remains for you to do is to give Mr. Cleveland the sack."[21]

Inveighing against the Trusts, Democrats made their fight seem a war on the money power. In fact, financial interests avid for tariff reform and comforted to see the democracy in such "safe" hands bankrolled the campaign. The Republican alternative to the Mills bill, with tax cuts on tobacco and a spending hike for veterans and coastal defense, was easy to make fun of as a more costly grocery basket and a cheaper "chaw"—"much rye and little wool" for the workingman. Cleveland did better than in 1884. He ran ahead of the Republican candidate, Benjamin Harrison, by one hundred thousand votes, but he got them in the wrong places. Narrow defeats in Indiana and New York cost him the electoral college.[22]

Billion-Dollar Politics

Harrison has gone into history between Cleveland's two terms, like a thin slice of bologna sandwiched between two bulky slices of coarse bread. He was, in order of importance, the grandson of that momentary President, William Henry Harrison; a forgettable Indiana senator elected after a forgettable soldier's career; and a good vote-getter from a state that Republicans had to carry. A cooler customer there never was. Young Theodore Roosevelt, spotting him, was reminded of "a pig blinking in a cold wind." He was a good speaker, and occasionally showed a sharp wit: addressing the Washington press corps at the Gridiron banquet, he joked that the dinner was "the second time that I have been called upon this week to open a congress of American inventors." But legend said that he could make a crowd of twenty thousand his friends by addressing them, and turn them all back into enemies by shaking their hands. Already by 1889, the president-elect was portrayed as "Little Ben," submerged in his grandfather's hat and overshadowed by James G. Blaine, the new secretary of state and still uncrowned king of the party. Reporters hungry for human interest stories concentrated on his fondness for grandchild Benjamin "Baby" McKee, Postmaster-General John Wanamaker's evangelical activities, or Vice President Levi Morton's expensive taste in wines. As the jingle went,

> *The baby runs the White House,*
> *Levi runs the bar,*
> *Wanny runs the Sunday School,*
> *And dammit, here we are!*[23]

To Mugwumps, Harrison's advent seemed like more of a restoration to spoils politics than it really was. Choosing a head for the Civil Service Commission, he could not have chosen better than Theodore Roosevelt, but while the commissioner strove for reform, the assistant postmaster-general was sacking a postmaster every three minutes, newspaper editors by the hundreds were rewarded for their loyalty with public office. Even a few convicted vote-buyers found their way onto the payroll. Still, by the end of Harrison's term, the number of offices under the merit rules had grown. The navy yards, long foul nests for spoilsmen, had been transformed. The bosses of the party found Harrison so unresponsive that one senator dubbed him "the hitching post."[24]

Overworked, irascible, impatient with callers, Harrison took an interest in everything, down to the pettiest detail. He had neither the time nor the mind to propose bold initiatives, though he used gentle pressure and quiet chats with the leading men in Congress to affect results. A more dynamic (that is, a twentieth-century) president might have done much more, for the new administration had opportunities denied every predecessor for fifteen years. It controlled the Court, the Senate, and, by a slim majority, the House. That majority would take strong management; fortunately for the Republicans, the House had two leaders fit for action: William McKinley, chairman of the Ways and Means Committee, and the new Speaker of the House, Thomas Brackett Reed of Maine.

As bulky as Cleveland and much brighter, Reed was an uncommon politician. He had principles and scorned to admit it, concealing a zest for partisan warfare behind a languid Down East drawl. No man was more at home in the battles of the House. By contrast, the Senate was "where good Representatives went when they died."[25]

To legislate, the House must free itself from the "disappearing quorum," that custom letting the minority stop business by refusing to answer their names on rollcall. Reed ordered everybody present counted. Democrats broke silence just for him. They leaped to their feet, yelled, waved their fists. "The Chair is making a statement of fact that the gentleman from Kentucky is present," said the "czar" to one protestor. "Does he deny it?" Soon other rules were changed to speed business for the majority. "Mack," the Speaker would inform Benton McMillin, one of the Democratic leaders, "here is an outrage McKinley, Cannon and myself are about to perpetrate. You will have time to prepare your screams and usual denunciations." Republicans may not have wept with delight when Reed gave them a smile, but they rose when he waved his hand and sank into their chairs at his scowl.[26]

Between Reed's rules and the new Republican states brought into the Union, Republicans got their way and did more than any Congress in a generation. Henry Cabot Lodge's bill to protect fair elections down South, the so-called Force Bill, made it to the Senate. To still the clamor against monopolies, the Sherman Anti-Trust Act passed both houses, applying the law against "combinations in restraint of trade," whatever that meant. (Many supporters probably assumed it meant nothing at all.) To soothe the West, the Sherman Silver Purchase Act bought 4.5 million ounces of silver a month, and let the government issue legal tender notes with which to pay for it—a modest, and as it turned out, sham step to swell the money supply. What with the Dependent Pension Act and the big appropriation for launching a two-ocean navy, the surplus shrank to manageable proportions.[27] One critic carped about the "Billion-Dollar Congress." "Yes," an administration official agreed, "but this is a billion-dollar country."

St. Patrick's Day.
Taking the stereotype of brawling Irishmen, the
Republican cartoonist makes "Czar" Reed the
Orangeman, stopping the Democratic parade. (*Judge*,
1890)

It also made a billion-dollar mistake in tinkering with the tariff. Under McKinley's guidance, the House added thirty-seven articles to the free list, but left rates on
many other raw materials as high or higher than before.[28] The Senate patched the
bill with five hundred amendments. Wool growers and glassmakers got special attention. The final product spread protection broader and set the rates higher than any
other measure in that century. Farm goods like barley and bacon got protection. So
did the tin plate, an "infant industry" some distance from being born. Raw sugar was
allowed in free, but growers were sweetened with a bounty of two cents per pound.
With summer heat blanketing the Capitol and the Speaker presiding in a flannel shirt
with a black waist-sash (resembling "an honest rutabaga wound in a black ribbon"),
Democrats took comfort in lemonade heavily laced with Kentucky rye, and McKinley himself chivvied through a bill he found trouble recognizing. The final law cut
deep into the revenue and put the government close to bankruptcy the moment the
economy slumped. Consumers fearful of monopoly pricing, businessmen needing raw
materials from abroad, and idealists wanting a logical, professional adjustment of
rates all had cause for complaint. Blaine's remark about one change in particular fit
the whole bill: "Such movements as this for protection will protect the Republican
party into speedy retirement."[29]

When the midterm election returns came in, Blaine looked like a prophet. Already the year before, Democrats had carried northeastern states, and for the first time in forty years had elected governors in Iowa and Rhode Island. Now Republicans lost the House and McKinley his seat. Reed himself had to buy his margin in a "safe" district. The Billion-Dollar Congress, as one wag quipped, would give way to "the Five-Cent Congress."[30]

The whirligig of party had turned once more, the sharpest turn in sixteen years, but the causes went beyond "the mother of trusts." All of those pressures on the party system that the new industrial order had imposed had broken loose in the Billion-Dollar Congress, as lobbies defined the agenda for the Republican majority. But no agenda could satisfy such disparate interests as now had found voice. Nor could it do a thing to settle the quarrels that the new cultural order of cities and immigrants had raised. The "sideshows," as one Californian called the economic and moral crusades that formed their own parties in 1884, were worse than ever.[31]

The Party of Moral Ideals

The pressure came from Catholic and Protestant churches alike. By the 1880s, one American in six ascribed to the Catholic faith. Eight thousand priests ministered to their needs, and in just one year, four new bishoprics came into being. That fall, they celebrated with a vast procession through Baltimore. Venetian lanterns and Bengal lights, emblems and banners, and fraternal societies, white and black, on the march—it might have been mistaken for a political parade, except that a cardinal,

The American River Ganges.
The Catholic bishops in Nast's 1871 cartoon are about to devour the
Protestant public schoolchildren. (*Harper's Weekly,* 1871)

rather than a candidate, presided. As Catholics felt their power, they found their voice, demanding greater recognition. With Democratic help, they elected one of their faith as mayor of New York in 1880, and of Boston in 1884. Where Democratic governors could steer spoils their way, Irish-run political machines arose. Traditionally, states had permitted nonsectarian services in prisons, poorhouses, and asylums, but had closed the door on Catholic priests ministering to those of their own faith. There would be no mass, nor administering of the sacraments on public property. Now from Michigan to Massachusetts, Catholics were pressing for "freedom of worship."[32]

Most divisive of all was the split over the schools; for public education did not just teach mathematics but morals. Catholics saw nothing wrong with that. "The sectarianism of infidelity" was worse than the most bigoted Christian teaching. They objected to the way moralizing was weighted on the Protestant side. (It was weighted on the English side, as well. A Boston geography lesson declaimed Great Britain as "noted for its love of law and order, and fair dealings." Ireland, by contrast, was known for "peat, potatoes, poverty, and political disturbances.") Textbooks blazed with anti-Catholic stereotypes. Local laws barred Catholics from teaching. If there was Bible-reading in the schools (and there usually was), it was the King James version; if students said prayers (and they usually did), they were Protestant prayers. Catholics asked to be spared both ceremonies. At the same time, they demanded a share of public revenues for their own parochial schools.[33]

With "popery" threatening their children, evangelical Protestants were aghast. Ever more loudly, the demand rose for legislation to shore up the schools. Through public education, a Methodist minister asserted, nearly two million children had been weaned from Catholicism over a dozen years. But much yet remained to be done. If lawmakers wanted to keep America's old-fashioned values, they must act now, by making attendance compulsory. "The public school is needed to Americanize our youth," a Republican candidate for governor explained. It was "the great digestive apparatus" to make all nationalities one.[34]

At the same time, the 1880s loosed the second great drive for statewide Prohibition. For every state that passed an amendment ending the sale of liquor, three more defeated it. Usually, the proposal never got out of the legislature. Between 1887 and 1890, twelve statewide elections ended in defeat. Still, what mattered was not the final score, but the fervor that temperance advocates threw into the fray. When they could not get a comprehensive law, they settled for local option. When that eluded them, they pushed to raise the license fee levied on saloons beyond what most grog shops could afford to pay.[35]

If the major parties shrugged them off, they would back slates of their own. Prohibition parties had no chance of carrying states, but every chance of draining off enough Republican votes to turn a hair's breadth victory into a narrow defeat. When a presidency or governorship rested on less than a one percent margin, three percent could not be ignored. Republicans might be furious at John P. St. John's 1884 presidential bid. The angriest Kansas partisans proposed renaming the fourth book of the Gospels, and the legislature made St. John County into Logan, after "Black Jack" Logan, the Civil War general who once had St. John arrested. But writing off his backers was another matter. When the temperance Blue-Ribboners won 80,000 to the pledge in Pittsburgh and 120,000 in Philadelphia in two months' time, they became a force to parley with. That was one reason why in 1886 so many Republican conventions put themselves on record in favor of submitting Prohibition amendments to the voters.[36]

Harrison came in just as Republicans in the Old Northwest enlisted on the losing side of the culture wars. America's ethnic mix had changed too far for native-born Protestants to carry the day alone. Winning Irish Catholics was a luxury for Republicans, but the German Lutheran vote was a necessity. Taking up Prohibition or the school issue only bought trouble; unfortunately, by 1889, so would leaving the issues alone. The evangelical impulse beat too strongly among rank and file Republicans. At party conventions, Protestants found things going more and more their way. At times, the halls rang with cries of "amen!" and "hallelujah!"

Perhaps a prayer for guidance would have been more appropriate. A Sunday-closing law helped cost Republicans Ohio in 1889, turned their majority in Chicago into a Democratic sweep, and toppled one of their most reliable Midwestern states. "Iowa will go Democratic when Hell goes Methodist," one Republican had boasted; now, apparently, Hell went Methodist. Running a teetotaler for governor and backing a system of state-licensed saloons, the Democrats stood for regulation over prohibition, as well as low tariffs and clean politics. They carried every major city and most of the German vote.[37]

Other cultural issues turned the drift of Catholics and Germans to the Democratic side into a torrent. Let the British-American clubs and W.C.T.U. spearhead a drive to keep Catholics off of the Boston school board. Everybody knew which party benefited. Nothing could make French-Canadians clasp hands with Irish Democrats except an attack on Catholic schools and on the teaching of their children in their mother language. But that was just what Massachusetts lawmakers did, by debating a bill restricting teaching to the English language. The same provision in compulsory education laws of Wisconsin and Illinois provoked a storm. There, public school boards got full authority to inspect private institutions. Protestant officials used it to determine parochial schools' textbooks and close some schools down completely—for teaching Catholicism! Any child arrested by truant officers went to the nearest public school, no matter where originally enrolled. Lutherans and Catholics made common cause with German parents, whose schools would lose accreditation for continuing to teach in German. Democrats seized the issue gladly. Tariff and school law alike exposed the way Republicans would use government to play favorites, they cried. Immigrants, Catholics, and angry farmers agreed. The reigning party went to a thumping defeat in all three states.[38]

Among the fallen was John J. Ingalls. Up for reelection to the Senate that winter, he used all his organizational skills, only to find that Kansas farmers who until now had thought like Republicans were beginning to think like farmers. As the vote was announced, a legislator rose in triumph, to move "that as the decalogue and golden rule had a place in politics, the house adjourn . . . ."[39] From Topeka's capitol, the victors glimpsed, however vaguely, that the reform of parties, if not of politics, however iridescent it might be, had taken a somewhat more solid form than dream.

Chapter 16

Vox Pop

Just at the start of the 1890s, a story went around the West with a bite to it. It seemed there was a debate at a schoolhouse in one of the more remote Kansas villages. The topic: resolved, that Republican government has brought the state unparalleled prosperity. Up rose the proposition's defender, armed with irrefutable statistics. Railroad mileage, production rates, property assessments . . . the case was overwhelming. Then his opponent stood up. His rebuttal was short and direct. He walked to the coal scuttle, filled the shovel, heaved its contents into a pot-bellied stove, shut the stove door, said, "I rest my case," and sat down. He won overwhelmingly. There was no contest: the scuttle had been filled with corn. With prices as they were, it was cheaper for a Kansan to burn his crop than to sell it and buy coal.

"In Kansas We Busted"

Being a farmer had long been a dubious honor. Stereotype and myth glorified him as the mainstay of the republic. From the earliest days of settlement, producers in general had been rated as worthier than the money-changer, speculator, lawyer, banker, or shopkeeper. They, at least, made something of value. A sense of the toilers' special merit rallied the Knights of Labor against labor's oppressors. It roused Henry George to indignation against the land sharks and monopolists who levied a toll on the real makers of America's wealth. Still, among producers, the "yeoman

farmer" ranked first among equals as the personification of American independence. No wage slave he, no tool of faction! He could grow what he pleased and vote
as he pleased—the ideal defender for old-fashioned republican values like liberty and
self-denial. More than the city-dweller, he stayed in close touch with nature. The
change of seasons, the rich smell of the new-turned soil, the abundance of high summer's harvest all shaped his life. In that sense, he was closest to God and was Adam's
truest descendant.[1]

  A romantic vision, indeed! And, like all such visions, it was largely moonshine.
What with mortgages and creditors' liens, many a plowman no more owned the land
he worked than he did the air he breathed. As for the yeoman farmer myth, rural life's
hardships outweighed its romance. When L. Frank Baum set *The Wonderful Wizard of
Oz* in Kansas in 1900, he began some of the finest and most American fantasy books
ever written, but there was nothing fantastic in his depiction of Dorothy's home on
the gray prairies. Thin, spare Aunt Em had come to Kansas a red-cheeked, jolly girl,
but endless work took the color from her. She no longer smiled, and Uncle Henry
never laughed. "He worked hard from morning till night and did not know what joy
was," Baum wrote. Promise and hope had been drained from this world as completely
as from the mean, hungry streets of the Lower East Side in New York.[2]

  To survive on most farms, the whole family had to share the work. Margaret
Gebby, an Ohio farmer's wife, raised chickens and churned butter, to sell in town for
the sugar and coffee that went on the table and for the overalls her husband Elmer
wore. One dollar in five the family made came from her, and there were millions of
folks like the Gebbys—and millions of Margarets listed by census-takers merely as
"housewives."[3] Quite possibly, the heritage of toil explains why so many refugees from
the farms accepted child labor and long hours in the factories without complaint: they
were no strangers to eleven-hour workdays. "The basest fraud on earth is agriculture,"
one farmer swore. "No wonder Cain killed his brother. He was a tiller of the ground."[4]

  By the Gilded Age, the average American farm family depended on distant
markets as much as did any millhand, even if it got no closer than the crossroads store.
Corn ripening in Iowa fed hogs in Indiana; its price rose or fell with the news of har-
vests in India. To survive, tobacco growers needed to fertilize their fields with the phosphate that technology had found ways of mining. Sickle and flail could let a wheat
grower harvest a little under eight acres in prime reaping season; technology raised
the limit to 135 acres, but machines and vast domains cost money and bred a host of
hired laborers and tenants alongside a crowd of small farmers. New devices also only
paid for themselves if the farmer grew more, and for the national market. Of his own
free will, he became part of an international economy, but once in it, there was no
getting out again. The honor of being a yeoman farmer paid far below premium
prices.[5]

  Out west, it paid less every year. That was the story across the prairies in the
late 1880s. Wheat had sold for one dollar a bushel in 1870. By the 1890s, a farmer
was lucky to get sixty cents, and at times got only thirty-five cents. Forty-five cents a
bushel in 1870, corn went for ten cents two decades later.[6] In their own way, those
who tilled the soil had helped add to the value of the dollar that everyone else had

earned over the past two decades, and for wage earners who could fend off a pay cut, money that could buy more goods was welcome. For debtors forced to work harder just to pay off old obligations, the change meant real hardship. Railroad tycoons might hold rates steady by a "gentleman's agreement," and the Sugar Trust limit supply by buying every last refinery, but farmers had no chance of persuading several million neighbors to control production or fix prices. Too much land was being plowed. The Homestead Act and the railroad hucksters had seen to that. Farmers grew too much. The latest in farm machinery had done that. In the late 1880s, drought assured foreclosure on over eleven thousand farms in Kansas alone. "In God We Trusted, in Kansas We Busted," the sign on one wagon read.[7]

The Farmers' Alliance Aroused

Across the Plains as far south as Texas, through the cotton counties as far east as Georgia, farm families blamed a host of villains. There was the railroad tycoon, who charged more for carrying corn to Chicago in three days than the producer earned for growing it in ninety. There were the thousand or so makers of farm implements, whose control over their markets let them keep prices up while the crops machinery raised lost value. There was the mortgage holder, implacable and anonymous in a bank office east of the Mississippi, who had been ready to lend at eight percent in the 1880s and now calling for three to five times that much.[8]

As the Kansas dirt turned to dust and the land boom to bust, farmers began to stir. They had tried alternatives before. In the early 1870s, many had joined the Grange to help one another with advice, inspirational talk, and cooperative buying. In the 1880s, many farmers joined the Farmer's Alliances. At first, the members shared no more than ideas about the everyday problems they faced. What was the best means of fighting corn borers? Which fertilizer produced the best results? Gradually, they began to think in larger terms. The Grange showed the tug of public issues. An element of the mystical had surrounded it from the time that Oliver H. Kelley founded it in 1867; like the Knights of Labor, it had begun as a secret society, dedicated to cooperation. Women were encouraged to join and had the same right to vote or hold office that any man did. Out west, the Grange made common cause with the WCTU, made its members swear off alcohol, and endorsed women's suffrage. Many Grangers joined the short-lived Anti-Monopoly parties across the Old Northwest in the mid-1870s, which put a scare into the Republicans in power, and split the Grange so badly that it took years to recover. With the Farmers' Alliance, the important steps were economic. Firms made a larger profit by mass production; could farmers get their goods cheaper by mass purchases? If the Farmer's Alliance bought in bulk, it could then sell to its members without taking a middleman's profit. Indeed, joined together, farmers might force the manufacturers to bring their own prices down.[9]

In Texas, Alliance members took on the Jute Trust. Five cents a yard would make its bags for holding picked cotton profitable, but why charge so little when consumers had nowhere else to turn? When the price rose to eleven cents, the Southern Alliance launched a boycott and called on their members to use cotton cloth instead.

"Millions for cotton bagging—not one cent for jute!" the Atlanta *Constitution* trumpeted. Eventually, the Jute Trust caved in. Other victories followed, but the Alliances could not keep their cooperatives going and found the real changes needed too large for private organizations to handle. Some embraced government action instead.[10]

Already, farmers had turned their eyes to the political leadership, but the hopeful gaze changed swiftly into a glower. With farms threatened by foreclosure, stump speakers prated about Copperheads, Confederates, Carpetbaggers, or Negro rule, and took credit for an imperceptible prosperity. Was it possible that the major parties were hoaxing the hayseed, while they let the rich do the ruling? Some farmers may have remembered the published remark of one railroad man: "If you have to pay money to have the right thing done, it is only just and fair to do it."[11]

The Billion Dollar Congress completed the disillusionment. Thanks to the McKinley bill, farm machinery and finished goods would cost more, and if the farm family ended up in beggary, so would the very tin cup they extended for pennies. Across the South and the West, the Farmers' Alliance routed its enemies, Republican or Democrat. Within a year, some in the Alliance and other discontenteds had formed a party of their own, the People's or Populist Party. Within two years, its delegates had assembled in Omaha to nominate a presidential ticket and bid defiance to those who had seduced America from its heritage. "We meet in the midst of a nation brought to the verge of moral, political and material ruin," Ignatius Donnelly shouted, as he read the crowd his preamble to the People's platform. " . . . Assembled on the anniversary of the birth of the illustrious man who led the first great revolution on this continent against oppression, filled with the sentiments which actuated that grand generation, we seek to restore the government of the republic to the hands of the 'plain people' with whom it originated."[12]

Populists: "The Ash-Heap of Failure?"

Their enemies drew the Populists as ignorant, half-cracked hicks and mountebanks, "would-be assassins and anarchists," their program a combination of reactionary values and radical solutions. "What's the matter with Kansas?" asked William Allen White, a young editor in Emporia in 1896, in his indictment of the Populists who ran the state. "We all know. . . . We have an old mossback Jacksonian who snorts and howls because there is a bathtub in the Statehouse. We are running that old jay for governor. We have another shabby, wild-eyed, rattle-brained fanatic. . . . We are running him for Chief Justice. . . . We have raked the ash-heap of failure, . . . and found an old-hoop-skirt of a man who has failed as a businessman, and who has failed as an editor, who has failed as a preacher, and we are going to run him for congressman-at-large." The "Western farmer can out-ass anything on earth," a Chicago lawyer complained.[13]

Beyond question, their leader *did* look like political freaks. Many of them came from the edges of the political system, where the Prohibition, Greenback, and labor parties had trained a constant fire on the mainstream organizations. Kansas sent to the House Jeremiah Simpson, "the Sockless Cicero of the Sunflower State," whose claim to fame was his derision of his opponent's silk stockings and his apocryphal protest that he himself could not afford to wear any at all. Audiences cheered Mary Elizabeth Lease, "the Kansas Pythoness," a onetime lawyer and organizer for the Knights of Labor with show-stopping oratory. Farmers, she cried, should "raise less corn and more hell." Hostile reports gave a fanatic's reputation to Davis H. Waite, governor of Colorado, for having declared it better "that blood should flow to the horses' bridles rather than our national liberties shall be destroyed," an idea that, as one newspaper suggested, was unhygienic, at the very least.[14]

Yet on closer inspection, *extraordinary* is a fitter word than *freakish* for the Populists. The epitome of a bespectacled Victorian gentleman, "Bloody Bridles" Waite neither urged violence nor caused it. Other governors readily sent in the troops against strikers, while Waite worked tirelessly to end labor disputes by negotiation. Once he reached Washington, "Sockless Jerry" adopted a dress suit, a bicycle, and a rather conventional political posture. There were the others: former Union general and congressman James Baird Weaver of Iowa, as respectable a nominee for president as the party could have run; one-time Confederate general James G. Field, his running mate; and Senator William Peffer of Kansas, conscientious and innovative, whose long beard alone turned him into the cartoonists' symbol of everything zany in Populism.[15]

Wherever cotton, corn, and wheat grew and the existing parties had failed to keep their promises, Populism had a chance of setting down roots. A few sharecroppers and many small landed farmers backed the cause. So did their neighbors in nearby towns. Whether lawyers or storekeepers, their fortunes depended on those of the countryside around them. In drought-stricken western Kansas, dotted with new-built ghost towns, Populism found few converts. But just to the east, where farmers were just getting by, the movement took hold firmly. Miners and small stockmen in the mountain West joined up to resist employers and cattle barons, and, ultimately, to raise the market price for the silver that some of their neighbors were trying to sell.[16] Victims of the Southern Pacific in California, of the Northern Pacific land grabs in Montana, veterans of the Prohibitionist and Labor parties, women's suffragists, all came. All were welcome, for, as Jerry Simpson explained the Populist cause, "It is a struggle between the robbers and the robbed."[17]

Populism: "The Robbers and the Robbed"

Populists' doctrine was not at all mindless, nor their premises all that new. As they saw it, the new industrial order had led the country astray. Able to bring abundance within the reach of all, technology had done the opposite, humbling the producing classes and exalting the capitalists, lavishing wealth on the few who speculated and impoverishing the many who toiled. A system that treated human beings like machines, to work, wear out, and discard, corporate apologists protested, was the necessary price of progress. Populists denied it. Poverty, violence, and destructive competition were the system's doing—a system devised to make progress suit those with inside political connections, the monopolists, profit takers, and mortgage holders.[18]

Privilege and plutocracy had given this infamous "Money Power" control over everything that mattered. It depressed the price of grain and decreed the miners' wages at Cripple Creek, Colorado; manipulated the money supply and the laws; corrupted the courts; cornered the market in indispensable goods; and swallowed vast tracts of the public domain. Oceans apart, New York's Wall Street and London's Lombard Street ran a parallel course, with financiers like the Episcopalian J. P. Morgan and the Jewish Rothschilds worshiping at the altar of a gold-backed currency.

The system must be rearranged, and the Money Power's idols knocked down. Rearrangement had three parts: democracy, public power, and easy credit. New institutions must empower the people. Voters, not legislatures, should choose senators, and politicians' ability to threaten or corrupt must be taken away, by adoption of a real secret ballot. The monopoly on lawmaking that elected representatives had must be broken by measures permitting laws initiated by the voters and referred to referendum on election day. No official should defy the public will with impunity; nor would he, if the people had the right to recall him before his term ended. Return government to the people, and it could be trusted with new powers. If a business like railroads or telegraph lines worked best in one set of hands, they should be public, rather than private ones.[19]

Third, the banks' control over the money supply and credit must be broken. A network of postal savings banks and a subtreasury would give debtors some alternative. By permitting farmers to store their crops until the price rose, the subtreasury would give them more power in the marketplace; by letting them use their harvest as collateral for low-interest loans, it would permit them to escape the private bankers' rates. Less important at the beginning, but soon to overshadow all other issues, the Populists wanted to expand the nation's currency in ways that kept a handful of bankers from setting its value artificially high.

Populist belief at its most radical pitted producing West and South against bondholding East. It made a start at erasing the old dividing lines on which parties had played. As town dwellers, the Knights of Labor might not rub elbows with the Populist farmers, Terence V. Powderly acknowledged, "but in being skinned, squeezed, robbed, deceived, and made use of to pull chestnuts out of the fire for the monkeys of Wall Street they are one and the same." "You are kept apart that you may be separately fleeced of your earnings," Tom Watson told the whites and blacks of Georgia. "You are made to hate each other because upon that hatred is rested the keystone of the arch of financial despotism which enslaves you both."[20]

Just as the Grange and Alliances had built themselves on families, so did Populism. "Show us a sub-Alliance that is progressing and growing with no lady membership," a Texas paper declared, "and [we] will show you a dozen living churches of Christ with no women in them." In the West, women attended the conventions, drew up platforms, wrote pamphlets, and gave speeches. As good wives and mothers, they had no choice; in the struggle against the Money Power, their homes, their families, were at stake. Some of them were professionals, trained in public advocacy by work for the WCTU or among the Knights of Labor. They fought under a new banner for the same old causes: antimonopoly and temperance, and some of them formed a National Woman's Alliance to push the Populists towards putting a woman's suffrage

Tom Watson, the unlikely—and momentary—voice of equal rights. Later, the Georgia Populist would wage unending war on blacks, Jews, and Catholics. (James P. Boyd, *Parties, Problems and Leaders of 1896* [New York: Publishers' Union], p. 606)

plank in their platform. Whether the Populists actually had half a million "white-ribboners" in their ranks, they certainly had enough to make Prohibition a rallying cry among the faithful at every party convention out west, and women like Mary Lease and Sarah Emery, a high-ranking WCTU official, kept the cry ringing. Southern women held back more. Engaging in politics, they protested, was the opposite of ladylike conduct. Still, some of them wrote letters to the Populist newspapers and took local offices.[21]

In so many ways the movement promised a gentler, fairer social order than the one that Homestead and Haymarket exposed. To follow the Populist masses on their campaigns is to see visions: a People's Restaurant and People's Drug Store in Augusta; a Populist baseball team in Georgia called the Wool Hats; wagon trains for the Alliance, a mile long and festooned with evergreen as a token that they bore "living issues" in place of the dead; girls knitting socks for "Sockless Jerry"; and children sitting in Alabama schoolrooms, corncobs pinned to their coats to show their support for Reuben Kolb's race for governor.[22]

Shortcomings of the Populist Party

No movement is purer than one that failed, more noble than one wrecked by nefarious means—as indeed the means were. On closer inspection, however, Populism grows a little less distinct, and rather less noble. Consider, for example, its attitude on blacks. Members had good reason to assail the political uses of race baiting. Victory in the old Confederacy would take black votes. That did not make the southern wing of the party egalitarian. Among the most idealistic of Texas Populists was Tom Nugent, candidate for governor and Confederate veteran. Yet even with him, equality had its limits. Blacks had no place in white schoolrooms and railway cars, and if they deluded themselves into thinking otherwise, the state should pass laws to set things right. Let Tom Watson express good intentions in 1892 as he would; how deeply felt were they, after all? As legislator he did all he could to cut black school funds, and performed intellectual handsprings to find grounds for deciding a contested seat against a black candidate. In his own county, where his voice was gospel, the white community had seen to it that no blacks held any political rally or cast ballots against Tom Watson's original party. Floggings, threats, and night-riding went on there . . . until the Populists organized and began looking around for votes. In other counties, they took them however they could, which included the bullying of leaders of the Negro community and driving out those who counseled the rank and file to stick by the Republican ticket.[23]

The color line bent in the South. Occasionally it broke, but not generally, not even where Populism ran strongly. The insurgents had a program that should have attracted the poor in both races. They would end the convict lease; in the legislature, their votes went for a secret ballot and elections honestly held, free of intimidation. Blacks sat high in Populist councils in Texas and Georgia and argued the party's cause on the stump. And yet, the mass conversions that might have happened never did. Perhaps it was the patronizing air of the Watsons, lauding "a bright people's party darkey," or of the editors who thought it a devastating point against the Democrats that their president had sent a "democratic nigger" with a face "like an ordinary round two gallon pot" as consul to Madagascar. Possibly it was simply a distrust of those who for so long had behaved as enemies. Memory needed only go back to the summer of 1891, when the Colored Farmers' Alliance, 1.2 million members strong, seemed to promise a common cause with white Alliancemen. The bloody suppression of a strike by black cotton pickers showed otherwise.[24] Whatever the reason, when all three parties fielded tickets, blacks stuck by the Republican one.

In fact, Populism did badly all over the place. For all the Knights of Labor's promise to stand by the party "to the end of the furrow," the organization never had a foothold in cities. In 1892, forty thousand voters cast ballots in New Orleans. Only seventy-one were Populists. Nor did farmers east of the Mississippi and north of the Ohio take much fancy to it. Farmers in upstate New York had no tears for the plight of Nebraskans whose wheat undersold their own. Instead of protesting, New Englanders had kept the Grange going, built cooperative enterprises that actually made money, and, when consumer demand changed, switched from sheep to dairy cows. Those within range of eastern cities could scarcely grow enough fresh fruits and vegetables to meet demand. A farm family's life was hard anywhere. Beyond that, eastern farmers had little in common with western ones and little sympathy for their complaining.[25]

As for the program of the party, it may have served as a rallying cry in 1892, but the election returns muted the radical voices. Did they sense, perhaps, that for

most farmers the long-term programs had none of the appeal of more temporary solutions, and of those, the most popular were those most exclusively to the farmers'
benefit? Or was it the fear, in a year of mob violence and protest marches, of being
labeled "anarchists"—still the ugliest word in political lingo? Whatever the reasons,
Populism by 1894 had practically forgotten its program. Even the subtreasury was fading into recollection. On the stump, their every orator was silver-tongued. Old party
habits kept reemerging, defining what Populism meant, from one place to another.
Out west, many Populist legislators backed women's suffrage and temperance, the way
so many Republicans had. They supported conservation and banking regulation, and
even a few health and safety laws, as minor parties had. But southern Populists more
often spoke as Democratic farmers spoke, for cheap government and tax cuts. In
Georgia, Populist members urged the state to buy textbooks for the common schools
and legalize referenda, but nothing appealed to them as much as cutting the governor's salary and wiping the budget clear of such wasteful spending as paving for the
street in front of his mansion. Alabama's Populist lawmakers voted against abolishing
the convict lease, and for repealing all the laws against child labor. And even on the
prairies, advanced Populists found too many laggards in their ranks to get a clear commitment to Prohibition or woman's rights. South Dakota Populists used their power
to put through a law forbidding political gatherings within two hundred feet of a railroad track; they could not hire special trains and speak from the tail-end, after all,
while Democrats and Republicans could.[26]

Free Silver

The only plank that kept on winning votes was the one for restoring silver to its
traditional place in the money supply. Dressed up in flashy rhetoric, it could mas-
querade as the vanguard of revolution against the moneyed men. Ask any political
scientist from Harvard, and he would have called it a sucker game worked by rogues
on rubes. It was neither.

The plain fact was that America's debtors were carrying around currency strong
enough to kill them. Overproduction and labor-saving machinery were not the whole
story of why prices had been falling. Over twenty-five years, the money supply had
gone up more slowly than the population. That meant fewer dollars per person, and
the farther a place was from the banking centers of the Northeast, the worse the problem was.

Currency Issues as Political Rallying Points

The reason was not hard to discover. As any economist knew, paper dollars were
no more than paper, unless they had precious metal backing them up. A greenback,
as the government's currency was known, was essentially a promise to pay, to be redeemed at a bank in specie. Any other system would rely on the faith, or, worse, gulli-
bility of the people. It almost invited a panic, the moment they suddenly realized that
whoever stole their purse stole trash. In an emergency like the Civil War, the government might grind as much cash off the printing presses as the country's rag supply

would permit, but it was risky, and only a faith in their ultimate redemption and stiff taxation kept the United States from seeing the kind of inflation that Confederate "graybacks" suffered. Across the South, gold coins had been auctioned at infamous prices. Everyone knew the story of a woodcutter who agreed to sell a steamboat captain his timber for Confederate money at "cord for cord." Specie alone made "sound money," or, as its defenders called it, "honest money." So up to 1873, the United States used both gold and silver to back up its paper.[27]

Gold made a natural choice. California, Australia, and South Africa mined just enough to allow a little currency expansion, but not enough to boost prices. Silver was a trickier proposition. There was more of it, and its value dipped and soared unpredictably as new lodes turned up. By 1870, silver dollars had all but vanished. Anybody able to melt down a dollar coin and sell its metal for $1.03 was sure to do so. Then, suddenly, the price began to fall. Other countries took gold as their sole standard of value. Foreigners paying off debts or fulfilling contracts no longer were buying silver. For a while, too, there seemed to be a Comstock Lode born every minute. Worth $1.32 an ounce in 1872, $1.11 in 1884, and 63 cents in 1894, thirty-two ounces of silver were selling for the same price as one ounce of gold. That is, in the parlance of the day, it was valued at 32 to 1.[28]

Had the government still kept coining silver in the old amounts, the value would have been higher; so would prices—and not just silver's. But the Coinage Act of 1873 stopped the making of silver dollars. As prices fell in the years that followed, the so-called "Crime of '73" took on folklore status as the moment when a conspiracy of gold-harders did in the "dollar of the daddies." With a monopoly on one precious metal, they wanted the government to patronize no other. Avaricious bankers, it seemed, with Shylock's blood in their veins, dreamed of making their loans pay twice their original value, by making the products of the soil worth half as much. A deflated currency could do it. So politicians like Senator John Sherman of Ohio and reputedly sinister operators like the Jewish Baron Ernest Seyd, fugleman for the world's greatest banking house, that of the Rothschilds in London, arranged demonetization. "They as completely sold out the nation, as Judas sold out Christ," one bimetallist shrieked.[29]

Ending the bankers' grip took no radical departure. It took a restoration. Silver, "the poor man's money," must be coined again and made legal tender for all debts. Of course, the mines were turning out so much ore that even the inflationists who spoke of "free silver" did not mean absolute free coinage. They would set a limit: government purchases until silver's price in relation to gold reached 16 to 1. Prices would go up, farmers' burden of debt would go down.[30]

However correct the Populists may have been about some things, their views on silver were a mixture of truth and tommyrot, in just about the same proportions as politicians' views were about any other issue. Many of them were greenbackers, not silverites at all: for them, currency needed no more backing than a government endorsement. They preferred the people's paper dollars, but would accept two precious metals to back it up rather than one, if that stood a better chance of being enacted. Money was money, Robert Schilling told Milwaukeeans. It rested on the people's faith

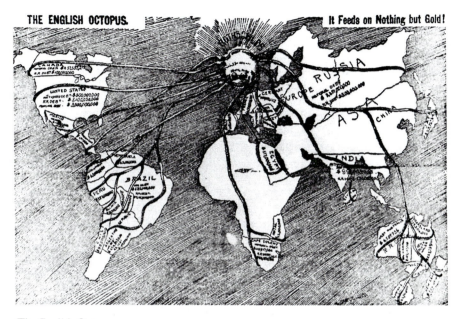

The English Octopus.
Coin's Financial School was pro-silver, not Populist, but the vision of a British money-power conspiracy was one they shared. (Coin's Financial School, 1895)

in its value, not on some arbitrary stockpile of material backing it up. What difference would it make if the government coined it from "gold, silver, copper, paper, sauerkraut or sausage"? (His audience found plenty of difference, and so did the voters.) In practice, bimetallism had always been a problem, because the comparative values of gold and silver kept shifting. That, and not a bankers' plot, explained "the Crime of '73." If that *was* a conspiracy, men in the Treasury were behind it, and for plausible reasons. By the fall of 1872, silver was pouring into the Treasury. More discoveries were expected. If the metal got back into circulation in a big way and could be used to pay off government bonds, bondholders who had bought securities expecting payment in gold would dump them at once, setting off a panic. Far from having spent $500,000 to finish off silver, poor decent Baron Seyd had been a spokesman in silver's favor.[31] Behind "16 to 1" stood not only the farmers' friends, but the mine owners of the Rocky Mountain states. A government that restored the Dollar of the Daddies would make silver investments as good as gold.

That does not mean that the "goldbugs" knew what they were talking about, either. Like silver men, they had turned a precious metal into something worth more than its market price. Gold was moral, the *only* moral money; it was the only possible backing for currency. Anything else was *dis*honest money, the scheme of selfish men out to cheat the creditor of his due. No honest man of any sense could believe differently. Obviously, then, a silverite was either a crank, a Bonanza King, a demagogue, a communist, or a hayseed.[32] Confederates had exchanged their gray uniform for a silver outfit; it was their revenge on the "substantial men" of the North for winning the war.

In fact, gold and silver both were overvalued, at least in what they could do and were doing. Even in the 1880s, the money supply grew faster than gold reserves. Strangely enough, the bankers deserved some of the credit, or at least bank deposits did. In 1879, they amounted to two dollars per dollar of currency, in 1892 they amounted to four dollars. More money in the bank meant more to lend out again.[33]

Later, historians would talk as if Populists turned the silver issue into a paying proposition, only to have Democrats jump their claim. The reverse was closer to the truth. From the late 1870s on, silver had cast its allure on those uneasy with a gold-backed currency. Every time the economy went into a slump, the cries went up for inflation, or, rather, since spokesmen simply wanted to bring dollars down to their old value, *reflation*. "We do not want a Wall Street silver dollar," one editor insisted, "but a people's silver dollar, a Mississippi Valley dollar, a dollar with an eagle on it, whose right wing shall fan Washington City while his left wing wafts the dust along the streets of San Francisco, and his tail spreads over Hudson's Bay, while his beak is dredging the mud from the steam between the jetties at South Pass."[34]

The loudest spokesmen came from the Democratic South, like "Silver Dick" Bland of Missouri. In 1878, they had managed to shove a free coinage bill through the House. In the Senate, it fell into the gingerly hands of William Boyd Allison, an Iowa Republican so cautious that it was said he could clump across the Senate in wooden shoes as silently as a fly along the ceiling. The Bland-Allison act, passed over President Hayes's veto, forced the Treasury to buy between $2 million and $4 million in silver each month, to coin into dollars that could be converted into silver certificates. However much conservatives might describe this as a firebrand of revolution, it hardly qualified as a safety match. No president went beyond the minimum, and even as they put the new coins into circulation, withdrew well over $100 million more to make up for it. Most of the silver dollars were simply piled up inside the Treasury vaults.[35]

In the recession of the mid-1880s, Bland and his friends were back with another coinage bill. It got nowhere, but by 1890, Republicans had pledged themselves hostage to the silverites when they brought in new Rocky Mountain states. With the newly minted senators adding their voices to the reflationists elsewhere and threatening to kill every bill until they had their way, Republicans gave in and passed the Sherman Silver Purchase Act. Every month, the Treasury must buy 4.5 million ounces of silver at its market value. In two years' time, the law created the potential for $180 million in silver money, which, however large a fraction of his fortune it would have been to Andrew Carnegie, mattered hardly at all to the total money supply. And that was all it was: potential. Unlike the Bland-Allison Act, nothing in the new law *made* the Treasury turn that bullion into coin. That only happened if someone wanted to be paid in silver, which just about no one asking redemption of Treasury notes did. In effect, the "reflationists," as the currency expansion advocates might be called, had exchanged a symbol for a substance, and soon lost even that.[36] So Southern Democrats and Far Western Republicans continued to clamor for silver.

As hard times stripped sixty million dollars out of circulation, the clamor became a thunderous roar. By the mid-1890s, the most widely read spokesman for free silver was William Harvey, a one-time owner of a silver mine and real estate promoter and author of *Coin's Financial School.* Published in 1894 as a set of lectures by "Coin," a young spokesman for silver who bested the bankers at every point, the book sold 5,000 copies a day—1.5 million in all. All the old arguments were there in fresh prose, and, better still, in biting caricature: gold conspirators, the American tradition of bimetallism, tight money as the Depression's sole cause, free silver as a cureall. Critics could deride "Coin." They could not ignore him. Many a reader actually imagined that the lectures had taken place, and as one Minnesotan complained, high school boys in his town were "about equally divided between silver and baseball, with a deciding leaning toward the former." Off the eastern printing presses flowed desperate replies: *Coin's Financial Fraud, Bullion vs. Coin, Farmer Hayseed in Town, Coin's Financial Fool, Silas Honest Money.* None came close to Harvey's original in impact.[37]

It was the Populists, then, who were the real claim jumpers, even in Montana, where copper miners, not silver miners, headed the party first.[38] To be sure, many of them had more radical visions of what bimetallism would do than had the two main parties. Smite the gold hoarders, they argued, and the Money Power's grip on debtors would be loosed. Supplies of one metal it could control, but not both, not when just about every state from the Pacific to the Plains had ore to sell, and foreigners unlimited supplies to dump on American markets. For pragmatists in the party, however, the issue's real appeal was its winning way. Democrats across the South, perhaps Republicans in the West, might desert their old allegiances, especially if the national parties continued to stand by gold. As Populists bled the Democracy of members, state organizations would be forced to join or die.

Friends of fusion had grounds for hope. Already they had tried alliances here and there and found Democrats willing to sustain more than the money plank for coalition's sake. Talk about sticking to the "middle of the road" free of contamination from the parties on either side was all very well, but where did that road go? If it did not lead to power, if a stern independence left the Populists out of office, how could any of their program be put through? How long could they feed members on hopes of eventual victory?[39]

The Democrats Tack to a Populist Gale

But the willingness of Democrats to give ground, and beyond the silver issue, was more ominous than it seemed. Not because so many of them were insincere—as a fair number of them were, especially in the heyday of the Farmer's Alliance. Many old-line officeholders were like Senator Pugh of Alabama, full of good homilies until after his reelection. From then on, the mere whiff of Alliance talk in a letter got it consigned to the wastebasket: as he put it, "I am out of the demagogue business for the next five years." But the Depression brought just the opposite problem: honest indignation at the way affairs were going. Hardship broke old ways of thinking before it broke party lines, and the same crisis that created a Populist movement was creating a radical wing in the Democratic party. The heirs of Jefferson would not let "the J. Pierpont Arnolds," those "moneyed sharks," sell out the government to coupon-clippers.[40] Reformers might not master the state organization everywhere or hold on long. But there would be a fight, and the conservatives would have to give ground.

Silver was part of the story, but only part. In Arkansas, the reformers took on the bondholders. Florida Democrats called on the federal government to take over the railroads and wipe out national banks. Georgia Democrats came out for an income tax and laws against speculators; Alabama's reformed the tax code, set up industrial schools, and put regulations on insurance companies; Missourians embraced the eight-hour day and fairer workmen's compensation laws. And everywhere, the reformers tried to set up or strengthen railroad regulatory commissions.[41]

Two southern states show how far reform could go. In South Carolina, a farmers' revolt threw out the Confederate brigadiers. The challenger, Ben Tillman, was no one-gallus farmer by any means. To work his upcountry estate took twenty tenants and thirty plows. But "the One-Eyed Plowboy" was far from the old gentility, and gloried in it. When he ran for governor in 1890, he spoke from a farm wagon seat decorated with corn tassels and pea vines. In power, he backed the subtreasury scheme, cut official salaries, pushed through a state primary, strengthened the railroad commission, set up an agricultural experiment station, and got funds for an agricultural college. He took on the fertilizer makers, who were mining phosphate deposits in state waters and paying a pittance. Banks and railroads would pay heavier taxes; textile owners would face limits on the hours they could work their employees. In Texas, a onetime sharecropper and self-taught lawyer named James Hogg made a name for himself as attorney-general by hectoring the railroad companies. When the legislature refused to set up a regulatory commission in 1890, Hogg led the fight to write one into the state constitution. As governor, he filled the commission with men no railroad could buy and shoved through new restrictions on the corporations. He tried, unsuccessfully, to get more money for schools and a more progressive tax system, and anointed a successor as progressive as himself. Populists could only sputter that Hogg had sold the people out—and swear that if elected, they would keep those laws intact.[42]

Obviously, a party able to remake itself was bad news for the Populist come-outers, and two parties able to do so was even worse. From the start, many in the Farmer's Alliance would break everything but the old party tie. Teaching the organization a lesson as they did in 1890 was one thing; abandoning it completely or endorsing the subtreasury quite another. They would need a far better excuse than the major parties gave them, and a constant reminder. When General Weaver took his presidential campaign south, Democrats pelted him. "That damned rotten egg that hit Mrs. Weaver smells all through Minnesota and the northwest," a Populist supporter wrote. His former Republican allies were so stirred up that they would vote Republican again, just to teach Democrats one more lesson. Every time Democrats bested the Money Power inside the party, they gave their own members that much less reason for giving up their old allegiances and members of the People's party that much more reason to make common cause with them; every time reform Democrats lost, they reached out for Populist recruits to shift the balance of power. And of course, as long as the major parties left the door ajar for reformers, there was always someplace for dissidents to go whenever a quarrel broke out in the Populist ranks—which was just about all the time. No outsider could outdo the venom of one Tennessee Populist, who called another "a moral coward, a spiteful villain, a treacherous wretch, a venomous reptile, and a voluminous liar," with "not even the vacuum where a conscience should be."[43]

So the farmers' revolt was real enough, but it never translated all that well into the People's Party. That left only one serious question: could the two national parties translate any better into the America of the 1890s?

Chapter 17

The Second Cleveland's Administration

Thanks to careful management and the latest techniques, the 1892 campaign was the deadest in generations. Processions, costumes, and kerosene lanterns gave way to pamphlets, reading clubs, and discourses printed on stereotyped plates for use in several thousand newspapers. Spectacle vanished. So did the crowds. Party organizers insisted that voters were too busy mulling over the issues—that Election Day would be different. It was. Not since 1872 had the turnout been so low.[1]

Most of the stay-at-homes were Republicans. Harrison was admired, but not beloved, and, as Boss Platt later wrote, his renomination "caused a chattering of the teeth among the warm-blooded Republicans of the East. . . . Many of the New York delegates, including myself, wrapped ourselves in overcoats and earmuffs, hurried from the convention hall, and took the first train to New York." With his wife passing through her last illness, the president had no time to mend fences, and not much desire to do so. Nor would he do what more craven allies wanted him to do and abandon black Republicans to their fate by giving up his support for a federal bill to protect voting rights.[2]

Four years away from the trough made Democrats more willing to take Grover Cleveland. Not all of them liked the idea. "It is a funeral!" a leading New York delegate shouted, as the convention gave the ex-president victory on the first ballot (the thought may have been on his mind for other reasons; the week before, a cyclone had ripped the roof off of the convention hall, and the hastily built replacement had shown its defects partway through proceedings when the electric lights—wires and all—fell from the ceiling, nearly killing the governor of New York).[3]

If so, at first it seemed to be the Republicans' funeral. With strikes in the coal fields and open war at the Homestead mills, and the specter of Negro rule to brandish before white southerners, the Democrats had issues all their own way. The Populists polled over a million votes for their nominee, General Weaver. Out west they carried three governorships, five senate seats, and as many as ten congressmen. But Weaver got less than 9 percent of the vote, and even where he did well, out west, Democrats, bent on beating Harrison, gave him a boost. Alabama produced Weaver's best southern showing, but he still lost it badly. Most places, ethnic or working-class discontent went Democratic. For the first time since 1859, Democrats would hold the House, Senate, and Executive Mansion. Every swing state in the Northeast went for Cleveland. Crowds sang:

Grover, Grover, four more years of Grover—
Out they go and in we come and we'll be in the clover.[4]

What they got, as it turned out, was short rations. Before the spring was out, so was the boom.

The Economic Boom Goes Bust

The signs had been gathering for quite some time. The economy had overheated, the railroad builders had overextended. Land values were too high in much of the country, and the banking system was utterly inadequate. Dependent on foreign funding and capital markets—England's in particular—Americans could not afford to have it let up, as it was doing. One of the greatest banking houses of the world, Baring Brothers of London, had invested heavily in lines in Massachusetts, Missouri, and elsewhere. Then, in 1890, the Barings came within a hair of collapse and were only saved by other financial houses shoring them up. Foreign investments (Argentine and South African, especially) had caused the crisis. From then on English financiers wanted nothing to do with them, American railroad securities included.[5]

Banking failures abroad also helped drain the gold supply at home. European investors, skittish about the future, dumped their American holdings, and took home what gold they were paid. With more superstition than science, businessmen had fixed on $100 million as the bottom line below which the Treasury's supply must never go, if gold payments were to continue. When Cleveland took office, government reserves hovered just above it. Treasury action checked the outflow for a few weeks. Then it resumed. On April 22, the minimum line was breached and business confidence fell apart. When the National Cordage Company, a would-be monopoly with $10 million in liabilities, failed on May 4, a skittish stock market started a steep tumble that went on for months.[6]

Not since 1873 had Wall Street taken so sustained, so irrecoverable a loss. By year's end, 160,000 businesses, starved for capital from overseas and unable to find backers at home, shut down. Four ironworkers in ten had lost their jobs. Most of the big transcontinental lines went bankrupt. By year's end, 583 banks had failed, including that owned by "Calico Charley" Foster, Harrison's Secretary of the Treasury.[7]

The hard times lingered for over four years, though they were worst that first winter. The economy gained in 1895, then slumped, reaching a second low point late in 1896. Editors advised townsfolk to go back to the land, but farming did so poorly that the tide of country people to the cities only quickened. Railroad dividends vanished. Securities lost value. Receivers took over 51,619 miles of track—and, in the South, one mile in every two. New building stopped. From steel billets to steam lard, prices dropped, but fewer people could buy them at any price. In some industrial states, unemployment reached 25 percent, and the national average was near 20 percent. Multitudes more were forced into lower paying jobs and part-time employment.[8]

To keep bread on the table, families coped however they could. They drew on their meager savings, moved to cheaper quarters, took in boarders, and went into debt, where the corner grocer would let them. Parents sent their children off to live with luckier relatives, or took them out of school to earn a living. Already more than occupied just running the household, wives took in neighbors' washing and ironing, opened the back room for boarders, or went off to look for work themselves; since employers paid them less than men, they hired them more willingly. Families dropped their insurance policies, skimped on doctors when the children were sick, scoured the streets looking for stray bits of coal and wood to keep their rooms heated, gave up gas lamps for candles, lived on bread rather than meat or fresh vegetables, or bought restaurant scraps. Only in the direst want would they go beyond their friends and neighbors to look for charity. Many people went hungry, and some took their own lives.[9]

Hard times brought lockouts, wage cuts, and union busting. At Cripple Creek, Colorado, mine owners tried to force their workers onto the ten-hour day. The Western Federation of Miners struck, and actually won, but they were exceptionally lucky. On midwestern railroads, management came together to set a standard wage and share blacklists. Long an empty alliance, the twenty-four lines in the General Managers' Association took on substance in the face of economic necessity.[10] More prone to downturns in demand than other industries, less able to control their output—much less how warm a winter consumers were having—bituminous coal miners in the Northeast felt hard times early. After a series of wage cuts, the United Mine Workers called members out in the spring of 1894. Some 180,000 miners walked off the job. With only twenty-six hundred dollars in the union treasury and nonunion workers in West Virginia producing coal, the strike was doomed. Mobs set coal shafts on fire in Illinois, and burned bridges carrying commerce in from out of state. Coal trains were halted, and a few were dynamited. States called out the national guard. By June, the strike was broken.[11]

In 1897, the UMW tried again. They threw their organizers into the Appalachians to enlist the holdouts of 1894. Union leaders were arrested for violating the Sabbath or set upon by sheriffs and company guards. Recruits were evicted. UMW vice president John Mitchell fled for his life, swimming an icy river to safety. The strike was won nationally, but as nonunion coal from West Virginia continued to pour into the Midwest, the gains dwindled away.[12]

Silver Purchase Repeal

The misery beyond his gates troubled Cleveland, but not enough to free his imagination. He was a stubborn man, and a sick one. Early in his term, doctors discovered a tumor on the roof of his mouth. If left there, it would have killed him, and financial markets were so jittery that the operation had to be done in secret. A surgeon removed it while the president "vacationed" on a yacht cruising the Hudson River. Much to his doctors'—and perhaps his own—surprise, the operation was a complete success. The tumor never came back, but Cleveland never recovered completely. He lost a hundred pounds, was easily tired, even more quickly exasperated. Gradually, the president became a recluse, shut off from press and public and all but a few of his closest political allies. Around him gathered a lackluster Cabinet of yes men and third choices, from Secretary of the Interior "Hoax Smith" to Richard Olney, the belligerent Attorney-General, whose outlook remained that of a high-paid Boston corporation lawyer.[13] They had no advice to give beyond what Cleveland already had decided upon. The solution lay in reviving business confidence. That could best be done in two ways: repeal the Sherman Silver Purchase Act of 1890 to show that gold alone would remain the backing for a nation's currency, and cut the McKinley Tariff to allow Americans to buy cheaper goods from abroad and open foreign markets to their own products.

Cleveland could make a decent case for his cure. Under the Sherman Act's provisions, the government had issued silver certificates, which bearers could redeem in gold or silver. They demanded gold only. The more they demanded, the lower the Treasury's supply fell, while the government was stuck with silver coin that no creditor wanted and no other country but Mexico would accept. There was no longer any chance of the Silver Purchase Act raising silver's price by purchasing a mere 4.5 million ounces a month.[14] On the other hand, repeal the act, and one of the drains on gold would end, and with it financiers might have hope. A return to the tariff for revenue would mean more money—gold in particular—for the Treasury.

But repeal had a high price tag. The president had kept a very calculated silence on the silver issue through the campaign. Unlimited coinage he would never accept, but he accepted a platform friendly to an inflated currency without so much as a grunt of protest. His first priority, he made clear, was fixing the tariff. Then, when the president summoned Congress into special session that summer, he did so on behalf of repeal, and that alone. With the assembling of "Cleveland's Circus," as one free-silver congressman called the session, the administration threw all its resources into winning an unconditional victory. Civil-service reform gave way to strong-arm pressure, hiring and firing to punish and reward congressmen. That had been one of the very things the Pendleton Act had been written to avoid; but as Cleveland put it, "a man had never yet been hung for breaking the spirit of the law."[15] Compromises were proposed. Cleveland brushed them aside. By the time he got the law he wanted, he had

THE LIGHT WON'T PENETRATE IT.

The Light Won't Penetrate It.
A perplexed Grover Cleveland cannot get sound-money
sense into the "free-silver crank's" brain. (*Puck*, 1895)

turned half his backers into bitter enemies. Months later Cleveland had a chance to
mend fences. The Treasury still held silver bought since 1878 and never coined—the
"seignorage," as it was called. Coining it would expand the money supply by a modest $55 million, and at least take the edge off silver Democrats' ire. Enough of repeal's
backers favored the idea to pass a bill. Cleveland vetoed it.

Was the fight over silver worth making? "All men of virtue and intelligence know
that all the ills of life—scarcity of money, baldness, the common bacillus, Home Rule,
... and the potato bug—are due to the Sherman Bill," jeered John Hay. "If it is repealed, sin and death will vanish from the world . . . the skies will fall, and we shall all
catch larks." Banks may have been failing at record rates, but not because of the sil-
ver-purchase act: most of them closed in the West and South, where silver coinage
was widely trusted and very popular. Repeal did not make the skies fall—only prices
and wages. It added to deflation already ripping through the economy. Before Congress acted, Pillsbury flour mills in the Midwest had to issue scrip for the wheat they
bought, and southern farmers found no buyer for their cotton because nobody had
the ready cash.[16] After it, farm prices kept dropping. So did the stock market and the
gold reserve.

"A full Treasury nobody looks at, and a half-full Treasury disturbs the whole world," Boston banker Henry L. Higginson wrote. "Every business man *knows* that—confidence, confidence—nothing else needed." The administration shared his opinion. At all costs, it had to keep gold levels up to the $100 million mark and knew only one way. It must sell government bonds for gold, preferably to those foreigners draining out so much American bullion in the first place. When Congress refused to give the president legal authority, he did it anyway. Four times the president authorized bond issues: $50 million in ten-year securities in February 1894, another $50 million the following November, $62 million the next February, and $100 million more a year later.[17]

The third arrangement caused the loudest outcry. The first two had been hawked in public, as the law required, with miserable results. Wall Street bankers had ended up buying the lion's share, for lack of any other takers. By the end of January 1895, the heart of the whole monetary system teetered on the verge of collapse. The Treasury gold reserve stood at $41.4 million, some $4 million less than the bullion drained from government vaults that month alone and more than the gold certificates still outstanding. Another bond issue could go begging, unless the administration made a private deal with J. P. Morgan and his syndicate friends, who would take a commission for selling the bonds to financiers worldwide. That happened in the end, though Cleveland wavered at the last minute, and had to have his backbone stiffened by Morgan and Olney. The president was bargaining from the weakest possible position. Still, he did what he could, refusing to go the full $100 million that Morgan wanted. Critics claimed that Morgan interests made a profit of $12 million to $16 million; it was, in fact, $1.5 million, and Morgan's own bank made $131,932.13.[18] But with those negotiations, the myth took hold that Cleveland had sold out fiscal policy to the bankers.

1894: The Terrible Year

Tariff reform proved an utter disaster. Drained of political capital by the Silver Purchase repeal, Cleveland had no leverage with the Congress of 1894. In the House, the frail, scholarly William L. Wilson of West Virginia put through a bill with a long free list of raw materials and some gingerly snips at rates on manufactured goods. House Democrats tacked an innovation onto it: a 2 percent tax on incomes greater than $4,000. The Senate patched it into something unrecognizable with 634 amendments. By the time a conference committee had completed its work on what one low-tariff man dubbed "the quintessence of wickedness," ad valorem rates of 35.5 percent had been raised to 38.68 percent—lower, indeed, than the 49.58 percent rate in the McKinley bill, but far from the reform Cleveland had promised. Disgustedly, the president let it pass without his signature (and with scant thanks for Wilson, who had done his very best; crushed, William "the best-beloved," as a colleague called him, broke down and cried like a child).[19] The measure did nothing for trade, nor for the Depression. Instead, it raised a howl among high-tariff men, including workers, convinced that they had been sold out to English competition.

Beyond this, the administration had nothing to suggest. After ordering staff reductions to save money—and letting the cuts fall on as many Republicans and blacks as it could—it had done all it thought should be done. One insider put it best, when he declared the government's main duty as resistance of every move towards "High Daddy government," and all those "'reforms' which mean that the Government is to rock the cradle and drive the hearse, weep over the grave and sit up with the widow, and pay every man for cracking his own lice."[20]

And the government supported inaction in the most active way. "Idle men throng the market places and congregate on street corners," Toledo's new mayor mused in 1897, "and yet on every hand there is work in abundance, that needs to be done." But no one on the city council dared propose a government jobs project. Already, the idea had met a stern rebuff at the nation's capital. With hunger and desperation shoving them on, armies of the jobless massed in the spring of 1894 for marches on Washington. At the head of the greatest of these was a self-made Ohio quarry owner and one-time Greenbacker, Jacob Coxey. Coxey had a passion for bicycles and, not too surprisingly, a love of good roads. Even in good times, he had backed a plan for putting the jobless to work at $1.50 a day building those roads. The federal government would issue $500 million in paper money to pay for it, and still more greenbacks to encourage local authorities to set up their own public works projects.[21]

Greater need gave Coxey's plan greater urgency and the faith that Congress could be forced to listen, if confronted with "a petition . . . with boots on." Out of New England the young men came, and across the mountains from Los Angeles, Seattle, and Portland. Across Ohio and Pennsylvania, Coxey's men found their way on handouts, or camped out in empty boxcars. Wherever the crowds went, unions welcomed them with provisions and recruits, and middle-class citizens enlisted in brand-new companies of state militia, complete with Gatling guns. State troops evicted them half-heartedly, letting one group off with a reprimand and a day's rations.[22]

Coxey's army got to Washington, but that was all it got except a bad press. Among the multitude of needy rode a modest, well-publicized assortment: astrologers, pamphleteers, cowboys, crackpots, and a self-proclaimed professor who boasted himself the loudest singer in the world. No one could take offense at the bespectacled commander of that host, riding in his carriage alongside his wife and baby "Legal Tender," but what could one say of lieutenants like Carl Browne, a Californian who detested bathing as much as he did the bondholders? Already depicted as "the longest free lunch on record," a mob of vagrants, and a well-organized army of revolutionaries, the crowd was actually so law abiding that it stopped at toll-gates—and Coxey would pay its way through. By the time it reached the capital, the army was swollen with journalists and Secret Service detectives reporting its every move. Even then, the hoped-for hundred thousand was ninety-nine thousand shy. Now Congress would not even let the marchers carry banners across the Capitol grounds. When Coxey did so anyway, club-wielding authorities set upon his backers. He was sentenced to twenty days in jail and fined five dollars for walking on the grass. It was rather a long sentence for a short banner: three inches long, pinned to his coat.[23] Unable to forage their way across the prairies, driven out of the railroad yards, other armies never reached

Jacob Coxey is Arrested for Walking on the Grass. (*Harper's Weekly*, 1894)

the District or arrived a few months late. They got even ruder treatment. If the president felt any sympathy for the marchers, he hid it well.

The Pullman Strike

That same summer, he showed how far his sympathies could be moved, when a railroad strike broke out across the Midwest. Built in 1881 by George M. Pullman to house the men who made his sleeping cars, the company town of Pullman seemed to outsiders the ideal example of capitalism at its most beneficent. Well-paved, tree-lined streets swept past some eighteen hundred dwellings, most of them roomy yellow brick houses with gas and indoor plumbing. Paternalism could offer no better, which was just the trouble. Pullman had given his workers the town he considered best for them, rather than one they would have devised for themselves: no town government or elected officers; no homeowners; no cemetery, orphanage, or public charity; no church but his own; no Democrats; and no free speech. Workers had to take gas and water at prices 80 percent higher than nearby Chicago demanded, and pay an annual fee for the library, whether they used it or not.[24]

With the Panic of 1893, Pullman's compulsory benevolence became a gift his workers could not afford. Wages were cut (70 percent in some cases), but not the town's rents; the community was a business proposition, and Pullman expected a good profit. Early in 1894, a second wage cut was announced, just as the firm announced an 8 percent dividend. A delegation of workers called on Pullman to ask that the cut be rescinded or rents reduced. Pullman not only refused; he laid off several members of the delegation. His workers struck. Their only hope lay in getting the railroads to boycott Pullman's product. So they turned for help to the fledgling American Railway

Union, headed by Eugene Victor Debs. Arbitration was proposed, and back came the word from Pullman's managers: "There is nothing to arbitrate." Wages were none of employees' business. With that, the ARU declared that it would run no train carrying Pullman cars.[25]

Debs had wanted desperately to avoid just such a crisis. His union had everything to lose, nothing to gain. It had no grievance of its own against the roads, had not tried negotiating the matter with them, and now was demanding that they break a contract with Pullman and open themselves to legal damages. A sympathetic boycott was almost sure to lead to a sympathetic strike, terrifically inconvenient for most Americans and sure to find no friends on the bench. For the same reasons, nothing could have pleased the General Managers' Association more than a quarrel with ARU on these terms.[26]

As one, the companies centering on Chicago warned that any employee who refused to handle Pullman cars would be dismissed. On road after road, the order was given and 150,000 trainmen struck. Traffic came to a standstill from Cincinnati to San Francisco. The Southern Pacific Railroad lost $200,000 a day. Across the Midwest, far more railroad workers were thrown out of work by the traffic tie-up than actually went on strike. With northern California's harvest season at its peak, crates of fruit piled up at the depot, only to rot. As coal trains stopped, the factories that were still running had to bank their fires.[27]

With a nation hampered and clamoring, the federal government could not avoid stepping in, but did so with flagrant partiality. Authorities tried neither mediation nor investigation. Already the managers had enlisted the help of the attorney general. Wealth, connections, and continuing retainers from some of the railroad men involved made Richard Olney more than receptive. His choleric disposition made him naturally hostile to disorder or wilfull behavior. It was made no better by having to give up his summer vacation to handle the crisis. He had made railroad men into judges and agents of the Justice Department before; now he did so again. Days before the boycott began, Olney was ready to send troops to protect strikebreakers. All he needed was the excuse. Violence might force Illinois's governor John Peter Altgeld to ask for aid, but the strikers refused to riot and the governor declared the state capable of handling any trouble. Olney and the railroads therefore turned to the federal courts and one of its newest weapons against labor, the injunction, for a ban on union activity so broad in scope and applied to so many thousands of people that it would be broken at once. Then a judge could call on the president for help enforcing the court's order. Working with company attorneys behind the scenes and friendly judges before the bar, the Justice Department soon had what an editor described as "a Gatling gun on paper."[28]

Within a day, the judge's injunction and request for help had been issued. Soldiers and a mob of deputy marshals—many of them railroad employees—fed, armed, and supervised by the managers, were dispatched to crush out anarchy, a state that had not existed until the troops arrived as strikebreakers. Then Chicago mobs went on a ten-day rampage, wrecking railroad cars by the hundred. Fresh from covering Coxey's march, a young reporter felt his sympathy for the workers clash against his horror at the pandemonium. "All southern Chicago seemed afire," he wrote later. State and local militia restored order there and elsewhere, but federal troops got the credit, such as it was, and the ARU, whose members took no part in the violence, got the blame. Some two dozen people were killed, none of them strikers.[29]

An equally hard blow fell from the AFL and the railroad craft unions, all of whom feared the idea on which the ARU had been founded, of one organization open to all railroad men. The Brotherhoods refused to join the strike and worked against it across the East. The AFL called on its members to stand clear. Even the men along the Great Northern Railroad, whose strike the ARU had helped win three months before, stood aloof. (The next year, Great Northern workers emerged again, to ask the ARU for more funds!) Perhaps no more than one trainman in ten went off the job.[30]

By mid-July, the strike had collapsed. Most of those who walked out got their old jobs back. The most active union men were blacklisted on every line the General Managers' Association ran. Debs was indicted for conspiracy to hamper interstate commerce. A juror's death brought a mistrial, but the government was already as good as beaten. As the jurors were dismissed, they all came up to shake Debs's hand.[31] Debs's violation of the blanket injunction, however, was another matter. Contempt of court took no jury trial. Spared the rigors of making a serious case, the government had no trouble convincing a judge to put Debs in jail for six months. By the time he emerged, the ARU was a wraith.

Between them, Debs, Coxey, and Pullman had initiated a revolution, but not a radical one. Before the panic, lawyers and jurists had differed over how far the courts must interfere on the conservative side, and the Supreme Court itself had left the states with plenty of power to regulate business. With the upheaval of 1894, the weight of the bench shifted decisively to the right. In the year that followed, the Supreme Court would block the most important steps government had taken to control predatory wealth. It knocked down a state maximum hours law, gave the judges the last word on what railroad rates were reasonable, and dealt a jarring blow to every regulatory commission in the land. When the American Sugar Refining Company, with nine-tenths of the nation's refinery capacity, was brought up under the Sherman Anti-Trust Act, it escaped scot-free, and the vast majority of enterprises with it. Interstate commerce, said the court, meant businesses moving across state lines, like railroads—not manufacturing. (The Court was not trying to make America safe for trusts; it simply felt that trust-busting was a job for the states.)[32]

The income tax had ninety-nine years of legal precedent. Usually, that was enough to sanctify any measure, but not now. A one-vote majority overturned what the Chief Justice called "a century of error." The income tax was a direct tax, and unconstitutional in any form except one based on each state's population. But the decision did not stand on law so much as politics. Accept this tax, Justice Stephen Field warned, and the first gun was fired in "a war of the poor against the rich; a war constantly growing in intensity and bitterness," leading to revolution.[33]

As far back as 1842, the courts had upheld the legality of unions and the right to strike. But by 1893, a few judges were starting to backtrack. Starting that year, jurists began touting the injunction as a remedy for labor disputes. Any railroad strike, Circuit Judge William Howard Taft announced, interfered with interstate commerce. If a union supported strikers, it was no longer a legal organization. A few lower courts declared it a crime for workers to quit their jobs at any time inconvenient to their employers. If a court ordered them to work and they refused to, they could be jailed for contempt of court. The Supreme Court did not carry the injunction quite that far, but to the distress of even some conservative legal scholars, it did uphold it, and Debs's conviction without trial by jury as well.[34]

Even so, the immediate public reaction was hard to mistake. To those who followed newspaper accounts, the real issue in the Pullman strike was the choice between the rule of street demonstrations and the rule of law. Middle-class Americans, even ministers sympathetic to the miseries of the lower classes, knew anarchy when they saw it, and, as in this case, even when they didn't:

In after years when people talk
Of present stirring times,
And of the action needful to
Sit down on public crimes,
They'll all of them acknowledge then
(The fact cannot be hid)
That whatever was the best to do
Is just what Grover did.[35]

Discontented voters did not respond to repression and judicial fiat by turning Populist. They shifted in record numbers to the conservative alternative to the administration. Even the beaten coal miners of Ohio did so.

We must never forget how deeply conservative values were rooted in American life. And yet this was not the whole story, by any means. Even some of those who spoke of the need for order blamed Pullman for making a labor dispute into a national crisis. "A man who won't meet his men half-way is a God-damn fool!" Ohio industrialist Mark Hanna exploded. As reporters revealed the destitution of the Pullman employees, donations poured in. That fall, the president's own investigating commission issued a scathing report on Pullman's role in bringing on the strike. When the old man died in 1897, his will left a million dollars for a manual-training school for boys. But Chicago had not forgotten. The funeral services took place at home in secret, the corpse borne to the tomb under the shroud of night. Over the lead-encased coffin in the concrete-lined grave, the family laid concrete-covered steel rails, to keep workers from exhuming and desecrating the body, as they explained it. California editor Ambrose Bierce offered another motive: "It is clear the family in their bereavement was making sure the son of a bitch wasn't going to get up and come back."[36]

To see the real impact of hard times, the Chicago railroad yards and the lawn of the Capitol may be the last place to look. Even as policemen and soldiers routed the forces of disorder, the old assumptions about poverty, progress, and competition were coming under greater challenge than ever before.

"Morganizing" the Railroads

The railroads' experience made this starkly clear. For twenty years, too many roads battled for too little trade, and built track with disregard for the realities of figures on their ledgers. "Gentlemen's agreements" had failed to make them work as one, but the panic made the job easier by removing quite a lot of the gentlemen. Bankruptcy led to consolidation, and consolidation hastened system building, but market forces were not the only influence in that direction. A stronger one came from Wall Street's investment bankers.

That of J. Pierpont Morgan towered above the others. Large, belligerent, with a bulbous nose which made him wary of snapshot photographers, Morgan grew gruffer as he grew older. "Will you lend me your ear?" one supplicant begged. "Certainly," Morgan told him. "But nothing else." Anyone meeting him during business hours would find it hard to imagine that the financier was also a sponsor of religious revivals, a founder of the local Society for the Suppression of Vice, and a committee member of the YMCA, and if they knew how he enjoyed being pallbearer at funerals, would have surmised that the pleasure came from attending the departure of one more potential rival. The legend of Morgan loomed larger than the man himself and gave him half his power: a big enough financier to bail out Grover Cleveland's government or stop a panic (as he did in 1907), or force commercial giants to make peace with each other. Surrounded by the best legal and technical talent that money could buy, he held a commanding interest in three of the largest insurance companies, assorted trust companies, and some of the biggest banks in New York.[37] Those seeking a financial villain in American life could not have chosen better. Even his yacht was named *Corsair*!

But Morgan was no wrecker of commerce. He took his place on railroads' boards of directors, not as a pirate boarding a passing ship, but as the invited guest of firms short on capital and business confidence. His name conveyed reliability, just what investors wanted most. No financier could provide so wide a range of services; his firm had the legal expertise and corporate accountants that jerry-built railroads so lacked; his partners included men with experience managing railroads. It was not power that Morgan craved, but stability and stable railroad rates, the kind shippers could depend on from one year to the next. By 1900, he had direct control of over 30,000 miles of railroad, and allies ran many thousand more. Most of those lines had been "Morganized" in the 1890s—thrown into receivership during hard times, handed over to Morgan for financial resurrection, their debts scaled or wiped out, new bond issues floated, and bankers promoted to spots on the boards of directors, bankers accountable to Morgan himself.[38]

Given the opportunity, competing roads became pieces of a regional monopoly, often more efficient and certainly more profitable than what had gone before. By 1900, a half-dozen firms owned four-fifths of the mileage in New England. Two companies held over half. Virtually all the track south of the Potomac belonged to ten railroad systems, all of which northerners controlled. In 1906, indeed, seven groups of railroads owned nearly two miles in every three nationwide.[39]

The quest for stability had an ironic side-effect. The Pullman strike had broken the biggest railroad union, but only after massive involvement by the federal government. A crisis like that must not happen again. While Debs sat in prison, Chicago's railroad magnates were meeting in boardrooms to set up machinery for cooperation. Bit by bit, they came around to the unthinkable, the notion that some kind of labor organization was not only tolerable, but essential, if the industry was to run smoothly. As the ARU was wiped out, the Brotherhoods found roads readier than ever to make an agreement with them—102 companies by 1902. With better times, leading railroads granted wage hikes before unions could organize to compel them or went halfway to meet workers' demands before a crisis developed. When the presidential commission called for a law setting up a permanent structure for arbitrating disputes, it found companies receptive. In time, so was Richard Olney himself. Allying himself with the surviving railroad unions, he supported the Erdman Act that made government-arranged, court-enforced arbitration possible. No longer could railroads issue yellow-dog contracts or impose the blacklist. Flawed though it was, the Erdman Act offered a token that the new century might escape the confrontation marring the close of the old.[40]

The Rediscovery of Poverty

In good times, the rigid Social Darwinism of William Graham Sumner had met a mounting attack from sociologists and polemicists. The panic reinforced those doubts and spread them further. As long as poverty remained half-hidden, Americans could convince themselves that self-reliance and character brought their due. When want touched relatives and kin, when neighbors went begging, when those in need were so visible, the idea that success remained open to all who were worthy of it looked absurd. With a new vigor, reformers made the argument that compassion, not clear-headed efficiency, must be the guiding principle of charity work.

Backing up their appeals was a growing library of evidence. State labor bureaus produced facts and tables to show how often accidents, not drink, made beggars of able-bodied workers. Roving through darkest New York with a camera to prove his case for the city health board, police reporter Jacob Riis caught a misery both diverse and monotonous. He came upon a two-room tenement holding fifteen sleepers. Most were lodgers finding a floor to lie on at five cents a night. In the Mulberry Bend neighborhood, where seventeen murders had occurred in a single block, Riis gathered the evidence to make the city tear the worst buildings down and build a park—where, on opening day, he was clubbed by a policeman for walking on the grass. By 1890, Riis had put his indictment of social neglect on paper. When *How the Other Half Lives* appeared, readers glimpsed poverty in all its grit, with helpless, often hard-working people, their communities breeding grounds for crime and disease. Traveling with the hobos, Josiah Flynt published an account of human beings who, however far they roamed, remained economic hostages with no hope of escape. With prosperity, the reports would continue: Robert Hunter's *Poverty*, which shocked the middle class with the news that, even in good times, ten million Americans lived in desperate circumstances, and John Spargo's *The Bitter Cry of the Children*.[41]

With the Academy of Design decreeing the canons of art, painters and sculptors had stuck to the pleasing, the tasteful. Art patrons preferred the awesome natural vistas that Bierstadt painted to the more honest, "damnably ugly" pictures of Thomas Eakins, or the realistic Union soldiers of Winslow Homer's paintings. One of John George Brown's bootblacks, now, fresh-faced and cheery—that might uplift viewers. The more horrific snapshots that Riis brought out of the New York slums went begging for a publisher, but only at first. With the publication of *How the Other Half Lives*, Riis made a breakthrough. Soon others, among them Lewis Hine, would capture the immigrant, the child laborer, even the prostitutes on film. By the end of the 1890s, Robert Henri, a prominent art teacher, had stirred a revolt among the painters. The "cult of the ugly," critics called it; it might better have been called the "cult of the city," for the new art caught the city's vitality, as well as its sordidness.[42]

Beyond the mass of novels that used the slums for blood-and-thunder tales and for cheap sentimentality, discriminating readers now might pick up fiction that gave a more graphic, far more chilling picture of industrialism's price and poverty's crippling effects. "Pittsburgh, Youngstown, Gary—they make their steel with men," the young poet Carl Sandburg would write. O. Henry's short stories mixed the old sentimentality with a city dweller's fondness for the wisecrack. But often, beneath the flippant style, the trick of the surprise twist, readers could see the drearier side to the city, where the poor had precious little to live on but fantasies. The slums that Stephen Crane depicted in *Maggie* provided neither sympathy nor a second chance for their inhabitants. Only the ruthless survived. In Theodore Dreiser's novels, poverty meant hopelessness and a spirit permanently stunted. Aspiring people rose any way they could.[43]

Literature and art both fostered and captured the way a sense of responsibility for the poor was widening, but those in need could find more solid proofs than words on a page. As the first winter of the depression hit, concerned citizens leaped into action. Relief could be as individual as the Pittsburgh shoe dealer who bought a thousand pounds of beef and five hundred loaves of bread for the needy over five weeks, or as well-coordinated as the emergency committees that set up five-cent restaurants in Boston and New York, to give full meals below cost to those unable to provide for themselves. The Women's Relief Corps visited the homes of the poor, while the Catholic Girls Home served unfortunates who came to them. Patrolmen chipped in part of their wages, trade unions helped members who had been laid off, women's clubs distributed food and clothing, and cities scrambled for some excuse to do street construction or extend sewer lines, just so that the unemployed might earn a paycheck again. But most of all, the poor helped the poor. As one tramp put it, "The kind that always helps you [is] the kind that's in hard luck themselves, and knows what it is."[44]

A New Breed of Urban Reformers

As the economic crisis deepened, liberal and moral reformers agreed that something had gone wrong with the system, though at first they rounded up the usual suspects: political corruption and moral breakdown. Admittedly, no reform in New York

City worth the name could sidestep a fight with what the Reverend Charles Parkhurst called "the dirtiest, crookedest, and ugliest lot of men ever combined in semi-military array outside of Japan and Turkey." Ministers could make a good case, too, that moral rottenness made city problems worse. Let good people glance at Chicago's nineteenth precinct, first ward, if they wanted to see how the two issues connected. It had eleven pawnshops, forty-six saloons, thirty-seven houses of prostitution, and a paid-off policeman presiding benevolently over them all.[45]

For years, churchgoers and the kind of people who filled Good Government Clubs ("goo-goos," as they were known) had won practically nothing but moral victories. By the 1890s, they had joined forces and were starting to win something better. New Orleans reformers wiped out the notorious Louisiana Lottery, Los Angeles activists shut down gambling dens. In Albany, Jersey City, and San Francisco, Irish-run political machines went to smash, and in 1894, the goo-goos, merchants, and evangelicals even beat Tammany Hall.

Still, the victories of the mid-1890s showed not just the possibilities, but the limits of nonpartisan politics, Gilded Age style. Honest administration and moral decrees could not keep the bosses out for long. Nor could they provide an answer for many of the cities' problems. The two limitations, in fact, were connected. Even while New York City's goo-goos were proving police corruption in one committee hearing, another commission was looking into the squalor of tenement life. "Say what you will, a man cannot live like a pig and vote like a man," Jacob Riis argued.[46] If poverty and political misrule went together, reformers had to broaden their program.

Some were already doing just that. In Detroit, Republicans had elected Hazen Pingree mayor in 1888. A shoe manufacturer who despised politics and boasted that he had gone to City Hall only to pay his taxes, Pingree gave the city the businesslike administration his backers expected. His administration paved streets, built parks, and erected school buildings. But Pingree also challenged the utility monopolies' rates for gas and electricity. Under his guidance, the city built its own streetcar line, telephone company, and electrical lighting plant. When the Depression hit, Pingree opened up vacant lots for the jobless to make into gardens and, to provide for themselves. He also remade the tax system to put a bigger load on those ablest to pay. Detractors mocked "Potato Patch" Pingree, but his plan worked. It fed nearly half the families on relief and helped send Pingree to the governor's mansion.[47]

Samuel M. Jones of Toledo strayed even farther from Mugwump thinking. Grown rich making oil-drilling equipment, he was quite an unusual employer, driven hard by Christian faith. Workers got an eight-hour day, with meals served on the job and regular paid vacations. Thinking only of a plausible frontman, the scandal-beleaguered Republican machine ran Jones for mayor, only to find him pushing for social reforms once he got into office. Under "Golden Rule" Jones's administration, Toledo built playgrounds, night schools, a city golf course, a municipal ball park, even a free lodging house for tramps. Most of all, he took up Pingree's fight for public ownership of franchises and utilities. By 1899, Jones stood alone. Both parties ran other candidates. Jones won anyhow, and stayed mayor for the rest of his life.[48]

Social Reform Movements Proliferate

In New York City itself, old-fashioned reformers edged forward into social reform because women pushed them there. Jacob Riis remembered how they overwhelmed state legislators with facts and the mayor with arguments. "They could worm a playground or a small park out of him when I should have been met with . . . a virtual invitation to be gone," he marveled. Though most women's clubs remained genteel middle-class affairs, content to talk literature and call for curfews, a minority took on broader concerns. They helped elect women to school boards and lobbied for increased funding for libraries and schools. Women in Milwaukee formed a Consumers' League, to put pressure on stores selling goods made from child labor, and all across the state lobbied officials to enforce the labor laws. By 1900, a National Consumers' League had begun, with Florence Kelley among its guiding spirits. Blacklisting firms for using sweatshop goods might break the law, so the ladies devised a "white list" instead. Manufacturers wanting the League's label had to sign contracts and agree to inspection of their factories by League members at any time.[49]

Jones, Pingree, and the women's clubs did not supersede the old reform movements. They supplemented it. What made the mid-1890s different was not the existence of reform, but its breadth and variety, from the Populists and reforming Democrats of the South and West to the crusaders of the cities. Fear, selfishness, intolerance—all these the hard times of the 1890s worsened; but they also spurred on the hope, idealism, creativity, and questioning spirit of Americans. Instead of a political system about to collapse from its own inability to change, Americans should have glimpsed a system open to transformation in countless ways.

Change even found a few supporters on the bench. As the events of 1894 receded into the past, so did the unanimity of judges and lawyers that order and the rights of property would need immediate protection. By early 1895, the moderate voices reasserted themselves, warning against that other subversive force threatening the republic, what Cleveland had called the "communism of pelf." The Supreme Court itself began to shift with the changing winds. Before the century was out, the court had reaffirmed the antitrust law's power to control cartels and railroad combination and the state's right to limit the working day, where health and safety were at stake. It even approved of levies open to the same objection as the federal income tax.[50]

So 1894 did not end reform. It just interrupted it. From everywhere there was an agreement that change would come—that it must come. In the clamor, they may have overlooked the unobtrusive fact: it was already happening.

Chapter 18

Cross of Gold

"The Democratic mortality will be so great next Fall that their dead will be buried in trenches and marked 'unknown,'" former Speaker Reed predicted in the spring of 1894. He was right, even more so when he amended it, "until the supply of trenches gives out." In twenty-four states, not a single Democrat was elected, in six more only one apiece. Most of those who left were gone for good, giving the Republicans pretty close to a solid North and a lock on the electoral college for the next twenty years. Populists had been waiting for such a break as this, only to discover that Republicans got all the converts. As for tariff reform, it was discredited for a generation.[1]

For one cause or another, voters felt betrayed—reform-minded Democrats as much as any. Glowering eyes turned ever more on Grover Cleveland. Was this the man who, as candidate, had denounced the Homestead lockout as one more proof of "the tender mercy the workingman receives from those made selfish and sordid by unjust governmental favoritism"? In the West, Democrats had beaten Harrison by fusing with the Populists. Cleveland let it happen. Did he imagine that the coalition was one without any sharing of principle, indeed? Or had he been willing to take the fruits that others had picked and then claim them all as his own exclusive property? "I hate the very ground that man walks on," an Alabama senator exclaimed.[2]

For years Democrats in the South and the West had flirted with the free silver notion. Now the flirtation became an infatuation. When Cabinet officers went west to stump for sound money, their audiences hooted, jeered, and threatened violence.

Arguing against free silver, the Postmaster-General lamented, was as impossible as talking down a cyclone.[3]

So the party lurched into its national convention in Chicago in 1896. When the money plank came up, "Goldbugs" of the East clashed with "Silverfish" and "Popocrats" from the South and the West. Who would win was not in question. Cleveland's friends were badly outnumbered. And yet the silver men sat discontented, waiting for some orator to capture the spirit of the larger cause for which they fought. Then a thirty-six-year-old Nebraskan rose to speak for the silver plank. This was the address of his life, the one he had been rehearsing for for years, from turns of phrase to waves of his hands.[4] And the silver men had been waiting to hear him speak, for already he had earned fame as a mighty orator. His name was William Jennings Bryan.

William Jennings Bryan and the "Cross of Gold"

The points of his speech were simple; others had made them before, countless times. But as he spoke, he put matters so plainly, poignantly, defiantly, that they sounded fresh. Bryan took the party's traditions, and the traditions of the republic, and put them on the side of reform. The fight he rallied his listeners to was the old, old one that Thomas Jefferson and Andrew Jackson had fought, for the producer against the predator, the toiler against the speculator. The people's appeals had gone unheard in the past. Now there could be no compromise:

> Having behind us the producing masses of this nation, and the world, supported by the commercial interests, the laboring interests, and the toilers everywhere, we will answer their demand for a gold standard by saying to them: *you shall not press down upon the brow of labor this crown of thorns; you shall not crucify mankind upon a cross of gold.*

As Bryan stood there, arms outstretched like a victim crucified, the crowd went mad. Delegates clambered on chairs, shouted, screamed, and wept. The silver plank was virtually yelled through, and before the convention was done, Bryan himself had become the presidential nominee.[5] To those who joined his crusade then, he would remain a hero all their lives long. "The bard and prophet of them all," the poet Vachel Lindsay called him,

> *Prairie avenger, mountain lion,*
> *Bryan, Bryan, Bryan, Bryan,*
> *Gigantic troubadour, speaking like a siege gun,*
> *Smashing Plymouth rock with his boulders from the West.*[6]

His last, sad years would dim his fame. Bryan the baldheaded dogmatist and defender of Prohibition, the huckster for Florida real estate and defender of Genesis as literal truth in the Scopes "monkey trial," voice and courage both apparently gone in his last Democratic convention, when it could have been used to force the party on record against the Klan—was this, indeed, the prophet of them all? Or was he the ambitious protector of a world already lost, the enemy of a new world he did not understand?

William Jennings Bryan. (Library of Congress)

When he died in 1925, he looked more like a relic than a reformer. Had he always been so?

Cosmopolitan critics found it easy to proclaim his nickname, "Boy Orator of the Platte" a particularly apt one: the river was six inches shallow, and a half-mile wide at the mouth. Bryan certainly had simple tastes and made simple judgments, but there was nothing shallow in the intensity of his belief. If his mind was uncluttered by complexities, he would have argued that it was because the great truths on which a government of free people must be based are themselves simple. Left to their own instincts, the people were right. Democracy in its broadest sense was right. True to the old republican thought drawn on by Populist, Knight, and Bourbon Democrat, Bryan believed that those who toiled and produced the goods had first claim to government's attention. Those he knew best, trusted most, were the farmers among which he had been raised. Bryan never understood the cities, but it was crystal clear to him that urban growth and industrial development had sapped the old values for which he stood. If Homestead and Haymarket, foreclosed mortgages and failed farmers were the fruits of progress, then economic theory needed replacing with the old moral principles applied in new ways. If the people were worthy of trust, then government of the people could put faith in its right to use what powers it had: strengthening its oversight over the railroads, regulating the stock exchanges and the grain gamblers, and enacting a graduated income tax.[7] If doing right was every individual's duty, it was also government's duty. The people's servants must act on moral questions, act against privilege, and act to take back the authority from Pittsburgh, London, and New York.

The Battle of the Standards, 1896

By custom, presidential candidates stayed home in statesmanlike dignity. Bryan could not afford to. With so many of his own party's press against him, and coverage lacking in places where it was not outright unfair, he had to muscle his way onto the front page. Boarding a train, he barnstormed the West, showing up for picnics, barbecues, and fairs, and addressing crowds at every whistlestop. Three million people heard him by the campaign's end.[8]

But did they heed? The more Bryan spoke, the less clear it became just what, besides free silver, he had to offer—and whether that was enough. The Democratic convention had come out for a low tariff, stronger antitrust laws, an income tax, and tougher controls on railroads. Bryan talked about them all now and then, but he talked silver all the time. A one-note crusade was worse than monotonous. For factory hands, it was just plain irrelevant. Workers who might have voted Democratic were baffled, disgusted, and, finally, bored. To hear that more money meant higher prices for wheat might attract Nebraska ploughmen, but not Chicago laborers, who would have to pay more for bread. Tight credit had nothing to do with the plight of eastern farmers. Texas cattle and western wheat were underselling them; trunk-line railroads gave Kansas preferred rates to eastern markets. Wipe out the plainsmen's debts and they could sell their goods for even less. If inflation would help them do that, the Ohio farmer wanted nothing to do with it.

Both sides oversimplified their case, and to undecided voters, the contradictory forecasts of what 16 to 1 would mean must have left utter bewilderment. That was part of the joke when the men in Mr. Dooley's bar wrestled with the topic:

> "You was saying something about the parity," said Mr. McKenna, "but what I want to know is this. What's the difference between a silver dollar today, a silver dollar before the massacre of '73, and a silver dollar after Altgeld . . . gets in his work?"
> "All the diff'rence in th' wurruld," said Mr. Hennessey. "Th' dollar ye have there is now worth on'y 50 cints; with free coinage it'd be worth $2."
> "D'ye mean to say that this buck is worth only 50 cents?" demanded Mr. McKenna.
> "I do," said Mr. Hennessey with a fine effort.
> "I'll give you 55 cents for all you have in your pocket," said Mr. McKenna.
> "I see," said Mr. Hennessey, "that I was deceived. Ye'er a frind of Cleveland."

Cleveland had more friends than free silver men could afford. Goldbugs and Mugwumps fielded their own ticket, strong on sound money, low tariff, and civil service reform. Republicans paid the bills. It carried no states, but robbed Bryan of victory in at least four.[9]

Republicans had nominated Governor William McKinley of Ohio on a sound-money platform. Partisan typecasting made him out as the darling of the Money

Power. Behind him was "Dollar Mark" Hanna, a Cleveland industrialist and voice for the new economic order. That said, it was not so harsh a voice. Hanna had never gone in for union-smashing, and despised those who did. His devotion to McKinley came from his heart, not his wallet, though he gave money freely enough: $100,000 just to win him the nomination. McKinley was worth loving. He was honest, principled, and flexible. He was nobody's fool and certainly not Hanna's tool. When novelist John Hay met him, whatever doubts he had about the governor's strength of will melted away. "I was more struck than ever with his mask," he wrote. "It was a genuine Italian ecclesiastical face of the fifteenth century. And there are idiots who think Mark Hanna will run him!"[10]

McKinley was far more appealing than stereotype made out and the ideal spokesman for the protective tariff, not as a preserver of privileges, but as a promoter of harmony. As governor of Ohio, he showed that conservatism meant neither a lack of sympathy for the workingman nor a blind faith in *laissez-faire*. If women got the vote in school elections, if corporation taxes were raised, if safety laws for industries and railroad workers were tightened substantially, McKinley deserved much of the credit.[11]

Now he was ready to run, not as the spokesman of the old order, but of the new, and at its best. It was not an industrial American he championed, but an America too complex to define by any one adjective. There was room for the immigrant and the native, the factory and the farm, the workingman and the capitalist. All needed justice and protection, and all would get it. There must be prosperity, but it must benefit all. So McKinley became the voice of sound money, but not so loudly, so stridently, that he ruled out the coining of silver entirely, if other countries would agree (which, as a Colorado senator had commented, when the idea was raised some years before, was like declaring a willingness to turn Quaker as long as the Pope would do so, too).[12] He argued for the tariff, and for the rights of immigrants, praised the employee and the employer.

With brass bands behind them, dignitaries marching in front, and arches overhead made of tariff-protected tin, delegations came calling at Canton, Ohio. Standing in his parlor or on his front porch, McKinley would listen to their address, which, since he had edited it beforehand, had no nasty surprises. Then came a welcome, a few remarks about the issues, and handshakes all around. The foremost men of the delegation were tickled to find that McKinley knew enough about them for a heart-to-heart chat. Callers gave him tons of flowers, sheets of tin, a host of live eagles named in his honor, watermelons, cheeses, canes, and flags. The front-porch campaign proved good campaign tactics, though 750,000 callers made a shambles of McKinley's house and made off with his picket-fence entirely.[13]

By contrast to Bryan's personal campaign, McKinley's look staid, conservative, and reassuring. Beyond the barnstorming campaign, however, the Democrats were the more old-fashioned canvassers. Every week, five million families got material from the Republican party. Wage earners read that free silver meant a higher cost of living, farmers were promised an international agreement to coin silver without uncontrolled inflation. There were special departments to write material for bicycle riders, traveling salesmen, blacks, and women. Ghost writers were hired to write speeches for party officials; pamphleteers sent out 250 million tracts before the campaign's end, and still could not keep up with the demand. Pamphlets in Hebrew, Spanish, Norwegian, and Swedish poured out of the Chicago office, where the mailing room alone required 100 workers. Some 250 speakers took to the stump. Hanna raised money enough for all expenses. Banks and insurance companies were assessed a contribution based on their assets, commercial firms paid in amounts that were based on how large a business they did. In all, the Republican war chest, $3.5 million, had doubled since 1892. It was quite a contrast to the underfunded Bryan Democrats, nowhere more so than in Boston. By October, the campaign organ had folded and the campaign headquarters had been cut to a handful of volunteers. The man managing things there could not even pay his washing bills, much less telephone charges (the company cut the line off) and did all his work on one typewriter—which was rented.[14]

Both sides gave the battle an apocalyptic significance. It was democracy's last chance—the republic's worst challenge. To Bryan's supporters, the campaign that followed was good against evil, the farmhouse against the counting-house. Businessmen were warned that Bryanism was Populism, and Populism anarchy. Insurance companies advised farmers that if Bryan won, policies would be canceled. Factory owners closed their mills for the fall and explained that if free silver triumphed, the gates would never open again. The Connecticut School Fund Commission declared that it would lend money to no farmer in Ohio or Indiana, unless McKinley won, and, indeed, would foreclose every mortgage at once.[15] On the suggestion of the *Railway Age* ("the tail-wagging, saliva-excreting yaller dog of the almighty dollar," as one editor branded it), railroad superintendents passed out cards to their employees pledging their vote to McKinley. Workers signed. They had no choice. Ministers called Heaven's wrath down against Bryan, and the few who went for "the Anarchistic, Socialistic, repudiation, Demo-popocratic ticket" found themselves out of a living. Churchgoers wore their yellow McKinley ribbons even to services. "The Campaign is simply disgusting," Godkin of the *Nation* wrote. "We shall win, but what a victory!"[16]

Bryan was trounced worse than any presidential candidate in twenty-four years. His defenders put the best face on it. He came so close to winning in so many states! If only 142 votes had changed sides in Kentucky, 1,000 in California, 1,100 in Oregon, 9,000 in Indiana, and 3,000 in North Dakota, all would have entered the Democratic column. True enough; and it was just as true that any fair election where blacks were permitted to vote would have lost him more electoral votes in the South than all those switchovers would have gained him. The Republican candidate could never win there, but, as one businessman put it, "neither could his Maker if he were on earth and running on a ticket that gave to every voter a guarantee that he would go to Heaven when he died." As it was, McKinley took all four border states east of the Mississippi. Bryan carried twenty-six states, but the ones that counted all went against him. Not a single state in the Midwest went for him; not a state in the Northeast, and only one county in all of New York. He lost the middle class, the rich, and the working class. McKinley even outpolled him in the countryside.[17]

No Democrat could have won, not with the Cleveland administration to explain away, and not with so many of the rank and file implacably opposed to any stand on the money question but their own. Industrial workers were manipulated by a campaign of hysteria, bigotry, and Republican flapdoodle, but it took no deceiving to tell them what they already knew: free trade had ruined them and free silver would beggar them. Bryan talked in the language of an old, rustic America—the country of self-sufficient farmers and journeymen shoemakers, who saw themselves as the keepers of a republican tradition. It rang strangely now in city streets, where open fields and independent craftsmen were a distant memory and where so many Americans came from foreign shores and other cultures. Within months, many of those same cities that went for McKinley threw out Republican mayors and elected Irish Democrats. Still, of all the Democratic leaders, Bryan had the greatest popular appeal by far. To his followers, he could do no wrong. No candidate could have called out so high a vote, both for and against himself, nor come closer to winning a free-silver victory. Hanna's comment was an apt one when he was asked whether the Democrats would hesitate before running him again: "Does a dog hesitate for a marriage licence?"[18]

Bryan would get a rematch, but neither the silver issue nor the Populists had the same luck. The new administration had a more industrial panacea: tariff hikes. Once again, the president had a good idea of what he wanted in legislation; once again, the lobbyists for everything from burlap to mustard seed and the senators from Lumber, Wool, Sugar, and Iron made a mess of the final result. "Tariffs are guesswork modified by compromise," one of the modifiers explained. Some rates went up a little, and sugar rose a lot. The best the president could manage was to cut a few escape hatches in the final law, which let him make deals with other countries in order to work out reciprocal cuts in duties.[19]

The Populists Undone

It scarcely mattered. Prosperity was already taking hold by mid-1897. A year later, it was too plain even for campaign orators to ignore. "Goldbugs" like McKinley were lucky. The argument against gold had always been its scarcity: world finance could not get along on an annual increase of five to six million ounces. What became of the argument if vast new gold fields opened up? or if ore, useless till now, could be made to unlock its riches? That was just what happened, with strikes in South Africa, Australia, and the Klondike, and with the development of a cyanide process for extracting gold. By 1910, output reached 22 million ounces a year. Gold was not flowing out of American vaults, but in, and the pace quickened, as flood and drought devastated European cropland in 1897, and the cry went out for American wheat. Before another year had passed, factory chimneys were blackening the skies again.[20]

By then the Populist party was done for. With so many of its members ready to support Bryan, it could have run a third candidate and let its own fortunes—local as well as national—go hang. Instead, it accepted him as its own candidate, with Tom Watson for vice president (Bryan accepted the nomination, but not the running mate). "The Democracy raped our convention while our own leaders held the struggling victim," Ignatius Donnelly wrote furiously. But at least western Democrats thought

Populist voters worth courting; southerners wanted them wiped out completely. That November, the Populists' separate ticket got 2 percent. Defeat took the heart out of many insurgents; good times dulled the anger in others. When a group of Kansas insurgents had money enough to buy up the national bank and become "one of the tentacles of the Money Octopus" themselves, their commitment was bound to slacken. One by one, the party's strongholds crumbled. Populist leaders drifted into the two old parties again.[21]

The Populists had been honestly beaten—and dishonestly. But in the South, Populists had allied with Republicans where they could. A coalition victory would not have meant Negro rule, as Democrats shouted, but it would certainly have thrown a few more local offices blacks' way. White conservatives found this concept intolerable.

Out of this came the bitterest sort of politics. Both sides sent out night-riders in Georgia. In Louisiana, Democrats abducted black women and flayed them with barbed wire. When biracial coalition loomed greatest, in 1896, the state had twenty-one lynchings, one-fifth of the national total. Two years later, the North Carolina Fusionist government was smashed by cries about

NEGRO CONGRESSMEN, NEGRO SOLICITORS, NEGRO REVENUE OFFICERS, NEGRO COLLECTORS OF CUSTOMS, NEGROES in charge of white institutions, NEGROES in charge of white schools, NEGROES holding inquests over white dead. NEGROES controlling the finances of great cities, NEGROES in control of the sanitation and police of cities, NEGRO CONSTABLES arresting white women and men, NEGRO MAGISTRATES trying white women and white men, white convicts chained to NEGRO CONVICTS, and forced to social equality with them.[22]

"If the white men can stand negro supremacy we neither can nor will," a North Carolina woman wrote her cousin. " . . . Solomon says, 'There is a time to kill,' That time seems to have come so get to work, and don't stop short of a complete clearing of the decks." Middling farmers provided the votes, but merchants, bankers, and prominent lawyers set the tone and raised the money. In Wilmington, Alfred M. Waddell, one of the Democratic leaders, swore that whites would rule "if we have to choke the current of the Cape Fear with carcasses." As soon as the votes were in, he and his allies burned the offices of the local Fusionist newspaper. As Republicans fled for their lives, white rioters led by the Wilmington Light Infantry Company, complete with artillery, rampaged through the Negro part of town, beating or killing blacks by the dozen. The Fusionist city government was forced to resign and was replaced by men off a list of names that the revolutionaries had prepared. Waddell became mayor.[23]

"It is the religious duty of Democrats to rob Populists and Republicans of their votes whenever and wherever the opportunity presents itself," a daily insisted; "and any failure to do so will be a violation of the true Democratic teaching. . . . Rob them! You bet! What are we here for?" And they *did* rob them. By any honest vote, the opposition would have carried Louisiana and Alabama. But as Henry Cabot Lodge remarked acidly, places in the Deep South outdid Caesar's Rome, where "the sheeted dead/Did squeak and gibber." Alabama's voted! In Georgia's tenth congressional district, two counties had 2,000 voters, 15,000 of which went Democratic. "We had to do it," one perpetrator pleaded. "Those d——d Populists would have ruined this country."[24]

A Jim Crow Electorate: Making a More Solid South

They never did, because Democrats went beyond stopgap remedies. Even before the People's Party was formed, they had begun "reforming" the vote to cut out as many of their enemies as possible. Now the pace quickened. Undoubtedly, the South did need reform—real reform. Of the six states without a law for registering voters in 1889, four were southern. Under the "Ouachita Plan," election officials kept heavy black majorities on the registration books in Louisiana's river parishes and saved them the trouble of voting by simply counting them for the Democrats, both in counting returns and in apportioning delegates for party conventions. "Sir," one delegate to Mississippi's 1890 constitutional convention exclaimed, "it is no secret that there has not been a full vote and a fair count in Mississippi since 1875—that we have been preserving the ascendancy of the white people by revolutionary methods. In plain words, we have been stuffing ballot boxes, committing perjury and . . . carrying the elections by fraud and violence. . . ."[25]

What was needed was an honest way of eliminating Negro voters. Of course, the Fifteenth Amendment stood in the way of any frank bar on a person based on color, but starting in the 1880s, the cotton states began to change the election laws in ways that, on paper, at least, treated all races equally. A voter must pay his poll tax, and might even be asked to brandish the county clerk's receipt for it. With Democrats in charge of registration, state registrars got new power to turn would-be voters away from the polls. Anyone wanting to cast a ballot had to be of "good character." Protesting the vagueness of the term, one delegate to Alabama's constitutional convention wanted to know who could pass it. Could Christ? "That would depend entirely on which way he was going to vote," one of the reform's backers responded. Some states put through a literacy test, though they had an escape clause for illiterates: they could vote, if they explained correctly what a passage in the state constitution meant (white Democrats, curiously, grasped the clause's meaning far better than black Republicans did). Louisiana, among others, gave an exemption to those whose grandfathers had voted—which cut out the descendants of slaves pretty neatly.[26]

The poll tax was the real killer. Everywhere it was tried, it wiped out the black vote, and it was tried all across the South. After that, the literacy test, "grandfather clause" and all, did more insult than injury. White supremacy could get along without it, which was just as well, since the Supreme Court knocked it down. It was not just white supremacy Democrats had been after, anyway, but Democratic supremacy. They were having to sweat harder for their victories all the time. A poll tax or literacy test could cut out poor white farmers quicker than they could say "Populist." "With the present election machinery we are not afraid of the old Devil, even," a Florida newspaper complained, "for we could count him out so quick that his head would swim. . . ."[27]

Still, white supremacy was the best way of bringing whites to vote for a government that would take their rights away after promising not to, and the disfranchisers needed every vote they could get. Negro voters would not strip themselves of what small share in power they had. Barred from the constitutional conventions, threatened at election time, they still had friends to speak out. White Populists knew that a "reformed" electorate would turn third parties into a minor nuisance, if that, and fought hard. So afraid of yeoman whites were the disfranchisers that they wrote provisions into new constitutions, and then declared them law without a popular vote.[28]

By the time Georgia completed her restrictions in 1908, the South had turned Solid indeed. In 1901, the last black congressman, George White of North Carolina, left the House and the state for unhappy exile. Wherever "reform" passed, voting fell: by half in South Carolina and Virginia, by two-thirds in Louisiana. Black turnout fell 100 percent in North Carolina, 96 percent in Alabama, 83 percent in Florida.[29] Opposition parties were wiped out.

What was happening in the South was, in fact, a savage version of a national revolution. Until the 1880s, most states allowed anyone to vote, without registration or an educational qualification. But new states required an ability to read and write English, and in the 1890s, older states made their restrictions tougher. Only ten states still let aliens vote on their first papers by the century's end.

Anti-Fusion Laws and the Australian Ballot

All this was part of a strong move to clean up the political process. Starting with New York in 1890, states forced campaigns to go public about how much they spent and where it came from. That was a beginning, nothing more. A dozen years after its passage, Connecticut's corrupt-practices act had yet to be put into action. As for voter registration, while many states put through measures affecting cities, and nearly all the laws grew stronger over time, full statewide record keeping had to wait into the twentieth century.[30]

Most important was the Australian ballot.[31] As long as partisans passed out their own tickets, buying or intimidating voters was easy. But the Australian ballot offered perfect secrecy. It took ballot printing out of parties' hands. Instead of a dozen kinds of ballots, the state would print an official one, containing all authorized candidates, and would distribute it at the polls. Massachusetts was the first state to give the idea a trial in 1888. By the end of 1889, ten states had passed the reform, by 1892 all but ten, by 1910, all but four (southern every one).[32]

The idea found favor all across the political system, for different reasons. To small-party radicals, the secret ballot would break employers' power to bully workers into voting right. Mugwumps proclaimed it the cure-all for "floaters" and lock-step party voting. Party organizations loved the idea of a system that made it harder for soreheads to bolt the ranks and run. For that matter, any process that gave the major parties—and only them—an automatic right to a place on the official ballot, and by taxing everybody, even those whose tickets failed to make the cut, was just fine with Republicans and Democrats.[33]

In Bad Company.
The case for the Australian ballot was as plain as the
stuffed ballot box and the bribery fund. (*Puck*, 1888)

Everyone was right. The Australian ballot did encourage ticket-splitting, which
meant more independence from voters, and that parties needed to show more discretion in whom they ran. It cut into vote-buying severely and set workers free of their
fear of employers' wrath. But in other ways it struck hard at the poor. When the official ballot listed candidates by party, illiterates might still cast a straight ticket, and all
the more so when each party printed its emblem alongside the name. But how could
they tell who was who, when, as happened in a dozen states, the ballot divided con-
testants up office by office? In effect, the governments had put through a literacy test.[34]

Before the advent of this system, anyone could field a ticket, simply by printing
up ballots and passing them out. Now, to gain access to the publicly printed ballot,
there were qualifications: it was necessary to collect a number of signatures that was
usually prohibitively high for anyone outside of the major party organizations. Already by 1890, the Prohibition party was being driven out of existence in local races
in New Jersey. In twenty years, the number of independents running for the legislature there fell two-thirds. After their poor showing in 1897, Iowa Populists were
knocked off the ballot and never got on again.[35]

None of this was accidental. Major parties wanted no trouble, and they wrote
the laws. And as Republicans knew, opposition parties could win by fusion when
neither could win alone, as long as the same nominees could run under their separate
labels or as a fusion ticket; getting Populists or Democrats to vote for the other party
ticket was much harder. The solution was obvious: "reform" voting so that no candidate could appear on the official ballot more than once, either as a Populist or as a

Democrat. Antifusion laws didn't kill the Populists exactly, but they kept them from crawling out of the grave, and served as a sovereign birth control on new third parties that might hold the balance of power in close contests.[36]

Bit by bit, the old political system was being transformed, its wilder possibilities tamed, its abuses limited. In the next twenty years, the movement to separate the party organizations from politics would spread far beyond ballot reform. States would put through innovations that the Populists had endorsed: the direct statewide primary to select candidates; the powers of referendum and initiative to permit voters to propose legislation and pass it without legislative encumbrance; the power to recall officials by popular vote before their terms had ended; and, most significantly, the Seventeenth Amendment, for the direct election of senators and the Nineteenth, which extended the vote to women.

Sports

Already, by 1896, in spite of the hoopla, the old party system was coming under a challenge more dangerous than the Australian ballot or any other political reform. Without spoils or spectacles to keep them interested, the voters were changing from participants to spectators, but matters having nothing to do with politics were drawing their attention elsewhere. The impulse that the Gilded Age gave to make people join and associate, the extra time that a shorter work week allowed—all were creating a host of diversions more regular in their appearance, more attractive in their variety, than processions and speechmaking.

Spectator sports like horseracing and boxing had drawn crowds since long before the Civil War. They still did. Boxing was illegal in most places and stayed that way until 1890, when New Orleans tried regulating it instead, by Marquis of Queensberry rules. With three-minute rounds and padded gloves, bruisers like John L. Sullivan attracted a bigger audience than ever. Even after "Gentleman Jim" Corbett ended his career by knocking him to the mat in the twenty-first round in an 1892 match, he remained America's biggest sports hero. But boxing stayed a masculine game, and a strictly working-class game at that. At the other end of the social scale, the city elites who formed athletic clubs built up track and field meets.[37]

Baseball was different. Beginning among the gentility of New York City, it had become a pastime for middle-class amateurs by the 1860s. In 1862, with the building of the first enclosed field in Brooklyn, a game largely for the pleasure of the players began to change into one for the delight of the audience. In 1869, the first professional team, the Cincinnati Red Stockings, took on comers nationwide. They even had their own uniform. In the centennial year, in baseball's version of the managerial revolution, eight big-city clubs founded the National League, set up to form a common set of rules, to coordinate schedules, and, most important, to limit the market: only big cities could field League teams, and only one team per city. Just after the Civil War, too, four northeastern colleges had adopted London Football Association rules to transmute an American cross between soccer and rugby into something unique. Over the next twenty years, the ball lengthened into an oblong, and players turned into coordinated teams. New rules let them tackle their opponents, rather than slugging them. Still, without helmets or padded uniforms, football stayed a pretty rough sport, with eye gouging, leg wrenching, and broken collarbones. Eighteen players died in 1905. Usually, Yale won.[38]

By century's end, sports events were winning the kinds of audiences that campaign rallies once enjoyed. Crowds felt the same kinship with anonymous thousands—while enjoying peanuts, popcorn, and crackerjack, to boot. Colleges quickly discovered that the way to raise funds was to rouse alumni, and a winning football team did that better than a renowned faculty. Eight million people attended baseball games in 1890. Newspapers published team schedules. So did a Chicago cigar store, on what may rank as the first baseball cards. Sporting goods shops did a thriving business. Ministers applied baseball's lessons to the Gospel; for that purpose, the text, "And Abner said to Joab, let the young men now arise, and play before us," was a natural. Some readers found it significant that when the poet John Greenleaf Whittier died in 1892, his obituary got one column, alongside twelve for John L.'s fight with "Gentleman Jim."[39]

The Chicago World's Fair of 1893 caught the change in mood. Like Philadelphia's Centennial Exhibition, visitors could find all the edification they wanted, and sages all the omens of the future, including the electric chair from Sing Sing, and a consumer extravaganza complete with innovations like Aunt Jemima's pancake mix and zippers. A woman graduate from M.I.T. had designed the Woman's Building, and women artists drew the murals and carved the statutes in it. And of course, there was Daniel Burnham's "White City."[40]

Yet many who came found all the inspiration beside the point. The "Midway" included all the foreign exhibits and all the fun. The big draw was the Streets of Cairo, and particularly the damsel doing the "national muscle dance," as exhibitors called it, wiggling her stomach to sensuous music. Not many people stayed around through the five historical papers given in one evening to hear Professor Frederick Jackson Turner propound his theory of the way the frontier had made Americans of Europeans and democracy out of aristocracy, but countless numbers gawked at "Buffalo Bill's" Wild West show. If the Corliss engine captured the sober purpose of Philadelphia in 1876, quite another spirit shone from Chicago's symbol: George Ferris's wheel, which was two hundred feet high.[41]

Saying that Americans gave up politics for baseball and turned out for hootchy-kootchy dancers rather than orators overstates what actually happened. Americans went to Coney Island and the polls, too. But the grip of the parties over the electorate was weakening in the 1890s, and one reason was that the political culture that made them so eager to vote—and vote a straight ticket—on Election Day was under challenge, both from inside the political process and from without. Taking away the force of party loyalty did not necessarily remove the impulse among involved Americans to remake society through government action. On the contrary, it hurried the process along. Issues, not partisanship, would play a larger role in deciding the results outside the South. Where once party organizations rousted out their own members, they now courted independents: those for whom a cause—campaign reform, say, or temperance or a tax break—mattered more than party labels.

Chapter 19

The Ceremony
of Innocence
Is Drowned: Empire

William McKinley looked every inch a president, even when it might not have been necessary. Typically, the one time his staff persuaded him to go fishing, he outfitted himself in a frock coat and silk hat—though, untypically of his luck, the fish he caught tipped the boat over. Congressmen might not get their way, but they left the White House half reconciled to McKinley's. "I ran into a bank of roses," one office seeker grumbled afterwards. To this "Epoch of Good Nature," as one cynic styled it, there was one tremendous exception.[1] The country went to war.

"Cuba Libre!"

For two hundred years, corruption, incompetence, bankruptcy, and revolution had been weakening the Spanish empire. Monarchs still sat on a tottering throne, and dominions spanned the globe from the Philippines to the West Indies, but Madrid's control had slackened dramatically, and colonists knew it. Throughout the nineteenth century, Cuba had raised one revolt after another. In February 1895, with the plantations beggared by the latest American tariff on raw sugar, a new uprising broke out. Unable to win on the battlefield, insurgents burned the cane fields instead. "Work is a crime against the revolution," General Maximo Gomez declared. As long as the sugar economy functioned, Spain would have the revenue to enforce its decrees. "Blessed be the torch!"[2]

Vainly, authorities tried to suppress the insurgents. In February 1896, they made Valereano Weyler captain-general of Cuba. "Butcher" Weyler quickly justified his thuggish reputation. On any given day, crowds could watch as scholars, lawyers, and professionals seeking home rule rather than outright independence trooped off to prison. To quarantine the populace from the infection of revolutionary doctrine, Weyler herded them into fortified towns. Anyone outside would be shot on sight. Pent up in cities unequipped to hold them, between one and four hundred thousand "reconcentrated" civilians died of hunger and disease. From coast to coast, Spain strung barbed wire, anchored in blockhouses. That did not stop the rebels, but it pinned down the Spanish army. Deprived of military protection and their labor supply, sugar planters watched their estates decay or go up in flames. By the end of 1897, even Spanish loyalists wanted Weyler recalled.[3]

Americans could not have missed the ruckus ninety miles offshore, even if their own properties escaped the torch (they didn't). Cuba's troubles were front-page stuff, especially for the new metropolitan presses. From the independent papers of the 1870s to William Randolph Hearst's San Francisco *Chronicle* in the 1890s, journalism had been changing. Partisan sheets found themselves rivaled by more sensational papers, with a much broader definition of news and a rich diet of crime, sports, and human interest stories. From fashion to society reporting, advice columns, and child-rearing advice, the new journalism brought women into the reading audience as never before. Under Joseph Pulitzer's guidance, a pair of broken-down St. Louis newspapers merged into one of national impact, the *Post-Dispatch*. Arriving in New York in 1883, he fashioned the remnants of a once-proud Democratic organ into a new *World*, the trendsetter of its time. Pulitzer added the daily editorial cartoon, sketches, and portraits. He threw headlines across several columns—even the whole front page—shortened paragraphs, and simplified the language. After only four years, Pulitzer's paper sold 250,000 copies a day. Eight years more, and Hearst came east to buy the *Journal*, spirit away Pulitzer's best talent, and give him a press-run for his money. When he stole the latest talent, R. F. Outcault, whose "Yellow Kid" series on Sundays was to prove the start of the funnies, Hearst gave a name to the sensationalism that he and dozens of papers nationwide had adopted: "yellow journalism."[4]

Pulitzer's paper embraced the Cuban cause first but left his polemics on the editorial page. Hearst gave Cuban events a rave review on page one. Expatriates of the Junta found a steady friend at *Journal* offices. With three packet boats to carry news into Key West and eight reporters hungry for sensation, Hearst produced shockers galore. Where else could readers find all about the "Cuban Girl Martyr," Evangelina Cisneros, jailed for refusing to surrender her chastity to Spanish lust, and rescued from durance vile by a *Journal* reporter? Leave it to Hearst to collect 200,000 signatures on a clemency petition from English women alone, or to telegraph the Pope to intercede. Soon the *World*, too, was printing crazy tales just to keep up: one insurgent general apparently died in battle a dozen times, committed suicide once, and ultimately was done in by a poisoned quail that Spanish peacemakers served him.[5]

When western artist Frederic Remington wired from Cuba that all was peaceful, with no war to draw, Hearst wired back, "Please remain. You supply the pictures and I'll supply the war." Did he supply it? Popular historians think so, but the cry of "Cuba Libre!" arose from deeper, stronger causes. Yellow journalism did stir up its readers, but out in the heartland, where seldom was read a sensational word, residents shared the same indignation. Leading men had few illusions about the revolutionaries, however much they liked the white, well-educated expatriates of the Junta.[6] But the Spanish conjured up worse images still: the haughty Castilian, treacherous, medieval—and Catholic. Mention Spain, and the average Protestant would draw on that best-selling collection of cruelties, Foxe's Book of Martyrs, or imagine the hooded judges and torture chambers of the Inquisition. And why look so far back? The State Department had trusted Madrid's promises of reform and self-government in the last Cuban uprising. Misled then, Americans suspected, it was being duped now (as indeed it was). Whether peace, freedom, or order was wanted, America would have to intervene to get it.

That something *did* need to be done owed more to the nation's sense of mission than to Hearst. When Hungarians rose against Austrian rule in 1849, and Greece fought for freedom in the 1820s, that idealism had burst forth. With revolution so much nearer, it burned brighter. And war would not only redeem the Cubans, who grew blonder and bluer-eyed the more Americans considered their woes (the insurgent leader showing an "Anglo-Saxon tenacity of purpose"), but America, too. It would give the nation a cause beyond the self-seeking that politics and prosperity encouraged—perhaps the same moral commitment that a dying generation of Civil War veterans had found, now so long ago.

True, some business interests hoped for intervention on their own behalf, as a distraction, or even as a bit of economic pump priming. "A lively war with some respectable antagonist would help all around," a railroad attorney assured one senator. Exports to Cuba had fallen from $20 million in 1894 to $8 million in 1897, and imports had dropped from $76 million to $18 million. American investors on the island had some $50 million at stake, mostly in sugar plantations. But most businessmen lobbied hard against war. Chambers of commerce and boards of trade warned that intervention would trample down the budding recovery. Their reluctance only added to the idealistic glow of "Cuba Libre."

> *Shall half a gross of merchants—*
> *The Shylocks of the trade—*
> *Barter your heart and conscience, too,*
> *While freedom is betrayed?*

Better "that the jingle of servile gold be drowned in the crash of sovereign steel," a Texas journalist announced.[7] Finally, in an age honoring manliness and competition, war appealed to some as the highest test for a man's personal mettle. It was Social Darwinism at its rawest, where the least fit died.

The New Colossus: Toward a More Assertive Foreign Policy, 1880–1895

Plainly, the forces impelling the country towards war went far beyond Spanish misrule and New York misinformation. Twenty years' industrial growth had turned America into a commercial giant, in its own eyes, if not the world's. Using that giant's strength grew ever more tempting, as European nations used theirs in Africa, Asia, and the South Pacific, but the first noticeable steps were taken by the American people and not their government. Missionaries, technicians, investors, promoters, and travelers planted American values and carried American goods practically everywhere. They expected protection from authorities back home. When Japan needed railroad builders, it hired American engineers. Americans set up the country's postal system and customs service, and even introduced their schools to a regimen of class calisthenics from Amherst. Businessmen content to supply the home market found themselves forced to think more broadly. As long as the country exported agricultural products, it could depend on European consumers, but by the 1890s, manufactured goods were needing a foreign market, as well—and that would require buyers in the nonindustrialized world. Americans had to look to Africa, China, and South America.[8]

The nationalism that Republicans used to justify high tariffs worked very well to justify an assertive foreign policy, too. Nation-states took care of their own people not just at home, but abroad. In the 1880s, the inclination mostly took the form of vague talk about running any canal that French promoters dared dig through Central America and a treaty with Hawaii allowing the United States to build a naval base at Pearl Harbor (and not doing a lick of work to build either one). The Samoan crisis of 1889 signaled a sea change, in more senses than one. On one South Pacific island, Pago Pago, America had built a naval station in 1878, which it shared with Germany and Great Britain. All three countries cast covetous eyes on the whole archipelago, and came near war. A typhoon that played no favorites kept the peace by smashing naval squadrons. The rival powers won time to find a peaceful way out and settled on a joint protectorate. (In 1899, Germany and the United States dissolved the arrangement and took islands outright.) Not long after that, the Harrison administration quarreled with Britain over fur-seal hunting in the Bering Sea off Alaska. Once again, war threatened, though in the end, the United States agreed to international arbitration and paid heavy damages. When two American sailors were killed in a brawl in Valparaiso, Harrison demanded "prompt and full reparation" from Chile, on pain of war. Chile handed over a $75,000 indemnity.

Four years later, a boundary dispute between British Guiana and Venezuela brought the Democratic administration its own chance to bluster. President Cleveland may have feared the quarrel as an excuse for one more British land-grab, this time in Latin America, but the chance to score political points was also too good for the president to resist. Richard Olney, recently promoted to Secretary of State, used the occasion to interpret the Monroe Doctrine afresh. Under its provisions, he insisted, the United States was "practically sovereign on this continent." England must accept international arbitration, rather than bully a Latin American nation. Neither the administration nor the British ministry wanted war. After much sabre rattling, both nations set up an impartial commission to draw the boundary. But the aggressiveness the administration showed was something new. Quite a few Americans were coming to believe, as one Ohioan did, that "A hard fist is a d——d sight better on the average . . . than so-called diplomacy."[9]

Hawaii Knocks at the Gate

An even more ominous note sounded in early 1893 in the Hawaiian islands. Since the 1820s, American missionaries and landowners had turned the kingdom into a home away from home. Though the island had six times as many Chinese, three times as many Japanese, and four times as many Portuguese as Americans, natives did business in dollars, and the English used in the legislature twanged with a Yankee accent. Over time, white planters made sugar growing a big business. In 1887, they even got King Kalakua to accept a new constitution taking power away from the throne and giving it to the American-born elite. (Kalakua, whose manners and fondness for the poker and banquet tables made him, in one contemporary's phrase, "a sort of Polynesian Prince of Wales," bore his loss philosophically, as long as his salary was paid regularly; he could use every penny of it, and plenty more besides.)[10]

Then the king died. His sister Liliuokalani was determined to put the native Hawaiian back in charge—and the native Hawaiian she had in mind was herself. When she tried a *coup d'etat*, a small group of American-born planters leaped into action. Helped by the American minister and a squadron of marines, they dethroned the queen, declared a republic with a constitution much like that of the United States, and arranged an annexation treaty. (From the first, opponents charged that the uprising "was a revolution of sugar, by sugar, and for sugar," but most planters on the islands and sugar refiners on the mainland shunned annexation schemes; American laws would cut off the flow of cheap contract field hands from Japan and China.) President Cleveland withdrew the treaty, but never found a way of putting Liliuokalani back on the throne. He left the issue to Congress, and Congress left the revolutionary government alone. Expansion had been checked, but only for now. A change in administrations might change official attitudes towards annexation. And Cleveland left no doubt in anyone's mind that the Monroe Doctrine applied to Hawaii: as a "stepping-stone to the growing trade of the Pacific," it was off-limits to European colonizers.[11]

Samoa, Chile, Hawaii, Venezuela: all these incidents in six years' time showed how the pulse of American activism was quickening. Each time force was threatened, the use of force on behalf of America's foreign policy objectives became a little less unthinkable. And each year, America's ability to deliver its force grew, as both parties expanded the steel navy. As will be clear, the army made no such advances—in numbers, it ranked behind Bulgaria's in the mid-1890s—but even there, the fading of the threat of Indian war made more soldiers available for action elsewhere.

So even before Cleveland's presidency ended, foreign policy had taken on a new importance. By 1897, the State Department was finding its hand forced by public opinion as well as its own conviction that the national security could not afford another ten years of chaos and bloodletting. The administration did not demand that Cuba go free, but it insisted on order being restored. Madrid's negotiators were willing to recall Weyler, ease up on reconcentration, and propose a new scheme for home rule. All the reforms lacked was real substance or enforcement; but then, that may have been the point. As one high Spanish official sneered, their reform program arose "for the purpose of printing it in the newspapers."[12]

"A Splendid Little War" with Spain

Then two incidents carried the situation virtually beyond the administration's control. After rioting in Havana, the *U.S.S. Maine,* spanking new and formidably armed, steamed into the harbor, officially on a goodwill tour. No one was fooled. It had come to protect American citizens. At 9:40 p.m. on February 15th, an explosion tore through the hull and sent it to the bottom of the bay, killing some 260 men. Yellow journalists accused the Spanish of planting a mine—though the last thing Spain wanted was an incident leading to war, especially a week after the *Journal* had published a private letter from the Dupuy de Lome, the Spanish minister in Washington, sneering at the president as "weak," labeling him as "a would-be politician," and suggesting how to baby American negotiators along. But with the cry of "Remember the Maine!" dinning against Congress and a sober report from an official naval board of inquiry laying blame for the explosion on outside sources that the mother country either would not or could not control, Spain could not escape war.[13]

Nor could McKinley. The president, Assistant Secretary of the Navy Theodore Roosevelt charged, had no more backbone than a chocolate eclair, but McKinley had personal motives, not just political reasons, for resisting the warmonger. A volunteer in the Civil War, "the Major" remembered its barbarities clearly. Politics really shoved him the other way: forbearance would cost Republicans the midterm elections that fall and cost McKinley his influence on Capitol Hill instantly. Sleepless, fretful, the president toyed with trying to buy the island. He asked Spain for an armistice and the authority to arbitrate the dispute, in essence by declaring Cuba independent. Madrid conceded just enough to allow the president an out, but by then it was too late for McKinley to rethink his decision to intervene. On April 11th, the president delivered the most halfhearted war message ever made, if war message it was. He hinted that negotiations with Spain were working out at last and failed to ask for a declaration of war, much less one on behalf of the insurgents. He requested only the power to act to bring peace to Cuba and set up an orderly government there. Still, he should have known what Congress would give him: an assertion of Cuba's independence, backed by American guns.[14]

The outpouring was tremendous. Wall Street brokers and clerks filled a regiment on their own. Confederates rallied to the Stars and Stripes, with "Fighting Joe" Wheeler commissioned in the army he had fought through dozens of engagements. (He never quite got the hang of it; once, charging the Spanish works, he shouted to his men, "We've got the damn Yankees on the run!")[15] Black regiments from the West assembled in Chickamauga and Key West, only to find foes closer than foreign soil: Jim Crow facilities. When barbers and bartenders refused to serve them, angry volunteers shot up the establishments or shut them down.[16]

With an army suddenly increased eightfold, the War Department was overwhelmed. The Secretary of War was Russell Alger, a lumber magnate and Civil War veteran, who combined fatuous optimism, befuddlement, and bad temper. But it would have taken a far greater man than he to have organized an invading force overnight, after two generations of skinflint budgets, or to have changed mobilization plans on the spot when Congress suddenly ordered the army to find some way of putting in thousands of raw recruits from the National Guard.[17] Thanks to Washington's unpreparedness, it took seven weeks to bear seventeen thousand men to Cuba, and fifteen boxcars of uniforms sat on a siding twenty-five miles from the ill-clad recruits in Tampa's training camps. Soon soldiers would march across tropic landscapes in midsummer, clad in wool. They would dine on cans of "embalmed beef" so disgusting in taste (except to the maggots, which got there before the soldiers did) that quite a few infantrymen wanted to embalm the suppliers. Only 345 volunteers died in battle, but 5,400 gave their lives in this war, most of them dying from yellow fever and cholera.[18]

American handicaps were nothing, compared to Spain's. Already, in one observer's image, she had thrown "her seed-corn into the hopper": recruits not yet out of their teens, ragged and barefoot, "as pitiful food for powder as was ever seen." Spain had no commissary department, no tents, no rations for lads on the march, and for lack of a single ambulance, the sick were strapped to the back of pack mules. Without food shipments from abroad, its armies would starve; even the horses would perish for lack of hay. Its navy could show but one first-class battleship to match America's four, and its fleet was poorly equipped and out of repair.[19] Unable to stop an invasion of Cuba, the Spanish fleet at Santiago steamed out to certain destruction. On the other side of the world, six ships from America's Asiatic Squadron, which had been sent from Hong Kong under Commodore George Dewey, sailed into Manila harbor at daybreak on a steamy May 1. The channel had been mined, and Corregidor's guns should have made scrap metal of invaders. But the mines (all fourteen of them) lacked fuses and many of the guns were museum pieces, muzzle-loaders and flintlocks. Dewey's men wiped out the enemy ships with ease. Then they destroyed shore batteries. By eleven in the morning, the fight was over, with eight Americans slightly wounded by flying splinters.[20] Dewey became an instant hero.

Oh, dewy was the morning
Upon the first of May,
And Dewey was the Admiral,
Down in Manila Bay.
And dewy were the Regent's eyes,
Them orbs of royal blue;
And dew we feel discouraged?
I dew not think we dew!

The commander got a promotion, a ceremonial sword, and a Congressional vote of thanks. Babies were named after him. So was a gum (Dewey's Chewies) and a laxative ("the 'Salt' of Salts"). Had he not married a Catholic (and deeded her the house that a grateful nation had given him as a reward), he might well have been nominated for president.[21]

Americans landing on Cuba found the fight easier than they expected. Their greatest glory came along the San Juan ridge on which a Spanish fort stood. There, regiments charged the blockhouses among what one soldier described as "a perfect hailstorm of bullets." Having resigned his government post, Theodore Roosevelt led black troops and his own "Rough Riders," a regiment of cowboy chums and aristocrats, up the slopes of a small outcropping, Kettle Hill, with more spirit than the enemy at the top was prepared for. Later, prisoners of war complained bitterly that the Americans refused to fight war in a sporting way. Fired upon, they just kept marching, and having reached the top, "they tried to catch us with their hands." Roosevelt shot a Spanish officer with his pistol and came home hero enough to be elected governor of New York that fall. Honors on that charge, as in the whole war, knew no color line. "If it had not been for the Negro cavalry," one of Roosevelt's men declared, "the Rough Riders would have been exterminated." In all, black soldiers in Cuba earned twenty-six Certificates of Merit and five Congressional Medals of Honor.[22]

With the Spanish suing for peace in five months' time, the fight was, as the new Secretary of State John Hay described it, "a splendid little war." By the end of August, the United States found itself custodian of Cuba, Puerto Rico, Guam, and the Philippines, as well as a few places that the Spanish never laid claim to: Wake Island and Hawaii. That bred a dilemma: what was to be done with them? Cuba must be freed eventually, if only to sue for annexation on its own. In ordering war, Congress had passed the Teller Amendment, promising not to turn the island into an American colony. But when the Spanish surrendered Santiago, they did so to Americans alone; Cuban insurgents were barred from the city, much less a share in running it. The Liberation Army was disbanded and a new military set up, purged of Negro officers and outlandish notions like independence. Cubans must rule Cuba—eventually—but light-skinned ones, and then after proper tutelage.[23] The other territories did not even have the Teller Amendment for a guarantee. Even before peace was agreed on, the president had decided to buy them for $20 million from Spain.

Why Empire?

From republic to empire seemed a fateful step. What caused the sudden change from liberator to oppressor? Imperial theorists have proposed a number of possibilities. Empire, they argue, provided a diversion from injustices at home. It served big business interests by allowing them "sheltered markets," areas forced to buy our goods exclusively, and a cheap source for raw materials. None of these arguments works very well. For one thing, businessmen were halfhearted backers of overseas expansion. Certainly the few who traded with China wanted markets there kept open. As Europeans carved out spheres of influence, it worried exporters nearly as much as it did the English, who had their own sphere already. Both lobbied the State Department hard. When Secretary Hay sent notes to the great powers in 1899, asking that they let trade flow where it would, textile-makers might have seen visions of Chinese by the million, dressed in Carolina cotton—though, in fact, nobody in any government took the request all that seriously, Hay included. Whether exporters felt half so keen on the next Open Door note ten months later, committing American policy to protecting China's territorial integrity, is another matter. Foreign adventures cost money. An empire would require a large army to police it, and higher taxes to pay for it. Caribbean colonies would glut sugar markets at home, which was fine for the consumer and death to the Sugar Trust. The last thing beet-sugar producers wanted was Cuban cane. Filipinos did not seem a likely market for American steel, woolens, wheat, or cotton. Europe continued to offer America its best market for agricultural produce, and the best opportunities for investment.[24]

Much of the ardor may have come from the sense that an empire had become the kind of status symbol that would distinguish major powers from insignificant ones. Since the early 1880s, European world powers had divided up Africa and most of Asia. By 1898, China seemed sure to follow. Already a Russian fleet sat off Port Arthur, not far from the new British concession at Weihaiwei and the German troops occupying Shantung province. As an American colony, the Philippines might add to our cachet internationally; to win a war and take only a coaling station or even one island, as the president explained, would make us "the laughing-stock of the world."[25]

It also might leave the United States in greater peril than before. Let the Philippines go free, and they would fall prey to German or English expansion instantly. So might Hawaii. Alfred T. Mahan had set the terms already in 1890, with *The Influence of Sea Power on History*. Mahan's thesis was simple: while commerce made nations rich and strong, the nations that ruled the sea ruled the world. In an age of steamships, nations wanting to protect their trade needed coaling stations and bases along the way. The wealth of the Indies depended on American ports at Guam, Hawaii, and the Philippines, and still more on a canal across Central America, which would be protected by naval bases in the Caribbean. Commoners did not read Mahan, but members of the power elite did: Roosevelt, Senator Henry Cabot Lodge, and Secretary of State John Hay. His book may not have converted them; they already had a strong sense of national security and prestige, but it gave them bookish basis for what they wanted to believe already.[26]

Still, none of these arguments would have convinced the public as much as the one that McKinley chose, of uplift and mission. It certainly suited America's Protestant clergymen. "Has it ever occurred to you that Jesus was the most imperial of the imperialists?" the *Missionary Record* inquired. That missionary spirit flavored American policy in the Philippines. Their government dredged and improved harbor facilities, laid down thousands of miles of roads, and deepened river channels. Daniel Burnham went to design Manila anew. Hundreds of schoolteachers crossed the Pacific to educate the children. Imperial authorities built classrooms, taught the Filipinos English, introduced them to basketball, and founded the University of the Philippines.[27]

Guerrilla War in the Philippines, 1899–1902

They also killed them. Even before Dewey's arrival, insurgents under Emilio Aguinaldo had been wresting the countryside from Spanish control. Appalled to find one overlord swapped from another, they rose again in 1899. Americans carried the field easily, but Aguinaldo's army faded into the forest. It proved a minor nuisance in some places and a constant menace in others. Filipinos joined both sides; Aguinaldo's recruits included crowds of unwilling conscripts, following their feudal overlords, while many inhabitants who neither shared the culture nor religion of the insurgents were glad to act as scouts or torture folks just down the road. Finally, in 1901, American soldiers nabbed Aguinaldo, who, to anti-imperialists' chagrin, promptly made peace with his captors and ordered insurgents to submit. Most of them did.[28]

It was, in short, a guerrilla war that the United States slowly won, but at a great cost and growing frustration. This revelation shared the front page with reports of heavy losses after one more Filipino ambush. "We have bought ten million Malays at $2 a head—unpicked," "Czar" Reed remarked; "and nobody knows what it will cost to pick them."[29] It cost over $400 million and three years of jungle warfare, with seventy thousand American soldiers stationed in the Philippines at any one time. Seven thousand died in battle or from wounds. So did two hundred thousand civilians, destroyed by famine or disease in a war where Americans applied the Spanish reconcentration policy themselves. Neither side followed the rules. Both armies burned crops and farms and slaughtered cattle, though American soldiers committed arson more efficiently with a steam fire engine that could spray oil on villages beforehand. Filipino insurgents buried prisoners alive. American interrogators used siphons and bamboo pipes to force water ("the filthier the better," one recruit advised) into captives' stomachs. On northern Luzon, the universal rule was to take no prisoners at all.[30]

American soldiers did not object. "Our fighting blood was up and we all wanted to kill 'niggers,'" an infantryman wrote home after one fight. "This shooting human beings is a 'hot game,' and beats rabbit hunting all to pieces." Guerrilla warfare's treachery turned their contempt for Filipinos into a general hatred for all of them, women and children included. "The country won't be pacified until the niggers are killed off like the Indians," one Kansas infantryman argued.[31]

In the spring of 1901, the Supreme Court put its seal on empire by declaring that the inhabitants of the Philippines had whatever rights Congress saw fit to grant, beyond certain fundamental civil rights. Representation, citizenship, even the right to a jury trial, would take Congressional dispensation. "Ye-es, as near as I can make out the Constitution follows the flag," Secretary of War Elihu Root commented, "—but doesn't quite catch up with it." Puerto Ricans had already seen that; under the Foraker Act the year before, they had received all the exactions of American law, without American citizenship.[32]

Assumptions of superiority actually had underlain the expansionist ideal all along; for the assumption of uplift was that the conquerors were morally, culturally, even racially superior to those to whom they imparted values. It could be as harmless

The first step towards lightening

"The White Man's Burden"

is through teaching the virtues of cleanliness.

Pears' Soap

An advertisement that brought together imperialism, Admiral Dewey, and clean hands. (*Collier's*, October 14, 1899)

as the advertisement for Pear's Soap, showing Admiral Dewey washing his hands. "The first step towards lightening 'The White Man's Burden' is through teaching the virtues of cleanliness," the ad explained. "O, Aguinaldo leads a sloppy life," a jingle ran,

> *He eats potatoes with his knife,*
> *And once a year he takes a scrub,*
> *And leaves the water in the tub.*[33]

That sense of an international world order, with major powers applying civilization through smokeless powder, blended easily into the assumption that some races were born to rule and others to serve.

American soldiers with not such clean hands. The troops destroy Caloocan, in the Philippines, 1899. (Library of Congress)

The unworthiness of America's insurgent allies struck soldiers the moment they reached Cuba. The Spanish took defeat with becoming gratitude and good manners. A Yankee could treat Castilian gents to drinks at the cafe. But the Cubans themselves! Barefoot, half-starved, unlettered, "they were the dirtiest, most slovenly looking lot of men" that Roosevelt had ever seen. "The valiant Cuban!" a lieutenant exclaimed. "He strikes you first by his color. It ranges from chocolate yellow through all the shades to deepest black with kinky hair." What city had they captured, what battles won? Soon the press was describing its erstwhile George Washingtons as savages who stole American provisions, shot at sailors swimming away from sinking ships, and murdered messengers sent under a flag of truce. Could free government be trusted to the "monkey man" of the Philippines, or races "only partially civilized," "a horde of dirty Cuban beggars and ragamuffins"? "Self-government!" General William Shafter exclaimed. "Why those people are no more fit for self-government than gunpowder is for hell!"[34]

Against that image, set the American soldier as Senator Albert Beveridge of Indiana idealized him, Anglo-Saxon and fair-skinned, the "fine-featured, delicate-nostriled, thin-eared, and generally clean-cut featured man." Black infantrymen in the Philippines, listening to their white comrades singing "I Don't Like a Nigger Nohow," and barred from hotels and brothels for their skin color, might have drawn a different picture, but when England's poet Rudyard Kipling invited Americans to join England in taking up "the white man's burden," the general public response was rhapsodic.[35]

"Stumbled and Sinned in the Dark": Anti-Imperialism

In both parties, prominent men spoke of McKinley's adventure as a betrayal of national ideals. "Take up the White Man's Burden," Ernest Crosby challenged his countrymen,

> *Send forth your sturdy sons;*
> *And load them down with whiskey*
> *And Testaments and guns.*
> *Throw in a few diseases*
> *To spread in tropic climes,*
> *For there the healthy niggers*
> *Are quite behind the times.*

Writers like Ambrose Bierce and Mark Twain, old Mugwumps like Carl Schurz, and the last champions of equal rights like George Frisbie Hoar of Massachusetts, all agitated against empire, and found themselves in the company of Southern Democrats quivering at the prospect that mongrel millions might call themselves Americans— one hundred thousand Chinese on the island of Luzon alone, not to mention "crossbreeds" and Malays, as one Boston businessman warned. Speaker Reed so detested the policy that he quit public life rather than do the administration's will in the House. "The command 'Go ye into all the world and preach the Gospel to every creature' has no Gatling gun attachment," Bryan gibed. Bigotry, parochialism, and idealism mixed, then, on both sides, but the anti-imperialists were not just angry. They were afraid. How long could a country that flouted its ideals abroad be expected to keep them at home? "Let him never dream that his bullet's scream went wide of its island mark," a poet wrote savagely on "a Soldier Fallen in the Philippines": "Home to the heart of his darling land where she stumbled and sinned in the dark"[36]

The issue of empire could not help spilling into politics, especially since McKinley was sure to be renominated. The only surprise at the Republican convention was in the choice of a running mate, the young New York governor and war hero, Theodore Roosevelt. Proud to think himself "the best Governor of my time," Roosevelt had been insisting for months that he would not consider the vice presidency; he even came to Washington to tell the president and his associates, and was chagrined to find them just as reluctant. But the cheers of the crowd overcame even the "Emperor of Expediency," as Reed dubbed McKinley. He accepted the inevitable wryly, wondering how Roosevelt could bear sitting still "long enough to preside in the Senate."[37]

Even with blood flowing in the Philippines, Republicans had a right to feel confident, especially since they would be running against Bryan again. In imperialism, the "Great Commoner," as he was coming to be known, thought he had found a winning issue, even among the Gold Democrats who had quit the party in 1896. But by accepting a renomination and hammering 16-to-1 back into the platform, Bryan gave them something else to vote against.[38] In the end, a host of anti-imperialists went for

McKinley. "It is a choice between evils," one conservative wrote, "and I am going to shut my eyes, hold my nose, vote, go home and disinfect myself."

"I niver knew annything so dead," Mr. Dooley's favorite customer complained that September, as the campaign began. "They ain't been so much as a black eye give or took in th' ward, and it's less thin two months to th' big day." McKinley could not match Bryan's barb that America dared not educate the Filipinos, lest they learn to read the Constitution. Nor did he try. He refused to speak even from his front porch. Others did the talking, including Mark Hanna and young Senator Beveridge, who gave addresses so eloquent that, as Mr. Dooley remarked, "you could waltz to them." Roosevelt barnstormed, making up in energy what he lacked in polish. "I talked two words to [Bryan's] one," he recalled later. "Maybe he was an oratorical cocktail, but I was his chaser."[39]

Money did the real talking, in two senses. Again, Democrats were miserably outspent. The Republican war chest took in more contributions than it knew what to do with, so much that when the election was done with, it sent Standard Oil a $50,000 refund.[40] But every newspaper financial page was in its own way a McKinley tract. The full dinner pail beat Bryan in 1900, and it stayed full long enough to keep Republicans in office for a dozen years more. From 1900 to 1910, the price of farm products rose 50 percent. Railroad companies issued $67 million in securities in 1898, and $527 million in 1902. They found eager takers. Steel magnate emeritus Henry Clay Frick dubbed them "the Rembrandts of investment." (Frick meanwhile was buying Old Masters as if they were the railroad securities of art.) Lesser companies were recapitalized and launched to a lasting success: Union Carbide and National Biscuit in 1898; Diamond Match, National Distillers, United Fruit, and Borden's Condensed Milk in 1899. By 1901, an average day saw half a million shares traded, and the Stock Exchange had to move to roomier quarters, just in time for traders to sell 3.25 million.[41] Now seemed the time for optimism, even complacency.

So Bryan, who should have done better, did worse. His campaign turned into a desperate effort to find a winning issue. Silver was dropped, imperialism downplayed, and for a while the trusts were made the foremost issue. All three, in their own ways, fit together; all three fit his commitment to restore the promise of democracy, economic as well as political. But listeners knew a loser when they saw one. When someone in one audience yelled that Mrs. Bryan would be sleeping in the White House next March, a heckler shot back that in that case, she would be sleeping with McKinley.[42] When Election Day came, turnout dropped to a new low. Carrying only 52 percent of the popular vote, McKinley still won the Electoral College handily. Bryan lost his own state, county, city, and precinct.

Retreat from Empire

There would be no retreat from McKinleyism, not if that term meant mixing in the world's affairs. In the summer of 1900, Chinese nationalists, led by secret societies like the Fists of Righteous Harmony (or Boxers, as an American press quickly dubbed them), rose against outsiders. Native converts to Christianity were butchered, foreign missions burned, diplomats killed, and Western legations in Peking put under siege. When the empires mustered an army to rescue their countrymen, the Boxer Rebellion collapsed. Yet the closing scenes may have been more significant than the main event. Incidents like these had happened before, in other places, and always a European victory set off a land-grab. Not this time. China paid a heavy indemnity, and the foreigners kept their privileges, but the United States saw to it that Chinese territory stayed Chinese.[43]

The Boxer Rebellion, not the Philippines, pointed toward America's real future. By that same election-year summer, the president had signed a bill giving Hawaii a territorial government, no different in rights from Oklahoma. Anyone able to write English or Hawaiian could vote. Already, too, McKinley was setting confines on our imperial design in Cuba, where military rule continued, with 11,000 soldiers under arms there. In 1900, the president called in General Leonard Wood to manage things. "I want you to go down there to get the people ready for a republican form of government," he explained. " . . . We want to do all we can for them and to get out of the island as soon as we safely can." Wood, who would rather have seen those "stupid, downtrodden people" remain American subjects, settled for making Cuba a trusty client state. The general worked eighteen hours a day, and drove his subordinates just as hard.

> *There is no time for food.*
> *Write till the ink runs dry.*
> *The man who works for Wood*
> *Is one who wants to die.*

Just as the emperor Augustus found ancient Rome brick and left it marble, one of the general's defenders boasted, so Wood had "found Cuba a den of filth and disease and left it a sewer system." But the general did more than put up-to-date plumbing in the hospitals and buy schoolbooks and desks for 100,000 children. Under his protection, American investors took over plantations and refineries. Under his tutelage, a conservative republican constitution was drawn up. The Platt Amendment made the protectorate, and Cuba's nominal independence, official in 1901. The new nation could not make any treaty putting its independence at risk; the United States could intervene to preserve the republic; the country's finances must remain solvent; and the United States got a naval base at Guantanamo. By 1902, Cuba had restored its old sugar economy, as dependent on American consumers as it had once been on Spain's. The island had its own president and legislature: a legislature chosen by white, literate, propertied Cubans, and a president hand-picked by General Wood and elected without leaving his home in upstate in New York to campaign.[44] Yet limited independence was a significant step away from empire.

Elsewhere, American policy followed the same course. In the Philippines, an American-run commission tried to remodel local government, spark the economy, and train the natives in political democracy. Starting in 1907, a national assembly shared power with the commissioners. Nine years later, Congress made official the promise to set the Philippines free eventually, and a few months later, it gave Puerto Ricans the full American citizenship denied them in 1900.

Gunboat Diplomacy: The American Presence in the Caribbean

In the first two decades of the new century, the United States would treat the Caribbean very much like an American lake, with an unofficial protectorate blanketing nations unable to keep order or a sound balance on their ledgers. In 1903, when Colombia's government refused to agree to a treaty leasing a strip of land on the Isthmus of Panama for American interests to build a canal, President Theodore Roosevelt lost his temper with "those jack-rabbits." For years, Panamanians had tried to make their own republic. With an American battleship backing them up, they called a revolution, and when the smoke (not much more than a few wisps) cleared, the United States had its treaty. "Gunboat diplomacy" sent troops to Cuba in 1906 and 1917, to the Dominican Republic in 1916, and to Vera Cruz, Mexico's essential Gulf port, in 1914. Marines helped out a Nicaraguan revolution in 1909 and came ashore to occupy the country in 1912. Stability mattered more to the United States than democracy or good drainage, and it did a better job of building up the Dominican Republic's army than its railroad lines. In time, the United States came to administer ten Latin American countries' financial policies. Still, what failed to happen may be what matters most. For years, Europeans had used unpaid debts and unprotected nationals as an excuse for taking new territory. There were more oppressive "white men's burdens" than an American official acting as customs collector. American forces landed in Haiti in 1915. They stayed until 1934, but they left, and had meant to all along. Far from extending its own empire, the United States kept half a dozen others out, by making itself constable for the Caribbean. That, in effect, was what the Roosevelt Corollary meant, when McKinley's successor announced it in his annual message in 1904.

Naval officers clamored for bases in China, the Dominican Republic, and Haiti. Colombia offered to sell some of its islands. Roosevelt would have none of them; he even declined two of the four bases that the Platt Amendment allowed in Cuba and drew the borders for the base at Guantanamo so narrowly that it lacked an adequate water supply on its own. So discreetly did he handle his intervention in Cuba that the soldiers had friendly crowds on hand to bid them goodbye when they left. Roosevelt's remark about the Dominican Republic summed up the reluctant imperialist perfectly: he no more wanted to annex it "than a gorged boa constrictor . . . to swallow a porcupine wrong-end-to."[45]

So, in the end, the gap between Roosevelt in action and Bryan in speech did not yawn so widely after all. When Bryan became secretary of state himself in 1913, he showed his commitment to peace by melting swords into plowshare-shaped paperweights and by getting crowds of countries to sign arbitration treaties. (Roosevelt never cared for parchment peace, but he won the Nobel prize for arranging the negotiations that ended a short, bitter war between Russia and Japan.) But it was Bryan who tried to arrange for a protectorate over Nicaragua that was markedly similar to the Platt Amendment; it was during his tenure that troops landed in Vera Cruz to help topple Mexico's dictator, and the decision, for all Bryan's reluctance, was the logical outcome of a policy already a year old, based on that same combination of pragmatism and moral outrage that had sent Americans into their tropical adventures in 1898.[46]

Epilogue: "The Right Is More Precious Than Peace," 1917

Problems changed, but that combination still impelled American policy, no matter who ran it. No one would have called the conflict that engulfed Europe in 1914 a "splendid little war." Rightly, contemporaries dubbed it the Great War, made more horrible by the technological genius devised in a century of peace: poison gas, tanks, and reconnaissance planes; the barbed wire that could slow an attack across open ground; the machine guns able to kill oncoming soldiers by the hundreds; the artillery able to hit enemy lines from miles behind the front. No charge up San Juan Hill could win this kind of fight. When the United States did enter the war in 1917, the administration acted from a sense of real threat to national interests. The sudden expansion of submarine warfare that winter had narrowed American options to a humiliating peace, with foreign trade cut off now and the prospect of the British empire in German hands a few years hence, and the first serious war in half a century. It was therefore as a pragmatist, as much as McKinley or Roosevelt had been, that the president went to Capitol Hill on April 2, 1917.

Yet the president's call to arms could depend on a wide, sympathetic audience of Americans whose hearts were more than halfway on the Allies' side already. And beyond the language of a duty taken painfully, with uncertainty over the outcome and choices taken because they could no longer be avoided, listeners might have heard the echo of that spirit that justified war with Spain, that coated the Philippine occupation with Christian benevolence—if not a forgetfulness about the whole imperial adventure eighteen years before. The "right is more precious than peace," Wilson ended,

> and we shall fight for the things which we have always carried nearest our hearts—for democracy, for the right of those who submit to authority to have a voice in their own governments, for the rights and liberties of small nations, for a universal domination of right by such a concert of free peoples as shall bring peace and safety to all nations and make the world itself at last free.[47]

Chapter 20

The Promised Land

'Tis well an old age is out,
And time to begin anew.

—*John Dryden*

Ever the symbol of conservatism
and confidence, President McKinley began his second term under a cloud only literally—it poured on Inauguration Day. His tours that summer brought out big, friendly crowds, and gave the president the chance to do what he liked most, shake hands. Such affability had worried his friend, Mark Hanna, for years. "What would happen, do you think, if some crank got in there with a revolver in his pants?" he asked once.[1] On September 6, 1901, some crank did. As McKinley stood greeting well-wishers at the Temple of Music in Buffalo's Exposition, he was shot from point-blank range by a pistol concealed in the handkerchief-bandaged hand of Leon Czolgosz, an anarchist. "My wife—be careful, Cortelyou, how you tell her—oh, be careful!" the president murmured. A week and a day, and McKinley was dead.[2]

It is tempting to say that the Gilded Age died with him, though, of course, it didn't. The world did not change all at once, but in countless small ways over a score of years. Many of the changes may have made more of a difference to people's lives than one president succeeding another.

The Advent of the Automobile: Americans Take to the Open Road

Among the most dramatic changes was the gradual adoption of the automobile. Germans had developed the internal combustion engine in the 1870s and 1880s, and there had been steam-driven automobiles since the 1820s, which railroad interests drove out of existence. Carriage works like Studebaker adapted their buggies for motors, and other handymen took the idea of ball-bearings and pneumatic tires from the great travel fad of those years, the bicycle. It was no accident that America's first automakers were Charles and Frank Duryea, Massachusetts bicycle designers, who by 1898 had made thirteen cars, each different from the one before it.[3] Only in 1900, when the Olds Motor Works started the mass production of automobiles, did they go much beyond the novelty stage. Olds turned out six hundred of them in the first year and four thousand by the third, and sold them for less than $700 apiece. American life transformed just a little, each time a consumer bought one (though in 1900 the machine was too new to have a fixed name; in one contest, "motocycle" came in first over contenders like "mocle," "petrocar," and "viamote"). Where some three hundred cars wheezed, sputtered, and jerked forward nationwide in 1895, enough soon were on the move for states to begin setting speed limits (with twenty miles an hour as the absolute maximum, and, in Tennessee, the additional safeguard that no journey could be started without a week's public notice). By 1910, 460,000 cars had take to the roads—axle-deep, often enough, since few roads outside city limits were paved.[4]

They did not stay so for long. Thanks in part to the automobile, the Good Roads movement that had begun with bicyclists picked up speed. "Who can keep in a good humor with clay on his feet?" one proponent argued. ". . . Locomotion is freedom, and good roads make freedom easy." Another lobbyist gave paved roads the credit for the decline in malaria cases. Certainly roads fit for automobiles transformed rural life. For one thing, farmers no longer had to go into town once a week to pick up their mail at the post office. Starting in 1899 in a Maryland county, expanding to cover over 35,000 postal routes by 1905, the government was able to give them free mail delivery; in 1913, it added free parcel delivery, too. Changes in recreation, mail delivery, and freight hauling had only begun to end the isolation of the farm, but the beginning itself was revolutionary. By the second decade of the century, the internal combustion engine had carried Americans into a world increasingly unlike the one where the Duryeas learned their trade.[5]

Not at once, but bit by bit, invention would change the world of the Gilded Age into something rich and strange. Between 1890 and 1920, newspapers announced the making of the wireless telegraph, synthetic resins, mechanical refrigeration, and oil-burning steamships. Ever improving, Edison's kinetoscope transformed the theater more into a movie palace. On December 17, 1903, Wilbur and Orville Wright's airplane lifted off at Kitty Hawk (for twelve seconds).[6]

Scientific and Artistic Achievements Punctuate the Era

In public health, the same steady flow of discoveries was doing more than remaking American life. It was in the summer of 1900, for example, that Dr. Walter Reed and his colleagues traced yellow fever to its carrier, the mosquito.[7] Within months, Dr. William Gorgas, chief surgeon for the American military government in Havana, went after the breeding grounds to wipe out the disease itself.[8] Already, a revolution in public health was well under way. One could date it to the start of professional medical societies in the 1880s, or to the reorganization of the American Medical Association in 1901, or, better still, to the founding of the first professional medical school in 1893, at Johns Hopkins, which was open to women as well as men. Thanks to the pasteurization of milk (thanks still more to lawmakers who forced it on dairy farmers, who resisted it as bitterly as basic sanitary regulations), "summer complaint" no longer killed its infant thousands. Parasitology had tracked down the sources for malaria, leprosy, tuberculosis, and diphtheria. Little changes over time had great effects: disposable drinking cups at public water dispensers, for example, or the use of incinerators in place of festering garbage dumps, or the adoption of screen doors and windows. "Swat the Fly!" campaigns, and grisly pictures of disease-bearing flies, enlarged for Sunday newspaper readers to goggle at, were one more reason why between 1900 and 1925, average life expectancy would lengthen by some six years.[9]

America even sounded different. Theodore Thomas, that most gifted conductor, had fed his audiences a diet of the highest-minded classical works at the Chicago Fair, to a cool reception. "Why does Mr. Thomas play the soggy tunes of Bach, Brahms, and Bruckner?" one critic complained. "Has he never heard of Victor Herbert and Sousa?" But even Victor Herbert sounded old-fashioned by 1900, compared to the jumping syncopation—the ragged time—of Scott Joplin's ragtime.

Let other countries carry on their *fin de siecle* until 1914. Here, literature, art, music, social thought, economics, and politics all bespoke a new world, as fresh and vital as Charles Dana Gibson's creation, that perfect combination of independence, patrician superiority, and feminine allure: the Gibson girl. What *Harper's Weekly* had been to the Gilded Age, new mass-market periodicals—*Ladies' Home Journal, Saturday Evening Post,* and *Liberty*—were to the Progressive Era. Already, before the old century ended, Stephen Crane, Theodore Dreiser, Jack London, and Frank Norris were changing the American novel into something hard, realistic, and modeled on the naturalism of Emile Zola, or, as critics grumbled, something sordid and depressing. By 1914, critics were speaking of a poetic Renaissance, with Robert Frost, Carl Sandburg, Amy Lowell, Edgar Lee Masters, Vachel Lindsay, and Edward Arlington Robinson taking first rank. In New York, the "Ash-Can school" of painting had provoked stormy criticism, and shattered the tradition of realism.[10]

What changes might another century bring? Nothing seemed impossible in 1901. Pundits predicted that by the year 2000, science would have developed strawberries as big as apples, and a cantaloupe sufficient to feed a whole family. Philadelphia would be able to grow its own oranges, rats and mice would be extinct and the horse practically so, and homeowners could turn on a spigot to pipe hot or cold air into their houses. Trolley fare would be reduced to a penny—assuming there *were* trolleys—which, in a city filled with automobiles "with cushioned wheels," seemed unlikely. Conceivably, Americans might even travel to England in two days![11]

In fact and in popular imagination, then, a new age seemed well under way long before McKinley made his journey to Buffalo, and it was still in the making ten years later. Yet, in other ways, what carried 1901 out of the Gilded Age were the very forces that had given the era its character.

More than ever, Americans basked in the glow of self-congratulation. Grounds for optimism lay before them on the business page. "McKinley Prosperity" meant ten-cent cotton, the highest price in years, full freight yards and money for railroads to make themselves safer and swifter. Managers built new lines and modernized the old ones, and the smart ones would take as their model Edward H. Harriman of the Illinois Central, one of Wall Street's canniest speculators. Under his command, the Union Pacific underwent a complete overhaul. Harriman overlooked nothing, down to the savings from shortening the bolts holding rail and tie together. "You see, what I want to do is to put the road in such shape that if I were to die and you succeeded me, not even *you* would be able to undo my work," he told a banker. In spite of the expense, Union Pacific earned a princely income.[12]

The U.S. Economy Matures: Exports Exceed Imports

McKinley got credit for recovery. In fact, good times advanced on thirty years of capital investment. Though modernization of the steel industry began in the 1870s, the United States only overtook all rivals in world production of iron and steel after 1890; railroad building into the Appalachians over a quarter of a century paid off just at the century's end, as the country became first among nations in coal production. Starting in 1893, the country exported more than it imported. In 1897, it passed all records: a trade surplus of $286 million, and a billion dollars worth of exports. By 1901, the figures would be $615 million and $1.5 billion respectively.[13]

All signs pointed to a maturing economy. So did the growth of bigger businesses, some taking in every step in production to save on costs and others absorbing rivals to keep up prices. The depression had thrown plenty of firms into receivership. As soon as recovery began, the weaker properties went at bargain rates. Hard times had only worsened existing problems of competition, price wars and all. The Sherman Anti-Trust Law, as interpreted by the Supreme Court, forbade pools, trade associations, or gentlemen's agreements. But the law did not forbid one set of hands to do what many working together could not. As a result, in 1897, the greatest merger wave in history hit Wall Street with the blessing—even the encouragement—of investment bankers. It lasted for six years and bred a host of giants. When the American Tobacco Trust formed in 1903, it combined seven businesses organized from 162 mergers. Only eight industrial firms had more than $50 million in capitalization in 1897; by 1903, forty did.[14]

Two events in 1901 brought home how far the Gilded Age drive toward bigger business had changed the old competitive system. The first came with the retirement of Andrew Carnegie, the enterprising spirit of the Gilded Age made flesh. He had ended the century by breaking one last set of competitors, those backed by J. P. Morgan and others. To get the railroad connections he needed, he even threatened to build competitors to Morgan's lines across the Northeast. Before the fight could convulse the securities market, Morgan sued for terms; how much would Carnegie ask to sell his steel empire? It was worth $320 million. He wanted and got $480 million.[15] Combining it with other firms already under his command, Morgan formed the first billion-dollar corporation: U.S. Steel.

An unlikely combination: steel king Andrew Carnegie, William Jennings Bryan, railroad magnate James J. Hill, and John Mitchell of the UMW. (Library of Congress)

A few months later, Morgan acted as a midwife to a second financial giant, this time in the railroad industry. Northern Securities made a fitting symbol for the end of the age of railroad competition. Already virtually every mile of track worth owning belonged to six groups of financiers. Harriman and Hill ran the strongest rail systems west of the Mississippi, and by 1901 their battle for the remaining transcontinental lines set off a sharp little Wall Street panic. Speculators by the thousands lost everything. To keep peace on the Exchange, Morgan persuaded the rivals to pool their securities in a new holding company.[16]

The merger wave made a much smaller revolution than people expected. Some industries never could consolidate: textiles, for example, or coal. They would pay dearly for it in low profits, low wages, and depressed conditions in prosperous times. For others, consolidation lay far in the future. Not until the 1920s would the number of automobile companies fall below a hundred, and among makers of soft drinks, customer preference left room for dozens of competitors well into the 1950s. Oil was oil, after all, but chocolate Yoo-Hoo and Grape NeHi were as different from Coca-Cola as wood and stone.

As for the consolidators, they overlooked a few obvious facts. Bigness was not enough. By making and selling more, by owning every step in the process, a firm could cut costs. But just absorbing one's rivals without streamlining management saved nothing, except, perhaps the cost of printing separate letterheads on official stationery. Going into debt to consolidate actually could cut into profits. That was why so many mergers failed, and others, U.S. Steel included, did only a middling business, and why, suddenly, in 1903, the merger wave stopped.[17]

But Americans were not gifted with second sight. They found the mergers quite impressive, indeed—and a little terrifying. The very components that became U.S. Steel had been immense themselves. Morgan's tin-plate firm had taken in 265 factories. Now 800 mills, and 170 different companies, had come under one board of directors. U.S. Steel's capitalization was the equivalent of a stack of five-dollar gold pieces rising up twenty miles, and amounted to 26 percent of the value of all mergers between 1895 and 1904. It employed 148,000 workers and paid more in wages than the army and navy combined. Not just consumers, but businessmen had reason to worry when so much economic power had gone into so few hands. If Northern Securities dominated the Northwest from Chicago to the Pacific, for example, what happened to competitive prices? What would protect the shipper or the consumer from being robbed? How widely would a maturing capitalism share its benefits?[18]

That question was one that workers and consumers could answer easily enough. For the middle class and consumers, a rising money supply showed itself most plainly in prices outpacing income, and in the feeling that they were being taken advantage of. This became clearest every winter, when home owners sought a steady, reliable coal supply, and yelped at the price. When food cost 16 percent more in 1903 than it had in 1896, and coal 40 percent more, wages would have to rise pretty steeply to catch up. They didn't. On average, laborers made 10 percent less in 1900 then they had before the Panic, and their real earnings would continue to fall all through the next dozen years. Experts set the minimum income that it would take for the average family to live decently at somewhere between $800 and $1,100. Yet in the paper box, shirt, and millinery industries, the median pay lay between $8 and $9 a week. In New York's canneries, workers put in fifteen-hour days at ten cents an hour. "I didn't live," a woman on a six-dollar wage testified. "I simply existed. I couldn't live what you would call living."[19]

Not too surprisingly, labor relations in the years to come would be a convulsive as ever. In the first nine months of 1904, seventy-seven thousand workers went on strike in Chicago. A thousand policemen walked out. So did bakery employees, cigar makers, machinists, and steel workers. By many measures, indeed, the number of strikes per million employees rose to its highest point in the first decade of the century, and did not fall very far until the 1920s.[20]

Progressivism

Indeed, for those Americans easily alarmed, 1901 had a slightly apocalyptic quality. In July, they might sense the conclusive proof that class conflict would define the new century: the Left came together to form the Socialist Party of America. Leading it was Eugene Victor Debs, as rousing a speechmaker or fetching a presidential candidate as the movement had. Members calling each other "comrade" made one Socialist squirm, but, he added, "when Debs says comrade, it is all right. He means it. The old man . . . actually believes that there can be such a thing as the brotherhood of man. And that's not the funniest part of it. As long as he's around, I believe it myself." Behind him rallied miners, lumberjacks, tenant farmers, and intellectuals, fierce revolutionaries and pragmatic reformers ("slowcialists," the radical wing called them),

German-speaking trade unionists, Yiddish-speaking garment workers, and even a few of Frances Willard's disciples, who saw in Socialism the logical successor to the WCTU.[21]

Obviously, then, complacency was not the only emotion that this rather uneven recovery inspired in Americans. Amid the self-congratulatory platitudes rose murmurs of discontent, and from highly respectable figures. Regular Republicans, middle-class civic societies, women's clubs, trade journals—even some academics— were challenging the new order that the Gilded Age had wrought. Reform had not come into its own in 1901—not quite. But across middle America, one could catch hints of an uprising to come.

That spring, Galveston won a new charter that carried the fight against partisan politics to its proper end by setting up a city-commission form of government. New York voters threw out Tammany Hall—again; and Cleveland's chose Tom Johnson, who would take "gas and water socialism," as he called it, further than "Golden Rule" Jones and "Potato Patch" Pingree had. What Johnson would be to urban reform, "Fighting Bob" La Follette, the new governor of Wisconsin, would be to action at the state level.[22]

What was emerging, as time would show, was the connection of forces pressing for political change into an often contradictory movement. For simplicity's sake, historians call it Progressivism, but there was really nothing simple about its agenda. A few financiers and businessmen looking for stability thought that government could give the economy a rationality that free markets clearly had not provided—closing the national forests to reckless harvesting of timber, say, or keeping cattle from stripping the public land bare.[23] Other businessmen wanted competition restored, by a crusade against monopoly. From the settlement houses and the churches came cries for action against poverty. Out of the temperance forces came added pressure to break the saloons' power to destroy families and debauch politics. Millionaires, workers, Protestant evangelicals, urban immigrants, and even a few bosses all were on the way to alliances that, ten years before, they would have considered unthinkable. Not one movement, but dozens, based on a variety of motives, took shape. This, then, was the force putting the political progressivism into the Progressive Era.

What held the reformers together? No two historians, possibly no two Progressives, would agree, but three values, merging and conflicting, covered most of the agenda: democracy, stability, and morality. To restore government to the public interest, power must flow away from the privileged and back to the people. The voters must have the power to write laws and vote on them, through initiative and referendum, to select candidates through the direct primary, to recall judges, and elect senators. Government power must even the odds between the economically powerful and the powerless, either by busting the trusts or putting them under regulation, and using the law to shelter the unprotected, whether child laborer or consumer. In place of cutthroat competition, the public sector must give the economy stability, through regulatory agencies and federal control of the money supply. It must apply scientific management to the public lands and balance long-term needs against short-term demands. Finally, most simply, government must act as moral agent. Graft, drunkenness, prostitution, un-American customs, and untrammeled greed must give way to government control.[24]

As should be pretty obvious, the bloom of reform that emerged in the new century had grown from seed sown in the old. The trend towards home rule in the cities, nonpartisan elections, and a professional civil service had begun long since. Railroad regulation rested on commissions begun, tested, and strengthened during the Gilded Age. The forces that remade Democratic thought and nominated Bryan in 1896 would persist, adding their power to the Progressive movement and helping define its program. Urban reform owed much to the mayors and settlement houses of the 1890s. That Prohibition found a Progressive following would not be surprising to anyone who had paid attention to the platform of St. John and the causes that Frances Willard's WCTU advanced.

Progressivism worked from the same heritage of moral commitment that propelled so many Gilded Age reformers. It also worked within the same limits. The split between moralists out to change city habits and urban dwellers would intensify. So would the fears about the New Immigration. What could be more modern, say, than the "New Woman"? Whether swinging a tennis-racket or debating the issues of the day, she was the image of up-to-date notions. She wanted more from marriage than a master and provider, and more for herself than a career as a kitchen-drudge. Independence meant a balancing of career and child rearing, and just possibly fewer children. "I think it would be a fearful thing to die and have done nothing for the race but to have babies," one lady commented, "—a rat or a cow could do as much." Led by Margaret Sanger and Mary Ware Dennett, the National Birth Control League campaigned to end the ban on sending information about contraception through the mails. It even opened a clinic—which police raided at once.[25]

The moral core to Progressivism made reforming women's work more necessary than ever. "Dante is dead," one activist proclaimed. ". . . I think it is time we dropped the study of his *Inferno* and turned our attention to our own." That could include lobbying for pure food and drug laws, providing school lunches for Boston's children, or having the state set up special juvenile courts. The National Association of Colored Women, fifty thousand strong, the General Federation of Women's Clubs, and settlement house workers, white and black, carried food baskets to the needy and built day nurseries, but they also battled to make the cities shoulder their responsibilities for cleaner streets and purer politics.[26]

Finally, the Progressive Era saw the fulfillment of the suffragists' hopes. Taking up the parades and spectacle that the two major parties had abandoned, and combining them with the latest advertising techniques, women in yellow sashes marched, exhorted, and petitioned. Under the firm hand of Carrie Chapman Catt, the National Woman Suffrage Association turned itself into a political powerhouse. Its more militant rival, Alice Paul's National Woman's Party, fixed its sights on a national constitutional amendment. There were hunger strikes, picketings, and arrests—and victories. "The foxes have holes, and birds of the air have nests, but the politician has no hiding place when the suffragists get after him," one newspaper commented. Congress passed the amendment in 1919. It was ratified barely a year later.[27]

Revolutionary! and yet. . . . Being a "New Woman" took more money, education, and leisure than most Americans had. Thanks to readymade clothing and commercial laundries, middle-class housewives might spend less time sewing and scrubbing, but new domestic chores replaced old ones. Beyond urban limits, the days of electrical washers, stoves, and toasters lay far in the future. For theorists like Charlotte Perkins Gilman, woman's salvation required economic independence. Home crimped and confined. But press, politicians, and perhaps most women themselves saw their proper role in life pretty much in the same old way, as wife and mother above all. Failing there, they failed in a vital part of life. Even as radicals in Greenwich Village discussed Freud and radical Emma Goldman compared middle-class marriage to prostitution, leading Progressives were warning that unless Anglo-Saxon mothers got back to having four children apiece at the least, America's finest ethnic stock would be committing "race suicide."[28]

Some women, even the professionals with a passion for reforming society, wanted nothing to do with the ballot box. That belonged to men's world, and a cynical, corrupting place it was. For every crowd of yellow ribbons, there were at least a few red roses worn by the anti-suffragists. Being a good voter was not what mattered to the thousands who joined the National Congress of Mothers; being a good parent was. As far as members of the Parent-Teacher Associations were concerned, fresh-air camps and infant health clinics would do more to change people's lives than electing a woman to Congress. Clubwomen entered politics most willingly and got the most respectful attention when they could show that their cause was an extension of "women's role." Who had a better right to call for laws protecting children or to save the family? Even rousting out the bosses could be sold as "municipal housekeeping." So there were more activists than suffragists, and far more suffragists than feminists. They might agree on getting the vote; they could never unite on just what to do with it. There would be no equal rights amendment and only a brief second wind for moral reform after 1920, which as one feminist lamented, was to be expected, "women being fools because God made them to match the men."[29]

Most of all, Progressivism left Jim Crow as strong as ever. Admittedly, white supremacists suffered a few setbacks. Maryland Democrats failed in their effort to disfranchise blacks. The Supreme Court knocked down the grandfather clause in 1910, forbade peonage as a form of slavery in 1911, and overturned city ordinances that mandated black neighborhoods in 1917. The judges even gave a little added emphasis to the "equal" in "separate but equal" when Oklahoma tried to get out of providing blacks with their own railroad dining cars.[30] Leading the fight against discrimination, William E. Du Bois was able to carry the black elite with him. In 1905, twenty-nine black professionals and scholars met in Canada to form the Niagara movement and issue a declaration of war on discrimination. In 1909 the movement took another step forward. Shocked by a race riot in Lincoln's own Springfield, Illinois, in 1909, black and white activists met to discuss the race problem. Out of their talks came the first lasting civil rights group, the National Association for the Advancement of Colored People. Among its founders were Jane Addams and Ida Wells-Barnett.

The Patterns of Racism Persist in the Twentieth Century

Blacks continued to work, and some prospered. "There are always places for the coloured man at the bottom," one black northerner assured a reporter, who also saw black miners, paper-hangers, policemen, and plumbers. The quality of life rested on many small accomplishments, and not just on outside prejudice. In Indianapolis, for example, the Coloured Women's Club opened a day nursery for the children of black working women. "Forty years ago the white man emancipated us," a reporter was told, "but we are only just now discovering that we must emancipate ourselves."[31]

But the essential pattern set late in the Gilded Age persisted, and, if anything, became more indelible across the North. Most settlement houses drew the color line. Northern medical schools closed their doors to black applicants. So did the American Bar Association and the American Medical Association. Even in Boston, where black policemen, firemen, and schoolteachers worked alongside white ones, restaurants and hotels put Jim Crow service into effect. Leases and deeds nationwide included a "restrictive covenant," which barred black residents. In Philadelphia, one compassionate white minister offered to set up a Sunday school for Negro children—until it was suggested that his church might find room for it. "Why, we couldn't do that!" he protested. "We should have to air all the cushions afterward!"[32]

Lynching persisted, and became directed ever more against blacks alone. In one month alone during 1901, mobs burned four victims to death. In southern states, the new century saw a spate of "vagrancy" laws to allow planters to round up all the black labor they needed, and of laws to keep emigrant agents from enticing blacks away from their landlords with prohibitive licenses. Cases of involuntary servitude—of peonage—went up sharply and would not fully vanish for forty years. The gap between funding for black and white schools widened. Politicians ranted against northern philanthropists for funding black education, called for repeal of the Fifteenth Amendment, and endorsed deportation of all blacks to Africa. "Yes, we have stuffed ballot-boxes, and will stuff them again," Senator Ben Tillman cried; "we have cheated niggers in elections, and will cheat them again; . . . we have burned niggers at the stake and will burn others; a nigger has no right to live anyhow, unless a white man wants him to live." Starting in 1913, the federal civil service required prospective employees to attach a photograph to their application, to make sure that blacks got none but the most menial government posts. "A Negro's place is in the corn-field," one official explained.[33]

President Theodore Roosevelt Ushers In a New Era

Progressivism, then, betrayed its origins, but it was more than the Gilded Age written in bolder strokes. Like the era from which it emerged, it picked and discarded from past experience, past ideals, to fit a changed world. That is why, in the end, the death of McKinley makes as good a breaking point as any—that and the character of his successor. Forty-two years old in 1901, Theodore Roosevelt would not just inhabit the White House. He would fill it, spilling out for headlong walks, tennis games, horseback canters, and hunting sprees into the southern canebrake. Secret service agents chased after him, desperately trying to get close enough to guard him, but they need not have bothered. Roosevelt kept a revolver by his bedside and often packed a pistol while on the go. "Well, sir, they'll be great times down there f'r a few years," Mr. Dooley told Hennessey. "A movement is on foot f'r to establish an emergency hospital f'r office-holders an' politicians acrost th' sthreet fr'm th' White House where they can be threated f'r infractions iv th' Civil Sarvice law followed be pers'nal injuries. I'll be watchin' th' pa-apers ivry mornin.' 'Rayciption at the White House. Among th' casualties was so-an-so.'"[34]

The energy that drove on the Gilded Age sent T. R. rushing through it, a self-made man in every sense but that of a Horatio Alger hero. Near-sighted and sickly as a boy, he had willed his own regeneration, growing into a stocky young dude of solid muscle and iron will. He read two books a day or more, had vehement opinions on them all, and wrote twenty-four himself. But the college picture that sums him up best shows him stripped to the waist, scowling and belligerent, ready to box. His fondness for the sport would cost him sight in one eye during his presidency. Whether as a goo-goo New York assemblyman helping pass one of the first state civil service laws; as the Republican candidate for mayor in the Henry George campaign of 1886; as Harrison and Cleveland's civil service commissioner; as Jacob Riis's ally against the slums; as a rancher wrecked in the collapse of the "Beef Bonanza"; as the nemesis of New York saloons and grafting cops; or as a pistol-waving amateur soldier in Cuba, Roosevelt loved a good scrap.[35]

That vitality and aggressiveness helped to remake the presidency itself (though again, the first big steps came, with much less ballyhoo, under McKinley). As Justice Oliver Wendell Holmes, his first, best Supreme Court selection put it later, "He played all his cards—if not more." In seven years, he virtually recreated the presidency, enhancing its power as "bully pulpit" in shaping public opinion and its influence as policymaker. Even before architects finished adding a permanent pressroom to the White House in 1902, T. R. had made cultivating the press corps a fine art. Instead of deferring to Cabinet members, he went straight to clerks or bureau chiefs to get the facts and make his own judgments. From his lips flowed an unprecedented torrent of messages and letters, dictated as he paced the room, edited between strides. Cleveland had used his annual message to call for tariff reform; Roosevelt offered a full program. Instead of writing treaties that required Senate consent, the president made agreements, some of which remained secret for years. Whatever powers the law did not forbid him, he took.[36]

Not just the presidency, but the federal government took on new life. Early in 1902, the Justice Department announced that it meant to use the Sherman Anti-Trust Act against Northern Securities. Morgan himself rushed down to Washington for an audience at the White House. "If we have done anything wrong," he pleaded, "send your man to my man and they can fix it up." "We don't want to fix it up," the Attorney-General responded, "we want to stop it."[37] In 1904, the Supreme Court upheld the government's case and gave the Sherman Act latitude enough to be used against bigness, however free the market remained.

The second proof of the "Square Deal" that Roosevelt championed found its symbol in late 1902, five months after a coal strike in eastern Pennsylvania's anthracite

Theodore Roosevelt makes music at the Trusts' expense.
(Luther Bradley cartoon, Chicago *Daily News*, 1905)

fields sent 147,000 workers out, demanding union recognition for the United Mine Workers and disrupting an economy dependent on coal. By the end of August, prices had leaped by half. With winter approaching and no resolution near, the country faced the prospect of cold hearths, closed factories and schools, and coal going from $2.40 to $30 a ton. UMW president John Mitchell welcomed federal mediation, but the operators held fast against union and government interference. As John M. Baer, speaking for the managers, expressed it, the rights must be left to "the Christian men to whom God in His infinite wisdom has given the control of the property interests of the country. . . ." When the president invited both sides to confer in Washington, the mine owners not only balked at concessions. They gave Roosevelt a dressing-down for associating with radicals like Mitchell. Only when it became clear that the government might take over the mines, put them into receivership, and dig the coal itself did the management agree to arbitration. The miners ended up getting much of what they wanted.[38]

Summary

Progressivism built on the precedents that the Gilded Age had set. It improved upon them, and, over time, deflected further from the principles that guided them. But to the end, it owed a debt to the society passing away. "There is a deeper and more vital continuity than that of policy," one magazine wrote; "it is the continuity of character." The editors were trying to prove that Roosevelt would behave like a second

McKinley, but their statement fit the age better than the man. America's character held true, for good and evil, in the new century, changing imperceptibly from day to day.[39]

That character, with all the energy, ambition, and conscience that it displayed over the Gilded Age, was capable of committing terrible wrongs. The United States was everything every critic said of it: a country that had proceeded from barbarism to decadence without passing through civilization, a "chromo-civilization" of cheap goods and cheap values, a dollar-mad society of go-getters. Yet in the striving lay the possibilities for greatness of spirit, as well, and the possibility was one often realized. Penning snide, often grotesquely unfair pen-portraits of America as he traveled the West in the late 1880s, the English writer Rudyard Kipling discovered, to his surprise, that for all their cocksure style, there lay something behind Americans worthy of his respect. "I admit everything," he told a scornful Englishman.

> Their Government's provisional; their law's the notion of the moment; their railways are made of hairpins and match-sticks, and most of their good luck lives in their woods and mines and rivers and not in their brains; but for all that, they be the biggest, finest, and best people on the surface of the globe! Just you wait a hundred years and see how they'll behave when they've had the screw put on them. . . . There is nothing known to man that he will not be, and his country will sway the world with one foot as a man tilts a see-saw plank![40]

Endnotes

AHR—*American Historical Review*
GHQ—*Georgia Historical Quarterly*
JAH—*Journal of American History*
JSH—*Journal of Southern History*
LC—*Library of Congress*
LH—*Labor History*
NYHSQ—*New York Historical Society Quarterly*
WHQ—*Western Historical Quarterly*

Introduction

1. Sean Cashman, *America in the Gilded Age: From the Death of Lincoln to the Rise of Theodore Roosevelt* (New York: New York University Press, 1984), 330–31; William Minturn, *Travels West* (London, Samuel Tinsley, 1877), 75.
2. Ray Ginger, *Age of Excess: The United States from 1877 to 1914* (New York: Macmillan, 1965), 319–28; Robert H. Wiebe, *The Search for Order, 1877–1920* (New York: Hill and Wang, 1967), xiii–xiv; Nell Irvin Painter, *Standing at Armageddon: The United States, 1877–1919* (New York: Norton, 1987).
3. J. T. Trowbridge, "Ancestors," *Atlantic*, 43 (January 1879): 11.

Chapter 1: Progress Backward, 1876

1. E. A. Tozier, "Centennial Record" (memorandum book), Historical Society of Pennsylvania, Philadelphia; Charles R. Anderson and Aubrey H. Starke, eds., *Sidney Lanier: Letters, 1874–1877* (Baltimore: Johns Hopkins, 1945), 300–91.
2. Dee Brown, *The Year of the Century* (New York: Scribner's, 1966), 132–33; Robert V. Bruce, *Bell: Alexander Graham Bell and the Conquest of Solitude* (Boston: Little, Brown & Co., 1973), 188–98.
3. Daniel Boorstin, *The Americans: The Democratic Experience* (New York: Random House, 1973), 379–80.

4. Robert Friedel and Paul Israel, with Bernard S. Finn, *Edison's Electric Light: Biography of an Invention* (New Brunswick, NJ: Rutgers University Press, 1986), 7–8, 33–117.
5. *Ibid.*, 381–82; *Scientific American*, March 9, April 20, 1901.
6. Francis E. Leupp, *George Westinghouse: His Life and Achievements* (London: John Murray, 1919), 131–42.
7. Joseph Frazier Wall, *Andrew Carnegie* (New York: Oxford University Press, 1970), 637–38.
8. Frank G. Carpenter, *Carp's Washington* (New York: McGraw-Hill, 1960), 192–93.
9. "Machinery," in Finley Peter Dunne, *Observations by Mr. Dooley* (New York: R. H. Russell, 1906), 215–16.
10. John Bach McMaster, "A Century of Social Betterment," *Atlantic*, 79 (January 1897): 26; *Railroad Trainmen's Journal*, 13 (October 1896): 735–36; Glenna Matthews, *"Just a Housewife": The Rise and Fall of Domesticity in America* (New York: Oxford University Press, 1987), 100–05.
11. Joe B. Frantz, *Gail Borden: Dairyman to a Nation* (Norman: University of Oklahoma Press, 1951), 197–221; Boorstin, *Americans: The Democratic Experience*, 309–15.
12. "The Skyscrapers of New York," *Collier's*, 26 (December 1, 1900): 28–29; Edward C. Kirkland, *Industry Comes of Age: Business, Labor and Public Policy, 1860–1897* (New York: Holt, Rinehart and Winston, 1961), 256–57; John Anderson Miller, *Fares, Please! From Horse-Cars to Streamliners* (New York: D. Appleton-Century Co., 1941), 29, 70–81, 102, 115–16.
13. Ann Durkin Keating, *Building Chicago: Suburban Developers and the Creation of a Divided Metropolis* (Columbus: Ohio State University Press, 1988), 22–26; Walter Wellman, "Rise of the American City," *McClure's*, 17 (September 1901): 470–75.
14. Gunther Barth, *City People: The Rise of Modern City Culture in Nineteenth-Century America* (New York: Oxford University Press, 1980), 29–56.
15. David Nasaw, *Children of the City: At Work and at Play* (New York: Oxford University Press, 1985), 2–8.
16. Arthur Reed Kimball, "The Age of Disfigurement," *Outlook*, 57 (October 30, 1897): 521; William Minturn, *Travels West* (London: Samuel Tinsley, 1877), 12–13.
17. Dunne, "Machinery," *Observations by Mr. Dooley*, 218.
18. U.S. Bureau of the Census, *The Statistical History of the United States: From Colonial Times to the Present* (New York: Basic Books, 1976), 8; Lowell, "An Ode for the Fourth of July, 1876," in *The Complete Poetical Works of James Russell Lowell* (Boston: Houghton Mifflin 1896), 372.
19. Wolfgang Schivelbusch, *Disenchanted Night: The Industrialization of Light in the Nineteenth Century* (Berkeley: University of California Press, 1988), 64–69.
20. U.S. Bureau of the Census, *Abstract of the Twelfth Census* (1900), 330; *Statistical History*, 11–12, 509–12.
21. Philip Sandhurst and others, *The Great Centennial Exhibition Critically Illustrated and Described* (Philadelphia: P. W. Ziegler & Co., 1876), 25, 53, 548–61.
22. Elisabeth Griffith, *In Her Own Right: The Life of Elizabeth Cady Stanton* (New York: Oxford, 1984), 166–67.
23. Jack S. Blocker, Jr., *"Give to the Winds Thy Fears": The Women's Temperance Crusade, 1873–1874* (Westport: Greenwood Press, 1985), 7–51, 85–146; Jed Dannenbaum, *Drink and Disorder: Temperance Reform in Cincinnati from the Washingtonian Revival to the WCTU* (Urbana: University of Illinois Press, 1984), 214–17.
24. Blocker, *"Give to the Winds Thy Fears,"* 31–51, 62–67, 166–69.
25. Dannenbaum, *Drink and Disorder*, 227–30.
26. Hjalmar Horth Boyesen, "The Chautauqua Movement," *Cosmopolitan*, 19 (June 1895): 147–58.
27. Helen E. Smith, "Village Improvement Societies and Good Roads," *Independent*, February 6, 1896, p. 7; Jayme A. Sokolow and Mary Ann Lamanno, "Woman and Utopia: The Woman's Commonwealth of Belton, Texas," *Southwest Historical Quarterly*, 87 (April 1984): 371–92.

Chapter 2: *A New Stillbirth of Freedom?*

1. *Independent*, May 2, 1861.
2. Philip Shaw Paludan, *"A People's Contest": The Union and Civil War, 1861–1865* (New York: Harper & Row, 1988), 316–17, 325–26, 337; Grady McWhiney and Perry D. Jamieson, *Attack and Die: Civil War Military Tactics and the Southern Heritage* (University: University of Alabama, 1980), 3–24; Walter Lowenfels, comp. and ed., *Walt Whitman's Civil War* (New York: Knopf, 1961), 5–8.
3. Catherine Clinton and Nina Silber, eds., *Divided Houses: Gender and the Civil War* (New York: Oxford University Press, 1992), 16–18, 171–99.
4. Paludan, *"A People's Contest,"* 118–21.
5. Paludan, *"A People's Contest,"* 129–35; Harold M. Hyman, *A More Perfect Union: The Impact of the Civil War and Reconstruction on the Constitution* (New York: Knopf, 1973), 381.
6. Eric Foner, *Reconstruction: America's Unfinished Revolution, 1863–1877* (New York: Harper & Row, 1988), 29;

James M. McPherson, *Abraham Lincoln and the Second American Revolution* (New York: Oxford University Press, 1990), 12–13.

7. Leon F. Litwack, *Been in the Storm So Long: The Aftermath of Slavery* (New York: Vintage, 1979), 98–103.

8. Michael Les Benedict, *A Compromise of Principle: Congressional Republicans and Reconstruction, 1863–1869* (New York: Norton, 1974), 122–26, 134–38; Detroit *Free Press*, November 1, 1868; Fawn M. Brodie, *Thaddeus Stevens: Scourge of the South* (New York: Norton, 1966), 231–32, 266–72.

9. New York *Independent*, June 14, 1866; Chicago *Tribune*, August 25, 1868; Cincinnati *Enquirer*, October 9, 1879; Milwaukee *Wisconsin*, June 25, 1868; David Donald, *Charles Sumner and the Rights of Man* (New York: Knopf, 1970), 41–42, 248–54.

10. Cincinnati *Enquirer*, October 9, 1879; Jacob D. Cox to James A. Garfield, May 4, 1866, Garfield MSS, LC; Chicago *Tribune*, August 25, 1868; *Flake's Daily Galveston Bulletin*, October 9, 1867.

11. Hans L. Trefousse, *Andrew Johnson: A Biography* (New York: Norton, 1989), 165–69, 234–42; *Papers of Andrew Johnson* (Knoxville: University of Tennessee Press), 3:379; New York Herald, February 8, 1866.

12. Kenneth M. Stampp, *The Era of Reconstruction, 1865–1877* (New York: Knopf, 1965), 50–61; Jacob D. Cox to James Monroe, November 21, 1866, Cox MSS, Oberlin.

13. Willie Lee Rose, *Rehearsal for Reconstruction: The Port Royal Experiment* (New York: Vintage, 1964), 346–57; New York *World*, December 15, 30, 1865; D. K. Cartter to Benjamin F. Butler, August 29, 1865, Benjamin F. Butler MSS, LC.

14. Sidney Andrews, *The South Since the War* (Boston: Ticknor & Fields, 1866), 219, 344; Alvan C. Gillem to Joseph Fowler, May 1, 1866, Joseph Fowler MSS, Southern Historical Collections, University of North Carolina; B. Dally to Nathaniel P. Banks, July 31, 1866, Nathaniel P. Banks, MSS, LC.

15. New York *Herald*, October 20, 1866; Foner, *Reconstruction*, 199–215.

16. James M. McPherson, *The Struggle for Equality: Abolitionists and the Negro in the Civil War and Reconstruction* (Princeton: Princeton University Press, 1964), 393; Eric L. McKitrick, *Andrew Johnson and Reconstruction* (Chicago: University of Chicago Press, 1960), 274–325; Trefousse, *Andrew Johnson*, 247; Samuel S. Cox, *Why We Laugh*, 282.

17. Stampp, *Era of Reconstruction*, 136–38; New York *Independent*, June 21, 1866.

18. New York *Citizen*, March 17, 1866; McKitrick, *Andrew Johnson and Reconstruction*, 394–447.

19. Michael Les Benedict, *The Impeachment and Trial of Andrew Johnson* (New York: Norton, 1973), 89–180; Donald, *Charles Sumner and the Rights of Man*, 337.

20. Fredrickson, *Inner Civil War*, 192–93; Herman Belz, *Emancipation and Equal Rights: Politics and Constitutionalism in the Civil War Era* (New York: Norton, 1978), 73, 102–03; James A. Garfield to Jacob D. Cox, July 26, 1865, Cox MSS.

21. Eric Foner, *Reconstruction*, 446–48; Cincinnati *Enquirer*, September 28, 1869.

22. Foner, *Reconstruction*, 256, 473; Carrie Chapman Catt and Nettie Rogers Shuler, *Woman Suffrage and Politics: The Inner Story of the Suffrage Movement* (Seattle: University of Washington Press, 1970), 108–31; White, "*It's Your Misfortune and None of My Own*", 355–59.

23. Frederick E. Hoxie, *A Final Promise: The Campaign to Assimilate the Indians, 1880–1920* (Lincoln: University of Nebraska Press, 1984), 210–38; R. Alton Lee, "Indian Citizenship and the Fourteenth Amendment," *South Dakota History*, 4 (Spring 1974): 198–221.

24. Miriam Gurko, *Ladies of Seneca Falls: The Birth of the Woman's Rights Movement* (New York: Schocken, 1974), 233–37.

25. George M. Fredrickson, *The Inner Civil War: Northern Intellectuals and the Crisis of the Union* (New York: Harper & Row, 1965), 130–50, 183–89.

26. Thomas Bailey Aldrich, *Poems*, 372.

27. Summers, *Era of Good Stealings*, 118–20, 146–48.

28. William Gillette, *Retreat from Reconstruction, 1869–1879* (Baton Rouge: Louisiana State University Press, 1979), 34–36; Morton Keller, *Affairs of State: Public Life in Late Nineteenth Century America* (Cambridge: Harvard University Press, 1977), 114.

29. Mark Twain and Charles Dudley Warner, *The Gilded Age: A Tale of Today*; James Bryce *The American Commonwealth* (London: Macmillan, 1891), 1:521.

30. Glyndon van Deusen, *William Henry Seward* (New York: Oxford University Press, 1967), 255–63, 403; Ernest Duvergier de Hauranne, *A Frenchman in Lincoln's America* (Chicago: Lakeside Press, 1974–75), 1:72–73; Charles S. Campbell, *The Transformation of American Foreign Relations, 1865–1900* (New York: Harper & Row, 1976), 12–19.

31. Van Deusen, *William Henry Seward*, 365–70, 515–16, 537–49; Campbell, *Transformation of American Foreign Relations*, 16–18.

32. James B. Chapin, "Hamilton Fish and American Expansion," Ph.D. Dissertation, Cornell, 1971,

pp. 246–49; William S. McFeely, *Grant* (New York: Norton, 1981), 336–41, 350; Donald, *Charles Sumner and the Rights of Man*, 374–96, 434–36; New York *Herald*, January 12, 1869.

33. Hugh Thomas, *Cuba: The Pursuit of Freedom* (New York: Harper & Row, 1971), 247–69; Richard Bradford, *The Virginius Affair* (Boulder: Colorado Association University Press, 1980), 75; Chapin, "Hamilton Fish and American Expansion," 249–94, 436–94; Washington *Sunday Capital*, March 16, 1873.

34. William F. Weld to Benjamin F. Butler, April 2, 1870, Butler MSS; "Gath," Chicago *Tribune*, June 14, 1870.

35. McFeely, *Grant*, 351–52; Cincinnati *Gazette*, February 2, 1870; "D.P.," Cincinnati *Commercial*, January 7, 1871; New York *World*, January 12, 1871.

36. The full story is in Paul S. Holbo, *Tarnished Expansion: The Alaska Scandal, the Press, and Congress, 1867–1871* (Knoxville: University of Tennessee Press, 1983).

37. Glyndon G. Van Deusen, *Horace Greeley: Nineteenth-Century Crusader* (Philadelphia: University of Pennsylvania Press, 1953), 353–56, 382–408; Foner, *Reconstruction*, 497–509.

38. Forrest G. Wood, *Black Scare: The Racist Response to Emancipation and Reconstruction* (Berkeley: University of California Press, 1970), 54, 151; Washington *New National Era*, January 2, 1873; Cincinnati *Commercial*, August 17, 1874; Charles Fairman, *Reconstruction and Reunion, 1864–88* (New York: Macmillan Publishing Co., 1987), 2:550–88.

39. McPherson, *Struggle for Equality*, 431.

Chapter 3: "Gentlemen, We Are Not Yet Over": Reconstruction

1. The joke may play on Thomas Nelson Page's remark in his novel *Red Rock*, "even the moonlight was richer and mellower . . . than it is now." Paul Gaston, *The New South Creed: A Study in Southern Mythmaking* (New York: Vintage, 1970), 172.

2. John W. Blassingame, *Black New Orleans, 1860–1880* (Chicago: University of Chicago Press, 1973), 152; Foner, *Reconstruction*, 90–93.

3. Leon Litwack, *Been in the Storm So Long: The Aftermath of Slavery* (New York: Random House, 1979), 472–85.

4. McPherson, *Lincoln and the Second American Revolution*, 16–17; Litwack, *Been in the Storm So Long*, 245–51, 256–59.

5. New York *World*, April 28, 1871.

6. New York *World*, February 21, 1871; Richard N. Current, *Those Terrible Carpetbaggers* (New York: Oxford University Press, 1988), 243–45; Foner, *Reconstruction*, 356, 363, 386–89.

7. Foner, *Reconstruction*, 351–61.

8. Mark W. Summers, *Railroads, Reconstruction, and the Gospel of Prosperity: Aid under the Radical Republicans, 1865–1877* (Princeton: Princeton University Press, 1984), 35–45, 116; Foner, *Reconstruction*, 390.

9. Eric Foner, *Nothing but Freedom: Emancipation and Its Legacy* (Baton Rouge: Louisiana State University Press, 1983), 55–58.

10. Current, *Those Terrible Carpetbaggers*, 148–52, 233–35, 240–42, 248–55, 276–81; W. McKee Evans, *Ballots and Fence Rails: Reconstruction on the Lower Cape Fear* (Chapel Hill: University of North Carolina, 1966), 162.

11. Foner, *Reconstruction*, 430–39, 457–58; Stephen Cresswell, "Enforcing the Enforcement Acts: The Department of Justice in Northern Mississippi, 1870–1890," *JSH*, 53 (August 1987): 421–40.

12. Mark W. Summers, *The Era of Good Stealings* (New York: Oxford University Press, 1992).

13. Irwin Unger, *The Greenback Era: A Social and Political History of American Finance, 1865–1879* (Princeton: Princeton University Press, 1964), 293–302, 314–21.

14. Hyman, *A More Perfect Union*, 480; Gillette, *Retreat from Reconstruction*, 36.

15. Foner, *Reconstruction*, 558–63, 573–75; Vernon Lane Wharton, *The Negro in Mississippi, 1865–1890* (Chapel Hill: University of North Carolina, 1947), 181–98.

16. Keith I. Polakoff, *The Politics of Inertia: The Election of 1876 and the End of Reconstruction* (Baton Rouge: Louisiana State University Press, 1973), 71–73; Gillette, *Retreat from Reconstruction*, 312–14.

17. Gillette, *Retreat from Reconstruction*, 300–21.

18. Polakoff, *Politics of Inertia*, 201–92.

19. Polakoff, *Politics of Inertia*, 292–314; Foner, *Reconstruction*, 581.

20. Stanley P. Hirshson, *Farewell to the Bloody Shirt: Northern Republicans and the Southern Negro, 1877–1893* (Bloomington: Indiana University Press, 1962), 27–44; Gillette, *Retreat from Reconstruction*, 353–54.

21. Lawrence D. Rice, *The Negro in Texas, 1874–1900* (Baton Rouge: Louisiana State University Press, 1971), 86–112; William J. Cooper, Jr., *The Conservative Regime: South Carolina, 1877–1890* (Baltimore: Johns Hopkins, 1968), 87–88.

22. Gordon McKinney, *Southern Mountain Republicans, 1865–1900* (Chapel Hill: University of North Carolina Press, 1978), 119–21; Roger L. Hart, *Redeemers, Bourbons and Populists: Tennessee, 1870–1896* (Baton Rouge: Louisiana State University Press, 1975), 97; Edmund L. Drago, *Black Politicians and Reconstruction in Georgia* (Baton Rouge: Louisiana State University Press, 1982), 157.

23. Foner, *Reconstruction*, 590; Eric Anderson, *Race and Politics in North Carolina, 1872–1901: The Black Second* (Baton Rouge: Louisiana State University, 1981), 340–41; Evans, *Ballots and Fence-Rails*, 172; Jimmie F. Gross, "Alabama Politics and the Negro," Ph.D. Dissertation, p. 88.

24. Carl Degler, *The Other South: Southern Dissenters in the Nineteenth Century* (New York: Harper & Row, 1974), 267–69.

25. Hirshson, *Farewell to the Bloody Shirt*, 123–26, 143–89; Allen W. Moger, *Virginia, Bourbonism to Byrd: 1870–1925* (Charlottesville: University Press of Virginia, 1968), 63–66.

26. Hirshson, *Farewell to the Bloody Shirt*, 200–35; H. Wayne Morgan, *From Hayes to McKinley: National Party Politics, 1877–1896* (Syracuse: Syracuse University Press, 1969), 340–42; Richard E. Welch, Jr., "The Federal Elections Bill of 1890: Postscripts and Prelude," *JAH*, 52 (December 1965): 511–26.

27. Rayford W. Logan, *The Betrayal of the Negro, from Rutherford B. Hayes to Woodrow Wilson* (New York: Collier, 1965), 378; Twain and Warner, *Gilded Age*, 153; New York *Evening Post*, January 5, 1884.

28. Joseph C. Furnas, *Goodbye to Uncle Tom* (New York: William Sloane Associates, 1956), 262–84; Joyce Appleby, "Reconciliation and the Northern Novelist, 1865–1880," *Civil War History*, 10 (June 1964): 117–29; Gaston, *New South Creed*, 170–71, 180–87; Mrs. D. B. Dyer, "Some Types in Dixieland," *Cosmopolitan*, 22 (January 1897): 238–40.

29. Charles A. Lofgren, *The Plessy Case: A Legal-Historical Interpretation* (New York: Oxford University Press, 1987).

30. William I. Hair, *Bourbonism and Agrarian Protest: Louisiana Politics, 1877–1900* (Baton Rouge: Louisiana State University Press, 1969), 129–33; *Outlook*, 57 (September 4, 1897): 11; Wharton, *Negro in Mississippi, 1865–1890*, 240–42.

31. Hair, *Bourbonism and Agrarian Protest*, 127–29.

32. William A. Sinclair, *The Aftermath of Slavery* (Boston: Small, Maynard & Co., 1905), 172–73.

33. Tallahassee *Weekly Floridian*, August 18, 1893; Louis R. Harlan, *Separate and Unequal: Public School Campaigns and Racism in the Southern Seaboard States, 1901–1915* (Chapel Hill: University of North Carolina Press, 1958), 9–21; Hair, *Bourbonism and Agrarian Protest*, 120–27.

34. James R. Young, "Confederate Pensions in Georgia, 1886–1929," *GHQ Quarterly*, 66 (Spring 1982): 48–49; *Harper's Weekly*, February 10, 1894.

35. *Debates and Proceedings of the Convention which Assembled at Little Rock* (Little Rock: J. G. Price, 1868), 681.

Chapter 4: Redeeming the Past, 1875–1898

1. Frederick A. Bode, "Religion and Class Hegemony: A Populist Critique in North Carolina," *JSH* 37 (August 1971): 425–27; Gaston, *New South Creed*, 17–42, 83–92.

2. Ralph Lowell Eckert, *John Brown Gordon: Soldier, Southerner, American* (Baton Rouge: Louisiana State University Press, 1989), 242–58; Cooper, *Conservative Regime*, 120–25.

3. C. Vann Woodward, *Origins of the New South, 1877–1913* (Baton Rouge: Louisiana State University Press, 1951), 115–36; John J. Beck, "Building the New South: A Revolution from Above in a Piedmont County," *JSH*, 53 (August 1987): 441–70; Edward L. Ayers, *The Promise of the New South: Life after Reconstruction* (New York: Oxford University Press, 1992), 104–22.

4. Arthur P. Hudson, "An Attala Boyhood," *Journal of Mississippi History*, 4 (July 1942): 142; James M. Clifton, "Twilight Comes to the Rice Kingdom," *GHQ*, 62 (Summer 1978): 146–64; John A. Heitmann, "Organization as Power: The Louisiana Sugar Planters' Association and the Creation of Scientific and Technical Institutions, 1877–1910," *Louisiana History*, 27 (Summer 1986): 281–94; Ayers, *Promise of the New South*, 190–91.

5. Numan V. Bartley, *The Creation of Modern Georgia* (Athens: University of Georgia Press, 1983), 37.

6. Bartley, *Creation of Modern Georgia*, 89; J. Wayne Flynt, *Dixie's Forgotten People: The South's Poor Whites* (Bloomington: Indiana University Press, 1979), 61.

7. Foner, *Reconstruction*, 400.

8. Jonathan Wiener, "Planter Persistence and Social Change: Alabama, 1850–1870," *Journal of Interdisci-*

plinary History, 7 (Autumn 1976): 235–60; Michael Wayne, *The Reshaping of Plantation Society: The Natchez District, 1860–1880* (Baton Rouge: Louisiana State University Press, 1983), 75–91.

9. Harold D. Woodman, *King Cotton and His Retainers: Financing and Marketing the Cotton Crop of the South, 1800–1925* (Lexington: University of Kentucky Press, 1968), 246–49; Wayne, *Reshaping of Plantation Society*, 91–98; Foner, *Reconstruction*, 376.

10. Wayne, *Reshaping of Plantation Society*, 111–12, 140–49.

11. Bartley, *Creation of Modern Georgia*, 36–38.

12. Wayne, *Reshaping of Plantation Society*, 120–24.

13. Drago, *Black Politicians and Reconstruction*, 126; Eric Anderson and Alfred A. Moss, Jr., eds., *The Facts of Reconstruction: Essays in Honor of John Hope Franklin* (Baton Rouge: Louisiana State University Press, 1991), 179–81, 187–88; Loren Schweninger, *Black Property Owners in the South, 1790–1915* (Urbana: University of Chicago Press, 1990), 144–76.

14. Jay R. Mandle, *The Roots of Black Poverty: The Southern Plantation Economy after the Civil War* (Durham: Duke University Press, 1978), 28–51; Roger L. Ransom and Richard Sutch, *One Kind of Freedom: The Economic Consequences of Emancipation* (Cambridge: Cambridge University Press, 1977), 64–105, 149–70.

15. Michael Perman, *Road to Redemption: Southern Politics, 1869–1879* (Chapel Hill: University of North Carolina Press, 1984), 223–28, 234; Albert D. Kirwan, *Revolt of the Rednecks: Mississippi Politics: 1876–1925* (New York: Harper & Row, 1951), 48.

16. Wayne, *Reshaping of Plantation Society*, 183–87; Perman, *Road to Redemption*, 242–52.

17. "Corn," in *Poems of Sidney Lanier* (New York: Charles Scribner's Sons, 1929), 56; Hart, *Redeemers, Bourbons and Populists*, 40.

18. Barton C. Shaw, *The Wool-Hat Boys: Georgia's Populist Party* (Baton Rouge: Louisiana State University Press, 1984), 17–19, 124.

19. "Fredricksburg," in Thomas Bailey Aldrich, *Poems*, 382.

20. Mary P. Dearing, *Veterans in Politics: The Story of the G.A.R.* (Baton Rouge: Louisiana State University Press, 1952), 80–96, 106–08, 308; Stuart McConnell, *Glorious Contentment: The Grand Army of the Republic, 1865–1900* (Chapel Hill: University of North Carolina Press, 1992).

21. Charles Reagan Wilson, "The Religion of the Lost Cause: Ritual and Organization of the Southern Civil Religion, 1865–1920, "*JSH*, 46 (May 1980): 219–38; Gaines M. Foster, *Ghosts of the Confederacy: Defeat, the Lost Cause, and the Emergence of the New South, 1865 to 1913* (New York: Oxford University Press, 1987), 106–112, 131–39.

22. John A. Simpson, "The Cult of the 'Lost Cause,'" *Tennessee Historical Quarterly*, 34 (Winter 1975): 350–61; *Society of the Army of the Cumberland, 31st Reunion: Washington D.C., 1903* (Cincinnati: Robert Clarke Co., 1904), 23, 26, 28, 105, 118.

23. Kyle S. Sinisi, "Veterans as Political Activists: The Kansas Grand Army of the Republic, 1880–1893," *Kansas History*, 14 (Summer 1991): 89–99.

24. William D. Foulke, *Life of Oliver P. Morgan*, 2 vols. (Indianapolis: Bowen-Merrill Co., 1899), 474–75.

25. Hudson Strode, *Jefferson Davis: Tragic Hero* (New York: Harcourt, Brace & World, Inc., 1964), 478–524; but see also Michael Kammen, *Mystic Chords of Memory: The Transformation of Tradition in American Culture* (New York: Alfred A. Knopf, 1991), 126.

26. Dearing, *Veterans in Politics*, 343–47; Allan Nevins, *Grover Cleveland: A Study in Courage* (New York: Dodd, Mead, 1932), 332–36.

27. Thomas L. Miller, "Texas Land Grants to Confederate Veterans and Widows," *Southwestern Historical Quarterly*, 69 (July 1965): 59–65; Theda Skocpol, *Protecting Soldiers and Mothers: The Political Origins of Social Policy in the United States* (Cambridge: Harvard University Press, 1992), 103–43; Dearing, *Veterans in Politics*, 247–50, 330–33, 393–401.

28. *Nation*, February 9, 16, April 13, May 4, 25, 1893; Finley Peter Dunne, "Hanging Aldermen" in *Mr. Dooley in the Hearts of His Countrymen* (Boston: Small, Maynard & Co., 1899), 29; *Nation*, October 2, 1890, p. 268. Mr. Dooley was referring specifically to the excuse for awarding swindling transit contracts, but the general point fits perfectly. Pensions for service in the War of 1812 were even more scandalous. In 1897, only three actual veterans were still collecting—and three thousand widows! *Outlook*, 57 (December 18, 1897): 935.

29. *Society of the ... Cumberland, 1903*, 26, 105.

30. Dearing, *Veterans in Politics*, 176–69, 214–16, 349–50.

31. Buck, *Road to Reunion*, 238–39; Eckert, *John Brown Gordon*, 328–29.

32. Foster, *Ghosts of the Confederacy*, 120–21, 135–36; Buck, *Road to Reunion*, 247.

33. McConnell, *Glorious Contentment*, 167–73; Buck, *Road to Reunion*, 247, Eckert, *John Brown Gordon*, 316–21; Howard Dorgan, "A Case Study in Reconciliation: General Gordon ...", *Quarterly Journal of Speech*, 60 (February 1974): 83–91.

34. Kammen, *Mystic Chords of Memory*, 98–99, 122–25.

35. Kammen, *Mystic Chords of Memory*, 240–42, 259–60, 266–69.

36. *The Spirit of the Union League Club, 1879–1926* (Chicago: The Club, 1926); Skocpol, *Protecting Soldiers and Mothers*, 424–79.

37. B. L. T., "Sectionalism and School Histories," *Outlook*, 56 (August 28, 1897): 1033–36; Dearing, *Veterans in Politics*, 471–78; *Journal of the 31st National Encampment of the Grand Army of the Republic, Buffalo, N.Y.: August 25, 26, 27, 1897* (Lincoln, Neb.: State Journal Company, 1897), 148.

38. *Public Opinion*, September 2, 1897.

39. McConnell, *Glorious Contentment*, 103–110, 205–224; George C. Rable, *Civil Wars: Women and the Crisis of Southern Nationalism* (Urbana: University of Chicago Press, 1989), 236–39.

40. Fredrickson, *Inner Civil War*, 187–88, 217–222; Edmund Wilson, *Patriotic Gore: Studies in the Literature of the American Civil War* (New York: Oxford University Press, 1962), 758–61.

Chapter 5: Wasteland

1. Joseph G. Rosa and Robin May, *Buffalo Bill and His Wild West* (Lawrence: University Press of Kansas, 1989), 7–10, 51.

2. Wilton Eckley, *The American Circus* (Boston: Twayne, 1984), 9–19; Rosa and May, *Buffalo Bill and His Wild West*, 81–83, 140–57.

3. Jane Tompkins, "At the Buffalo Bill Museum—June 1988," *South Atlantic Quarterly*, 89 (Summer 1990): 540–46.

4. Larsen, *The Urban West at the End of the Frontier*, 118–20.

5. Walter Prescott Webb, *The Great Plains* (Boston: Ginn and Company, 1931), 27–32.

6. Hiram M. Drache, *The Challenge of the Prairie: Life and Times of Red River Pioneers* (Fargo: North Dakota Institute for Regional Studies, 1970), 165–68; Webb, *Great Plains*, 19–26; Shannon, *Farmer's Last Frontier*, 150–53.

7. Drache, *Challenge of the Prairie*, 35–44; Craig Miner, *West of Wichita: Settling the High Plains of Kansas, 1865–1890* (Lawrence: University Press of Kansas, 1986), 148–49.

8. Shannon, *Farmer's Last Frontier*, 149; Webb, *Great Plains*, 321–82; Miner, *West of Wichita*, 158–60.

9. Webb, *Great Plains*, 40–44; Tom McHugh, *The Time of the Buffalo* (New York: Knopf, 1972), 3–17, 83–109; E. Douglas Branch, *The Hunting of the Buffalo* (New York: D. Appleton and Company, 1929), 26–51, 109–111, 119–20.

10. J. Frank Dobie, *The Longhorns* (New York: Grosset & Dunlap), 3–42, 176–220; Webb, *Great Plains*, 280–312; Paul, *Far West and the Great Plains in Transition*, 188–89.

11. Webb, *Great Plains*, 60–68, 79–83; Richard White, *The Roots of Dependency: Subsistence, Environment, and Social Change among the Choctaws, Pawnees, and Navajos* (Lincoln: University of Nebraska Press, 1983), 152–54, 179–88.

12. Richard White, "The Winning of the West: The Expansion of the Western Sioux in the Eighteenth and Nineteenth Centuries," *JAH*, 65 (September 1978): 319–43.

13. Martha Royce Blaine, *Pawnee Passage: 1870–1875* (Norman: University of Oklahoma Press, 1990), 98–142; John C. Ewers, "Intertribal Warfare as the Precursor of Indian-White Warfare on the Northern Great Plains," *WHQ*, 6 (October 1975): 397–410.

14. Brian W. Dippie, *The Vanishing American: White Attitudes and U.S. Indian Policy* (Lawrence: University Press of Kansas, 1982), 134; Alvin M. Josephy, Jr., *The Civil War in the American West* (New York: Knopf, 1991), 95–154.

15. Gerald F. Kreyche, *Visitors of the American West* (Lexington: University Press of Kentucky, 1989), 216–18; Don Russell, "How Many Indians Were Killed? White Man versus Red Man: The Facts and the Legend," *American West*, 10 (July 1973): 42–47, 61–63.

16. Kipling, *American Notes*, 176.

17. Frederic Remington, "Vagabonding with the Tenth Horse," *Cosmopolitan*, 22 (February 1897): 349.

18. Robert Wooster, *The Military and United States Indian Policy, 1865–1903* (New Haven: Yale University Press, 1988), 144–75; Robert M. Utley, "A Chained Dog: The Indian-Fighting Army: Military Strategy on the Western Frontier," *American West*, 10 (July 1973): 18–24.

19. Jerome A. Green, "George Crook," in Paul Andrew Hutton, ed., *Soldiers West: Biographies from the Military Frontier* (Lincoln: University of Nebraska Press, 1987), 120–21; Paul Andrew Hutton, ed., *The Custer Reader* (Lincoln: University of Nebraska Press, 1992), 229–77.

20. Josephy, *Nez Perce Indians and the Opening of the Northwest*, 499–506, 591; Greene, "George Crook," in Hutton, ed., *Soldiers West*, 121, 126–29.

21. Josephy, *The Nez Perce Indians and the Opening of the Northwest* (New Haven: Yale University Press, 1965), 527–633.

22. *Life*, August 21, 1884, p. 5; Josephy, *The Nez Perce Indians and the Opening of the Northwest*, 634–44.

23. George B. Grinnell, *The Fighting Cheyennes* (Norman: University of Oklahoma Press, 1956), 406–27.

24. White, *Roots of Dependency*, 189–92; *Eleventh Census*, 1890, pp. 17–18, 24–25; Kipling, *American Notes*, 178.

25. White, *"It's Your Misfortune and None of My Own,"* 238–41.

26. Athearn, *Union Pacific Country*, 146; Minturn, *Travels West*, 76.

27. Smalley, *History of the Northern Pacific*, 334–42; Bryant, *Atchison, Topeka & the Santa Fe*, 64–70; Overton, *Burlington West*, 341–69; Webb, *Great Plains*, 375–82.

28. Bryant, *Atchison, Topeka & the Santa Fe*, 70–72.

29. George Augustus Sala, *America Revisited* (London: Vizetelly & Co., 1886), 386–87; Robert G. Athearn, *Union Pacific Country* (Lincoln: University of Nebraska Press, 1971), 60, 143–44; Shelton Stromquist, *A Generation of Boomers: The Pattern of Railroad Labor Conflict in Nineteenth-Century America* (Urbana: University of Illinois Press, 1987), 152–53, 157–58.

30. Webb, *Great Plains*, 282–83, 393–412.

31. Webb, *Great Plains*, 412–18.

32. Paul, *Far West and Great Plains in Transition*, 288; Webb, *Great Plains*, 308–10.

33. *Harper's Weekly*, January 6, 1894.

34. Paul, *Far West and the Great Plains in Transition*, 191–94.

35. John B. Jackson, *American Space: the Centennial Years* (New York: Norton, 1972), 178–79; Paul, *Far West and the Great Plains in Transition*, 195; Edward E. Dale, *Cow Country* (Norman: University of Oklahoma Press, 1942), 80–86.

36. Atherton, *Cattle Kings*, 160–70, 193–217.

37. Dobie, *Longhorns*, 87–121; Weston, *Real American Cowboy*, 43–49, 59–60.

38. James C. Olson, *History of Nebraska* (Lincoln: University of Nebraska Press, 1966), 159; Webb, *Great Plains*, 343; Drache, *Challenge of the Prairie*, 230–47, 319.

39. Elwyn B. Robinson, *History of North Dakota* (Lincoln: University of Nebraska Press, 1966), 154.

40. Lewis Atherton, *The Cattle Kings* (Bloomington: Indiana University Press, 1962), 18–20; Jimmy M. Skaggs, *The Cattle-Trailing Industry: Between Supply and Demand, 1866–1890* (Norman: University of Oklahoma, 1973), 1–11; Weston, *Real American Cowboy*, 13–15; Kenneth O. Porter, "Negro Labor in the Western Cattle Industry, 1866–1900," *LH*, 10 (Summer 1969): 346–74.

41. Edward Everett Dale, *Cow Country* (Norman: University of Oklahoma Press, 1942), 89–105; Cronon, *Nature's Metropolis*, 180–82; *Statistical Atlas of the Eleventh Census* (1890), p. 60.

42. White, *"It's Your Misfortune and None of My Own,"* 232–34; Larry M. Dilsaver, "After the Gold Rush," *Geographical Review*, 75 (January 1985): 10–12.

43. White, *"It's Your Misfortune and None of My Own,"* 124–27.

44. E. Gregory McPherson and Renee A. Haip, "Emerging Desert Landscape in Tucson," *Geographical Review*, 79 (October 1989): 435–40; Robin W. Doughty, "Settlement and Environmental Change in Texas, 1820–1900," *Southwestern Historical Quarterly*, 89 (April 1986): 438–42; Daniel W. Gade, "Weeds in Vermont as Tokens of Socioeconomic Change," *Geographical Review*, 81 (April 1991): 159.

45. Branch, *Hunting of the Buffalo*, 148–70, 185–220; *Ladies' Home Journal*, February 1901, p. 5.

46. White, *"It's Your Misfortune and None of My Own,"* 220.

47. Hoxie, *A Final Promise*, 21–39, 70–73.

48. Michael C. Coleman "Problematic Panacea: Presbyterian Missionaries and the Allotment of Indian Lands in the Late Nineteenth Century," *Pacific Historical Quarterly*, 54 (May 1985): 143–59; Leonard A. Carlson, *Indians, Bureaucrats, and Land: The Dawes Act and the Decline of Indian Farming* (Westport: Greenwood Press, 1981), 11–13, 115–60.

49. Hoxie, *A Final Promise*, 198–200.

50. Robert M. Utley, *The Last Days of the Sioux Nation* (New Haven: Yale University Press, 1963), 60–270.

Chapter 6: Main Line to **E Pluribus Unum**

1. Frank Norris, *The Pit: A Story of Chicago* (New York: Doubleday, Page & Co., 1903), 62.

2. Mark W. Summers, "Radical Reconstruction and the Gospel of Prosperity," unpublished Ph.D. Dissertation, University of California, 1980, pp. 162–69.

3. Summers, "Radical Reconstruction and the Gospel of Prosperity," 172–78.

4. Mark W. Summers, *The Plundering Generation: Corruption and the Crisis of the Union, 1849–1861* (New York:

Oxford University Press, 1987), 108–112; Carter Goodrich, *Government Promotion of American Canals and Rail-roads, 1800–1890* (New York: Columbia University Press, 1960), 227–53.

5. Athearn, *Union Pacific Country*, 28–30; Wallace D. Farnham, "The Pacific Railroad Act of 1862," *Nebraska History*, 43 (September 1962): 141–67; John F. Stover, *American Railroads* (Chicago: University of Chicago Press, 1961), 45, 67–68, 70, 76, 80–82, 87–89.

6. Stover, *American Railroads*, 91–92; Lloyd J. Mercer, "Taxpayers or Investors: Who Paid for the Land Grant Roads?," *Business History Review*, 46 (Autumn 1972): 279–94; for Texas demagoguery, and the plain facts, see S. G. Reed, *A History of the Texas Railroads* (Houston: St. Clair Publishing Co., 1941), 164–87.

7. Stover, *American Railroads*, 76, 88–90; Henry Kirke White, *History of the Union Pacific Railway* (Chicago: University of Chicago Press, 1895), 80–84, 91–92; Richard C. Overton, *Burlington West: A Colonization History of the Burlington Railroad* (Cambridge: Harvard University Press, 1941), 477–78; Lawrence L. Waters, *Steel Rails to Santa Fe* (Lawrence: University of Kanasa Press, 1950), 255–58; Leslie E. Decker, *Railroads, Lands, and Politics: The Taxation of Railroad Land Grants, 1864–1897* (Providence: Brown University Press, 1964), 246–50.

8. Smalley, *History of the Northern Pacific*, 204; Martin, *James J. Hill and the Opening of the Northwest*, 116, 180–81, 213–17, 225–27.

9. Charles Edgar Ames, *Pioneering the Union Pacific: A Reappraisal of the Builders of the Railroad* (New York: Appleton-Century-Crofts, 1969), 42–49.

10. Summers, *Era of Good Stealings*, 50–54, 231–37.

11. Oscar O. Winther, *The Transportation Frontier: Trans-Mississippi West, 1865–1890* (New York: Holt, Rine-hart and Winston, 1964), 108–10.

12. Winther, *Transportation Frontier*, 111–12.

13. Athearn, *Union Pacific Country*, 98–100; Winther, *Transportation Frontier*, 113–15.

14. Winther, *Transportation Frontier*, 100–04.

15. *Poor's Manual* (1895), v; Albro Martin, *Railroads Triumphant: The Growth, Rejection, and Rebirth of a Vital American Force* (New York: Oxford University Press, 1992), 24–30, 52–55; *Annual Report of the Interstate Commerce Commission* (1890), pp. 67–73; Stover, *American Railroads*, 171–72, 179.

16. Bryant, *Atchison, Topeka & Santa Fe*, 144–45; Stover, *American Railroads*, 159–70.

17. Waters, *Steel Rails to Santa Fe*, 167; Stover, *American Railroads*, 156–57; Leupp, *George Westinghouse*, 47–56; *Poor's Manual* (1895), 10 (advertisements); Martin, *Railroads Triumphant*, 88.

18. Martin, *Railroads Triumphant*, 83–91; Stover, *American Railroads*, 166–68; Sala, *America Revisited*, 93–97.

19. *Railway World*, January 23, February 20, 1892; Daniel W. Gade, "Weeds in Vermont as Tokens of Socioeconomic Change," *Geographical Review*, 81 (April 1991): 155–59; Stover, *American Railroads*, 98; Bryant, *Atchison, Topeka & Santa Fe*, 65.

20. Ginger, *Age of Excess*, 22–23; Martin, *James J. Hill and the Opening of the Northwest*, 276–79, 310–11; Stover, *American Railroads* 98.

21. Smalley, *History of the Northern Pacific*, 312. Julesburg was not wiped out—not quite. And as a visitor noted, "becoming nearly deserted" improved its moral tone immensely. Minturn, *Travels West*, 86.

22. Nollie Hickman, *Mississippi Harvest: Lumbering in the Longleaf Pine Belt, 1840–1915* (University: University of Mississippi, 1962), 57–67.

23. Ronald D. Eller, *Miners, Millhands, and Mountaineers: Industrialization of the Appalachian South, 1880–1930* (Knoxville: University of Tennessee Press, 1982), 93–112.

24. Martin, *Railroads Triumphant*, 145–51; Eller, *Miners, Millhands, and Mountaineers*, 65–80; Joseph L. Nimmo, Jr., *The Anti-Trust Law and the Railraod Problem* (Washington: Rufus H. Darby Printing Co., 1901), 25.

25. Boorstin, *Americans: The Democratic Experience*, 121–24.

26. Boorstin, *Americans: The Democratic Experience*, 124–28; Alfred D. Chandler, Jr., *The Visible Hand: The Managerial Revolution in American Business* (Cambridge: Belknap Press of Harvard University Press, 1977), 230–31; Gordon L. Weil, *Sears, Roebuck, U.S.A.: The Great American Catalog Store and How It Grew* (New York: Stein and Day, 1977), 5–40.

27. Nimmo, *Anti-Trust Law and the Railroad Problem*, 24; White, *History of the Union Pacific*, 88; *Poor's Manual* (1895), vii; Stover, *American Railroads*, 100–01, 171.

28. Kirkland, *Industry Comes of Age*, 217; Mansel G. Blackford and G. Austin Kerr, *Business Enterprise in American History* (Boston: Houghton Mifflin, 1986), 154.

29. Chandler, *Visible Hand*, 90–93; Kirkland, *Industry Comes of Age*, 225–26; Robert Sobel, *The Big Board: A History of the New York Stock Market* (New York: Free Press, 1965), 40.

30. The story is too good to leave out, and too silly to believe. Drew was no fool; a cattle-drover sells to the same clients on a regular basis. If he cheated them once, he could depend on them never trusting him there-

after—which, from all contemporary accounts they did. See Clifford Browder, *The Money Game in Old New York: Daniel Drew and His Times* (Lexington: University Press of Kentucky, 1986), 16–17, 21–22.

31. Kirkland, *Industry Comes of Age*, 55–57.

32. Sobel, *Big Board*, 86–87; Kirkland, *Industry Comes of Age*, 233–34.

33. Chandler, *Visible Hand*, 94–98.

34. Chandler, *Visible Hand*, 109–20.

35. Albro Martin, *Enterprise Denied: Origins of the Decline of American Railroads, 1897–1917* (New York: Columbia University Press, 1971), 71–76; Keith L. Bryant, Jr., "Cathedrals, Castles and Roman Baths: Railway Station Architecture in the Urban South, 1890–1920," *Journal of Urban History*, 2 (February 1976): 195–230.

36. Washington *Post*, November 17, 1883; Hair, *Bourbonism and Agrarian Protest*, 111–112. The infamous Gould bulks large in Matthew Josephson, *The Robber Barons: The Great American Capitalists, 1861–1901* (New York: Harcourt, Brace & World, Inc., 1934), 121–48, 153–59, 193–209; for a more sympathetic and not wholly persuasive portrait, see Maury Klein, *The Life and Legend of Jay Gould* (Baltimore: Johns Hopkins, 1986).

37. For restrictions, see *Poor's Manual* (1895), 1204–1372.

38. Stover, *American Railraods*, 154–59.

39. Kirkland, *Industry Comes of Age: 1860–1897*, 85–88; Chandler, *Visible Hand*, 133–43.

40. Maury Klein, *The Great Richmond Terminal: A Study in Businessmen and Business Strategy* (Charlottesville: University Press of Virginia, 1970); Waters, *Steel Rails to Santa Fe*, 194–204; Klein, *Life and Legend of Jay Gould*, 446–47; Chandler, *Visible Hand*, 148–50, 159–60.

41. On accidents, see *Railroad Trainmen's Journal*, 13 (February 1896): 83–86; *Annual Report of the Interstate Commerce Commission* (1900), pp. 23, 74.

42. Moger, *Virginia: From Bourbonism to Byrd*, 87.

43. David Thelen, *Paths of Resistance: Tradition and Democracy in Industrializing Missouri* (Columbia: University of Missouri Press, 1986), 70–77.

44. Robert V. Bruce, *1877: Year of Violence* (New York: Bobbs-Merrill, 1959); Melvyn Dubofsky, *The State and Labor in Modern America* (Chapel Hill: University of North Carolina, 1994), 8–12.

45. Bruce, *1877: Year of Violence*, 292–320.

46. Bruce, *1877: Year of Violence*, 320; see also New York *Herald*, October 8, 1877.

47. New York *Herald*, October 2, 1877; *Railway World*, July 10, 1886, March 12, 1892.

Chapter 7: Industrialism Unleashed

1. Bureau of the Census, *Statistical History*, 224, 600.

2. Atlas for Twelfth Census, 1900, Plate 198; David R. Meyer, "Midwestern Industrialization and the American Manufacturing Belt in the Nineteenth Century," *Journal of Economic History*, 49 (December 1989): 921–37.

3. Alfred D. Chandler, *Visible Hand*, 249–53, 290–95; William C. Edgar, *The Medal of Gold: A Story of Industrial Achievement* (Minneapolis: Bellman Co., 1925), 102–09; Shannon, *Farmer's Last Frontier*, 157–58.

4. Chicago *Tribune*, February 24, 27, 1875; Rudyard Kipling, *American Notes* (New York: Manhattan Press, n.d.), 227–29.

5. James R. Barrett, *Work and Community in the Jungle: Chicago's Packinghouse Workers, 1894–1922* (Urbana: University of Illinois, 1987), 19, 22-27.

6. Wall, *Andrew Carnegie*, 340–45, 499–505, 532–33.

7. Harold C. Livesay, *Andrew Carnegie and the Rise of Big Business* (Boston: Little, Brown and Company, 1975), 97–100, 109–21.

8. *Ibid.*, 109–16, 128, 155–56; Wall, *Andrew Carnegie*, 346–47.

9. Harold F. Williamson, Arnold R. Daum, *The American Petroleum Industry: The Age of Illumination, 1859–1899* (Evanston: Northwestern University Press, 1959), 3–60.

10. Daniel Yergin, *The Prize: The Epic Quest for Oil, Money, and Power* (New York: Simon & Schuster, 1991), 19–30.

11. New York *Citizen*, March 4, 1865; Yergin, *The Prize*, 30–32.

12. Robert C. Alberts, *The Good Provider: H. J. Heinz and his 57 Varieties* (Boston: Houghton Mifflin Co., 1973), 1–39.

13. Alberts, *Good Provider*, 41–46.

14. Edward C. Hampe, Jr. and Merle Wittenberg, *The Lifeline of America: Development of the Food Industry* (New York: McGraw-Hill, 1964), 113–20, 129; Chandler, *Visible Hand*, 253. Canned goods did not, in fact, catch

on until the 1920s. Even in 1900, American firms produced barely fifty million cases. By 1931, they were making 160 million, by 1940, 400 million.

15. Chandler, *Visible Hand*, 253; Frank Presbrey, *The History and Development of Advertising* (Garden City, NY: Doubleday, Doran & Co., Inc., 1929), 507; Alberts, *Good Provider*, 120–31; Strasser, *Satisfaction Guaranteed*, 121–22, 180–81, 195–98.

16. Presbrey, *History and Development of Advertising*, 250–75, 338–48; Strasser, *Satisfaction Guaranteed*, 29–57; Sala, *America Revisited*, 96–97.

17. Ayers, *Promise of the New South*, 86; Boorstin, *Americans: The Democratic Experience*, 137–48; Presbrey, *History and Development of Advertising*, 338–48, 365–79.

18. Presbrey, *History and Development of Advertising*, 210, 348, 489; Sidney Ratner and James H. Soltow, *The Evolution of the American Economy: Growth, Welfare and Decision Making* (New York: Basic Books, 1979), 381–82.

19. Bertram B. Fowler, *Men, Meat and Miracles* (New York: Julian Messner, 1952), 59–60; Ayers, *Promise of the New South*, 87–88; William Cahn, *Out of the Cracker Barrel: The Nabisco Story from Animal Crackers to Zuzus* (New York: Simon & Schuster, 1969), 31–32; New York *World*, January 2, 28, 1869; Strasser, *Satisfaction Guaranteed*, 215–19, 255–63.

20. Mary Yeager Kujovich, "The Refrigerated Car and the Growth of the American Dressed Beef Industry," *Business History Review*, 44 (Winter 1970): 460–82.

21. Chandler, *Visible Hand*, 295–96; Stanley W. Baron, *Brewed in America: A History of Beer and Ale in the United States* (Boston: Little, Brown & Co., 1962), 258–59, 272; Perry R. Duis, *The Saloon: Public Drinking in Chicago and Boston, 1880–1920* (Urbana: University of Illinois Press, 1983), 25–26.

22. Allan Nevins, *Study in Power: John D. Rockefeller, Industrialist and Philanthropist* (New York: Charles Scribner's Sons, 1953), 1:20–21; Chandler, *Visible Hand*, 254–56.

23. David Freeman Hawke, *John D.: The Founding Father of the Rockefellers* (New York: Harper & Row, 1980), 2–14, 24.

24. Hawke, *John D.*, 15–31.

25. For competitive practice, see John S. Magee, "Predatory Price Cutting: The Standard Oil Case," *Journal of Law and Economics*, 1 (October 1958): 137. For the origins of the industrial pools, see Kirkland, *Industry Comes of Age*, 201–02; also Chandler, *Visible Hand*, 321–26.

26. Williamson and Daum, *American Petroleum Industry*.

27. Hawke, *John D.*, 173–78.

28. Joseph A. Pratt, *The Growth of a Refining Region* (Greenwich, CT.: JAI Press, 1980), 33–37.

29. See Harold F. Williamson and Ralph L. Andreano, "Competitive Structure of the Petroleum Industry, 1880–1911: A Reappraisal," *Oil's First Century* (Boston: Harvard Graduate School of Business Administration, 1960), 71–84.

30. Wall, *Andrew Carnegie*, 347; Duis, *The Saloon*, 78–80; Baron, *Brewed in America*, 269–72.

31. Ruth Brandon, *A Capitalist Romance: Singer and the Sewing Machine* (Philadelphia: J. B. Lippincott Co., 1977), 42–73; Alan Dawley, *Class and Community: The Industrial Revolution in Lynn* (Cambridge: Harvard University Press, 1976), 92–93.

32. Boorstin, *Americans: The Democratic Experience*, 101–09; Strasser, *Satisfaction Guaranteed*, 206–12. Macy, Stewart, and Wanamaker were not really visionaries who saw selling in a fresh, new way. Worrisome figures on the ledger shoved them to sell a wider array than they planned in order to grab customers they could get no other way. But when they found that new methods worked, they never turned back. Susan Porter Benson, *Counter Cultures: Saleswomen, Managers, and Customers in American Department Stores, 1890–1940* (Urbana: University of Illinois Press, 1986), 12–17. See also Peter Samson, "The Department Store, Its Past and Its Future: A Review Article," *Business History Review*, 55 (Spring 1981): 26–34.

33. Boorstin, *Americans: The Democratic Experience*, 109–15; Strasser, *Satisfaction Guaranteed*, 206–12. Macy, ing of Organization Men, 1880–1940," *Business History Review*, 65 (Spring 1991): 130–39.

34. Gerald Carson, *The Old Country Store* (New York: Oxford University Press, 1954), 191–97; Ayers, *Promise of the New South*, 81–92, 100, 187–88.

35. Barth, *City People*, 143–46.

36. David Brody, *Steelworkers in America: The Nonunion Era* (New York: Harper & Row, 1960), 30–35.

37. Brody, *Steelworkers in America*, 29–49; S. J. Kleinberg, *The Shadow of the Mills: Working-Class Families in Pittsburgh, 1870–1907* (Pittsburgh: University of Pittsburgh Press, 1989), 8–10.

38. Elizabeth W. Etheridge, "Pellagra: An Unappreciated Reminder of Southern Distinctiveness," in Todd L. Savitt and James H. Young, *Disease and Distinctiveness in the American South* (Knoxville: University of Tennessee Press, 1988), 100–19.

39. Ayers, *Promise of the New South*, 96–99.

Chapter 8: The Unhuddled Masses

1. Heinrich E. Jacob, *The World of Emma Lazarus* (New York: Schocken, 1949), 177–80.

2. Thomas Kessner, *The Golden Door: Italian and Jewish Immigrant Mobility in New York City, 1880–1915* (New York: Oxford University Press, 1977), 5.

3. Maldwyn A. Jones, *Destination America* (New York: Holt, Rinehart and Winston, 1976), 168–70; Maldwyn A. Jones, *American Immigration* (Chicago: University of Chicago, 1960), 201–02.

4. Jones, *American Immigration*, 194.

5. Ewa Morawska, *For Bread with Butter: The Life-Worlds of East Central Europeans in Johnstown, Pennsylvania, 1890–1940* (Cambridge: Cambridge University Press, 1985), 24–25.

6. Henry V. Poor, *Twenty-Two Years of Protection* (New York: H. V. & H. W. Poor, 1888), 179.

7. John J. Bukowczyk, *And My Children Did Not Know Me: A History of the Polish-Americans* (Bloomington: Indiana University Press, 1987), 12–14.

8. Jon Gjerde, *From Peasants to Farmers: The Migration from Balestrand, Norway, to the Upper Middle West* (Cambridge: Cambridge University Press, 1985), 125; Morawska, *For Bread with Butter*, 66; Susan A. Glenn, *Daughters of the Shtetl: Life and Labor in the Immigrant Generation* (Ithaca: Cornell University Press, 1990), 54–55; Gary Ross Mormino, *Immigrants on the Hill: Italian-Americans in St. Louis, 1882–1982* (Urbana: University of Illinois Press, 1986), 43–44.

9. Jones, *Destination America*, 195; June G. Alexander, *The Immigrant Church and Community: Pittsburgh's Slovak Catholics and Lutherans, 1880–1915* (Pittsburgh: University of Pittsburgh Press, 1987), 7; Morawska, *For Bread with Butter*, 28–30, 38; Mormino, *Immigrants on the Hill*, 38.

10. Alexander, *Immigrant Church and Community*, 9; Morawska, *For Bread with Butter*, 72; Jones, *Destination America*, 196–97.

11. Virginia Yans-McLaughlin, *Family and Community: Italian Immigrants in Buffalo, 1880–1930* (Urbana: University of Illinois Press, 1982), 70–71; Sydney Stahl Weinberg, *The World of Our Mothers: The Lives of Jewish Immigrant Women* (New York: Schocken, 1988), 77.

12. Irving Howe, *World of Our Fathers* (New York: Harcourt, Brace, Jovanovich, 1976), 36–42.

13. Oscar Handlin, *The Uprooted: The Epic Story of the Great Migrations that Made the American People* (New York: Grosset & Dunlap, 1951), 54–59; Howe, *World of Our Fathers*, 43–46.

14. Morawska, *For Bread with Butter*, 113; Michael La Sorte, *La Merica: Images of Italian Greenhorn Experience* (Philadelphia: Temple University Press, 1985), 118; Howe, *World of Our Fathers*, 149–50.

15. John Bodnar, *Immigration and Industrialization: Ethnicity in an American Mill Town* (Pittsburgh: University of Pittsburgh Press, 1977), 38.

16. Yans-McLaughlin, *Family and Community*, 82–83; Weinberg, *World of Our Mothers*, 88–97, 115.

17. Terence V. Powderly to Patrick McCool, April 12, 1892, Terence V. Powderly MSS, Catholic University; Lars Ljungmark, *Swedish Exodus* (Carbondale: Southern Illinois University Press, 1979), 54; Morawska, *For Bread with Butter*, 68–69, 136; Barrett, *Work and Community*, 105–06.

18. Bayrd Still, *Milwaukee: The History of a City* (Madison: State Historical Society of Wisconsin, 1965), 268; see also Rowland Berthoff, "The Social Order of the Anthracite Region," *Pennsylvania Magazine of History and Biography*, 89 (July 1965): 269.

19. Stanley Feldstein, *The Land I Show You: Three Centuries of Jewish Life in America* (Garden City: Doubleday, 1978), 153; Weinberg, *World of Our Mothers*, 116.

20. Ingalls, *Urban Vigilantes in the New South*, 36–37, 43–50, 56; Gary R. Mormino and George E. Pozzetta, *The Immigrant World of Ybor City: Italians and Their Latin Neighbors in Tampa, 1885–1985* (Urbana: University of Illinois Press, 1987), 104–05.

21. Yans-McLaughlin, *Family and Community*, 185–92.

22. Stanley Nadel, "Kleindeutschland: New York City's Germans, 1845–1880," Ph.D. Dissertation, Columbia, 1981, 103–04; Gjerde, *From Peasant to Farmer*, 141–42; Mormino, *Immigrants on the Hill*, 71–74; Alexander, *Immigrant Church and Community*, 6, 100–08; Paul A. Spengler, *Yankee, Swedish and Italian Acculturation and Economic Mobility in Jamestown, New York, from 1860 to 1920* (New York: Arno Press, 1980), 125–26; William M. DeMarco, *Ethnics and Enclaves: Boston's Italian North End* (Ann Arbor: UMI Research Press, 1981).

23. Victor A. Walsh, " 'A Fanatic Heart': The Cause of Irish-American Nationalism in Pittsburgh During the Gilded Age," *Journal of Social History*, 15 (Winter 1981): 187–204; Timothy J. Meagher, " 'Why Should We Care for a Little Trouble or a Walk Through the Mud': St. Patrick's and Columbus Day Parades in Worcester, Massachusetts, 1845–1915," *New England Quarterly*, 58 (March 1985): 5–26; Feldstein, *Land I Show You*, 168.

24. La Sorte, *La Merica*, 153–55; Weinberg, *World of Our Mothers*, 114.

25. La Sorte, *La Merica*, 159–69.

26. *Ibid.*, 177–78.

27. Gjerde, *From Peasants to Farmers*, 168–201; Glenn, *Daughters of the Shtetl*, 64–79.

28. Annegret S. Ogden, *The Great American Housewife: From Helpmate to Wage Earner, 1776–1986* (Westport: Greenwood Press, 1986), 119.

29. Spengler, *Yankee, Swedish and Italian Acculturation*, 179–83; Andrew R. Heinze, *Adapting to Abundance: Jewish Immigrants, Mass Consumption, and the Search for American Identity* (New York: Columbia University Press, 1990), 54–76; Charles M. Harger, "Singing 'The Messiah' on the Plains," *Ladies' Home Journal*, April 1900, p. 15.

30. Heinze, *Adapting to Abundance*, 60–61; Weinberg, *World of Our Mothers*, 112–14.

31. Carl Wittke, *We Who Built America: The Saga of the Immigrant* (Cleveland: Case Western Reserve University, 1939), 365–401.

32. Terence V. Powderly to Patrick McCool, April 12, 1892, Powderly MSS; W. S. Wood to William E. Chandler, November 17, 1892, Henry Henchcliff to Chandler, November 28, 1892, William E. Chandler MSS, LC.

33. John T. Christian, *Americanism or Romanism, Which?* (Louisville: Baptist Book Concern, 1895), 44–89; Mary F. Cusack, *What Rome Teaches* (New York: Baker & Taylor Co., 1891), 235; W. S. Wood to William E. Chandler, November 17, 1892, Chandler MSS; Wittke, *We Who Built America*, 513–17.

34. Edward R. Kantowicz, "To Build a Catholic City," *Chicago History*, 14 (Summer 1985): 4–14; Yans-McLaughlin, *Family and Community*, 112–20; La Sorte, *La Merica*, 148–50; Feldstein, *Land I Show You*, 157–58.

35. Weinberg, *World of Our Mothers*, 96.

36. W. Eugene Holton, *Frontier Violence: Another Look* (New York: Oxford University Press, 1974), 80–95; Minturn, *Travels West*, 339.

37. Royce D. Delmatier, Charles F. McIntosh, and Earl G. Walters, eds., *The Rumble of California Politics, 1848–1970* (New York: John Wiley & Sons, 1970), 70–92.

38. Keller, *Affairs of State*, 443–45; S. L. Baldwin, "Beauties of Our Anti-Chinese Legislation," *Independent*, April 17, 1890.

39. Alan M. Kraut, *The Huddled Masses: The Immigration in American Society, 1880–1921* (Arlington Heights, IL: Harlan Davidson, 1982), 162–64; Keller, *Affairs of State*, 445–47.

40. Aldrich, *Poems*, 275–76.

Chapter 9: Opportunity?

1. Richard O'Connor, *The Golden Summers: An Antic History of Newport* (New York: G. P. Putnam's Sons, 1974), 242–55; Josephson, *Robber Barons*, 338–40.

2. G. M. Searle, "Evolution and Darwinism," *Catholic World*, 56 (November 1892): 223–24; Richard Hofstadter, *Social Darwinism in American Thought* (Philadelphia: University of Pennsylvania Press, 1944; Revised Edition, Boston: Beacon Press, 1955), 33–50; Sidney Fine, *Laissez-Faire and the General-Welfare State: A Study of Conflict in American Thought, 1865–1901* (Ann Arbor: University of Michigan, 1956), 32–34.

3. Fine, *Laissez-Faire and the General-Welfare State*, 34–41.

4. John Burdick, "From Virtue to Fitness: The Accommodation of a Planter Family to Postbellum Virginia," *Virginia Magazine of History and Biography*, 93 (January 1985): 14–35; Hofstadter, *Social Darwinism in American Thought*, 34–35.

5. Harris E. Starr, *William Graham Sumner* (New York: Henry Holt & Co., 1925), 399–496.

6. Henry F. May, *Protestant Churches and Industrial America* (New York: Harper & Row, 1949), 58–59, 70–72; Samuel M. Jones to Bolton Hall, June 13, 1898, Samuel Milton Jones MSS; Charles Loring Brace, *The Dangerous Classes of New York, and Twenty Years' Work Among Them* (New York: Wynkoop & Hallenbeck, Publishers, 1872), 44–45.

7. Ray Stannard Baker, *Following the Color Line* (New York: Doubleday, Page & Co., 1908), 221; Max Bennett Thrasher, "The Tuskegee Negro Conference," *Outlook*, 67 (March 2, 1901): 486; "Booker Washington and Tuskegee: A Southerner's View," *Ibid.* (April 13, 1901): 871.

8. Wall, *Andrew Carnegie*, 815–20.

9. Roy Rosenszweig, *Eight Hours for What We Will: Workers and Leisure in an Industrial City, 1870–1920* (Cambridge: Cambridge University Press, 1983), 49, 52–53; R. L. Smith, "Village Improvement among the Negroes," *Outlook*, 64 (March 31, 1900): 733–36; Thrasher, "The Tuskegee Negro Conference," *Ibid.*, 67 (March 2, 1901): 486.

10. Heinze, *Adapting to Abundance*, 20–43; Stephan Thernstrom, *Poverty and Progress: Social Mobility in a Nineteenth Century City* (Cambridge: Harvard University Press, 1964), 184, 223.

11. Thomas J. Schlereth, *Victorian America: Transformations in Everyday Life, 1876–1915* (New York: Harper Collins, 1991), 33–34, 78–84.

12. John A. Garraty, *The New Commonwealth, 1877–1890* (New York: Harper & Row, 1968), 130–33; Schlereth, *Victorian America*, 67; Richard J. Oestreicher, *Solidarity and Fragmentation: Working People and Class Consciousness in Detroit, 1875–1900* (Urbana: University of Illinois Press, 1986), 10–14; Carroll D. Wright, "Are the Rich Growing Richer and the Poor Poorer?" *Atlantic*, 80 (September 1897): 300–09.

13. John G. Cawelti, *Apostles of the Self-Made Man: Changing Concepts of Success in America* (Chicago: University of Chicago, 1965), 102–03; 109–120.

14. Doyle, *Nashville in the New South*, 65–67; James Michael Russell, *Atlanta, 1847–1890: City Building in the Old South and the New* (Baton Rouge: Louisiana State University Press, 1988), 251–58.

15. Berthoff, "Social Order of the Anthracite Region," 275; Francis W. Gregory and Irene Neu, "The American Industrial Elite in the 1870's: Their Social Origins," in William E. Miller, ed., *Men in Business: Essays in the History of Entrepreneurship* (Cambridge: Harvard University Press, 1952): 193–211; John N. Ingham, "Rags to Riches Revisited: The Effect of City Size and Related Factors on the Recruitment of Business Leaders," *Journal of American History*, 63 (December 1976): 615–37.

16. Wendy Gamber, "A Precarious Independence: Milliners and Dressmakers in Boston, 1860–1890," *Journal of Women's History*, 4 (Spring 1992): 68; Stephan Thernstrom, *The Other Bostonians: Poverty and Progress in the American Metropolis, 1880–1970* (Cambridge: Harvard University Press, 1973), 131–34.

17. Bodnar, *Immigration and Industrialization*, 36–38.

18. Schweninger, *Black Property Owners in the South*, 197–226; James S. Fisher, "Negro Farm Ownership in the South," *Annals of American Geography*, 63 (December 1973): 478–89; Willard B. Gatewood, Jr., "Aristocrats of Color: South and North. The Black Elite, 1880–1920," *JSH*, 54 (February 1988): 3–20.

19. Howard N. Rabinowitz, *Race Relations in the Urban South, 1865–1890* (Urbana: University of Illinois Press, 1980), 62–67; Doyle, *Nashville in the New South*, 116; Kenneth L. Kusmer, *A Ghetto Takes Shape: Black Cleveland, 1870–1930* (Urbana: University of Illinois Press, 1976), 66–78; Savannah *Tribune*, February 23, 1889.

20. I. A. Newby, *Black Carolinians: A History of Blacks in South Carolina from 1895 to 1968* (Columbia: University of South Carolina Press, 1973), 134–35; Hair, *Bourbonism and Agrarian Protest*, 190–91; Schweninger, *Black Property Owners in the South*, 226–32.

21. Gamber, "Precarious Independence," 60–88; Lucy E. Murphy, "Her Own Boss: Businesswomen and Separate Spheres in the Midwest, 1850–1880," *Illinois Historical Journal*, 80 (Autumn 1987): 155–76; Lynn Y. Weiner, *From Working Girl to Working Mother: The Female Labor Force in the United States, 1820–1980* (Chapel Hill: University of North Carolina Press, 1985), 27–29; Schlereth, *Victorian America*, 67–68, 74–75.

22. Lisa M. Fine, *The Souls of the Skyscraper: Female Clerical Workers in Chicago, 1870–1930* (Philadelphia: Temple University Press, 1990), 56; Margery W. Davies, *Women's Place is at the Typewriter: Office Work and Office Workers, 1870–1930* (Philadelphia: Temple University Press, 1982), 58, 89–96.

23. Schlereth, *Victorian America*, 68; Fine, *Souls of the Skyscraper*, 80–103.

24. Kessler-Harris, *Out to Work*, 109–22.

25. Wright, "Are the Rich Growing Richer," 301.

26. Kleinberg, *Shadow of the Mills*, 102–115.

27. Kleinberg, *Shadow of the Mills*, 232–36, 240–57.

28. Kleinberg, *Shadow of the Mills*, 262–64.

29. J. C. Furnas, *The Americans: A Social History of the United States, 1587–1914* (New York: G. P. Putnam's Sons, 1969), 680–81.

30. Eric H. Monkkonen, *Walking to Work: Tramps in America, 1790–1935* (Lincoln: University of Nebraska Press, 1984), 87–132, 141, 151; David Bensman, *The Practice of Solidarity: American Hat Finishers in the Nineteenth Century* (Urbana: University of Illinois Press, 1985), 48–49, 71–72; "The Great Wool Market of the West," *Collier's*, 31:8 (September 12, 1903).

31. Monkkonen, ed., *Walking to Work*, 151.

32. Furnas, *The Americans*, 680; Jacob Riis, *How the Other Half Lives* (New York: Hill & Wang, 1957), 61–67.

33. William Cowper Brann, *The Complete Works of Brann the Iconoclast* (New York: Brann, 1919), 7:169.

34. Fine, *Laissez-Faire and the General-Welfare State*, 44. That was true, as far as it went. But Youmans also opened up his magazine's pages to George's articles; published a friendly review of George's *Progress and Poverty*, which was anything but *laissez-faire* and despairing; and did his best to make the book famous. Charles Albro Barker, *Henry George* (New York: Oxford University Press, 1955), 321, 325–26, 579–80.

35. John L. Thomas, *Alternative America: Henry George, Edward Bellamy, Henry Demarest Lloyd and the Adversary Tradition* (Cambridge: Belknap Press of Harvard University Press, 1983), 102–31; Daniel Aaron, *Men of Good Hope: A Story of American Progressives* (New York: Oxford University Press, 1951), 58–61; Henry George, *Progress and Poverty* (Modern Library, 1929), 3, 5, 392–93.

36. Aaron, *Men of Good Hope*, 58, 69–87.
37. Thomas, *Alternative America*, 112–23; Barker, *Henry George*, 296–302.
38. Kirkland, *Industry Comes of Age*, 52; Poor, *Railroad Manual*, 1885, v.
39. Wall, *Andrew Carnegie*, 381–97.
40. Fine, *Laissez-Faire and the General Welfare State*, 252–64.
41. Wilson, *Patriotic Gore*, 766; Holmes, *The Common Law* (Boston: Little, Brown, 1881), 10.

Chapter 10: More? Labor's Revolutionary Tradition

1. New York *Herald*, August 1, 5, 12, September 27, 1876.
2. New York *Herald*, September 27, 1876, October 26, 1877; Milwaukee *News*, October 17, 1873.
3. Donald L. Miller and Richard E. Sharpless, *The Kingdom of Coal: Work, Enterprise, and Ethnic Communities in the Mine Fields* (Philadelphia: University of Pennsylvania Press, 1985), 118, 125–29.
4. Robert P. Ingalls, *Urban Vigilantes in the New South: Tampa, 1882–1936* (Knoxville: University of Tennessee Press, 1988), 33–34; Patricia A. Cooper, *Once a Cigar Maker: Men, Women, and Work Culture in American Cigar Factories, 1900–1919* (Urbana: University of Illinois Press, 1987), 41–68; Bensman, *Practice of Solidarity*, 73–76.
5. Chandler, *Visible Hand*, 242–44.
6. David Montgomery, "Workers' Control of Machine Production in the Nineteenth Century," *Labor History*, 17 (Fall 1976): 485–509; Harry A. Corbin, *The Men's Clothing Industry: Colonial through Modern Times* (New York: Fairchild Publications, Inc. 1970), 64–73.
7. Herbert Gutman and Donald H. Bell, eds., *The New England Working Class and the New Labor History* (Urbana: University of Illinois Press, 1987), 233; Garraty, *New Commonwealth*, 154–55.
8. New York *Herald*, November 6, 1877; Miller and Sharpless, *Kingdom of Coal*, 104–22; Berthoff. "Social Order of the Anthracite Region," 279.
9. Miller and Sharpless, *Kingdom of Coal*, 116.
10. David Montgomery, *Beyond Equality: Labor and the Radical Republicans, 1862–1872* (New York: Knopf, 1967), 231, 235; Kleinberg, *Shadow of the Mills*, 238–39.
11. Walter Licht, *Working for the Railroad: The Organization of Work in the Ninteenth Century* (Princeton: Princeton University Press, 1983), 80–89.
12. Benson, *Counter Cultures*, 128–59, 231–32; Schlereth, *Victorian America*, 65, 75.
13. Berthoff, "Social Order of the Anthracite Region," 278–81; Kleinberg, *Shadow of the Mills*, 265.
14. Benson, *Counter Cultures*, 231–53; Licht, *Working for the Railroad*, 93–101; David M. Katzman, *Seven Days a Week: Women and Domestic Service in Industrializing America* (Urbana: University of Illinois Press, 1978), 160–74, 220–48.
15. Montgomery, *Beyond Equality*, 176–87.
16. Montgomery, *Beyond Equality*, 223–29; David Montgomery, "William H. Sylvis and the Search for Working-Class Citizenship," in Melvyn Dubofsky and Warren Van Tine, eds., *Labor Leaders in America* (Urbana: University of Illinois Press, 1987), 17; Jonathan Grossman, *William Sylvis, Pioneer of American Labor* (New York: Columbia University Press, 1945), 216–19.
17. Montgomery, *Beyond Equality*, 185–88, 279–303; Henry Pelling, *American Labor* (Chicago: University of Chicago Press, 1960), 54–55.
18. Vincent J. Falzone, *Terence V. Powderly: Middle Class Reformer* (Washington, D.C.: University Press of America, 1978), 9–30; Samuel Walker, "Terence V. Powderly, Machinist: 1866–1877," *LH* (Spring 1978).
19. Garraty, *New Commonwealth*, 162–63; Bruce Laurie, *Artisans into Workers: Labor in Nineteenth-Century America* (New York: Farrar, Straus and Giroux, 1989), 146–55.
20. Laurie, *Artisans into Workers*, 150–51; Ken Fones-Wolf, *Trade Union Gospel: Christianity and Labor in Industrial Philadelphia, 1865–1915* (Philadelphia: Temple University Press, 1989), 82–84; William M. Dick, *Labor and Socialism in America: The Gompers Era* (Port Washington, N.Y.: Kennikat Press, 1972), 18.
21. Richard Oestreicher, "Terence Powderly, the Knights of Labor, and Artisanal Republicanism," in Dubofsky and Van Tine, eds., *Labor Leaders in America*, 46–48; Susan Levine, *Labor's True Woman: Carpet Weavers, Industrialization, and Labor Reform in the Gilded Age* (Philadelphia: Temple University Press, 1984), 63–153; Melton Alonza McLaurin, *The Knights of Labor in the South* (Westport, CT: Greenwood Press, 1978), 131–48.
22. Bruce C. Nelson, "Revival and Upheaval: Religion, Irreligion, and Chicago's Working Class in 1886," *Journal of Social History*, 25 (Winter 1991): 245–47.
23. Laurie, *Arisans into Workers*, 157–58; Oestreicher, "Terence Powderly," 51–54.
24. Bensman, *Practice of Solidarity*, 104–106.

25. Keyssar, "Unemployment and the Labor Movement," 240–42; Oestreicher, *Solidarity and Fragmentation*, 145–59; McLaurin, *Knights of Labor in the South*, 56–79; Ross, *Workers on the Edge*, 274–78.
26. Paul Avrich, *The Haymarket Tragedy* (Princeton: Princeton University Press, 1984), 185–86; Oestreicher, *Solidarity and Fragmentation*, 160–62.
27. Laurie, *Artisans into Workers*, 170–74; Klein, *Jay Gould*, 357–63; Merl E. Reed, "The Augusta Textile Mills and the Strike of 1886," *LH*, 14 (Spring 1973): 239–44.
28. Laurie, *Artisans into Workers*, 174–75; Oestreicher, "Terence Powderly," in Dubofsky and Van Tine, eds., *Labor Leaders in America*, 54–56.
29. Harold Livesay, *Samuel Gompers and Organized Labor in America* (Boston: Little, Brown & Co., 1978), 1–47; John M. Laslett, "Samuel Gompers and the Rise of American Business Unionism," in Dubofsky and Van Tine, eds., *Labor Leaders in America*, 73; Dick, *Labor and Socialism in America*, 31–36, 45–48; Stuart B. Kaufman, *Samuel Gompers and the Origins of the American Federation of Labor, 1848–1896* (Westport, CT: Greenwood Press, 1973), 47–48, 114–15, 214–22.
30. Cooper, *Once A Cigar Maker*, 80–84, 98–104; see also Bensman, *Practice of Solidarity*, 77–84.
31. Kaufman, *Samuel Gompers and the Origins of the AFL*, 162; Dick, *Labor and Socialism in America*, 67–80.
32. Livesay, *Samuel Gompers*, 113–15.
33. Warren R. Van Tine, *The Making of the Labor Bureaucrat: Union Leadership in the United States, 1870–1920* (Amherst: University of Massachusetts Press, 1973), 90–119, 140–80; Dick, *Labor and Socialism in America*, 127–30.
34. Van Tine, *Making of the Labor Bureaucrat*, 34–54.
35. Fred Greenbaum, "The Social Ideas of Samuel Gompers," *Labor History*, 7 (Winter 1986): 50–51.
36. Meredith Tax, *The Rising of the Women: Feminist Solidarity and Class Conflict, 1880–1917* (New York: Monthly Review Press, 1980), 56–63.
37. Livesay, *Samuel Gompers*, 92–95; 115–19, Laslett, "Samuel Gompers," 69, 76, 82–84; Dick, *Labor and Socialism in America*, 114; Philip A. Taft, *The A.F. of L. in the Time of Gompers* (New York: Harper & Brothers, 1957), 305–14.
38. Wall, *Andrew Carnegie*, 537–82.
39. Laslett, "Samuel Gompers," 75; Taft, *A.F. of L. in the Time of Gompers*, 80–82.
40. Herbert G. Gutman, "Two Lockouts in Pennsylvania, 1873–1874," *Pennsylvania Magazine of History and Biography*, 83 (July 1959): 307–26; Gutman, "Trouble on the Railroads in 1873–1874; Prelude to the 1877 Crisis?" *LH*, 2 (Spring 1961): 225–28; New York *Herald*, August 3, 1876, October 29, 1877.

Chapter 11: Anarchy with Police

1. All material on the Haymarket incident, unless otherwise indicated, is from Avrich, *Haymarket Tragedy*, 187–218.
2. Avrich, *Haymarket Tragedy*, 260–78.
3. Avrich, *Haymarket Tragedy*, 355–93.
4. Harry Barnard, *"Eagle Forgotten": The Life of John Peter Altgeld* (Indianapolis: Bobbs-Merrill, 1938), 183–267.
5. Robert M. Utley, *Billy the Kid: A Short and Violent Life* (Lincoln: University of Nebraska Press, 1989), 202–07.
6. Holton, *Frontier Violence*, 116–17.
7. Holton, *Frontier Violence*, 147–93; Robert N. Mullin, ed., *Maurice G. Fulton's History of the Lincoln Country War* (Tucson: University of Arizona Press, 1968).
8. Theodore N. Ferdinand, "The Criminal Patterns of Boston Since 1849," *American Journal of Sociology*, 73 (July 1867): 84–99; Herbert Asbury, *The Gangs of New York: An Informal History of the Underworld* (New York: Knopf, 1928), 225–33, 252–53; Asbury, *Gem of the Prairie: An Informal History of the Chicago Underworld* (New York: Garden City, 1942), 144–76; David R. Goldfield, *Cotton Fields and Skyscrapers: Southern City and Region* (Baton Rouge: Louisiana State University Press, 1982), 93–94.
9. Pamela Haag, "The 'Ill-Use of a Wife': Patterns of Working-Class Violence in Domestic and Public New York City, 1860–1880," *Journal of Social History*, 25 (Spring 1992): 447–78.
10. Asbury, *French Quarter*, 404–12.
11. *Papers on Out-Door Relief and Tramps, Read at the Saratoga Meeting of the American Social Science Association, Before the Conference of State Charities, September 5th & 6th, 1877* (New York, n.p. 1877), 10–12; Monkkonen, eds., *Walking to Work*, 15–16; Furnas, *The Americans*, 681–82.
12. For a similar view, see *Papers on Out-Door Relief and Tramps*, 15.
13. Cincinnati *Gazette*, August 12, 1871.

14. Herbert G. Gutman, "The Tompkins Square 'Riot' in New York City on January 13, 1874: A Re-Examination of Its Causes and Its Aftermath," *LH*, 6 (Winter 1965): 44–70.

15. Harry A. Millis, "The Law Affecting Immigrants and Tramps," *Charities Review*, 7 (September 1897): 587–94; for Ohio court decision, see Michael Davis, "Forced to Tramp: the Perspective of the Labor Press, 1870–1900," in Monkkonen, ed., *Walking to Work*, 161–62.

16. Thomas, *Alternative Americas*, 140; "Twenty Thousand Harvest Hands Wanted in Kansas," *Collier's*, 29:29 (May 10, 1902): Sidney Harring and Lorraine M. McMullin, "Class Conflict and the Suppression of Tramps in Buffalo, 1892–1894," *Law and Society Review*, 11 (1977): 5–14; but see Lynne M. Adrain and Joan E. Crowley, "Hoboes and Homeboys: The Demography of Misdemeanor Convictions in Allegheny Co. Jail, 1892–1923," *Journal of Social History*, 25 (Winter 1991): 345–72.

17. Allen Steinberg, "'The Spirit of Litigation': Private Prosecution and Criminal Justice in Nineteenth Century Philadelphia," *Journal of Social History*, 20 (Winter 1986): 231–50; John C. Schneider, *Detroit and the Problem of Order, 1830–1880: A Geography of Crime, Riot, and Policing* (Lincoln: University of Nebraska Press, 1980); Eric H. Monkkonen, *Police in Urban America, 1860–1920* (Cambridge: Cambridge University Press, 1981).

18. John F. Kasson, *Rudeness & Civility: Manners in Nineteenth-Century Urban America* (New York: HarperCollins, 1990).

19. *Nation*, June 2, 1870, May 25, June 15, 1871; Griffith, *In Her Own Right*, 147–52.

20. Elizabeth Pleck, "Feminist Responses to 'Crimes Against Women,' 1868–1896," *Signs*, 8 (Spring 1983): 454–61; Keller, *Affairs of State*, 467–72; Richard L. Griswold, "The Evolution of the Doctrine of Mental Cruelty in Victorian American Divorce, 1790–1900," *Journal of Social History*, 20 (Fall 1986): 127–48; Griswold, "Law, Sex, Cruelty, and Divorce in Victorian America, 1840–1900," *American Quarterly*, 38 (Winter 1986): 721–45: Michael Grossberg, "Who Gets the Child? Custody, Guardianship, and the Rise of a Judicial Patriarchy in Nineteenth-Century America," *Feminist Studies*, 9 (Summer 1983): 235–60.

21. Elizabeth Pleck, "Wife-Beating in Nineteenth-Century America," *Victimology*, 4 (Fall 1979): 62–74; Robert M. Ireland, "Frenzied and Fallen Females: Women and Sexual Dishonor in the Nineteenth-Century United States," *Journal of Woman's History*, 3 (Winter 1992): 109.

22. Kasson, *Rudeness & Civility*, 132–39; New York *Tribune*, June 7, 1870; Robert Ireland, "The Libertine Must Die: Sexual Dishonor and the Unwritten Law in the Nineteenth-Century United States," *Journal of Social History*, 23 (Fall 1989): 27–44; Ireland, "Frenzied and Fallen Females," 95–107.

23. Rabinowitz, *Race Relations in the Urban South*, 182–97; there were exceptions, to be sure. See Dale A. Somers, "Black and White in New Orleans: A Study in Urban Race Relations, 1865–1900," *JSH*, 40 (February 1974): 30–36.

24. Joel Williamson, *A Rage for Order: Black-White Relations in the American South Since Emancipation* (New York: Oxford University Press, 1986), 98–115, 193–95; Davenport, "Thomas Dixon's Mythology of Southern History," *JSH* 36 (August 1970): 350–67.

25. Williamson, *A Rage for Order*, 86–90; "Brother to the Ox," *Collier's*, 31:6 (August 29, 1903).

26. Ayers, *Promise of the New South*, 156–58; Sinclair, *Aftermath of Slavery*, 246–48; Tallahassee *Weekly Floridian*, July 15, 1893.

27. Williamson, *Rage for Order*, 120–36; Bartley, *Creation of Modern Georgia*, 140; Hair, *Carnival of Fury*, 107–08.

28. Ayers, *Promise of the New South*, 141–43; Linda M. Matthews, "Keeping Down Jim Crow: The Railroads and the Separate Coach Bills in South Carolina," *South Atlantic Quarterly*, 73 (Winter 1974): 117–29.

29. Woodward, *Origins of the New South*, 211–12, 355; Bartley, *Creation of Modern Georgia*, 147–48; Doyle, *Nashville in the New South*, 115; Du Bois, "The Savings of Black Georgia," *Outlook*, 69 (September 14, 1901): 130; John Dittmer, *Black Georgia in the Progressive Era, 1900–1920* (Urbana: University of Illinois Press, 1977), 20–21; Savannah *Tribune*, February 2, 1889.

30. Estelle Freedman, "Separatism as Strategy: Female Institution Building and American Feminism, 1870–1930," *Feminist Studies*, 5 (Fall 1979): 512–29.

31. Baker, *Following the Color Line*, 220. Washington's "Compromise" was not new. Other champions of equal rights had made the same argument for years. See Savannah *Tribune*, February 9, 1889.

32. Logan, *Betrayal of the Negro*, 275–86; Max Bennett Thrasher, "Booker Washington's Personality," *Outlook*, 69 (November 9, 1901): 632; "Booker Washington and Tuskegee: A Southerner's View," *Ibid.*, 68 (April 13, 1901): 872; John M. F. Erwin, "The Negro: A Business Proposition," *Outlook*, 69 (November 30, 1901): 815–20; Thrasher, "The Tuskegee Negro Conference," *Outlook*, 67 (March 2, 1901): 486.

33. Dittmer, *Black Georgia in the Progressive Era*, 17–21; Doyle *Nashville in the New South*, 117–19; William Ivy Hair, *Carnival of Fury: Robert Charles and the New Orleans Race Riot of 1900* (Baton Rouge: Louisiana State University Press, 1976).

34. Du Bois, "The Savings of Black Georgia," *Outlook*, 69 (September 14, 1901): 128–30; Baker, *Following the Color Line*, 221.

35. Asbury, *French Quarter*, 411–22.

36. David A. Johnson, "Vigilance and the Law: The Moral Authority of Popular Justice in the Far West," *American Quarterly*, 33 (Winter 1981): 558–86.

37. May, *Protestant Churches and Industrial America*, 92–93.

38. Sala, *America Revisited*, 176–77; Asbury, *Gangs of New York*, 235–37, 249–52.

Chapter 12: Salvation Armies: Self-Help and Virtue's Legions

1. Ayers, *Promise of the New South*, 165–66.

2. Daniel E. Sutherland, *The Expansion of Everyday Life, 1860–1876* (New York: Harper & Row, 1989), 79–80.

3. Sutherland, *Expansion of Everyday Life*, 79–86; Ayers, *Promise of the New South*, 16; Cincinnati *Enquirer*, July 28, 1876.

4. Ayers, *Promise of the New South*, 162–64.

5. Ayers, *Promise of the New South*, 160–64; Sinclair, *Aftermath of Slavery*, 278–79; *Independent*, January 2, 1896.

6. Kusmer, *Ghetto Takes Shape*, 91–96; *Locomotive Firemen's Magazine*, October 1893, p. 872; Anne M. Boylan, "Evangelical Womanhood in the Nineteenth Century: The Role of Women in the Sunday Schools," *Feminist Studies*, 4 (October 1978): 62–80; Nancy Grey Osterud, *Bonds of Community: The Lives of Farm Women in Nineteenth-Century New York* (Ithaca: Cornell University Press, 1991), 262–68.

7. Ayers, *Promise of the New South*, 16; Christopher Waldrep, "'So Much Sin': The Decline of Religious Discipline and the 'Tidal Wave of Crime,'" *Journal of Social History*, 23 (Spring 1990): 535–54; David E. Harrell, Jr., "Sin and Sectionalism: A Case Study of Morality in the Nineteenth-Century South," *Mississippi Quarterly*, 19 (Fall 1966): 157–70; Clarence Poe, *My First 80 Years* (Chapel Hill: University of North Carolina Press, 1963), 52.

8. Samuel M. Jones to Graham Taylor, June 24, 1898, Samuel Milton Jones MSS, Toledo Public Library.

9. May, *Protestant Churches and Industrial America*, 40, 145–4; De Hauranne, *A Frenchman in Lincoln's America*, 2:162–63.

10. Helen L. Horowitz, *Culture and the City: Cultural Philanthropy in Chicago from the 1880s to 1917* (Chicago: University of Chicago Press, 1976), 61–69, 98–101; Frederick Lewis Allen, *The Great Pierpont Morgan* (New York: Harper & Brothers, 1949), 129–51.

11. Ray Stannard Baker, "J. Pierpont Morgan," *McClure's*, 17 (October 1901): 518, John Ensor Harr and Peter J. Johnson, *The Rockefeller Century* (New York: Charles Scribner's Sons, 1988), 62; Wall, *Andrew Carnegie*, 815–84; Livesay, *Andrew Carnegie*, 3–70, 188.

12. Wall, *Andrew Carnegie*, 828–29; Finley Peter Dunne, "The Carnegie Libraries," *Dissertations by Mr. Dooley* (Harper & Brothers, 1906).

13. Edward N. Gale, "Two Women's Gifts of Twenty-Five Millions," *Ladies Home Journal*, December 1900, p. 11; Daniel A. Wren, "American Business Philanthropy and Higher Education in the Nineteenth Century," *Business History Review*, 57 (Autumn 1983): 321–46.

14. Nevins, *John D. Rockefeller*, 1:18, 31, 340–44.

15. Robert H. Bremner, *The Public Good: Philanthropy and Welfare in the Civil War Era* (New York: Alfred A. Knopf, 1980), 65–69.

16. Bremner, *Public Good*, 196–98; Clara Barton, *The Red Cross in Peace and War* (Washington, D.C.: American Historical Press, 1910), 60–69.

17. Bremner, *Public Good*, 152–58, 203.

18. Bremner, *Public Good*, 203; *Papers on Out-Door Relief and Tramps, Read at the Saratoga Meeting of the American Social Science Association, Before the Conference of State Charities, September 5 and 6, 1877* (New York: n.p., 1877), 3–4; see also Brace, *Dangerous Classes of New York*, 22–23.

19. Paul Boyer, *Urban Masses and Moral Order in America, 1820–1920* (Cambridge: Harvard University Press, 1978), 143–61; John T. Cumbler, "The Politics of Charity: Gender and Class in Late Nineteenth Century Charity Policy," *Journal of Social History*, 14 (Fall 1980): 99–112.

20. Bremner, *Public Good*, 199–204; Cumbler, "Politics of Charity," 105–06; Ayers, *Promise of the New South*, 170.

21. *Harper's Weekly*, June 9, 1894; Barton, *Red Cross in Peace and War*, 226–27; Clara Barton, *A Story of the Red Cross: Glimpses of Field Work* (New York: D. Appleton and Company, 1918), 75–93.

22. *Railway and Engineering Review*, June 9, 1900, p. 316; *Independent*, May 28, June 4, 1896, pp. 8–12; *Outlook*, May 1, 1897, pp. 61–67; April 20, 1901, p. 930; Kusmer, *Ghetto Takes Shape*, 148.

23. Belle Kearney, *A Slaveholder's Daughter* (New York: Abbey Press, 1900), 164–67.

24. May, *Protestant Churches and Industrial America*, 112–24; Boyer, *Urban Masses and Moral Order*, 123–31.

25. Asbury, *Gem of the Prairie*, 95–141, 249–61; Asbury, *French Quarter*, 424–26; New York *Tribune*, July 21, 1870.

26. David C. Humphrey, "Prostitution and Public Policy in Austin, Texas, 1870–1915," *Southwest Historical Quarterly*, 86 (April 1983): 473–516; Anne M. Butler, *Daughters of Joy, Sisters of Misery: Prostitutes in the American West, 1865–90* (Urbana: University of Illinois Press, 1985), 50–69; Ruth Rosen, *The Lost Sisterhood: Prostitution in America, 1900–1918* (Baltimore: Johns Hopkins University Press, 1982), 69–99.

27. David R. Dungan, *Rum and Ruin: The Remedy Found* (Oskaloosa, Iowa: Central Book Concern, 1879), 52–54, 85, "A Revelation of the Census," *Catholic World*, 41 (July 1885): 465–71.

28. Robert C. Allen, *Horrible Prettiness: Burlesque and American Culture* (Chapel Hill: University of North Carolina Press, 1991).

29. Cincinnati *Enquirer*, August 6, 1876; New York *Herald*, December 14, 1876.

30. *Independent*, January 2, 1896; Boyer, *Urban Masses and Moral Order*, 134–41.

31. Asbury, *Gangs of New York*, 182–88; Boyer, *Urban Masses and Moral Order*, 269.

32. Boyer, *Urban Masses and Moral Order*, 271–74; James Gilbert, *Perfect Cities: Chicago's Utopias of 1893* (Chicago: University of Chicago Press, 1991), 78–107.

33. Boyer, *Urban Masses and Moral Order*, 262–68; Doyle, *Nashville in the New South*, 80.

34. Paul Kleppner, *The Third Electoral System, 1853–1892* (Chapel Hill: University of North Carolina Press, 1979), 190–91; Louis A. Banks, *The Lincoln Legion: The Story of Its Founder and Forerunners* (New York: Mershon Co., 1905), 161–68; Dungan, *Rum and Ruin*, 124–28; Anthony Comstock, "Health and Morals," *Independent*, July 16, 1896, p. 5.

35. Heywood Broun and Margaret Leech, *Anthony Comstock: Roundsman of the Lord* (New York: Literary Guild of America, 1927), 15–18, 130–36, 225–35.

36. Cincinnati *Gazette*, July 24, 25, August 5, 1871; *Railway Age*, February 11, 25, 1887.

37. Lula Barnes Ansley, *History of the Georgia Woman's Christian Temperance Union from its Organization, 1883 to 1907* (Columbus, GA: Gilbert Printing Co., 1914), 70–75; Dungan, *Rum and Ruin*, 61–78; William H. Daniels, *The Temperance Reform and its Great Reformers* (New York: Nelson & Phillips, 1877), 373–510; Ruth Bordin, *Woman and Temperance: The Quest for Power and Liberty, 1873–1900* (Philadelphia: Temple University Press, 1981), 94.

38. Bordin, *Woman and Temperance*, 42–51, 67–85.

39. Richard Jensen, *The Winning of the Midwest: Social and Political Conflict, 1888–1896* (Chicago: University of Chicago Press, 1971), 74–75.

40. Carl V. Harris, *Political Power in Birmingham, 1871–1921* (Knoxville: University of Tennessee Press, 1977), 193–95; Bordin, *Woman and Temperance*, 82–85; John Hammond Moore, "The Negro and Prohibition in Atlanta, 1885–1887," *South Atlantic Quarterly*, 69 (Winter 1970): 38–57; Ansley, *Georgia Woman's Christian Temperance Union*, 76–78, 84–87; Russell, *Atlanta, 1847–1890*, 210–15.

41. Charles W. Eliot, "A Study of American Liquor Laws," *Atlantic*, 79 (February 1897): 181–83; Ernest H. Cherrington, *The Evolution of Prohibition in the United States of America* (Westerville, Ohio: The American Issue Press, 1920), 176–83.

42. Allan J. Lichtman, "Political Realignment and 'Ethnocultural' Voting in late Nineteenth Century America," *Journal of Social History*, 16 (Spring 1983): 72–74.

43. Robert J. Kolesar, "Politics and Policy in a Developing Industrial City: Worcester, Massachusetts in the Late Nineteenth Century," Ph.D. Dissertation, Clark University, 1987, pp. 158–80; Bordin, *Woman and Temperance*, 85–87; Christian, *Americanism or Romanism, Which?*, 33–37; Cusack, *What Rome Teaches*, 252–59.

44. Schlereth, *Victorian America*, 225–29; George L. McNutt, "Why Workingmen Drink," *Outlook*, 69 (September 14, 1901): 116–17; Samuel M. Jones to the Rev. D. M. Fisk, January 8, 1898, Jones MSS.

45. Schlereth, *Victorian America*, 230–40; Lewis A. Erenberg, "Ain't We Got Fun?" *Chicago History*, 14 (Winter 1985–86): 4–21.

46. Erik Amfitheatrof, *The Children of Columbus* (Boston: Little, Brown and Company, 1973), 121–34; David Ewen, *Music Comes to America* (New York: Thomas Y. Crowell Company, 1942), 26–44, 60–71, 84–87.

47. Allen F. Davis, *Spearheads for Reform: The Social Settlements and the Progressive Movement, 1890–1914* (New York: Oxford University Press, 1967), 3–39; Helen Lefkowitz Horowitz, "Hull-House as Women's Space," *Chicago History*, 12 (Winter 1983–84): 40–55.

48. Robert Smith Bader, *Prohibition in Kansas: A History* (Lawrence: University Press of Kansas, 1986), 82–87.

49. White, "*It's Your Misfortune and None of My Own*," 358–59.

Chapter 13: "What Are We Here For?"

1. Justus D. Doenecke, *The Presidencies of James A. Garfield and Chester A. Arthur* (Lawrence: University of Kansas Press, 1981), 26.

2. Joel H. Silbey, *The American Political Nation, 1838–1893* (Stanford: Stanford University Press, 1991), 54–62, 102–05; Michael E. McGerr, *The Decline of Popular Politics: The American North, 1865–1928* (New York: Oxford University Press, 1986), 17–20.

3. Morton Keller, *The Art and Politics of Thomas Nast* (New York: Oxford University Press, 1968); Richard S. West, *Satire on Stone: The Political Cartoons of Joseph Keppler* (Urbana: University of Illinois Press, 1988).

4. New York *Herald*, October 28, November 4, 1888; Jensen, *Winning of the Midwest*, 12–13.

5. Thernstrom, *Poverty and Progress*, 180; Jensen, *Winning of the Midwest*, 6–9; Dale Baum, "The Massachusetts Voter: Party Loyalty in the Gilded Age, 1872–1896," in Jack Tager and John W. Ifkovic, eds., *Massachusetts in the Gilded Age: Selected Essays* (Amherst: University of Massachusetts Press, 1985), 40–43.

6. Silbey, *American Political Nation*, 141–47, 218–19; *Outlook*, 56 (June 12, 1897): 407; *Ibid.*, 57 (October 9, 1897): 361; Carrie Chapman Catt, "Woman's Place in Politics," *Collier's*, 26:19 (October 20, 1900).

7. Chicago *Times*, April 15, 1876.

8. James A. Kehl, *Boss Rule in the Gilded Age: Matt Quay of Pennsylvania* (Pittsburgh: University of Pittsburgh Press, 1981), 63–64.

9. Alexander B. Callow, Jr., *The Tweed Ring* (New York: Oxford University Press, 1965), 135–43, 166–67, 176–78, 198–213.

10. Jon C. Teaford, *The Unheralded Triumph: City Government in America, 1870–1900* (Baltimore: Johns Hopkins University Press, 1984), 43–54; Theodore Lothrop Stoddard, *Master of Manhattan: The Life of Richard Croker* (New York: Longman's, 1931), 256–59.

11. Teaford, *Unheralded Triumph*, 175–87; Morgan, *From Hayes to McKinley*, 303–04; Richard L. McCormick, *From Realignment to Reform: Political Change in New York State, 1893–1910* (Ithaca: Cornell University Press, 1981), 70–84.

12. Lincoln Steffens, *The Autobiography of Lincoln Steffens* (New York: Harcourt, Brace & World, Inc., 1931), 1:236.

13. "Women in New York's Political Campaign," *Collier's Weekly*, 29:23–24 (September 13, 1902); see also Daniel Czitrom, "Underworlds and Underdogs: Big Tim Sullivan and Metropolitan Politics in New York, 1889–1913," *JAH*, 78 (September 1991): 542–47.

14. "Women in New York's Political Campaign," *Collier's*, 29:23 (September 13, 1902).

15. Melvin G. Holli, *Reform in Detroit: Hazen S. Pingree and Urban Politics* (New York: Oxford University Press, 1969), 24–26.

16. James B. Crooks, *Politics and Progress: The Rise of Urban Progressivism in Baltimore, 1895 to 1911* (Baton Rouge: Louisiana State University Press, 1968), 19–20.

17. Ivor Spencer, *The Victor and the Spoils: A Life of William L. Marcy* (Providence: Brown University Press, 1959), 61n; Harry J. Sievers, *Benjamin Harrison, Hoosier President: The White House and After* (New York: Bobbs-Merrill Co., Inc., 1968), 40–43.

18. C. K. Yearley, *The Money Machines: The Breakdown and Reform of Governmental and Party Finance in the North, 1860–1920* (Albany: State University of New York Press, 1970), 104–06; "Electoral Reform with the Massachusetts Ballot Act and the New York (Stanton) Bill" (New York: Society for Political Education, 1889), 11–12.

19. *Nation*, July 24, 1890; Morgan, *From Hayes to McKinley*, 21; Teaford, *Unheralded Triumph*, 168.

20. Yearley, *Money Machines*, 108–118.

21. Diana Klebanow, "E. L. Godkin, the City, and Civic Responsibility," *NYHSQ*, 55 (January 1971): 52–75; Ari Hoogenboom, *Outlawing the Spoils: A History of the Civil Service Reform Movement, 1865–1883* (Urbana: University of Illinois Press, 1961), 186–97; for women's roles, see "A Notable Competition," *Collier's*, 26:18 (November 3, 1900).

22. John Sproat, *"The Best Men": Liberal Reformers in the Gilded Age* (New York: Oxford University Press, 1968).

23. Robert Muccigrosso, "The City Reform Club," *NYHSQ*, 52 (July 1968): 239–40; Albert B. Paine, *Thomas Nast: His Period and His Pictures* (New York, 1904), 491.

24. Teaford, *Unheralded Triumph*, 66–80.

25. Teaford, *Unheralded Triumph*, 133–62; for the role of engineers in making cleaner, safer cities, see Stanley K. Schultz and Clay McShane, "To Engineer the Metropolis: Sewers, Sanitation, and City Planning in Late-Nineteenth Century America," *Journal of American History*, 65 (September 1978): 389–411.

26. Teaford, *Unheralded Triumph*, 162–71.

27. Summers, *Era of Good Stealings*, 95–103.

28. Ari Hoogenboom, *The Presidency of Rutherford B. Hayes* (Lawrence: University Press of Kansas, 1988), 217–19; Ben: Perley Poore, *Perley's Reminiscences of Sixty Years in the National Metropolis* (Philadelphia: Hubbard Brothers, 1886), 2:349–50.
29. Morgan, *From Hayes to McKinley*, 15–17.
30. "G. G.," New York *Tribune*, April 9, 1870; Hoogenboom, *Outlawing the Spoils*, 152–54; Hoogenboom, *Presidency of Rutherford B. Hayes*, 149–51, 194, 206–07.
31. Morgan, *From Hayes to McKinley*, 32–34, 37; New York *Times*, March 22, 1873; David M. Jordan, *Roscoe Conkling of New York: Voice in the Senate* (Ithaca: Cornell University Press, 1971), 146–53, 281–301.
32. Sala, *American Revisited*, 138; Jordan, *Roscoe Conkling*, 322–37; David Saville Muzzey, *James G. Blaine: A Political Idol of Other Days* (New York: Dodd, Mead & Co., 1934), 110, 162–72; Herbert J. Clancy, *The Presidential Election of 1880* (Chicago: Loyola University Press, 1958), 82–119. Blaine actually disliked the name "Plumed Knight." After all, what was a plume but the white feather? and what bold statesman shows the white feather?
33. Allan Peskin, *Garfield* (Kent State: Kent State University Press, 1979), 484–92, 500–13; Leon B. Richardson, *William E. Chandler: Republican* (New York: Dodd, Mead & Co., 1940), 265–67.
34. Muzzey, *James G. Blaine*, 60–61; Peskin, *Garfield*, 517–29, 533–35, 551–72.
35. Morgan, *From Hayes to McKinley*, 146–49; Thomas C. Reeves, *Gentleman Boss* (New York: Knopf, 1975), 268–76.
36. Hoogenboom, *Outlawing the Spoils*, 200–02, 236–53; Thomas B. Reed to George Gifford, December 20, 1882, Reed MSS, Bowdoin College.
37. Hoogenboom, *Outlawing the Spoils*, 260–64; annual reports of the Civil Service Reform Association of Philadelphia (Philadelphia: H. Ferkler, 1883–1907).
38. Morgan, *From Hayes to McKinley*, 30.
39. Nelson W. Polsby, "The Institutionalization of the U.S. House of Representatives," *American Political Science Review*, 62 (March 1968): 144–68; Nelson W. Polsby, Miram Gallaher, and Barry S. Rundquist, "The Growth of the Seniority System in the U.S. House of Representatives," *Ibid.*, 63 (September 1969): 787–807.
40. Richard J. Evans, *Death in Hamburg: Society and Politics in the Cholera Years, 1830–1910* (New York: Oxford University Press, 1987), 226–56, 372–79, 403–69; Jon Teaford, *Unheralded Triumph*, 247–48; see also Edward Meeker, "The Social Rate of Return on Investment in Public Health, 1880–1910," *Journal of Economic History*, 34 (June 1974): 392–421; Meeker, "The Improving Health of the United States, 1850–1915," *Explorations in Economic History*, 9 (Summer 1972): 366–73.
41. Carroll D. Wright, "The Working of the Department of Labor," *Cosmopolitan*, 13: 230; Gilkeson, *Middle-Class Providence*, 125–26.
42. John D. Buenker, *Urban Liberalism and Progressive Reform* (New York: Charles Scribner's, 1973), 25–27.

Chapter 14: The Myth of Laissez-Unfaire

1. Michael R. Hyman, *The Anti-Redeemers: Hill-Country Political Dissenters in the Lower South from Redemption to Populism* (Baton Rouge: Louisiana State University Press, 1990), 111; Shaw, *Wool-Hat Boys*, 126.
2. Ambrose Bierce, *Collected Works* (New York: Gordian Press, 1966), 6:267.
3. Woodward, *Origins of the New South*, 66–74.
4. *Sixty-second Annual Report of the New York Association for Improving the Condition of the Poor* (New York: United Charities Building, 1905), 18–19; St. Louis *Globe-Democrat*, March 25, 1891.
5. Pennsylvania Laws (1885), Acts 37, 58, 186; Bessie Louise Pierce, *A History of Chicago, 1871–1893* (New York: Knopf, 1957), 322; Keller, *Affairs of State*, 409–14, 509–11.
6. Alan I. Marcus, "Setting the Standard: Fertilizers, State Chemists, and Early National Commercial Regulation, 1880–1887," *Agricultural History*, 61 (Winter 1987): 47–73; Conner Sorenson, "The Rise of Government-Sponsored Applied Entomology, 1840–1870," *Agricultural History* 62 (Spring 1988): 114–15; James A. Young, "The Public Response to the Catastrophic Spread of Russian Thistle (1880) and Halogeton (1945)," *Agricultural History*, 62 (Spring 1988): 122–26.
7. Garraty, *New Commonwealth*, 144–45; Keller, *Affairs of State*, 419–22.
8. Leonard D. White, *The Republican Era: A Study in Administrative History, 1869–1901* (New York: Free Press, 1965), 232–56; Shannon, *Farmer's Last Frontier*, 270–71, 282–90.
9. Morgan, *From Hayes to McKinley*, 407–08; Robert C. Cotner, *James Stephen Hogg: A Biography* (Austin: University of Texas Press, 1959), 469.
10. Barker, *Henry George*, 455–81; David C. Hammack, *Power and Society: Greater New York at the Turn of the Century* (New York: Columbia University Press, 1982), 174–81.

11. Herbert J. Bass, *"I Am a Democrat": The Political Career of David Bennett Hill* (Syracuse: Syracuse University Press, 1961), 51–71; Michael A. Gordon, "The Labor Boycott in New York City, 1880–1886," *LH*, 16 (Spring 1975): 288–89; F. J. Stimson, "Democracy and the Laboring Man," *Atlantic*, 80 (November 1897): 605–19.

12. William H. Becker, "American Manufacturers and Foreign Markets, 1870–1900: Business Historians and the 'New Economic Determinists,'" *Business History Review*, 47 (Winter 1973): 466–81; Barrett, *Work and Community*, 18.

13. "Curiosities of American Export Trade," *Collier's*, 31:20 (May 23, 1903); "America's Debt to the Russian Jew," *Ibid.*, 31:10 (June 6, 1903); David M. Pletcher, *The Awkward Years: American Foreign Relations under Garfield and Arthur* (Columbia: University of Missouri Press, 1962), 158–91; Paul J. Zingg, "To the Shores of Barbary: The Ideology and Pursuit of American Commercial Expansion, 1816–1906," *South Atlantic Quarterly*, 79 (Autumn 1980): 417–18.

14. *Independent*, July 9, 1896; Henry B. Fuller, "The Upward Movement in Chicago," *Atlantic*, 80 (October 1897): 535–36; Ralph Scharnau, "Elizabeth Morgan, Crusader for Labor Reform," *LH*, 14 (Summer 1973): 340–51.

15. McCormick, *From Realignment to Reform*, 146–47.

16. Jacob Riis, *The Making of An American* (New York: Grosset & Dunlap, 1901), 311; Riis, *How the Other Half Lives*, 33–34; Doyle, *Nashville in the New South*, 100–01.

17. *Nation*, August 8, 1889, p. 103; Russell, *Atlanta, 1847–1890*, 194; Minturn, *Travels West*, 20–21.

18. J. W. Howard, "City Streets and Asphalt Pavement," *Independent*, February 6, 1896, p. 6; Perry Duis, "Whose City? Public and Private Places in Nineteenth-Century Chicago," *Chicago History*, 12 (Summer 1983): 4–7.

19. *Outlook* (April 20, 1901): 894–95; Harris, *Political Power in Birmingham*, 167, 146–75; Teaford, *Unheralded Triumph*, 226–29, 231–32, 274; Russell, *Atlanta, 1847–1890*, 228.

20. Doyle, *Nashville in the New South*, 84; Teaford, *Unheralded Triumph*, 221–31, 252–65.

21. Pierce, *History of Chicago*, 3:313–15; Teaford, *Unheralded Triumph*, 254, 292–93; Kolesar, "Politics and Policy," 92–117.

22. Edward Chase Kirkland, *Charles Francis Adams, Jr., 1835–1915: The Patrician at Bay* (Cambridge: Harvard University Press, 1965), 1–41; Thomas K. McCraw, *Prophets of Regulation* (Cambridge: Belknap Press, 1984), 1–15.

23. Kirkland, *Charles Francis Adams, Jr.*, 42–57; McCraw, *Prophets of Regulation*, 23–44.

24. Kirkland, *Industry Comes of Age*, 118–20; George H. Miller, *Railroads and the Granger Laws* (Madison: University of Wisconsin Press, 1971), 75–96, 114–16, 128–39, 161–68. For a study of weaker regulators, see 186–98; Paul J. Miranti, Jr., "The Mind's Eye of Reform: The ICC's Bureau of Statistics and Accounts and a Vision of Regulation, 1887–1940," *Business History Review*, 63 (Autumn 1989): 472–73. For an analysis of free passes, see Thomas C. Cochran, *Railroad Leaders, 1845–1890: The Business Mind in Action* (Cambridge: Harvard University Press, 1953), 192–96. For trouble on western railroads, see Bryant, *Atchison, Topeka & Santa Fe*, 207–08. A full comparison of state commissions' powers appears in *28th Annual Report of the Commission of Railroads in Michigan* (1900), 25–29.

25. Arnold M. Paul, *Conservative Crisis and the Rule of Law: Attitudes of Bar and Bench, 1887–1895* (Ithaca: Cornell University Press, 1960), 10–11; George W. Hilton, "The Consistency of the Interstate Commerce Act," *Journal of Law and Economics*, 19 (October 1966): 87–113; Gerald D. Nash, "Origins of the Interstate Commerce Act of 1887," *Pennsylvania History*, 24 (July 1957): 181–90.

26. Gabriel Kolko, *Railroads and Regulation, 1877–1916* (Princeton: Princeton University Press, 1964); Robert B. Carson, "Railroads and Regulation Revisited: A Note on Problems of Historiography and Ideology," *Historian*, 34 (1972): 437–446.

27. Purcell, "Ideas and Interests: Businessmen and the Interstate Commerce Act," *Journal of American History* 54 (1967): 561–78; Cochran, *Railroad Leaders*, 190–92; *Railway Review*, January 22, 1887, p. 47; *Railway Age*, February 18, 1887, p. 107.

28. For the rate-cutting catastrophe, see Maury Klein, "Competition and Regulation: The Railroad Model," *Business History Review*, 64 (Summer 1990): 314–18.

29. Miranti, "Mind's Eye of Reform," *Business History Review*, 63 (Autumn 1989): 476–82; Stover, *American Railroads*, 153–54; Steven W. Usselman, "Air Brakes for Freight Trains: Technological Innovation in the American Railroad Industry, 1869–1900," *Business History Review*, 58 (Spring 1984): 30–50. On ICC action see *Railway Age*, January 18, 1901, p. 41; *Annual Report of the Interstate Commerce Commission* (1900), 6, 78.

30. *Railway and Engineering Review*, June 2, 1900, p. 302; Philip L. Merkel, "The Origins of an Expanded Federal Court Jurisdiction: Railroad Development and the Ascendancy of the Federal Judiciary," *Business History Review*, 58 (Autumn 1984): 336–58; Miller, *Railroads and the Granger Laws*, 192–93.

31. Kolko, *Railroads and Regulation*, 81–83; Miranti, "Mind's Eye of Reform," 485.

32. Keller, *Affairs of State*, 358–70; Paul, *Conservative Crisis*, 29–35.

33. Paul, *Conservative Crisis*, 15–16.

34. Loren P. Beth, *The Development of the American Constitution, 1877–1917* (New York: Harper Torchbooks, 1971), 170–72.

35. Sidney G. Tarrow, "Lochner versus New York: A Political Analysis," *LH*, 5 (Fall 1964): 277–97; Catherine Drinker Bowen, *Yankee from Olympus: Justice Holmes and His Family* (Boston: Little, Brown and Co., 1944), 374–75.

36. *Railway World*, January 30, 1892, p. 102; Merkel, "Origins of an Expanded Federal Court Jurisdiction," *Business History Review*, 58 (Autumn 1894): 358; *Railway Age*, February 2, 1901, p. 78.

37. Tarrow, "Lochner versus New York," 298–312.

38. Leon Fink, *Workingmen's Democracy: The Knights of Labor and American Politics* (Urbana: University of Illinois Press, 1983).

39. McLaurin, *Knights of Labor in the South*, 80–112.

Chapter 15: Tariff Wars in the Billion-Dollar Country, 1884–1890

1. Burton J. Williams, *Senator John James Ingalls: Kansas' Iridescent Republican* (Lawrence: University Press of Kansas, 1972), 119.

2. Jean H. Baker, *Affairs of Party: The Political Culture of Northern Democrats in the Mid-Nineteenth Century* (Ithaca: Cornell University Press, 1983), 287–91, 300; McGerr, *Decline of Popular Politics*, 25.

3. *Railway World*, April 23, 1892; Garraty, *New Commonwealth*, 298; Paul Kleppner, *The Cross of Culture: A Social Analysis of Midwestern Politics, 1850–1900* (New York: Free Press, 1970), esp. pp. 5–91.

4. Kleppner, *Third Electoral System*, 143–237; Ballard C. Campbell, *Representative Democracy: Public Policy and Midwestern Legislatures in the Late Nineteenth Century* (Cambridge: Harvard, 1980), 120–30; William A. Robinson, *Thomas B. Reed, Parliamentarian* (New York: Dodd, Mead & Co., 1930), 99, 271.

5. *Nation*, October 21, 1880.

6. Baker, *Affairs of Party*, 143–46; Cleveland *Plain Dealer*, August 4, 1884; Raleigh *Sentinel*, March 2, 1876.

7. *Railway World*, April 23, 1892; Festus P. Summers, *William L. Wilson and Tariff Reform* (New Brunswick: Rutgers University Press, 1953), 86–87; Morgan, *From Hayes to McKinley*, 165–73.

8. Edwin A. Hartshorn, *Wages, Living, and Tariff* (Troy: William H. Young, 1884), 12; Thomas E. Fernon, "Free Trade Means Serf Pay and Famine Fare" (Philadelphia: Henry B. Ashmead, 1880), 56–57.

9. See Hartshorn, *Wages, Living, and Tariff*, 68–69; Poor, *Twenty-Two Years of Protection*, 180–200; Lucien Sanial, "The True American Policy" (New York: Association of American Economists, 1884), 11, 15.

10. Tom E. Terrill, "David A. Wells, the Democracy, and Tariff Reduction, 1877–1894," *JAH*, 61 (December 1969): 540–55; Henry C. Rew, "'Protection': Both Sides of the Question" (New York: Benjamin H. Tyrrell, 1888), 5–19; Augustus Mongredien, "The Western Farmer of America" (New York: Cassell, Petter, Galpin & Co., 1880), 7–10; New York *World*, December 21, 1888.

11. Stephen M. White to A. B. Butler, May 16, 1894, Stephen Mallory White MSS, Stanford University; Clancy, *Presidential Election of 1880*, 220–21. For arguments aimed at businessmen, see J. S. Moore, "Friendly Sermons to the Protectionist Manufacturers of the United States" (New York: B. P. Putnam's Sons, 1877), 46, 48.

12. Hirshson, *Farewell to the Bloody Shirt*, 124–26; Fernon, "Free Trade Means Serf Pay and Famine Fare," 65; D. G. Harriman, *American Tariffs from Plymouth Rock to McKinley* (New York: American Protective Tariff League, 1892), 74–76; Geoffrey Blodgett, *The Gentle Reformers: Massachusetts Democrats in the Cleveland Era* (Cambridge: Harvard University Press, 1966), 73–81.

13. Reeves, *Gentleman Boss*, 358–59; Muzzey, *James G. Blaine*, 84-99.

14. William M. Armstrong, ed., *The Gilded Age Letters of E. L. Godkin* (Albany: State University of New York Press, 1974), 315; Blodgett, *Gentle Reformers*, 1–11; Nevins, *Grover Cleveland*, 146–54.

15. Nevins, *Grover Cleveland*, 162–69.

16. Morgan, *From Hayes to McKinley*, 223; Muzzey, *James G. Blaine*, 307–20; Nevins, *Grover Cleveland*, 185–88.

17. Carpenter, *Carp's Washington*, 40, 48–49; Morgan, *From Hayes to McKinley*, 246–47; Nevins, *Grover Cleveland*, 82, 212–14, 310–13.

18. Nevins, *Grover Cleveland*, 763; Woodrow Wilson, "Mr. Cleveland as President," *Atlantic*, 79 (March 1897): 289–90; Charles R. Jones to Matt Ransom, Matt Ransom MSS, Southern Historical Collection, University of North Carolina; P. L. Robertson, "Cleveland's Constructive Use of the Pension Vetoes," *Mid-America*, 44 (January 1962): 33–45.

19. Nevins, *Grover Cleveland*, 123–24, 142–44; Geoffrey Blodgett, "The Political Leadership of Grover Cleveland," *South Atlantic Quarterly*, 82 (Summer 1983): 293–95; Richard E. Welch, Jr., *The Presidencies of Grover Cleveland* (Lawrence: University Press of Kansas, 1988), 77–79; Reeves, *Gentleman Boss*, 350.

20. *Puck*, August 29, 1888; Nevins, *Grover Cleveland*, 388–94, 400–01; Horace Samuel Merrill, *Bourbon Leader: Grover Cleveland and the Democratic Party* (Boston: Little, Brown & Co., 1957), 123–28.

21. Nevins, *Grover Cleveland*, 428–31; New York *Herald*, October 28, November 4, 1888; Morgan, *From Hayes to McKinley*, 314–16.

22. Nevins, *Grover Cleveland*, 398–400; *Puck*, September 26, 1888; James L. Baumgardner, "The 1888 Presidential Election: How Corrupt?" *Presidential Studies*, 14 (Summer 1984): 416–27.

23. Morgan, *From Hayes to McKinley*, 287–89; Arthur W. Dunn, *Gridiron Nights: Humorous and Satirical Views of Politics and Statesmen as Presented by the Famous Dining Club* (New York: Frederick A. Stokes Co., 1915), 19; Sievers, *Benjamin Harrison: Hoosier President*, 42–43, 55–57.

24. *Nation*, August 1, 1889, p. 81; Edmund Morris, *The Rise of Theodore Roosevelt* (New York: Coward, McCann & Geoghegan, Inc., 1979), 397–406.

25. Champ Clark, *My Quarter-Century of American Politics* (New York: Harper & Brothers, 1920), 1:276–85.

26. Clark, *My Quarter-Century*, 294; Washington *Post*, February 22, 1892; Robinson, *Thomas B. Reed*, 188–234.

27. Clarence A. Stern, *Golden Republicanism: The Crusade for Hard Money* (Ann Arbor: Edwards Brothers, 1964), 14–23.

28. Indeed, as one defender noted, some half of all American imports would come in duty-free—more than at any time in thirty years. Tea, coffee, cocoa, chicory, and dried fruit all went on the free list. Harriman, *American Tariffs*, 66–67.

29. H. Wayne Morgan, *William McKinley and His America* (Syracuse: Syracuse University Press, 1963), 128–47.

30. Kleppner, *Third Electoral System*, 298–306; Clipping, December 19, 1891, Francis G. Carpenter Scrapbook, LC.

31. John F. Swift to Stephen M. White, April 29, 1890, White MSS.

32. C. de Meaux, "A Catholic Centennial in the U.S.," *Catholic World*, 51 (June 1890): 376–94; George M. Searle, "Religious Liberty as Understood by the 'Evangelical Alliance,'" *Ibid.*, 39 (June 1884): 400–06; Steven P. Erie, *Rainbow's End: Irish-Americans and the Dilemmas of Urban Machine Politics, 1840–1985* (Berkeley: University of California Press, 1988), 35–41.

33. Lloyd P. Jorgenson, *The State and the Nonpublic School, 1825–1925* (Columbia: University of Missouri Press, 1987), 111–45; M. M. Sheedy, "The School Question in the Pennsylvania Legislature," *Catholic World*, 53 (July 1891): 491–93; Walter Elliott, "Honest Protestants and the Public Schools," *Ibid.*, 39 (July 1884): 420–26; Kleppner, *Third Electoral System*, 221–32.

34. Sheedy, "School Question," 487; Kleppner, *Third Electoral System*, 349–53.

35. Cherrington, *Evolution of Prohibition*, 176–83.

36. Banks, *The Lincoln Legion: The Story of Its Founder and Forerunner* (New York: Mershon Co., 1905), 166; Bader, *Prohibition in Kansas*, 77–78.

37. Kleppner, *Cross of Culture*, 143–44; Jensen, *Winning of the Midwest*, 83–121.

38. Kleppner, *Third Electoral System*, 300–06, 349–53; E. A. Higgins, "The American State and the Private School," *Catholic World*, 53 (July 1891): 521–27; Joanne Wheeler, "The Origins of Populism in the Political Structure of a Midwestern State: Partisan Preference in Illinois, 1876–1892," unpublished Ph.D. Dissertation, SUNY at Buffalo, 1976, pp. 145–56; Jensen, *Winning of the Midwest*, 122–53.

39. Williams, *Senator John James Ingalls*, 123.

Chapter 16: Vox Pop

1. Richard Hofstadter, *The Age of Reform: From Bryan to F.D.R.* (New York: Vintage, 1955), 23–36.

2. Thomas F. Averill, "Oz and Kansas Culture," *Kansas History*, 12 (Spring 1989): 2–7.

3. Virginia E. McCormick, "Butter and Egg Business: Implications from the Records of a Nineteenth-Century Ohio Farm Wife," *Ohio History*, 100 (Winter-Spring 1991): 57–67.

4. Ginger, *Age of Excess*, 68.

5. Hofstadter, *Age of Reform*, 34–46.

6. John D. Hicks, *The Populist Revolt* (Minneapolis: University of Minnesota Press, 1931), 56.

7. Shannon, *Farmer's Last Frontier*, 144–46, 308; Hicks, *Populist Revolt*, 32.

8. Shannon, *Farmer's Last Frontier*, 139–40, 301, 313.

9. D. Sven Nordin, *Rich Harvest: A History of the Grange, 1867–1900* (Jackson: University Press of Mississippi,

1974); Mari Jo Buhle, *Women and American Socialism, 1879–1920* (Champaign-Urbana: University of Illinois Press, 1983), 82–85.

10. Jacqueline P. Bull, "The General Store in the Southern Agrarian Economy from 1865–1910," Ph.D. Dissertation, University of Kentucky, 1948, pp. 65–66; Robert C. McMath, *American Populism: A Social History, 1877–1898* (New York: Hill and Wang, 1993), 94–107.

11. Josephson, *Robber Barons*, 352.

12. McMath, *American Populism*, 143–63.

13. T. J. Kerns to Stephen Mallory White, February 7, 1893, White MSS; Walter T. Nugent, *The Tolerant Populists: Kansas Populism and Nativism* (Chicago: University of Chicago Press, 1963), 190–91; Kenesaw Mountain Landis to Daniel Lamont, May 23, 1896, Daniel Lamont MSS, LC.

14. Nugent, *Tolerant Populists*, 76–84; clipping, November 17, 1891, Francis G. Carpenter Scrapbook, LC; Tallahassee *Floridian*, July 15, 1893.

15. John R. Morris, *David H. Waite: The Ideology of a Western Populist* (Washington, D.C.: University Press of America, 1982), 82–93; Karel Denis Bicha, "Jerry Simpson: Populist Without Principles," *JAH*, 54 (September 1967): 271–90; Peter H. Argersinger, *Populism and Politics: William Alfred Peffer and the People's Party* (Lexington: University Press of Kentucky, 1974); Janet Jennings, "Our Washington Letter," *Independent*, January 16, 1896, p. 6.

16. John Dibbern, "Who Were the Populists?: A Study of Grass-Roots Alliancemen in Dakota," *Agricultural History*, 56 (October 1982): 677–91; Shannon, *Farmer's Last Frontier*, 308; Robert W. Larson, *Populism in the Mountain West* (University of New Mexico Press, 1986), 3–4, 44–46, 74–75.

17. For Briton-baiting, and some Jewish stereotypes, see Ignatius Donnelly, *The American People's Money* (Chicago: Laird & Lee, 1896), 102, 136–37, 162. But for a defense of the Populists, and Donnelly in particular, see Norman Pollack, "Handlin on Anti-Semitism: A Critique of 'American Views of the Jew,'" *JAH*, 51 (December 1964): 391–403.

18. Norman Pollack, *The Populist Response to Industrial America: Midwestern Populist Thought* (Cambridge: Harvard University Press, 1962), 21–33, 68–71.

19. Larson, *Populism in the Mountain West*, 46–51, 86–90.

20. Bruce Palmer, *"Man Over Money": The Southern Populist Critique of American Capitalism* (Chapel Hill: University of North Carolina Press, 1980), 50–51; Terence V. Powderly to W. L. Stark, April 7, 1892, Powderly MSS; C. Vann Woodward, *Tom Watson: Agrarian Rebel* (New York: Macmillan, 1938), 220–222.

21. McMath, *American Populism*, 125–26; O. Gene Clanton, "Intolerant Populist? The Disaffection of Mary Elizabeth Lease," *Kansas Historical Quarterly*, 34 (Spring 1968): 189–200; Mary Jo Wagner, "Farms, Families, and Reform: Women in the Farmers' Alliance and Populist Party," Ph.D. Dissertation 1986, University of Oregon; Julie Roy Jeffrey, "Women in the Southern Farmers' Alliance: A Reconstruction of the Role and Status of Women in the Late Nineteenth-Century South," *Feminist Studies*, 3 (Fall 1975): 72–91.

22. Barton Shaw, *The Wool-Hat Boys* (Baton Rouge: Louisiana State University Press, 1984), 94–96; Lawrence Goodwyn, *The Populist Moment: A Short History of the Agrarian Revolt in America* (New York: Oxford University Press, 1978), 296; Samuel L. Webb, "Two-Party Politics in the One-Party South: Alabama Hill Country, 1880–1920," Ph.D. Dissertation, Univ. of Arkansas, p. 135.

23. Shaw, *Wool-Hat Boys*, 82–90; Palmer, *"Man Over Money"*, 52–62.

24. Palmer, *"Man Over Money"*, 55, 62; William Holmes, "The Demise of the Colored Farmers' Alliance," *JSH*, 41 (May 1975): 187–200.

25. Terence V. Powderly to W. L. Stark, April 7, 1892, Powderly MSS; Degler, *Other South*, 322–23; Michael M. Bell, "Did New England Go Downhill?" *Geographical Review*, 79 (1989): 454–57; Howard S. Russell, *A Long, Deep Furrow: Three Centuries of Farming in New England* (Hanover: University Press of New England, 1976), 437–61.

26. Shaw, *Wool-Hat Boys*, 100–01, 108–09, 131–39, Peter H. Argersinger, "Ideology and Behavior: Legislative Politics and Western Populism" and Karel D. Bicha, "Some Observations on 'Ideology and Behavior: Legislative Politics and Western Populism,'" *Agricultural History*, 58 (January 1984): 43–69; Herbert Croly, *Marcus Alonzo Hanna, His Life and Work* (New York: Macmillan, 1919), 335–36; Sheldon Hackney, *Populism to Progressivism in Alabama* (Princeton: Princeton University Press, 1969), 71–76.

27. Arthur Nussbaum, *A History of the Dollar* (New York: Columbia University Press, 1957), 61–64, 81–91, 101–32.

28. Thomas Dickieson, "Plain Words About Silver Money," (New York: Engineering Press, 1892), 9, 19; Nussbaum, *History of the Dollar*, 137–39.

29. A. L. Fitzgerald, *The Thirty Years' War on Silver: Money Scientifically Treated and Logically Presented* (Ainsworth & Co., 1903), 327–29; E. J. Farmer, *The Conspiracy Against Silver, or a Plea for Bi-Metallism in the United States* (Hiles & Coggshall, 1886), 7; Donnelly, *American People's Money*, 150–62.

30. The argument is more temperately made than usual in Edward A. Ross, *Honest Dollars* (Chicago: Charles H. Kerr & Co., 1896). For the quote, see Tallahassee *Weekly Floridian*, July 8, 1893, p. 2.

31. Jensen, *Winning of the Midwest*, 292–93; Allen Weinstein, "Was There a 'Crime of 1873'?: The Case of the Demonetized Dollar," *JAH*, 54 (September 1967); 307–26; Walter T. K. Nugent, *Money and American Society, 1865–1880* (New York: Free Press, 1968), 140–61.

32. J. Howard Cowperthwait, *Money, Silver, and Finance* (1892), p. 221; Irwin Unger, *The Greenback Era: A Social and Political History of American Finance, 1865–1879* (Princeton: Princeton University Press, 1964), 120–60; *Nation*, May 7, 14, 1896.

33. Garraty, *New Commonwealth*, 250–51; Milton Friedman and Anna Jacobson Schwartz, *Monetary History of the United States*, 46, 120–33.

34. Morgan, *From Hayes to McKinley*, 44.

35. Morgan, *From Hayes to McKinley*, 46–50; Worthington C. Ford, "The Standard Silver Dollar and the Coinage Law of 1878," Economic Tracts No. 13 (New York: Society for Political Education, 1884), p. 24.

36. Shannon, *Farmer's Last Frontier*, 319.

37. Stanley L. Jones, *The Presidential Election of 1896* (Madison: University of Wisconsin Press, 1964), 32–34.

38. Larson, *Populism in the Mountain West*, 29–36.

39. Gregg Cantrell and D. Scott Barton, "Texas Populists and the Failure of Biracial Politics," *JSH*, 55 (November 1989): 659–92.

40. Clipping, December 8, 1891, Francis G. Carpenter Scrapbook, LC; Seymour C. Armstrong to Grover Cleveland, July 6, 1896, Lamont MSS; G. Bilderbeck to William C. Whitney, June 29, 1896, J. Milton to Whitney, June 25, 1896, William C. Whitney MSS, LC.

41. Raymond Arsenault, *The Wild Ass of the Ozarks: Jeff Davis and the Social Bases of Southern Politics* (Philadelphia: Temple University Press, 1984), 53–58; Hackney, *Populism to Progressivism in Alabama*, 139–46; Tallahassee *Weekly Floridian*, May 13, 1893.

42. Cooper, *Conservative Regime*, 143–206; Simkins, *Pitchfork Ben Tillman*, 232–33; Cotner, *James Stephen Hogg*, 118–29, 168–249, 320–52.

43. Terence V. Powderly to Buchanan, November 3, 1892, Powderly MSS; Worth Robert Miller, "Building a Progressive Coalition in Texas: The Populist-Reform Democrat Rapprochement, 1900–1907," *JSH*, 52 (May 1986): 163–82; Hart, *Redeemers, Bourbons, and Populists*, 207.

Chapter 17: The Second Cleveland's Administration

1. McGerr, *Decline of Popular Politics*, 95–103.

2. Thomas C. Platt, *The Autobiography of Thomas Collier Platt* (New York: B. W. Dodge, 1910), 246–47; Sievers, *Benjamin Harrison: Hoosier President*, 241–44.

3. Nevins, *Grover Cleveland*, 488–91; Murat Halstead, "The Chicago Convention of 1892," *Cosmopolitan*, 13 (1892): 591.

4. Hicks, *Populist Revolt*, 261–68; Halstead, "Chicago Convention of 1892," 586, 589.

5. Mira Wilkins, *The History of Foreign Investment in the United States to 1914* (Cambridge: Harvard University Press, 1989), 194–98, 470–72.

6. Charles Hoffman, *The Depression of the Nineties: An Economic History* (Westport: Greenwood, 1970), 47–63; Robert Sobel, *Panic on Wall Street: A History of America's Financial Disasters* (New York: Macmillan, 1968), 240–52.

7. Gerald T. White, *The United States and the Problem of Recovery after 1893* (University: University of Alabama Press, 1982), 1–5.

8. Hoffman, *Depression of the Nineties*, 48–89, 106–10.

9. *Harper's Weekly*, January 6, 1894; Alexander Keyssar, *Out of Work: The First Century of Unemployment in Massachusetts* (Cambridge: Cambridge University Press, 1986), 143–76.

10. Stromquist, *Generation of Boomers*, 248–55.

11. Andrew Roy, *A History of the Coal Miners of the United States* (Columbus: J. L. Trauger, 1906), 311–20; Jensen, *Winning of the Midwest*, 243–52; Morgan, *William McKinley and His America*, 177–78; Ray S. Baker to his father, April 5, 1894, Ray Stannard Baker MSS, LC.

12. David Alan Corbin, *Life, Work, and Rebellion in the Coal Fields: The Southern West Virginia Miners, 1880–1922* (Urbana: University of Illinois Press, 1981), 44–46.

13. Blodgett, "Political Leadership of Grover Cleveland," *South Atlantic Quarterly*, 82 (Summer 1983): 296–98; Gerald G. Eggert, *Richard Olney: Evolution of a Statesman* (University Park: Pennsylvania State University Press, 1974), 47–52.

14. Dickieson, "Plain Words About Silver Money," 19; Nevins, *Grover Cleveland*, 536.

15. R. Hal Williams, *The Democratic Party and California Politics, 1880–1896* (Stanford: Stanford University Press, 1973), 155–58, 185; Nevins, *Grover Cleveland*, 541–42.

16. Merrill, *Bourbon Leader*, 172–73, 175; Thomas H. Proctor, *The Banker's Dream: A Fiction* (Vineland, NJ: Progressive Book Publishing Co., 1895), 88; Nevins, *Grover Cleveland*, 536.

17. Vincent P. Carosso, *The Morgans: Private International Bankers, 1854–1913* (Cambridge: Harvard University Press, 1987), 340; Welch, *Presidencies of Grover Cleveland*, 125–26.

18. Carosso, *The Morgans*, 312–51.

19. Summers, *William L. Wilson*, 161–71; Washington *Post*, March 21, 1894; Champ Clark, *My Quarter-Century of American Politics* (New York: Harper and Brothers, 1920), 350–54.

20. Elting E. Morison, *Letters of Theodore Roosevelt* (Cambridge: Harvard University Press, 1951), 1:394; Williams, *Democratic Party and California Politics*, 181–82.

21. Samuel M. Jones to Henry Demarest Lloyd, May 28, 1897, Samuel Milton Jones MSS; Donald McMurry, *Coxey's Army: A Study of the Industrial Army Movement of 1894* (Seattle: University of Washington Press, 1929), 22–26.

22. John Alexander Williams, *West Virginia and the Captains of Industry* (Morgantown, West Virginia University Library, 1976), 60; Morgan, *William McKinley and His America*, 179.

23. Ray Stannard Baker, *American Chronicle: the Autobiography of Ray Stannard Baker* (New York: Charles Scribner's Sons, 1945), 7–13, 21–22; Morgan, *From Hayes to McKinley*, 466–67; Morgan, *William McKinley and His America*, 179; McMurry, *Coxey's Army*, 104–26. Browne gets a much better write-up in Henry Vincent, *The Story of the Commonweal* (Chicago: W. B. Conkey Company, 1894), 110–12.

24. Almont Lindsey, *The Pullman Strike: The Story of a Unique Experiment and of a Great Labor Upheaval* (Chicago: University of Chicago Press, 1942), 46–57; Ray Ginger, *Altgeld's America: The Lincoln Ideal versus Changing Realities* (New York: Funk & Wagnalls Company, 1958), 145–48.

25. Ginger, *Altgeld's America*, 151–57.

26. Stromquist, *Generation of Boomers*, 255–56.

27. Jensen, *Winning of the Midwest*, 263; Williams, *Democratic Party and California Politics*, 195–96; Nevins, *Grover Cleveland*, 612–14.

28. Gerald G. Eggert, "A Missed Alternative: Federal Court Arbitration of Railway Labor Disputes, 1877–1895," *LH*, 7 (Fall 1966): 287–302; Eggert, *Richard Olney*, 42–43, 133–39.

29. Baker, *American Chronicle*, 38–39; Lindsey, *Pullman Strike*, 205–18. The rioters, in fact, were many of them Chicago's packinghouse workers, themselves out on strike. A railroad stoppage, as they knew, was the key to their own strike succeeding. Barrett, *Work and Community*, 128–29.

30. Jensen, *Winning of the Midwest*, 263; Nick Salvatore, *Eugene V. Debs: Citizen and Socialist* (Urbana: University of Illinois Press, 1982), 135–39.

31. Eggert, *Richard Olney*, 164–65.

32. Paul, *Conservative Crisis*, 68–74, 175–76; *Reagan v. Farmers' Loan and Trust Co.*, 154 U.S. 362–97; Charles W. McCurdy, "The Knight Sugar Decision of 1895 and the Modernization of American Corporation Law, 1869–1903," *Business History Review*, 53 (Autumn 1979): 304–43.

33. Paul, *Conservative Crisis*, 164–74, 185–218.

34. Paul, *Conservative Crisis*, 106–27, 146–57.

35. Morgan, *From Hayes to McKinley*, 465; Matthew C. Lee, "Onward Christian Soldiers: The Social Gospel and the Pullman Strike," *Chicago History*, 20 (Spring-Summer 1991): 4–21; Welch, *Presidencies of Grover Cleveland*.

36. Baker, *American Chronicle*, 42–45; Thomas Beer, *Hanna* (New York: Knopf, 1929), 132–33; Ginger, *Altgeld's America*, 193, 342.

37. Allen, *Great Pierpont Morgan*, 63–93, 188–207; Carosso, *The Morgans*, 433–38.

38. Carosso, *The Morgans*, 352–90; Allen, *Great Pierpont Morgan*, 93–97.

39. Stover, *American Railroads*, 135–36, 146–47.

40. Stromquist, *Generation of Boomers*, 258–65; Martin, *Enterprise Denied*, 124–28; Dubofsky, *State and Labor in Modern America*, 31–35.

41. Riis, *Making of an American*, 263–309; Robert H. Bremner, *From the Depths: The Discovery of Poverty in the United States* (New York: New York University Press, 1956), 68–93.

42. Bremner, *From the Depths*, 111–120.

43. Bremner, *From the Depths*, 103–11.

44. David P. Thelen, *The New Citizenship: Origins of Progressivism in Wisconsin, 1893–1900* (Columbia: University of Missouri Press, 1972), 88–89; Leah H. Feder, *Unemployment Relief in Periods of Depression: A Study of Measures Adopted in Certain American Cities* (New York: Russell Sage, 1936), 98–187; *Harper's Weekly*, January 13, 20, 27, 1894; Keyssar, *Out of Work*, 165.

45. Hammack, *Power and Society*, 147–51; Riis, *Making of an American*, 321–24, 326; Boyer, *Urban Masses and Moral Order*, 162–89.
46. Riis, *Making of an American*, 319.
47. Holli, *Reform in Detroit*, 158.
48. "The Re-Election of Jones," *Collier's*, 31:17–18 (April 18, 1903).
49. Riis, *Making of an American*, 362–65; Tax, *Rising of the Women*, 66–89; Thelen, *New Citizenship*, 86–99; "Round the Hearth," *Collier's*, 26 (January 19, 1901): 17.
50. Dubofsky, *State and Labor in Modern America*, 31; Beth, *Development of the American Constitution*, 159; Florence Kelley, "The United States Supreme Court and the Utah Eight-Hours' Law," *American Sociological Review* (1898–99), 21–34; Hans B. Thorelli, *The Federal Anti-Trust Policy* (Baltimore: Johns Hopkins University Press, 1955), 477.

Chapter 18: Cross of Gold

1. Robinson, *Thomas B. Reed*, 321; Blodgett, *Gentle Reformers*, 194.
2. Nevins, *Grover Cleveland*, 501, 675.
3. Festus Summers, ed., *Cabinet Diary of William L. Wilson* (Chapel Hill: University of North Carolina, 1957), 91; Nevins, *Grover Cleveland*, 689–98.
4. Paolo E. Coletta, *William Jennings Bryan: Political Evangelist, 1860–1908* (Lincoln: University of Nebraska Press, 1964), 49–103; Louis W. Koenig, *Bryan: A Political Biography of William Jennings Bryan* (New York: G. P. Putnam's Sons, 1971), 135.
5. Jones, *Presidential Election of 1896*, 224–29.
6. Vachel Lindsay, *The Golden Whales of California and Other Rhymes in the American Language* (New York: Macmillan, 1920), 22.
7. Paul W. Glad, *The Trumpet Soundeth: William Jennings Bryan and His Democracy, 1896–1912* (Lincoln: University of Nebraska Press, 1960), 27–42, 58.
8. R. Hal Williams, *Years of Decision: American Politics in the 1890s* (New York: Knopf, 1978), 117–19. The comparison slandered the Platte, which was actually only three-fourths of a mile wide, and on average *six* inches deep. Minturn, *Travels West*, 81.
9. Blodgett, *Gentle Reformers*, 214–39; Bass, "*I Am a Democrat*," 245.
10. Croly, *Marcus Alonzo Hanna*, 84–95; Morgan, *William McKinley and His America*, 231.
11. Morgan, *William McKinley and His America*, 59–64, 158–61, 177–80.
12. "Silver Speech of Hon. E. O. Wolcott of Colorado, April 6, 1892" (Washington, DC: 1892), p. 4.
13. Jensen, *Winning of the Midwest*, 287.
14. Gilbert C. Fite, "Republican Strategy and the Farm Vote in the Presidential Campaign of 1896," *American Historical Review* 55 (1960): 790–803; *Railway Age*, September 11, 1896, p. 197; Williams, *Years of Decision*, 120–21; Blodgett, *Gentle Reformers*, 236.
15. Thomas Page Grant to William C. Whitney, July 25, 1896, William C. Whitney MSS, LC; Coletta, *William Jennings Bryan*, 180, 201–02.
16. *Railway Age*, November 6, 1896, p. 358; *Railroad Trainmen's Journal*, 12 (November 1896): 881–83; Brann, *Works of Brann the Iconoclast*, 7:186; *Independent*, July 16, 1896, p. 10; Jensen, *Winning of the Midwest*, 286, 291. Armstrong, ed., *Gilded Age Letters of E. L. Godkin*, 484.
17. George W. Perkins to Albert J. Beveridge, October 19, 1896, Albert J. Beveridge MSS, LC; Williams, *Years of Decision*, 123–25; Jensen, *Winning of the Midwest*, 292–99.
18. Beer, *Hanna*, 203.
19. Jules Klein to Stephen M. White, June 24, 1897, White MSS; Morgan, *William McKinley and His America*, 278–80; Taussig, *Tariff History of the United States*, 325–55.
20. *Outlook*, 57 (September 4, 1897): 7–8; White, *United States and the Problem of Recovery*, 72–81; Samuel M. Jones to John H. Jones, June 7, 1897, Jones MSS.
21. Martin Ridge, *Ignatius Donnelly: The Portrait of a Politician* (Chicago: University of Chicago Press, 1962), 356–57; *Independent*, August 13, 1896, p. 13; C. A. Barlow to Thomas V. Cator, March 9, 1898, Thomas V. Cator MSS, Stanford; William A. White, "The Building Up of the Prairie West," *Collier's*, 29:10 (May 10, 1902).
22. Hair, *Bourbonism and Agrarian Protest*, 260–61; Escott, *Many Excellent People*, 254–58.
23. Ayers, *Promise of the New South*, 299–304. For an equally violent extirpation, see Lawrence E. Goodwyn, "Populist Dreams and Negro Rights: East Texas as a Case Study," *AHR*, 76 (December 1971): 1435–56.
24. Shreveport *Evening Judge*, December 15, 1895; Champ Clark, *My Quarter-Century of American Politics*, 1:349; Hair, *Bourbonism and Agrarian Protest*, 262–67; Shaw, *Wool-Hat Boys*, 75–76, 115–18.

25. Keller, *Affairs of State*, 525; Henry C. Dethloff and Robert R. Jones, "Race Relations in Louisiana, 1877–98," *Louisiana History*, 9 (Fall 1968): 308; Wharton, *Negro in Mississippi*, 1865–1890, 206.
26. Woodward, *Origins of the New South*, 327; Kousser, *Shaping of Southern Politics*, 47–62; Hackney, *Populism to Progressivism in Alabama*, 194; Hair, *Bourbonism and Agrarian Protest*, 276–77; Kirwan, *Revolt of the Rednecks*, 71.
27. Jones, "James L. Kemper and the Virginia Redeemers Face the Race Question: A Reconsideration," *JSH*, 38 (August 1972): 406; Kousser, *Shaping of Southern Politics*, 63–72, 190; Tallahassee *Weekly Floridian*, May 13, 1893, p. 2.
28. Woodward, *Origins of the New South*, 341–42; Kousser, *Shaping of Southern Politics*, 180–81.
29. Kousser, *Shaping of Southern Politics*, 194–95; 218, 224–29, 240–42; Samuel L. Webb, "Two-Party Politics in the One-Party South: Alabama Hill Country, 1880–1920," Ph.D. Dissertation, University of Arkansas, 185.
30. James K. Pollock, *Party Campaign Funds* (New York: Knopf, 1926), 7–8; Blodgett, *Gentle Reformers*, 116–17; Newman Smyth, "Political Corruption in Connecticut," *Outlook*, March 18, 1905, p. 690; Joseph P. Harris, *Registration of Voters in the United States* (Washington: Brookings Institution, 1929), 65–85.
31. This is so-called because several provinces in Australia adopted it first. By the 1880s, Great Britain and Canada had put it into law, as well.
32. L. E. Fredman, *The Australian Ballot: The Story of an American Reform* (East Lansing: Michigan State University Press, 1968), 5–19, 31–32, 46–48.
33. Terence V. Powderly to W. L. Stark, April 7, 1892, Powderly MSS; *Nation*, August 29, 1889, p. 165; Henry George, "Money in Elections," *North American Review*, 136 (March 1883): 201–11; Fredman, *Australian Ballot*, 33–36; Reynolds, *Testing Democracy*, 9, 58–59.
34. N. Matthews to Timothy S. Williams, March 14, 1890, Williams to David Bennett Hill, April 8, 1893, Timothy S. Williams MSS, New York Public Library; Fredman, *Australian Ballot*, 48.
35. Fredman, *Australian Ballot*, 48; *Nation*, June 4, 18, 1891; Reynolds, *Testing Democracy*, 66–67; Peter J. Argersinger, "To Disfranchise the People: The Iowa Ballot Law and the Election of 1897," *Mid-America* 63 (January 1981): 33.
36. Terence V. Powderly to H. P. Dempsey, March 31, 1892, Powderly MSS; Peter J. Argersinger, "'A Place on the Ballot': Fusion Politics and Anti-Fusion Laws," *AHR*, 85 (April 1980): 287–306.
37. Benjamin G. Rader, *American Sports: From the Age of Folk Games to the Age of Spectators* (Prentice Hall, 1983), 50–57, 97–103.
38. Harold Seymour, *Baseball: The Early Years* (New York: Oxford University Press, 1960); Rader, *American Sports*, 80–85; Douglas A. Noverr and Lawrence E. Ziewacz, *The Games They Played: Sports in American History, 1865–1980* (Chicago: Nelson-Hall, 1983), 28–29; *Independent*, December 6, 1894, p. 11.
39. Rader, *American Sports*, 75–79; Seymour, *Baseball*, 346–54.
40. Schlereth, *Victorian America*, 169–75; Gilbert, *Perfect Cities*, 75–130.
41. Furnas, *The Americans*, 761–66; Gilbert, *Perfect Cities*, 118–28.

Chapter 19: The Ceremony of Innocence Is Drowned: Empire

1. Morgan, *William McKinley and His America*, 319; *Nation*, March 7, 1901.
2. Elizabeth M. Howe, "The Passing of Spain," *Outlook*, 57 (October 30, 1897): 516; Louis A. Perez, Jr., *Cuba Between Empires, 1878–1902* (Pittsburgh: University of Pittsburgh Press, 1983), 126–36.
3. Graham A. Cosmas, *An Army for Empire: The United States Army in the Spanish-American War* (Columbia: University of Missouri Press, 1971), 76–79; Perez, *Cuba between Empires*, 120–24, 150–52. But see the *Nation's* defense of "reconcentration," November 18, 1897, p. 387.
4. David J. Burrell, "The Mighty Printing Presses," *Independent*, December 31, 1896; McGerr, *Decline of Popular Politics*, 122–30; W. A. Swanberg, *Pulitzer* (New York: Scribner's Sons, 1967), 237–39.
5. Swanberg, *Pulitzer*, 259–60, 264–67, 272–75; Walter Millis, *The Martial Spirit* (Cambridge: Riverside Press, 1931), 67–68.
6. Perez, *Cuba between Empires*, 120–32.
7. Perez, *Cuba between Empires*, 197–98; A. B. Hotchkiss to Stephen M. White, August 22, 1897, White MSS; W. P. Willett, "The Cuban Insurrection," *Independent*, January 30, 1896; Campbell, *Transformation of American Foreign Relations*, 247; Brann, *Brann the Iconoclast*, 7:72–76.
8. Milton Plesur, *America's Outward Thrust: Approaches to Foreign Affairs, 1865–1890* (DeKalb: Northern Illinois University Press, 1971), 74–86, 116–17; Walter LaFeber, *The New Empire: An Interpretation of American Expansion, 1860–1898* (Ithaca: Cornell University Press, 1963), 150–96.

9. LaFeber, *New Empire*, 242–83; C. W. Woolley to Samuel J. Randall, August 6, 1887, Samuel J. Randall MSS, University of Pennsylvania.

10. Casper Whitney, *Hawaiian America* (New York: Harper & Brothers, 1899), 2–7, 21–25, 45; "C.S.N.," Washington *Star*, August 9, 1890.

11. *Nation*, March 2, 1893; Thomas J. Osborne, *"Empire Can Wait": American Opposition to Hawaiian Annexation, 1893–1898* (Kent: Kent State University Press, 1981), 6–41.

12. Margaret Leech, *In the Days of McKinley* (New York: Harper Brothers, 1959), 150; Campbell, *Transformation of American Foreign Relations*, 250–51; Morgan, *William McKinley and His America*, 354; *Nation*, December 30, 1897, p. 510.

13. Millis, *Martial Spirit*, 102–06, 127–29; James M. Mayo, *War Memorials as Political Landscape* (Westport: Praeger, 1988), 159–60.

14. Morris, *Rise of Theodore Roosevelt*, 610; Morgan, *William McKinley and His America*, 340; Campbell, *Transformation of American Foreign Relations*, 268–73.

15. Millis, *Martial Spirit*, 162–63; Morgan, *William McKinley and His America*, 380–83, 391.

16. Williard B. Gatewood, Jr., *Black Americans and the White Man's Burden, 1898–1903* (Urbana: University of Illinois Press, 1975), 42–51.

17. Cosmas, *An Army for Empire*, 5–15, 73–75, 89–98.

18. Millis, *Martial Spirit*, 213–16; Cosmas, *An Army for Empire*, 164, 266–76, 287–94.

19. Elizabeth M. Howe, "The Passing of Spain," *Outlook*, 57 (October 30, 1897): 516; J. Frank Clark, "Cuba's Struggle for Freedom," *Cosmopolitan*, 19 (October 1895): 609–10; Cosmas, *An Army for Empire*, 79–81.

20. Foster Rhea Dulles, *The Imperial Years: The History of America's Brief Moment of Imperial Fervor* (New York: Crowell, 1956), 133.

21. Millis, *Martial Spirit*, 183–95; Swanberg, *Pulitzer*, 301; Sullivan, *Our Times: America Finding Herself*, 324–25, 331–43.

22. Morris, *Rise of Theodore Roosevelt*, 632–56; Gatewood, *Black Americans and the White Man's Burden*, 58–59, 103; James F. J. Archibald, "Our Legion of Honor," *Overland Monthly*, 38 (July 1901): 12–24.

23. Perez, *Cuba Between Empires*, 206–10, 218, 330–44.

24. Campbell, *Transformation of American Foreign Relations*, 309–11; Richard E. Welch, *Response to Imperialism: The United States and the Philippine-American War, 1899–1902* (Chapel Hill: University of North Carolina Press, 1979), 75–88; Robert L. Beisner, *Twelve against Empire: The Anti-Imperialists, 1898–1900* (New York: McGraw-Hill, 1968), 165–85.

25. Morgan, *William McKinley and His America*, 412.

26. Louis J. Halle, *The United States Acquires the Philippines: Consensus vs. Reality* (New York: University Press of America, 1985), 16–32. But see Wallace Rice, "Some Current Fallacies of Captain Mahan," *The Dial*, 28 (March 16, 1900): 199; Morris, *Rise of Theodore Roosevelt*, 424, 574–75; William C. Widenor, *Henry Cabot Lodge and the Search for an American Foreign Policy* (Berkeley: University of California Press, 1980), 88–93.

27. Glenn Anthony May, *Social Engineering in the Philippines: The Aims, Execution, and Impact of American Colonial Policy, 1900–1913* (Westport, CT: Greenwood, 1980), 123–26, 140–48; "Government Employees in Our New Possessions," *Collier's*, 26:22–23 (March 2, 1901).

28. Miller, *"Benevolent Assimilation,"* 31–40, 254–55; Peter W. Stanley, ed., *Reappraising an Empire: New Perspectives on Philippine-American History* (Cambridge: Harvard University Press, 1984), 50–53; Brian McAllister Linn, *The U.S. Army and Counterinsurgency in the Philippine War, 1899–1902* (Chapel Hill: University of North Carolina Press, 1989), 127–29, 163–70.

29. Miller, *"Benevolent Assimilation,"* 100–02.

30. Slotkin, *Gunfighter Nation*, 119–20; Stanley, ed., *Reappraising an Empire*, 43; John M. Gates, "War-Related Deaths in the Philippines, 1898–1902," *Pacific Historical Review*, 53 (August 1984): 367–78; Miller, *"Benevolent Assimilation,"* 73; *Nation*, August 30, 1900.

31. Gatewood, *Black Americans and the White Man's Burden*, 285; Miller, *"Benevolent Assimilation,"* 176–80, 182–88; Slotkin, *Gunfighter Nation*, 106–21.

32. Beth, *Development of the American Constitution*, 161–62.

33. Welch, *Response to Imperialism*, 102–04.

34. Perez, *Cuba between Empires*, 199–206, 213–14, 220–22.

35. Welch, *Responses to Imperialism*, 101; Gatewood, *Black Americans and the White Man's Burden*, 281–87. Mr. Dooley caught the irony in his play on the poem's first line: "Take up th' white man's burden an' hand it to th' coons."

36. Daniel R. Schirmer, *Republic or Empire: American Resistance to the Philippine War* (Cambridge: Schenkman Publishing Co., 1972), 83–104, 187–204; E. Berkeley Tompkins, *Anti-Imperialism in the United States: The Great*

Debate, 1890–1920, (Philadelphia: University of Pennsylvania Press, 1970), 120–60, 241; Samuel M. Jones to Herbert Welsh, November 11, 1899, Welsh, "The Philippine Question from the Christian and American Point of View," Herbert Welsh MSS, HSP; *Nation,* August 2, 1900; Edward Atkinson to Stephen M. White, January 19, 1899, White MSS, Christopher Lasch, "The Anti-Imperialists, the Philippines, and the Inequality of Man," *JSH,* 14 (August 1958): 319–31; New York *Times,* February 15, 1899; Hollingsworth, *Whirligig of Politics,* 173; William Vaughn Moody, "On a Soldier Fallen in the Philippines," *Atlantic,* 87 (February 1901): 288.

37. Morgan, *William McKinley and His America,* 491, 497–98.
38. Coletta, *William Jennings Bryan: Political Evangelist,* 244–62.
39. Hollingsworth, *Whirligig of Politics,* 180; Croly, *Marcus Alonzo Hanna,* 332–40.
40. Croly, *Marcus Alonzo Hanna,* 325.
41. Mowry, *Era of Theodore Roosevelt,* 3; Sullivan, *Our Times: Turn of the Century,* 522; Martin, *Enterprise Denied,* 96–98, 60–61; Sobel, *Big Board,* 152–56.
42. Morgan, *William McKinley and His America,* 500, 502.
43. Dulles, *Imperial Years,* 210–19.
44. Sullivan, *Our Times: Turn of the Century,* 522; Morgan, *William McKinley and His America,* 445–47; Perez, *Cuba between Empires,* 274–327, 371–73; Jack C. Lane, *Armed Progressive: General Leonard Wood* (San Rafael, CA: Presidio Press, 1978), 74–76, 98–100; "The Condition of Affairs in Cuba," *Collier's,* 26:5 (November 3, 1900).
45. David McCullough, *The Path between the Seas: The Creation of the Panama Canal, 1870–1914* (New York: Simon & Schuster, 1977), 305–86; Frederick W. Marks, *Velvet on Iron: The Diplomacy of Theodore Roosevelt* (Lincoln: University of Nebraska Press, 1979), 96–105, 140–42.
46. Marks, *Velvet on Iron,* 65–66; Paolo E. Coletta, *William Jennings Bryan: Progressive Politician and Moral Statesman, 1909–1915* (Lincoln: University of Nebraska Press, 1969), 179–81, 193–94, 239–49.
47. Edward R. S. Baker and W. E. Dodd, *Public Papers of Woodrow Wilson* (New York: Harper, 1927), 5:16.

Chapter 20: The Promised Land

1. Morgan, *William McKinley and His America,* 318, 511.
2. Leech, *In the Days of McKinley,* 586–603.
3. Sullivan, *Our Times: Turn of the Century,* 478–81, 484; David Beasley, *The Suppression of the Automobile: Skulduggery at the Crossroads* (Westport: Greenwood Press, 1988).
4. John B. Rae, *The American Automobile Industry* (Boston: Twayne Publishers, 1984), 11–41; Sullivan, *Our Times: Turn of the Century,* 491–50.
5. *Independent,* February 6, 1896; Peter J. Hugill, "Good Roads and the Automobile in the United States, 1880–1929," *Geographical Review,* 72 (1972): 330.
6. Sullivan, *Our Times: America Finding Herself,* 594–606.
7. This backed up what a prominent Cuban physician, Dr. Carlos Finlay, had been trying to tell Americans all along.
8. Sullivan, *Our Times: Turn of the Century,* 432–54.
9. Furnas, *The Americans,* 908–11.
10. Furnas, *The Americans,* 886–87; Sarah Barnwell Elliott, "The Spirit of the Nineteenth Century in Fiction," *Outlook,* January 19, 1901; Sullivan, *Our Times: The War Begins, 1909–1914,* 101–13.
11. John Elfreth Watkins, Jr., "What May Happen in the Next Hundred Years," *Ladies' Home Journal,* December 1900, p. 8.
12. Max B. Thrasher, "In the Cotton-field," *Outlook,* September 7, 1901, 59–68; Frederick Lewis Allen, *The Lords of Creation* (New York: Harper & Brothers, 1935), 46–48; Martin, *Enterprise Denied,* 99–101.
13. "The Financial Year," *Nation,* January 3, 1901; Frederic Emory, "The Foreign Trade of the United States," *Popular Science Monthly,* 58 (April 1901): 626–40; George E. Mowry, *The Era of Theodore Roosevelt and the Birth of Modern America, 1900–1912* (New York: Harper & Row, 1958), 4–5.
14. Sobel, *Big Board,* 152–57.
15. Wall, *Andrew Carnegie,* 767–93.
16. Allen, *Lords of Creation,* 49–65; Martin, *James J. Hill,* 508–11.
17. *Outlook,* October 5, 1901, p. 245; Gabriel Kolko, *The Triumph of Conservatism: A Reinterpretation of American History, 1900–1916* (New York: Macmillan, 1963), 26–56.
18. Allen, *Lords of Creation,* 28–29; Charles J. Bullock, "Trusts and Public Policy," *Atlantic,* 87 (June 1901): 737–45; William D. Washburn, Jr., "Minnesota and the Railway Trust," *Outlook,* 69 (December 14, 1901): 975–78.

19. *The Socialist Spirit*, 1 (September 1901): 6; *Outlook*, December 14, 1901, p. 967; Eric Foner, *History of the Labor Movement in the United States* (New York: International Publishers, 1964), 3:11–18.

20. Brody, *Steelworkers in America*, 68–78; Foner, *History of the Labor Movement in the United States*, 3:78–86; Barrett, *Work and Community*, 176–79; P. K. Edwards, *Strikes in the United States*, 14–15, 42.

21. Ray Ginger, *The Bending Cross: A Biography of Eugene Victor Debs* (New Brunswick: Rutgers University Press, 1949), 284–85; David A. Shannon, *The Socialist Party of America: A History* (New York: Macmillan, 1955), 1–61; James R. Green, *Grass-Roots Socialism: Radical Movements in the Southwest, 1895–1943* (Baton Rouge: Louisiana State University Press, 1978).

22. *Outlook*, 69 (October 12, 1901): 339; Bradley Robert Rice, *Progressive Cities: The Commission Government Movement in America, 1901–1920* (Austin: University of Texas Press, 1977), 6–33; Tom L. Johnson, *My Story* (New York: B. W. Huebsch, 1913), 121–23; Warner, *Progressivism in Ohio*, 72–78; Eric F. Goldman, *Rendezvous with Destiny*, 168–71.

23. Kolko, *Triumph of Conservatism*, 26–56; Robert H. Wiebe, *Businessmen and Reform: A Study of the Progressive Movement* (Cambridge: Harvard University Press, 1962); Samuel P. Hays, *Conservation and the Gospel of Efficiency: The Progressive Conservation Movement, 1890–1920* (Cambridge: Harvard University Press, 1959), 27–31, 49–65.

24. Robert M. Crunden, *Ministers of Reform: The Progressives' Achievement in American Civilization, 1889–1920* (Urbana: University of Illinois Press, 1984), 3–63.

25. Dorothy Schneider and Carl J. Schneider, *American Women in the Progressive Era, 1900–1920* (New York: Doubleday, 1993), 138–47.

26. Stephen J. Shaw, "Black Club Women and the Creation of the National Association of Colored Women," *Journal of Women's History*, 3 (Fall 1991): 10–25; Maureen A. Flanagan, "Gender and Urban Political Reform: The City Club and the Woman's City Club of Chicago in the Progressive Era," *AHR*, 95 (October 1990): 1032–50.

27. Schneider and Schneider, *American Women in the Progressive Era*, 165–90.

28. Molly Ladd-Taylor, *Mother-Work: Women, Child Welfare, and the State, 1890–1930* (Urbana: University of Illinois Press, 1994), 17–34, 107; *Ladies' Home Journal*, 23 (February 1906): 21.

29. Ladd-Taylor, *Mother-Work*, 43–55; Manuela Thurner, "Better Citizens Without the Ballot: American Antisuffrage Women and Their Rationale During the Progressive Era," *Journal of Women's History*, 5 (Spring 1993): 33–60; J. Stanley Lemons, *The Woman Citizen: Social Feminism in the 1920s* (Urbana: University of Illinois Press, 1973); Robert B. Fowler, *Carrie Catt: Feminist Politician* (Boston: Northeastern University Press, 1986), 155.

30. Beth, *Development of the American Constitution*, 198–99.

31. Baker, *Following the Color Line*, 138–47.

32. Baker, *Following the Color Line*, 113–29.

33. "The Epidemic of Savagery," *Outlook*, 69 (September 7, 1901): 9–11; William F. Holmes, "Labor Agents and The Georgia Exodus, 1899–1900," *South Atlantic Quarterly*, 79 (Autumn 1980): 436–48; William Cohen, *At Freedom's Edge: Black Mobility and the Southern White Quest for Racial Control* (Baton Rouge: Louisiana State University, 1991), 238–47, 288–94; Sinclair, *Aftermath of Slavery*, 222–23.

34. Sullivan, *Our Times: America Finds Itself*, 593–98.

35. All of which is chronicled superbly in Morris, *Rise of Theodore Roosevelt*.

36. Bowen, *Yankee from Olympus*, 370–71; Arthur M. Schlesinger, Jr., *The Imperial Presidency* (New York: Popular Library, 1973), 90–95, 122–23, 219; Morris, *Rise of Theodore Roosevelt*, 11.

37. Allen, *Great Pierpont Morgan*, 220–22.

38. Foner, *Labor Movement in the United States*, 86–87; Harbaugh, *Power and Responsibility*, 168–80.

39. *Outlook*, 69 (September 21, 1901): 158.

40. Kipling, *American Notes*, 192–93.

Index